The Dominion of Youth

Adolescence and the Making of
Modern Canada
1920–1950

Studies in Childhood and Family in Canada

Studies in Childhood and Family in Canada is a multidisciplinary series devoted to new perspectives on these subjects as they evolve. The series features studies that focus on the intersections of age, class, race, gender, and region as they contribute to a Canadian understanding of childhood and family, both historically and currently.

Series Editor
Cynthia Comacchio
Department of History
Wilfrid Laurier University

Manuscripts to be sent to
Brian Henderson, Director
Wilfrid Laurier University Press
75 University Avenue West
Waterloo, Ontario, Canada, N2L 3C5

The Dominion of Youth

Adolescence and the Making of
Modern Canada
1920–1950

Cynthia Comacchio

Studies in Childhood and Family in Canada

Wilfrid Laurier University Press
[WLU]

This book has been published with the help of a grant from the Canadian Federation for the Humanities and Social Sciences through the Aid to Scholarly Publications Programme, using funds provided by the Social Sciences and Humanities Research Council of Canada. We acknowledge the financial support of the Government of Canada through the Book Publishing Industry Development Program for our publishing activities.

Library and Archives Canada Cataloguing in Publication

Comacchio, Cynthia R., 1957-
    The dominion of youth : adolescence and the making of modern Canada, 1920–1950 / Cynthia R. Comacchio

(Studies in childhood and family in Canada)
Includes bibliographical references and index.
ISBN 978-1-55458-151-1 (pbk.)

    1. Teenagers—Canada—History—20th century. 2. Teenagers—Canada—Social life and customs. I. Title. II. Series

HQ799.C3C64 2006   306.2350971'09042   C2006-902348-4

© 2006 Wilfrid Laurier University Press
Waterloo, Ontario, Canada N2L 3C5
www.wlupress.wlu.ca

Cover design by Pam Woodland. Front cover photograph: Girl skaters from the Old Orchard Skating Club, Toronto, c. 1920. William James, photographer. City of Toronto Archives, SC 244-1367. With permission of the City of Toronto Archives.
Text design by Kathy Joslin.

Every reasonable effort has been made to acquire permission for copyright material used in this text, and to acknowledge all such indebtedness accurately. Any errors and omissions called to the publisher's attention will be corrected in future printings.

∞
This book is printed on Ancient Forest Friendly paper (100% post-consumer recycled).
Printed in Canada

Table of Contents

Preface

June 15, 1970

Dear Diary: Well, now I'm 13, I'm a teenager at last. I don't feel older yet. I'll feel more grown up in the fall when high school starts. That will be exciting.... I want things to change fast.

I have kept this old diary, with its gilded pink vinyl cover and its tiny padlock, through many years, moves, and life changes. Now and again I come across it; reading the careful scribbles, I am reminded that, at various times during the course of adolescence, the girl who wanted "things to change fast" would find herself wanting them to change back to their familiar form. That is the nature of "becoming adult." Where adolescence is concerned, there is probably as much looking backwards as forwards, as much a sense of exceptionality as commonality with peers, of aloneness as generational belonging, of being "a kid" as of being "grown up." The thirteen-year-old diarist could not have known, on the verge of stepping into high school, that looking backwards would become her life's work, and adolescence itself a consuming historical interest.

I became interested in the history of childhood and motherhood as a nervous new mother eager to know the "how-to" of scientific childrearing. Once my daughter reached the teen years, I found myself feeling as ignorant about parenting a "not-child-not-yet-adult" as I had when she was a fragile newborn. Coming of age in the late twentieth century, as my children did, was a complex and anxiety-provoking matter, and not only for them and for their parents. It was, and remains, a dominant social issue. Teenagers are seen to inhabit a world in which established values and their related customs are disintegrating, families are fragmenting, and parents and other elders are disregarded in favour of the peer group. This increasingly "wired" and media-saturated postmodern culture is considered to be fundamentally different than that of any previous generation—and eminently more dangerous. The young appear intent on "acting out" the worst fears of adult onlookers, as horribly manifested in the murder of fourteen-year-old Reena Virk in Victoria, British Columbia, and the high school shootings in Columbine, Colorado, among other acts of violence made all the more shocking in view of the youth of those involved. Most of the victims, and all of the perpetrators, were teenagers. What does this say about our world? More to the point, what does it portend about our future?

In reading the contemporary literature on adolescence, I felt compelled to delve into its precedents. What I uncovered were a few simple but salient themes and issues that call into question the newness of contemporary adolescent culture, as well as the unprecedented nature of public concerns about teenagers. The first of these might well appear obvious: adolescence is a socio-historic event as much as a personal experience. It changes over time to reflect its particular context, while maintaining certain cross-generational continuities that hinge on the usual variables of gender, class and race, and religion and culture. Although the focus varies, another "modern" theme is the tendency of society to project its every current anxiety onto the younger generation, citizens of the future. In the early twentieth century, as the eyes of so-called modern experts became fixed upon the young, certain long-lasting theories about the nature and meaning of adolescence were formulated. Once the Great War had passed and the "modern age" had truly arrived, the modern teenager emerged amidst the "new day's" intensive developments in technology, medicine, psychology, education, cultural anthropology, family sociology, and any number of other "scientific advances" and "modern innovations."

This creature, initially seen in a positive light as being more modern than its parents, quickly took on a certain resemblance to Frankenstein's infamous monster. Although it was not unlike its creators, both parents and the larger society, its very modernity made it a terror to behold: undisciplined, ungovernable, and ever challenging the "norm," hence threatening the future. This growing apprehension about the younger generation came to be classified—and still is—as the "youth problem." This book is about the ideas, policies, and projects that were devised, during the years from the end of one world war to the end of another, in hopes of ensuring the making of a certain type of modern young Canadian. It is also about the everyday experiences of growing up in what was itself a young Canada undertaking a parallel journey of transformation.

The problems associated with a long-term, often unwieldy and always exasperating project such as this one are borne not only by the historical actors but also by the historian trying to make sense of it all, not to mention the historian's hapless family, friends, and colleagues. While the work may be an individual effort, the related aggravations tend to be shared by all within reach, with or without their consent. With much appreciation and even more apology, then, I acknowledge all the moral support, encouragement, and technical, scholarly, and collegial assistance so kindly supplied by so many: Neil Sutherland, who pioneered family history in this country and continues, with much enthusiasm, energy, and generosity, to guide those who follow, myself included; my colleague Suzanne Zeller, who heard too much about all this and still made herself available for sustaining doses of coffee and cake; the good people at Wilfrid Laurier University Press, especially Sandra Woolfrey, Brian Henderson, Jacqueline Larson, Carroll Klein, and Leslie Macredie, all of whom remained remarkably straight-faced for all the years that it took to get the manuscript to them. And I very much appreciate the skill and imagination of Pam Woodland, who designed the cover.

Among other friends and colleagues who offered consistent encouragement, I thank also Terry Crowley and Jamie Snell, University of Guelph; Terry Copp, Wilfrid Laurier University; and the late Gerry Stortz, St. Jerome's University. A number of capable graduate student researchers gave much-appreciated assistance through the years, especially D.J. MacPherson, Inge Sanmiya, Alessandra Iozzo, and Laura Quirk. I am very grateful for the funding provided by grants and fellowships from the Social Sciences and Humanities Federation of Canada; the AMS-Hannah Institute for the History of Medicine; and the Office of Research, Wilfrid Laurier University, and especially for the support of Dr. Barry McPherson, former Dean of Research.

As always, I must thank my parents, Bruno and Maria Comacchio, and my sister and brother-in-law, Linda and Murray Calanchie, for helping me to raise my children while also "raising" this book. I feel strongly the ineffectiveness of trying to express what this means in the context of my life and the lives of my daughter and son. Stefanie, now twenty-three, and Evan, just leaving adolescence as this project comes to pass, pretty much came of age with it, this demanding, ever-present, un-human life form, also a "monster" of sorts, to extend the Frankenstein analogy. This might have been an interesting experience for them; it was more likely another thing to suffer through at a time when they had compelling projects of their own to take up. I am grateful for their patience and endurance, and for becoming such wonderful young adults, probably in spite of it all. Newcomers to our circle have been obliged to "live with it" as well. I thankfully acknowledge the supportive roles undertaken by my son-in-law, Long Ly, and my friend Murray Tucker.

Finally, I dedicate this one, with much love and constant amazement, to the "rising generation," as represented close to my heart by my grandson, Alexander Bruno Ly: *ti voglio tanto bene, carino mio.*

Introduction

Young Canada

Father of Nations!
Of our scant people mould a mighty state...
Whose forging on Thine anvil was begun
In blood late shed to purge the common shame
That so our hearts, the fever of faction done,
Banish old feud in our young nation's name.
　　　　　　　　　　　— Charles G.D. Roberts

*T*he young nation of Charles G.D. Roberts's[1] verse greeted the twentieth century with the assurance from its prime minister that this new era would be "filled by Canada." Throughout the Western world, "Canada's Century" was also heralded as "The Century of the Child." In 1900, American psychologist Granville Stanley Hall, pioneer of the child study movement and the century's foremost theorist of adolescence, asserted that "knowing the true nature and needs of childhood and adolescence" was the only sure means of "thread[ing] our way through all the mazes of culture and the distractions of modern life."[2] This was the setting within which the "scant people" that longed to raise "a mighty state" from the ashes of the Great War looked to its young to show the way forward.

Although not a modern discovery as such, adolescence, as life stage, experience, and culture, took on an identifiably modern form in the early twentieth century, thereby redefining conventional meanings of childhood and adulthood, of generational and familial relations, and of the state's role in the nurture and training of its future citizens. More than anything, modern adolescence entails a prolonged socialization of the young. But young Canadians were not merely recipients of these historical trends: they actively contributed to reconfiguring the institutions and practices that governed their age group. In the process, in keeping with the specific historic conditions of their "coming of age," they helped to define for their generation what made them "modern youth." During the years between the Great War and 1950, those who inhabited this life stage—this "dominion of youth"—would demarcate their territory in terms of distinctive generational cultures. The border between adulthood and childhood remained permeable, as always, but it was recognizable—and recognized—as never before. New ideas about adolescence informed new and "modern" networks of socialization and regulation.

Adolescence is ephemeral, as much conceptually as in its experience. More than a biological and demographic classification, it is, like childhood, a socio-historical product. It is subject to reformulation according to time-specific societal needs, evolving scientific theories, cultural precepts, national aspirations. While some form of adolescence, in the sense of physical and social maturation, has clearly always existed in human societies, the process of becoming adult is neither timeless nor universal. The experience of adolescence is as much "in process" as are the age group's human constituents. During the first half of the twentieth century, with its nature and needs subjected to increasingly rigorous scrutiny by the widening ranks of modern experts in the social sciences, medicine, and education, in social welfare organizations, and in state agencies, as well as by any number of commentators in the popular media, adolescence became a cultural phenomenon.[3] By 1950 the life stage had become, in the words of psychologist Erik Erikson, a publicly sanctioned "psychosocial moratorium," bridging the familial dependence of children and the worldly independence of adults.[4] The quaint-sounding notion of "coming of age," consequently, has as much to do with cultural meanings upheld, reproduced, and encoded by such institutions as family, church, school, and law—and, more recently, the state and its agencies—as with the biological changes of puberty.

The subject of "becoming adult" is as complicated for historians as it has been for both youth and the avid youth-watchers of the century just past who populate this study. At the most basic level, how do we locate the points of entry and exit, as well as the main physiological, psychological, sociological and cultural characteristics of so liminal and transitional—transitory, actually—a life stage? How do we avoid conjuring a universal adolescence, ensuring that we account for the ways in which class, gender, race, region, culture, and historical circumstance differentiate adolescent experiences? How does this necessary acknowledgement of the contingent and mutable nature of adolescence affect the ways in which historians make sense of adolescence in the past? Can we gauge in any meaningful manner how principal national and world-historic events shape a generation's collective biography?

In grappling with these issues, my objective is to capture a sense of what it meant for young Canadians to be "in process" within the context of a young nation caught up in its own self-formation and transformation during the years from 1920 to 1950. I am interested in the salient concerns of ordinary adolescent lives, those centring on family, peers and romantic interests, school, work, and leisure, to see how these played themselves out during this stage that was developmental for both youth and the nation. While the young defined their dominion, the Dominion itself was effectively working toward its own individuation, the formation of a modern identity that drew from but was self-consciously different from that of its British parent and its American peers. As Stanley Hall contended, to study the changing meaning of adolescence in the early twentieth century is to gain understanding of the nature of modernity: "Other oracles may grow dim," he argued, "but this one will never fail."[5]

For the sake of consistency and simplicity, I favour the term *adolescent* in describing the young Canadians under study here, even while acknowledging that the majority of my sources, published and private, most often make reference to *youth*—more colloquially to *youngsters*, or to boys and girls, individually and collectively—in a manner that takes in a wider age range than I deal with. The labels *teenage* and *teenager* were not consistently employed before the 1940s. Nonetheless, I have traced a growing attention to the "'teen-age" and the "'teen-ager" through the course of the interwar years. This preferred spelling in the press, with its carefully placed apostrophe, accentuates the definitive "in-between" nature of the life stage. The gradual public adoption of these terms, together with their historical spelling, points to my focus: the development of a modern constellation of meanings surrounding a life stage that, while comprising the teen years in biological and chronological terms, was refashioned into a distinct socio-cultural space between childhood's end and full adult citizenship.[6]

Although they lacked widespread public acknowledgement as "teenagers," modern adolescents were well on the scene by the close of the 1920s. The clearest evidence that they had arrived by this time is found in the mounting public discussion about them: there can be little doubt that the teenager was a steadily evolving and ever more vivid presence during these years. The 1950s brought about a consolidation of developing theories about what constituted modern youth, not the invention of that category. Reinforced, promoted, circulated, and made more accessible by mass media (especially television), the habits, behaviours, and "styles" that are recognizably adolescent and modern had entered the mainstream by mid-century. Yet modern adolescence had been very much in the making since at least the Great War. "Reformulating the chronology," as American historian Harvey Graff points out, is "central to reconceptualizing the historical development of growing up."[7] It matters where the modern adolescent is situated historically, and not just in light of academic positions. Mis-timing and mis-placing the subject skews our understandings of adolescence not only in the past but also in the present, in itself and in relation to childhood and adulthood, to family, and to the impact of historic change on life stages, age groups, institutions, self, and national identities.

To frame this study conceptually, I have borrowed from the sociological and psychological literature, both historical and current, especially generational theory and analysis. If the very term *adolescence* is weighted, so too is *generation*. The concept's popularity as an explanatory principle among social theorists and cultural critics can be traced to the early years of this period, testifying to the sense that both a new day and a new generation were emerging.[8] In our own time, partly in response to the aging of the population and the impact it has had on our social structure and agencies, there has been a resurgence of scholarly interest in the roles of age—and consequently generation—in social stratification, and also in the relationship of age to such traditional sociological variables as class, gender and race. Within the ambit of post–World War II politics and culture, generation has come to be seen as a critical factor that can at times supersede class in shaping ideology and behaviour.[9]

Among historians, generational analysis has long been employed as a viable approach to the history of the family. Its most common application is within the context of life-course studies, where it is usually restricted to parent-child generations or birth cohorts, as in Glen Elder's pioneering work on American families during the Great Depression.[10] Socio-cultural historians have also examined the nature and role of "special" or "strategic" generations, as exemplified by Robert Wohl's study of the "men of 1914," or Doug Owram's examination of the Canadian political and intellectual elite that constituted the "government generation" of the 1930s through the 1950s. In the realm of collective memory, the famed Baby Boom generation has produced or inspired a number of what can be classified as "generational biographies," in keeping with that generation's status as the most self-conscious in history. Also intriguing but ultimately less sustainable is the application of generational analysis to extrapolate from past or current trends as predictors of conditions and behavioural patterns, a type of history of the future premised on a "recurrent dynamic of generational behaviour" and demographic forecasting.[11] Twentieth-century literary works, including memoirs and fiction, have also sought to capture the collective psyche of particular generations, such as the "lost generation" of the post–World War I years immortalized in such novels as F. Scott Fitzgerald's *The Great Gatsby* (1925) or, more recently, the post-boomer cohorts classified by Douglas Coupland as *Generation X* (1991).[12]

The term's analytical application is obviously complicated by the difficulty of precise definition. Unlike *cohort*, which comprises everyone born at a certain time who came of age together, *generation* is a decidedly loose category.[13] In its basic sense, it refers to a group that is demographically identified by biological trends, whose members have certain shared historical experiences. These can be age-related—often on the level of popular culture, as in the "Jazz Age generation" or the "television generation"—or they can be defined by such world-historical events as war, economic depression, or moon landings. *Generation* is sometimes meant to take in people of varying ages, as occurs when parents are described in generational terms even though the group may well contain different generations. It is often used synonymously with *cohort*, and it is frequently conflated with *decade*, as in "the twenties generation" or "the sixties generation."[14]

It must be acknowledged, as well, that the selective, sentimental, mythic, and possibly arbitrary aspects of generational consciousness—and hence definition—may be impossible to account for. These elements affect the social construction of particular generations, both self-construction and construction by others, contemporaneously and through the historian's wary eyes. The generational fact that emerged in Western Europe on the eve of World War I drew much of its motivating force from a growing awareness of its significance among social critics, intellectuals, and social scientists of the day. Likewise, the "modern generation" that arose in Canada in that war's aftermath incited much public examination. It was hailed as a different species than its progenitors; it was acknowledged and explained as such; it was granted a specialness that, while often exaggerating the differences between young and old, nonetheless marked the generation's position in significant ways. "We are living in a new world," declared the editor of a rural newspaper in Ontario, as he insisted that "with all the dangers and difficulties of our times, there is a stimulating atmosphere around us; the very air we breathe is a tonic; and the call is for heroic youth to measure up to this demand."[15] At bottom, all these generational approaches—historical, contemporary, academic, discursive, fictive—centre on the relationship of generations to social change.

For the purposes of this study, I favour a concept of generations that emphasizes their historical location more than specific cohort dates. To borrow from sociologist Bryan Turner, my interest lies in "the social formation of distinct generations": their generational consciousness, what remains through history to identify their particular experience of youth, and the dynamic through which they transmit some aspects of their culture to successive generations to be modified, reshaped and reclaimed as "generational."[16] Despite the suspicions to which the term *generation* lends itself as applied in historical study, it is an effective organizational and analytical tool for considering the changes and continuities in the culture of adolescence as these relate to broader socio-cultural change over a fairly limited period. At the very least, *generation* identifies those who belonged to a certain social group—a category or class—within a specified range of ages, as is certainly the case where adolescents are the subject.[17]

Generations of youth, of course, do not exist in a historic vacuum. Their destinies invariably take shape in relation to the experiences of those who precede as well as those who follow them. Generational theorists stress that the collective consciousness underlying self-awareness of membership and a certain commonality of age-based experiences and interests—a generational consciousness—is most acute during the adolescent years. At this developmental stage, young people first become aware of their place in the arena of history, learn of their larger society and its expectations of them, begin to question established institutions and the conventions of their elders, and rehearse adult identities. The work of childhood self-formation that commonly takes place within the confined settings of family and community is impelled outward into a wider world, where the young undergo the final phase of individuation that will bring them to adulthood.[18] Where this self-formation is concerned, generational analysis also casts light on the role of collective and relational identities in the individuation process. For young people, especially women and minorities, the influence of these larger identities may override the individualist ideas that dominate Western societies. Literary scholar Helen Buss has observed the tendency of women to tell their life stories so as "to differentiate identity strands that are [their] own and those assumed by [their] community," the latter most often relational identities such as daughter, sister, wife, and mother. For those who lack status and power, not even pervasive individualism is capable of "prevent[ing] the self from being conceived collectively."[19]

Generational analysis attends to the under-studied status marker of age. Identities may be structured at birth through gender, class, ethnic, geographic, and historical position, but the status changes that take place over the life course and that are directly related to age are critical formative factors. Similarities of experience, function, and status within age groups and differences between age groups, uphold the hierarchy of age by means of which the roles and status of individuals and their age groups are delineated and power relations defined. Age has wide-ranging meanings for the individual as well as for the community. It is a point in the life cycle, a chronological identifier, a status position, a determinant of rights and responsibilities, and a sign of membership in a social grouping that stresses commonality without necessarily functioning "in common."[20] Cultural norms, often encoded in law, are frequently age-specific, thus discriminating between citizens of different ages and birth cohorts while ordering and regulating the life cycle.

Most important for the purposes of this study, age has become an increasingly dominant status-marker over the course of the twentieth century, even as its cultural meanings have shifted. Socio-cultural change requires adjustments in the age patterning of society as generational differences make themselves felt. Hence the age of majority dropped over the twentieth century while the age of school-leaving rose, both developments that affected the meanings of youth, adulthood, and citizenship and the dynamics of family. Modernity saw the waning of such traditional signposts of individual identity as birth and inheritance. Thus, comparison of self and others to a group that started out at the same time—identified by birth or completion of formal education or entry into the working world—gives individuals a way to gauge their own status, in the sense of being more or less successful in keeping up with the age group.[21] A number of other important demographic trends in full sway by the early twentieth century, such as increasing longevity, decreasing age gap between marital partners, and the reduced size of families, also consolidated generational mores and behaviour.[22] As literary critic Annie Krieger points out, "the age variable is perhaps not the one that produces the largest differences, but it is never negligible in any area," social, economic, political—or historical.[23]

By the time of the Great War, the "generational fact" transcended the simple demographic fact of successive human waves. It became a new implement in the expanding arsenal of the social sciences, another tool for measurement, assessment, standardization, regulation, and, most important, the age grading of the population. The rise of the social sciences lent impetus to the modern program of the state. The regulation of everyday life effectively rested on the uniform, the compulsory, the mandatory, all increasingly associated with the "correct" age for schooling, vocational training, wage labour, enfranchisement, marriage, and so on. Some of the new age-defined institutions inspired the development of others, similarly age-defined; each strengthened age identification both within the affected groups and for those excluded. Compulsory secondary schooling, for example, not only organized peer groups, but also introduced them to age-based activities outside of school, a vital modern source of generational consciousness. The new socializing institutions, especially the high school, widened the knowledge gap between parents and children, both in the sense of what traditionally constituted "learning" (or at least sufficient learning within certain restricted social parameters) and in the sense of a sophisticated grasp of new trends, new technologies, "modern" ways. Modernity inverted the social qualifications for wisdom and worldliness, once the privilege and prerogative of age. These qualities came to be identified with those previously regarded as unformed, callow youth. At the extreme, adulthood would now signify "banishment into the status of stranger to modernity."[24]

On a number of levels, then, the period considered here saw a growing recognition of the generation as a historical force, as a theory of social change as well as a means of identification. Especially after the Great War, the idea that a new, different—modern—generation was making its presence felt, an idea animated by a form of romantic historicism, became common ground among contemporary writers and intellectuals across North America and Western Europe.[25] In his influential 1928 essay on the subject, "The Problem of Generations," German sociologist Karl Mannheim posited that age is the fundamental category in any historical theory. As such, historical development is rooted in "the phenomenon of generations." Moments of intense social change and resultant anxieties tend to polarize age groups into oppositional "generation units." Such antagonistic elements, however, also exist within each generation. At times, members' other identifications—those of gender, class, race, religion—simply override that of age. Such conflicting responses from within the group remain generational reactions all the same.[26]

Mannheim also insisted on the relational and dialectical nature of the concept: what it means to be young affects the meaning of "old," and vice versa. Because power relations form the core of specific generational experiences, generations share certain defining traits with classes. Both self- and group identification, Mannheim contended, "endow the individuals sharing in them with a common location in the social and historical process, and thereby limit them to a specific range of potential experience, predisposing them for a certain characteristic mode of thought and experience, and a characteristic type of historically relevant action."[27] Through its ideas, actions, world view, and collective "style," each generation fashions its own *entelechy*, which reflects "the expression of the unity of its inner aim—of its inborn way of experiencing life and the world." The new generational style is not simply born with the generation, however. It is triggered by a societal experience of dynamic destabilization that makes traditional responses unacceptable to the young, encouraging the new and often discontiguous ideas that are the basis of generational consciousness and entelechy. Applied historically, then, the concept of generation defines an age cohort that acquires social significance by means of its formative cultural identity.[28]

For each of the three decades considered in this study, a world crisis—the Great War, the Great Depression, World War II—proved the necessary trigger for just such a generational consciousness. Each of the succeeding generations of youth carried through some aspects of its predecessors' mindsets, but each, due to its own historic context of dynamic destabilization, manifested its own generational consciousness. The most innovative generation in this regard was that of the 1920s. The effects of the historical experience of what we can call the first modern generation were consolidated by the generations that followed, even if modified by the world-historical and personal circumstances of the Great Depression and World War II. By 1950, as the period ended, certain experiences had become so clearly age-defined and "generational" as to justify classifying them as exclusively adolescent experiences, common to most young Canadians, however qualified by other factors. Among the most important of these were high school, certain forms of organized recreation, clothing, music, and language, and other aspects of a modern popular culture that, since the 1920s, was increasingly a youth culture, a mass culture fuelled by technological advances that the young, more than any other social group, were positioned to embrace.

Historic events affect people of all ages, but age shapes the experience of them. Each age group lives in what Mannheim described as "qualitatively quite different subjective eras," or different periods of self-formation, which can be effectively shared with others only at similar points in their personal histories.[29] For the "generation of 1914," both official and anecdotal evidence emphasize the youth of military recruits and suggest that many more than we can count lied about their age in order to enlist. Both ordinary recruits and junior officers could commit to service at the age of eighteen. Of the fifty-five men on the enlistment rolls of the Renfrew, Ontario, contingent in 1914, twenty-nine were twenty years old and under, and seventeen were just eighteen or nineteen. Sent to Canada as a Barnardo boy at the age of eleven, one young man ran away to join the expeditionary force as a sniper: "I gave me age as eighteen. I was between fourteen and fifteen." The last surviving Canadian veteran of Vimy Ridge, Clifford Holliday, endured that momentous battle before his seventeenth birthday, which was "just another day" in the trenches coping with rats, body lice, and the unrelenting enemy menace. Alice Strike, the last surviving female Great War veteran, joined the Royal Flying Corps (later the RAF) as a pay clerk when she was only seventeen, before marrying a Canadian soldier and emigrating to Winnipeg in 1919.[30] Well aware of the "under-age" phenomenon, the Great War Veterans Association lobbied the federal government to extend its veterans' vocational training program to those who had enlisted under the age of eighteen. The group pointed out that young men of fifteen and sixteen had sacrificed their chances for a good education to fight for their country, and that "no glory attaching to the experience" could compensate for the loss of opportunity, much less for the "broken down condition of many...which had rendered them helpless at practically the gate of a career."[31]

Those whom childhood largely spared from direct participation understood the watershed nature of the Great War as they became the "new generation" of the "new day." One rural Ontario woman remembered her intense impression that, after the armistice, "the world changed." Her prewar childhood now appeared to have been "just like a Strauss waltz" in contrast to the stepped-up pace of modern life.[32] In another Ontario town, a young boy recorded in his diary that "an old world was dying and a new one was waiting to be born."[33] Writer Hugh MacLennan, fourteen years old when the war began, believed that "the First World War haunted us.... We were all children of the First War, and its real horrors were just being revealed when we came of age."[34] In a letter to his adolescent daughter Dorothy in 1927, journalist and publisher J.F.B. Livesay would also refer to the war's generational legacy as he wondered, "Why are all you young people so sad? Is it because you missed the experience of the war, understand its horrors but not its beauties and its benefits and so blame us for it all?"[35]

During the 1930s, the crisis of imposed idleness was suffered by a great many Canadians of employable age, but probably by none more than the generation that finished school just as jobs disappeared. The Great Depression's impact was vastly different for the never-employed female teenager than for the middle-aged male breadwinner, and government relief policies were established on precisely that premise. Where the war had depended on youth for combat forces and home-front production, summoning them to active, selfless participation in the national cause, the Depression sidelined the young, curtailing their normal opportunities while reallocating limited resources to those already bearing adult responsibilities. Age and its concomitant social status effectively relegated youth to the furthest margins.[36] Writer Hugh Garner was fundamentally shaped by his Depression experiences, effectively captured in his autobiographical novel *Cabbagetown*. Seventeen years old in 1930, Garner spent years "riding the rods" across Canada, the United States, and Mexico in search of some means of subsistence. For all its hardship, the experience moulded his character and his craft: years later he would conclude that he would "not have wanted to miss the Great Depression for the world."[37]

Likewise, memories of a Depression childhood could not help but mark the outlook of those who were adolescents during World War II. Mordecai Richler, who was attending high school in Montreal, later wrote of his wartime youth, "I cannot remember it as a black time and I think it must be so for most boys of my generation. The truth is that for many of us to look back on the war is to recall the first time our fathers earned a good living."[38] For any number of young Canadians, the war would bestow the first opportunity since leaving school to be productively engaged, adequately clothed and fed, and earning wages. Writer Bill McNeil, growing up in the Depression-ravaged mining town of Glace Bay, Nova Scotia, remembered that, "that first wave of enlistment brought in the worst victims of the Depression, those poor lads who didn't know what it was like to have enough to eat or wear. I know, because many of them were my friends and neighbours. I would have been with them too, but in September 1939 I was only 15 years old, too young to fool the recruiting officer into thinking I was a mature man of 18. Not that I didn't try many times."[39] McNeil was "crushed, devastated and jealous beyond belief" when his friends were accepted, although only slightly older than he, at fifteen and seventeen years. They were among the first wave of casualties from his home town, killed shortly after being shipped overseas with a few months of basic training. At seventeen, Bill Marshall was probably the youngest of his platoon in the Highland Light Infantry, 9th Brigade, part of the second wave of the Canadian 3rd Division's landings at Juno Beach in June 1944. He survived D-Day but was wounded in Buron a month later, just three days past his eighteenth birthday.[40]

Among those who did not enlist, there was a marked sense of having "taken a short cut to adulthood."[41] During the anxious years of the war, the young were frequently called upon to defend themselves against charges of frivolity and even delinquency. There was considerable "scolding and yelping" in the press, in the juvenile courts, and among "those who deal with the youth of the country" about how teenagers were "letting the boys in service down." In response to one such reprimand by a *Toronto Star* columnist, three young women, aged seventeen to nineteen, tried to make a case for their generation and their gender:

> We the 'teen-age girls are the ones who are feeling this war most. Our brothers and fathers are away. Our mothers are working nights in munitions plants. We had to curtail our education in order to feel that we were doing our part in the war effort. We took jobs to help out. You accuse us of being asleep, of not knowing that there is such a serious thing as a war going on because you don't approve of the type of dancing we like or the things that stir us, as you put it. We would honestly like someone to tell us what is wrong with jitterbug dancing that makes you feel called upon to classify it with crime and juvenile delinquency.... Why pick on our generation?[42]

This sense of injustice translated into generational animosity, fuelled by the frustrations of youth at being constrained by historical circumstances and still not measuring up to the older generation's expectations. But the war also inspired generational solidarity, first in the cause of victory and finally in its celebration. At the end of it all, on VE Day in May 1945, in a scene likely repeated across the country, Vancouver's Magee High School was "intoxicated with joy." Having known only war for their entire high school stay, students "swarmed" into the auditorium "amid wild yells and hoots of pleasure" as the principal suspended classes. The whole school was "awarded a dance," and "students and teachers kicked up their heels on the long-awaited V-E Day."[43]

Historic events such as war and depression take on primacy in individual lives as in the collective generational experience, influencing both memory and lifelong impressions of social and political issues. Age and historical location, where personal and national history intersect, imprint generational consciousness. Just as much as class, race, and gender affect perception, experience, and outcome, so does age matter. The personal and the national, the biographical and the historical, connect in a generational framework.[44]

The rhetoric of generational opposition, or old versus young, often expressed in the antonymic categories wisdom/folly and virtue/vice, is also historically contingent. In the process of becoming adult as well as becoming modern, the young identified increasingly with their peer group, both on a generational basis and as part of the work of individuating from their parents. While intergenerational conflict is not "naturally" or biologically ordained, such clashes come about when, to quote Pierre Bourdieu, specific "conditions of existence...in imposing different definitions of the impossible, possible and the probable, cause one group to experience as natural or reasonable practices or aspirations which another group finds unthinkable or scandalous, and vice versa."[45] Norbert Elias, Mannheim's most gifted student, made the generational struggle for power and position the "social kernel" of all historic struggle. As Elias explains it, the success of the "rising generation" in improving its position depends upon the resources and opportunities offered to youth in any given moment.[46] When the usual generational rhythms of cultural transmission are disrupted by intense social change or world events, the authority of the older generation—and hence that of the dominant culture—cannot be as readily passed on to the receiving generation. As the young become unable to identify with the culture and values of their parents, intergenerational misunderstanding, if not conflict, also intensifies.[47]

Generational theorists postulate that this failure of cultural transmission may be ongoing in societies characterized by socio-cultural change as a "rapid, ineluctable and permanent feature of a technological civilization." An increase in peer-group socialization, consequently, is a key feature of the social changes of the past century. The historical context makes the peer group's experiences "unique" while emphasizing the similarities within and the differences between generations.[48] Rapid modernization had the net result of "crowd[ing] historical meaning into the family time span," providing for children a social content vastly different from that acquired by their parents. Alongside certain intrinsic differences between parents and youth, a set of extrinsic ones arose, heightening the potential for youth alienation and therefore generational opposition.[49]

"History" does not simply happen in particular ways to those born at a particular time; clearly they are participant, in varying degrees, in their own histories just as in "history." Whether they resist adult expectations, accommodate them, or embrace them outright, the young are not simply acted upon, despite the power imbalance imposed by age. And the generational conflict itself, however construed, does not play out merely as historical variations on the same melody, but is eminently variable in its rhythms. For all those adolescents who, like poet Dorothy Livesay, became "anti-family" during their teen years, there were those who "grew up very happily."[50] In the early 1950s, McGill University sociologists Frederick Elkin and William Westley challenged what had already become orthodoxy in regard to the inevitability of intergenerational conflict. Examining the situation of adolescents in "Suburbantown," a middle-class anglophone Montreal community characterized by "relative social and vicinal isolation," they found that the peer group did not serve as an oppositional group to the parents but rather tended "to encourage and reinforce many values and patterns of the adult world."[51]

It is also evident that the socio-cultural meanings assigned to adolescence—what it is seen to typify at particular moments—not infrequently reveal more about the pressing concerns of "society" (or at least of a sector that has political and economic influence) than about what the young were actually doing. The modern concept of adolescence catalyzed new ideas and new controversies about youth socialization that were—as they continue to be—direct referents to cultural change.[52] In his critical examination of what he aptly terms the "juvenilization" of the culture of our own times, anthropologist Marcel Danesi contends that the very act of keeping sexually mature young people in a state of enforced dependency is largely responsible for the "youth problem" of modernity, a problem that shows no sign of abating.[53]

The language of generational conflict became a sort of probe for exploring the tensions between the traditional and the modern and for examining evolving notions about national identity.[54] Although focused on the young, and especially on the "youth problem," public discourses throughout this period were also very much about the nation. A number of scholars have examined the relationship between early-twentieth-century anti-modernism and a nostalgic, mythic, even folkloric version of national history, demonstrating how differing views of past and future entwined with current issues of national identity that were regularly depicted as an outcome of generational differences.[55] Canada was, in effect, born a modern nation. The melding of its geographically and historically disparate units into a nation-state in the late nineteenth century depended as much upon the application of science and technology as upon political will, its gradual expansion "from sea unto sea" arranged by new technologies of communication and transportation.[56] But these forces, while elemental in accomplishing a nation, were also disruptive. For all that it signified progress, modernization also entailed rapid, unplanned industrialization and urbanization, rural out-migration, an unprecedented wave of immigration, the dispersal of Aboriginal peoples of the west in the interests of European settlement, and farm, labour, female, and regional discontent over widening economic disparities and inequitable political representation. While the young Dominion appeared poised to come into its own during the new century's opening decades, Canadians were also impelled to come to terms with modernizing forces by turns welcomed and feared. In many ways, it was not the structural changes entailed in modernization that disturbed Canadians as much as it was the condition engendered by these changes, a condition diagnosed as an ambiguous state of "modernity" or "modern times" or, even more succinctly, "the times."[57]

The new ideas and new things introduced in the new century made more apparent the existing cracks in a Victorian world view premised on continuity, stability, and progress as pathways of ongoing human achievement. Under the rubric of "modernism," the new order gave rise to a multitude of aesthetic styles and intellectual movements. By the eve of the Great War, cubism, Freudian psychoanalysis, atonal music, the theory of relativity, atomic science, and ideas about the divisibility of truth into "atomic propositions" were all in circulation.[58] For the majority, whose lives were far removed from the avant-garde and the intellectual elite, modernity was experienced more fundamentally in the everyday discordances of traditional ways with the new realities wrought by science and technology.[59] This is not to say that the modern simply and directly replaced the traditional, or that the spiritual was completely eclipsed by science and materialism: historical processes, like everyday life—like the very process of "growing up"—look backward and forward at once. This, too, characterizes experiences of both adolescence and modernity. The "war to end wars," in its nightmare force, blasted away much residual Victorianism or traditionalism, a loose body of ideas and approaches increasingly seen to be repressive and outmoded. Many influential Canadians agreed that the nation stood "at the parting of the ways." Yet if Canada's participation in the war had "elevated her to the status of nationhood and given her a world-wide renown and influence," the young Dominion, like its young citizens, was "merely on the threshold of her momentous development."[60]

By the 1920s, it appeared to many that "the times" had spawned certain destabilizing trends of fearsome potential. Contemporary discourses about a multitude of "modern problems" consistently reveal a subtext of ambivalence, if not outright anxiety, about the future: hope and fear are simultaneously discernible. Not coincidentally, it was at this time that a number of voices joined in ascending chorus to support a generational explanation. Thus, a "youth problem"—more specifically, "the problem of modern youth,"—distinguished the postwar generation from all its predecessors. Adolescents embodied the young Dominion's prospects. Carried along in an international tide of violence, working-class unrest, the undermining and collapse of political and social institutions, the proliferation of radical ideas, and the apparent loosening of moral standards, the generation born into the prewar world came of age in one that had changed irrevocably.[61] Simply for having attained that life stage during a tumultuous time, adolescents came to constitute a "youth problem" that their elders were duty-bound to set right.[62] The young were not merely confronting problems peculiar to their location in their personal life histories and in history—because they were young, they were a problem in and of themselves.

In attempting to grasp what is meant historically by adolescence, I share in the campaign to order, classify, categorize, and measure that energized the social and human sciences and their rising caste of "experts" in the early twentieth century. A number of these, ranging from physicians and those concerned more specifically with "mental hygiene" to educators, sociologists, and anthropologists, put together a remarkably cohesive body of theories concerning the "new" species that they termed "the modern adolescent." In doing so, they also took part in its making. The very premise of their work, as well as its rationale, reflected and reinforced a wider process of cultural transference: the traditional job of child socialization was less and less the business of families and more and more that of experts, themselves increasingly backed by new state agencies and policies. Whether they were invited by informed middle-class parents eager to be "modern" and "scientific" or dispatched by the new agencies to supervise the less fortunate and therefore problematic families, the admittance of public experts into the private domain was one of the most intently modern innovations in family life. It was also one that would profoundly affect the experiences of childhood, adolescence, and adulthood.

I support the idea of a multiplicity of youth experiences, both within specific time and culture contexts and over time, but I am focusing here on ordinary young Canadians and on what distinguished generational styles, with due consideration to race, ethnicity, language, religion, region, gender, and class. These all mattered—as they continue to matter—in shaping adolescence. While acknowledging that contemporaries often meant more than adolescents when they spoke of an amorphous category of "youth," at times even including unmarried adults up to age thirty, I use the terms *adolescent*, *youth*, and *teenager* to designate only those literally in the teen years, from thirteen to nineteen. The vast majority within this age group were finished with formal schooling by age sixteen, and only a tiny minority entered university, yet the records demonstrate that by the 1920s an unprecedented number were attending high school, and for longer periods than ever before. Most young Canadians of the time saw their adolescence roughly divided between school and work. I have consequently restricted my study to those in high school, in some form of job training, or at work, to the exclusion of the minority involved in postsecondary education.[63]

Although my scope is national, a tally of sources will show the prevalence of Ontario material. In large part the reasons are the familiar ones of practicality. But recognition must be given to the province's prototypical qualities in the period under study: it was the most modern component of the modernizing nation. Because Ontario was the most urban, most industrialized province, and the one most influenced by American technology and consumerism and related trends, much of the technology and popular culture that would become the heart of modern youth culture radiated outward from there. It was the media and advertising headquarters at a moment when mass media and advertising were fast becoming the major transmitters of messages about youth and modernity. I do not want to overplay Ontario's role in the making of a modern nation any more than in the making of modern youth, but that role is significant.

It has become standard practice among historians to focus on either the English Canadian or the French Canadian aspects of a given subject, and this study regretfully adheres to that convention. Wherever pertinent, I have referred to Quebec sources, both anglophone and francophone, but I have in no way done justice to what was unique to francophone Quebec youth. The experience of growing up in First Nations communities also merits its own study. While class, gender, and race are integral to any social group or socio-cultural phenomenon, the records lend themselves more to analysis of middle-class ideas and behaviour than to those of the working class; to urban rather than rural settings; to "white" or native-born Canadians over immigrants, Aboriginals, and people of colour; to Protestants over Catholics, Jews, and those of other faiths. I have also chosen not to look closely at the young people classified as "deviant," despite the fact that generalized deviance, as I have noted, was ascribed to young people. This is not a history of the aberrant, or of those represented as such. I have made "ordinary" adolescents my subject, in the awareness of how that label is itself a social construction.

In addition to the social historian's usual store of sources, I have tried to centre the stories of young Canadians themselves—excavated from a variety of print, oral, and electronic sources—in this larger story. This was easily the most challenging part of this project, since adult voices so often override those of the young and since adult perspectives form the basis of historical understandings of the meanings of youth and its experience. While recognizing the problematic role of memory as a historical source, I follow Neil Sutherland's inspirational path in regard to the "scripts of childhood": how people remember—what memory highlights for them as they look back over their own histories and over history writ large—is as significant as the veracity of detail or the accuracy of recall. There are certain themes, events, and issues—from entrance to high school or the working world to dating, extracurricular and other group leisure activities, participation in organizations, peer and familial relations, and the impact of national and world events—that not only are similar across class, gender, race, and regional divides but are also meaningful touchpoints in the personal histories of those remembering. Particular memories form a pattern that implies certain generational effects of certain events. From these can be discerned personal meanings that take on collective, or generational, significance, depending on the age of the individual at the time of the event.[64]

If the continuities in adolescent culture are relatively clear—adolescents' economic dependence, for example, and their lack of political power—what was "modernized" about adolescence during the first half of the twentieth century, and especially during the focal decades bounded by the wars? How did the changes transforming the nation shape the experience? How did changing experiences of youth affect Canadian society and culture? What follows is an attempt to understand the national, generational, and historical context for the evolution of ideas about modern adolescence and what these ideas signify for the Canada of the past, present, and future.

1

In Theory

The "Problem of Modern Youth"

Critic, with judgement crass
And too much haste, you say
That youth, on the primrose way
Steps on the gas.
Your ill-aimed cross-bow bolt
Quite misses youth's revolt.
Your missile hits
No bull's eye of this truth.
That ever flaming youth
Is a thing of opposites.
Its constant paradox
At your mad "magpie" mocks.
Wild youth, as ever thus,
Will not be bound by us.
—editorial, Toronto Star, *1926*

*A*ppearing at the ostensible height of the public furor over "flaming youth," the sardonic verse that is this chapter's epigraph acknowledges two fundamental facts in the history of adolescence: first, that social critics throughout all time have taken issue with the young; second, that they have achieved little in the way of their desired outcome. Public anxieties about "wild youth" are no more exclusive to modernity than they are unique to Canadian society.[1] Yet within the setting of a new worldwide awareness of youth as a modernizing force, as well as of the young Dominion's own experience of liminality in striving to become modern, adolescence was configured as "the problem of modern youth."[2] Perhaps even more than the material challenges facing Canadians in the early twentieth century, the socio-cultural implications of those challenges aroused a foreboding about the collapse of cherished institutions and the historical relations of authority that sustained them, including those between generations. Racialized and class-based apprehensions about disorder, degeneration and crisis—much of the rhetoric echoing concerns in Great Britain and the United States—took form in public discourses that often focused on the disintegration of "the family." Modern youth found a ready place in the ever-lengthening litany of the day's "social problems." The young became the cardinal symptoms of a widening urban pathology, just at the moment when doctors, psychologists, and educators were increasingly inclined to consider adolescence as a sort of psychosis. Proposals for the containment and supervision of youth in the name of health and social order were reinforced by particular ambitions for a "modern" Canada.[3] This chapter discusses the period's prevailing theories about adolescence, which were drawn from a variety of disciplines with much cross-fertilization and not a little imagination. The central question concerns what Mannheim posited as "the problem of generations": how and why did young Canadians constitute a profoundly modern "problem" from the Great War to 1950?[4]

Medicine and the social sciences, especially psychology, extended their reach beyond clinic and classroom just in time to supply an appropriate typology for the problems that appeared to be destabilizing youth, family, and nation in the early twentieth century. The much-studied Social Gospel movement, which aimed to bring an activist Christianity to bear upon the negative effects of modernization, also capitalized on the rise of these family "experts." These experts would provide the science to transform the movement's Christian middle-class objectives into the policies and agencies essential to national regeneration, especially where the critical matters of child and family welfare were concerned. In Canada as elsewhere, the language of citizenship permeated child welfare discourses. Especially in the Great War's aftermath, children and youth became "national assets" whose well-being was as much the concern of the expansionary state as it was of the private family. Eugenic theory—a distortion of genetics that sought to control the reproduction of the "unfit," classified in blatantly class and racialized terms—also captured the popular imagination, lending dubious support to child-saving campaigns. The futurist orientation of "the modern," as expressed in pervasive concerns about public health, national welfare, and "racial hygiene," simply demanded that youth be rescued from "the unholy trinity of Mammon, Bacchus and Priapus."[5] In many ways, this new obsession with the rising generation was a logical extension of the campaign to regulate the health and socialization of children in a manner befitting the goals of the Century of the Child.

The physiological changes known as *puberty* distinguish childhood's end, but even these measurable biological markers do not allow for more than a normal range of ages of entry into adolescence, which can manifest as early as ten years and as late as eighteen, with the years thirteen to sixteen being the most common. Gender, and such class, race, and regionally influenced elements as standard of living, nutrition, access to health care, general health status, and heredity are important causal factors in the timing of puberty. More to the point, while puberty is integral to the experience of adolescence, the two are not synonymous. Yet contemporary theories about that experience were resolutely biological, centring on the bodily changes associated with puberty, especially sexual maturation. Throughout the century—and to this day—public debates about adolescence rang with adult trepidation about youth sexuality. At base was an implicit understanding that sexual self-control, whether learned or somehow imposed, is the key to the successful regulation of the young.[6]

During the century's early years, a rising caste of modern experts articulated concepts of childhood and adolescence that would strongly influence policies of institutional age segregation and subordination. Since adolescence was the prime training grounds for citizenship, and since the wearing down of family, church, and other traditional agencies of socialization was considered the foremost of worrisome modern trends, expert direction and state involvement were entirely justified. The segmentation of the life course into self-contained stages, each critical in its own right, was part of the rationalization of modern living that encouraged new modes of social governance. In the schools, modernity's age-consciousness gave rise to universal age grading; to the development of curricula standardized to the life stage, especially in secondary schools; and to such "scientific" measuring systems for supposedly age-appropriate physical and mental development and behaviour as the intelligence quotient (IQ) testing that was widely adopted in North American classrooms by the interwar years.[7]

Growing public acceptance of ideas about childhood as an especially vulnerable stage that demanded parent education and expert supervision also helped to extend the experts' vigilance beyond childhood's end. By the 1920s, adolescence was seen to provide a unique opportunity for special—and specialized—attention to the needs of the young. The ideal was a partnership of informed parents and professionals, but the balance of power was steeply inclined toward the experts.[8] If the larger child welfare campaign was hobbled by insufficient regulation of parenting (given that parents could exercise their freedom in applying modern childrearing tenets) how much more might resistance be an issue when the object was the—by definition—intransigent adolescent? The point remains that the experts, in laying claim to adolescence, expanded their claim over parents and children of all ages, however much or little this was realized in day-to-day family living.

Despite experts' general embrace of the progress model of science, which sees each generation as rethinking and reformulating theories in the light of new evidence, there is an astonishing thematic continuity in those experts' ideas about adolescence straight through (and beyond) the period considered here. As the century opened, social scientists were intent on perfecting measures of the normal, and consequently of the deviant. These modern measures were derived not only from contemporary scientific currents but also from personal qualms about a social milieu that was being disrupted by modernizing forces. Recapitulation theory in particular influenced medical and psychological ideas about child development. Borrowing from evolutionary theory and cultural anthropology, recapitulationism correlated individual human development with the larger process of human evolution. The developmental stages of childhood and adolescence reflected the prehistoric state of humanity, the primitive and savage. Each succeeding stage of "normal" development, successfully negotiated, would bring the individual closer to the evolutionary apex of adulthood and thereby into the modern age.

The recapitulationist paradigm was most famously disseminated in the work of American psychologist Granville Stanley Hall. A pioneer in American experimental psychology and a leader in the international child study movement, Hall was a key figure in the project to establish age norms, and is easily the most renowned twentieth-century theorist of adolescent development. In his oft-cited multivolume work *Adolescence: Its Psychology and Its Relation to Physiology, Anthropology, Sociology, Sex, Crime, Religion, and Education* (1904), Hall framed his subject squarely in recapitulationist terms. Finding resonance within a context of conflicting and even contradictory ideas about the promises of modernity, his views affirmed that adolescence constituted the critical gap between primitive childhood and the "more perfect form" of civilized adulthood.[9]

Hall's conceptualization of adolescence emphasized at once youth's profoundly preparatory nature and the disjuncture between childhood and adulthood that typified this transitional stage. By focusing on the moral, sexual, and psychological upheaval that he saw as the principal trait of adolescence, and by identifying this storm and stress exclusively with the onset of biological puberty, he effectively distinguished the hallmarks of modern adolescence. The outcome has been an enduring portrayal of "normal" adolescence as a period of physical and mental anarchy, during which the young demonstrate, as Hall declared, a "peculiar proneness to be either very good or very bad."[10] Thus, they need careful direction by their elders. For parents, professionals, and all other concerned adults, the objective had to be "the stabilization of youth during this important period." Hall gave the physical manifestations of puberty less import than the psychological dimensions that really "made" adolescence, but his understanding of the adolescent psyche was resolutely biological.[11]

Hall's constitutive theory of adolescence was not modern in the sense of diverging greatly from its antecedents, many of which were medical in origin, most also asserting that puberty entailed interrelated physiological and emotional changes. More synthetic than innovative, moralistic than scientific, homiletic than analytical, his study was nonetheless the first comprehensive multidisciplinary treatment of the subject. But what made Hall's ideas inaugural and uniquely tenable was their introduction at a notable historical conjuncture. Socio-economic transformation had prepared a receptive audience for any number of 'scientific" theories that helped to explain current ills and suggested ways to resolve or at least regulate them.[12] Although the biological explanation influenced their work, sociologists and anthropologists of Hall's time tended to be more concerned about the environmental elements of the adolescent experience, specifically the role of the city, as the "youth problem" took on increasingly urban contours.[13] In the end, however, the early-twentieth-century experts were agreed upon one notion: that modern youth constituted a problem of alarming scope and potential.

This dedicated study of adolescence would give rise to numerous attempts to manage the actual members of that life stage. Such campaigns were not in and of themselves a modern phenomenon either, as the complex schooling, apprenticeship, inheritance, and marriage laws of earlier times easily demonstrate. What is different—modern—about early-twentieth-century approaches is the extent and uniformity of theorizing about and surveillance of young people, as manifested in the public discourses, professional studies, government surveys, and all manner of reform campaigns common to Western industrial nations at the time, including the young Dominion. Nor were such broadening (at times escalating) anxieties about young people contained at the discursive level. In Canada as elsewhere, they took form in an intricate network of state policies and legislation designed to address such related "problems" as those of youth recreation, labour, schooling, vocational training, "social hygiene," and juvenile corrections—to name the most prominent—that constituted the multifarious modern youth problem.

For all that worries about the young can be tracked throughout history, with the dawning of the Century of the Child, adolescents gained legitimacy as serious subjects for medicine, psychology, and the emerging social sciences. Contemporary studies did not simply expand the knowledge base: they operated in a fundamentally political manner as they interacted with public concerns about the national importance of childhood and youth, the cultural implications of modernity, the maintenance of civil order, and the training of a citizenry to meet certain prescribed "modern" ends. In these modern times, individual age and the age group became useful instruments for sorting and classifying human beings; identifying status, civic rights, and duties; and defining the appropriate means and methods of regulation. Class, race, and gender also remained key signifiers of what made the young a "problem"—or at least what made some young Canadians more of a problem than others.

The storm-and-stress model did not go unchallenged even in Hall's own time, but its imprint on the body of twentieth-century theories of adolescence has been remarkably tenacious.[14] While there is no obvious link between Hall's ideas and those of Sigmund Freud, Hall did much to introduce Americans to the Freudian thought that would come to characterize modern psychology. Freud's biological view of the psyche clearly fits with Hall's own biological determinism: both the psychoanalytic and the recapitulation approaches depict adolescence as phylogenetic (involving a staged process of psychosexual development that is genetic) and therefore not greatly affected by environment. Most important, like Hall, Freud stressed the critical relationship between the physiological manifestations of puberty and the growth of the psyche, reinforcing the storm-and-stress perspective on sexual maturation.[15]

Hall's ideas did much to shape Canadian perceptions of youth as a social problem of distinctly modern proportions.[16] Along with publications by other American experts and reformers who specialized in youth issues, such as Jane Addams, his writings were cited in Canadian publications, professional journals, newspapers, and mass-distribution magazines, and were read by Canadians in popular American publications. Presented without fail as though their findings were directly applicable to Canadian conditions, by the time of the Great War they reached a growing audience of both experts and ordinary, largely middle-class readers.[17] Canadian medicine, psychology, and sociology were increasingly affected by these new ideas about the nature of adolescence and its social impact. By the 1920s, sociology was opening up a promising area of specialization in family studies, especially at the renowned University of Chicago, from which emanated the modernization hypothesis that would dominate North American family sociology for at least the next half-century. Sociologists in Canada, many of them Chicago-trained and working out of Montreal's McGill University, took active part in examining the array of 'social problems" identified under the heading of modernization.

Concerns about "the family in crisis" made families particularly sensitive touchstones of wider change. While the purpose of such studies was to gauge the impact of modernization on internal family dynamics and on the relations of family and society, a necessary corollary was its generational impact. A number of surveys highlighted the complications of coming of age in a time of rapid change, emphasizing the generational conflict inherent in the relations of modern youth with their less-than-modern parents.[18] Chicago-trained sociologist Horace Miner, in his 1936 study of the "traditional" community of rural Catholic St. Denis, Quebec, contended that "every phase of life" had been touched by the "cultural changes" of the previous generation or two. Among the most notable changes was the growing number of youth who left the family farm and the community itself for urban employment, especially among those who came of age in the mid-1930s: 24 per cent of that generational cohort (aged fifteen to twenty-four) had out-migrated by 1947.[19] Studies by McGill sociologists Charles Young and Carl Dawson made similar observations about immigrant communities in western Canada. While these emphasized environment—the changes in the family's outer world and how these affected changes within—Young and Dawson nonetheless assumed adolescent angst to be a normal feature of the life stage, in these instances exacerbated by the tensions between old-world and new-world cultures.[20]

The most important critique of the storm-and-stress approach came from cultural anthropology, influenced particularly by Franz Boas's dismissal of biological determinism in human and cultural development.[21] Given its topical relevance, adolescence suggested the perfect test case: did biology make the tumultuous experience universal, or did culture act to reinforce, mitigate, or at least differentiate any presumed connection between biology and youthful turmoil? In 1928, Boas's student Margaret Mead produced *Coming of Age in Samoa*, probably the most widely read anthropological field study ever published. Mead's still-debated conclusion was that in societies such as the Samoan, where generational continuity in socialization and cultural conditioning are maintained, adolescent angst is minimal. A contemporary of Mead's and another of Boas's students, Ruth Benedict, further refined this understanding of the centrality of cultural conditioning, arguing that adolescence becomes conflict-ridden when modern societies codify vast differences in age-based rights and responsibilities.[22]

The closing years of the 1930s brought attempts to meld the biological and cultural approaches in a new synthesis that would see both nature and nurture at play in the adolescent experience. German psychologist Kurt Lewin's "field theory" placed adolescents within "a marginal and ambiguous life space," a situation that encourages both individual disequilibrium and adhesion to the peer group. The most important means of adolescent "social anchorage," this peer-group identification is also biologically supported: changes in the body directly affect changes in the life space, moving adolescents toward those who share these changes as they strive to detach from both parents and the "past child."[23] Following upon Mead and Benedict, Lewin contended that adolescence is most affected by the socially constructed barriers separating adults and children: rigid barriers exacerbate both individual and generational conflict. As did his contemporaries Karl Mannheim and Norbert Elias, Lewin argued that intensive social change sharpens the disjuncture between childhood and adulthood, amplifying adolescent tumult as the young are obliged, by accident of timing, to adjust on multiple levels at once.[24] In the 1950s, psychologist Erik Erikson would expand on this view, beginning with his *Childhood and Society* (1950), which dominated thinking on adolescence through much of the second half of the century. Employing contemporary anthropological findings to modify Freud's theories in two subsequent works, *Identity and the Life Cycle* (1959) and *Youth and Crisis* (1968), Erikson saw adolescence as principally a crisis of identity formation. In his perspective, despite cultural and historical differences in how the process is experienced, the experience itself remains a constant.[25]

When discussion of "this mysterious developmental process called adolescence" turned to socio-cultural factors, these were typically grafted onto the biological stem without much change in explanations of why the young posed such a challenge to modern society. As did many of the experts—on both sides of the biology/environment debate—commentators of all stripes gave signal importance to the "hectic modern times" that rendered adolescence "characteristic of and created by our form of civilization." Yet even while the historical moment was ascribed explanatory force, the young person's inability to cope with problems peculiar to both the age group and "the times" was still explained biologically.[26] In his popular advice manual for parents, *Normal Youth and Its Everyday Problems* (1932), whose very title captures the idea that the adolescent experience is "normally" troubled, American psychologist D.A. Thom found no "specific psychological principles applicable to the adolescent period." But he did find "certain physiological factors and psychological situations that are not met elsewhere, or are met here for the first time, or are met more frequently here than at any other time," so that adolescence was inevitably a stage "when all of life seems to be dominated by the intensity of the individual's own feelings."[27] The boundaries between mental and physical health and what was considered healthy social functioning were nowhere as ambiguous as in discussions about this life stage.[28]

The Hall paradigm sustains, even now, widespread assumptions about the nature of adolescence, testifying to the popular hold of the ideas that he first disseminated publicly a hundred years ago.[29] The core issue of biology versus environment has not been resolved. Each perspective has come into and fallen out of favour, often coexisting with varying degrees of comfort in both professional and public debates about children and more particularly about "the youth problem." Because they draw attention to the perpetually assailed family, moments of crisis lend weight to theories of biological causation; yet the proposed solutions tend to support environmental approaches. The seeming contradiction is understandable within the wider context of any given moment's crisis. During the first half of the twentieth century, experts' interventionism facilitated a biological causation theory that assuaged the responsibility of those who might reasonably have had some power to effect the environmental reforms needed. Turning to culture for the cure allowed—even demanded—expert participation in fixing what ailed, as they were trained to do.

Physicians and psychologists drew a direct line of causation between the rapid physical and mental growth of the teen years and their characteristic emotional confusion, while also faulting the socialization of adolescents, which found them thrust without adequate preparation into the hostile world of adult customs. Anxiety and alienation were the inevitable—indeed, the "natural"— outcome. As one Canadian doctor declared, it was "not to be wondered that so many... break down physically or mentally, but the wonder is that so many survive the ordeal with the little health supervision and health knowledge they receive."[30] If biology was destiny, the worried public needed to understand that destiny could be positively affected by intervention, regulation, and management of the problem—in this instance, of the adolescent.[31] Just as the liminal nature of adolescence explained many of its characteristics, organic and otherwise, it also pointed to an invaluable opportunity for expert intervention. In the interests of their safe passage to adulthood in the midst of a socio-historical swirl, the minds and bodies of adolescents became objects for much keener examination and regulation than ever before in history.[32]

By the Great War years, extended compulsory schooling and child protection legislation, child study, "child-saving" through new social agencies and family courts, and state-supported campaigns to supervise the health and upbringing of infants and schoolchildren indicated a childhood becoming modern by means of science and state regulation. The stage was set to support arguments, policies, and initiatives aimed at following these newly supervised children into the adolescent vortex, where they stood in danger of squandering all efforts previously extended on their behalf and in the nation's interest. If modernity were complex—tantalizing yet worrisome—what better means to its realize its benefits than through youth, modern citizens in the making?[33] The challenge lay in the fact that the young also appeared best qualified to adopt and popularize the modern age's darker elements.

At a time when child welfare was the foremost international reform objective, the boundaries between medicine and psychology were especially permeable, with pediatric specialists and child psychologists staking claims for their own expertise. As with their plans for infants and young children, the experts now argued that safeguarding the health of adolescents must become a national priority and the cornerstone of any program for youth. Supported by the new science of adolescence that construed this time as a form of organically based psychosis, experts in all fields argued for regular medical supervision and health education, the latter also encompassing "sex hygiene" or some basic high school training in the facts of life. It did not matter that there were no illnesses or defects, mental or physical, seen to be endemic to the age group, or that its general health status was excellent. The recommended supervision, like that for infants and schoolchildren, was to be all-embracing and focused on prevention. The adolescent's precarious condition meant that every part of life, from family relations through friendship, courtship, schooling, recreation, and work, might harbour threats to physical and mental health, and consequently to social or civic functioning. Expressed in intertwining discussions about public health, national welfare, and "racial hygiene," this futurist orientation demanded "the protection of parenthood."[34] This could be best accomplished by character training that made a specified and supervised regimen of self-care and self-control integral to adolescent socialization. In its broadest terms, this would take form as "a constructive education in citizenship and the ideals of national and individual life."[35]

With their shared biological emphasis, modern medicine and psychology upheld theories of an avowedly gendered adolescence, at a time when gender roles were actually more unsettled than ever. Categorical depictions of the "normal" characteristics of masculinity and femininity in youth perhaps reflected precisely that wider condition of insecurity and flux. Experts encouraged the cultivation of "manliness" through the co-development of muscular strength and "character," scarcely departing from Victorian ideas about muscular Christianity, imperialism, and the value of the school playing fields in the training of future military and political leaders, especially relevant while the young Dominion fought at Britain's side during the Great War.[36] Advice literature directed at boys and their parents promoted a virile but "civilized" manliness, as signified by the "vim," "push," "pluck," and "stick-to-it-iveness" that were held to make the "wholesome manly boy," traits that would ensure his future roles as citizen, father, and breadwinner.[37] By drawing attention to the poor physical health of recruits, the war further reinforced the importance of the "physical standard." Emerging boys' organizations such as the Tuxis asserted that "the men of the future must come from the boys, and if we put weaklings to the fore our country will go behind. The physical life of the boys must be developed to the utmost."[38]

Experts and youth-watchers alike, while insisting on the modernness of their views, maintained a traditional stance on feminine health and female social roles that upheld the primacy of the maternal. Much more than was the case for young men, however, such views were clearly at odds with the possibilities modernity was offering to young women, suggesting why worries about "the girl problem" were so resolutely biological. While the life stage was a dangerous passage for both sexes, young women were particularly predisposed by "nature" to an even wider variety of potential physical and mental health complications. Echoing the admonitions of Victorian medicine, the modern literature on female health distinguished little between the physical and the moral "protection" of women's reproductive capacity during the "critical years." Hall saw women as perpetually adolescent, their psychological formation never complete, never approaching the evolutionary apex represented by adult men. In his view, "woman's body and soul are phylectically older and more primitive, while man is more modern, variable and less conservative." He insisted that feminists were "persistently ignoring" the central importance of reproduction in women's lives, much to the physical and emotional detriment of adolescent girls.[39] Views of this type were hardly confined to male experts: an advice manual published the same year as Hall's study, by a female physician, which purported to be "The Twentieth Century Book for Every Woman," stressed how the young woman owed "much of her beauty and power" to the "regular healthy performance" of menstruation.[40]

Hall modernized his essentially traditional argument about women by fitting it to the recapitulationist perspective, contending that a more evolved society needs more, not less, defined gender roles. He acknowledged that gender roles are in part socially constructed to suit the needs and objectives of particular evolutionary stages. But he warned that, because they are biologically determined, their modification could not be countenanced in the long term: "Nature decrees with advancing civilisation that the sexes shall not approximate but differentiate." Young women were pushing beyond their "natural" limitations as they became caught up in such modern trends as urban living and employment. They were "fired" with ambitions that they could not safely and effectively attain, and therefore condemned to the unhealthy condition of "a suppressed semi-erotic state with never-culminating feeling." Unable to "fix their attentions properly" on womanly things, they were "lapsing into mannish ways, methods and ideals." Paradoxically, even as they became mannish, modern young women seemed to be transforming themselves into "mere figurines" and "grow(ing) dollish" by resorting to commercial amusements and shopping to pass their time rather than taking up their ordained vocation in homemaking.[41]

If the experts were generally critical of the modern young woman, social commentators were quite simply alarmed by the "girl of the new day," whose appearance and demeanour made her a visible affront to middle-class domestic ideals. One Torontonian was appalled at the sight of two young women on Yonge Street "with their overshoes flopping about loose" in the fashion that christened the flapper style of the 1920s. He suggested that "it would be a good scheme to have the police stop any young girl appearing out with her overshoes not fastened up and have her head examined," as the entire look was "so degrading."[42] Young women who adopted the style, and especially those who adopted the "manly" habits of public smoking and drinking that often accompanied it, set off warning bells about the decline of "womanliness," hence the family, the "race," and the nation. And the most dangerous flapper—due precisely to her precious youth—was the adolescent girl, now not so much "unnatural" in the Victorian manner for her flouting of middle-class convention and parental authority as psychologically and socially "unadjusted."[43]

In response to Hall's urging that women be trained to regard matrimony as their "one legitimate province," at least one contemporary female educator countered that "an inquiry so uncritical in method" as his own was a "relic of mediaeval times" that had no place in modern science.[44] Yet there was little of the modern in one doctor's declaration, in 1920, that "nothing in the whole range of life can compare in importance with the potential powers of reproduction" of the adolescent girl.[45] Amidst a postwar celebration of maternalism, even as more girls attended high school, pursued higher education, and launched careers, a new urgency surrounded earlier concerns about the ramifications of "intellectual development" on the physical health of "our girl life at a time when every attention should be given it."[46] For modern young women, expert opinion held that true adult status still signified motherhood. A modernized motherhood was the woman's badge of citizenship.

Concerns about reproduction, both biological and social, were often thinly veiled fears about sexuality in a modern age where it seemed to represent a mounting generational defiance of established moral conventions, gender ideals, and corresponding behaviour. The early-twentieth-century interest in sexual regulation stemmed from Victorian social-purity campaigns, which had brought sexual matters into the public forum. In turn, reformist campaigns had brought about legislative changes that narrowed the parameters of normal sexuality according to age and gender.[47] After the Great War, Freudian ideas acknowledging the primacy of sex in human experience and confirming the existence of the female sex drive were making incremental progress among the educated. More liberal practices, however, especially regarding the sexual freedom of unmarried youth, appear to have been limited to an avant-garde minority, notwithstanding the many fevered commentaries of the time. A 1930 American survey of 252 women under the age of twenty found that only one-fifth accepted petting as "natural" dating behaviour, while 92 per cent declared that premarital relations were "immoral or unwise."[48] Theories about adolescent sexuality marched in tandem with those about gender, adhering to the values associated with Victorian middle-class Christian morality. Modern science and the new openness of discourse about sexual matters encouraged the period's experts to discuss adolescence primarily—often exclusively—in terms of sexual maturation. At the same time, their views lent scientific support to a repressive educational crusade bent on making the life stage a sexual moratorium, contrary to "nature" as well as to modernity.

By and large, sexuality was seen to pose special dangers to adolescents simply because they were not adults. Even while she celebrated the supposed sexual expressiveness of Samoan adolescents, Margaret Mead believed that the pressures of modernity offered their American counterparts too many possibilities for being drawn into premature sexual relationships that intensified adolescent emotional turbulence through jealousy and competition.[49] Whatever the extent of the "new honesty" about healthy sexuality, anything to do with auto-erotic practices or same-sex attraction—indeed, youthful sexual experimentation of any kind—continued to be strictly proscribed. The inevitable physical consequences were made inseparable from mental and moral deterioration, which, for good measure, was linked to social degeneration, even to devolution. Sex was an adult domain, as evidenced in public discourses about the "flaming youth" of the 1920s, so labelled in large part because of their perceived "modern" sexual proclivities.[50]

The problem of modern youth was essentially about constraining youthful autonomy during a time when the experiences that traditionally distinguished life stages were changing within a wider context of shifting socio-cultural practices. The expanded regulation of adolescence—all to the purpose of training the ideal, responsible, conscientious adult citizen—had the ironic effect of extending dependence and infantilizing the young.[51] The wider social process was a juvenilization of culture that made the tastes, desires, and practices of youth increasingly the standard for all. In the 1920s, modernity was offering new and varied options to the "new generation." Adolescents of the "new day" were becoming adults in a manner so distinct from that of their elders that they appeared to be a collective social force cutting across all traditional barriers. Although this was often more illusory than real, what matters is that it was a widespread public perception about the younger generation. Media exaggeration and moral panic aside, modern youth were enjoying relatively greater personal freedom than had earlier generations, including their own parents. To adults looking on in fear and judgement, this translated into disproportionately greater moral licence, itself generally interpreted as sexual licence. Values, much like activities, were being increasingly defined by the newly important peer group, those biologically prepared for "the worst" while emotionally, psychologically, morally, open to temptation. It seemed that modern adolescence was sheltering the young from adult responsibilities while undermining the constraints customarily placed on the adult pleasures to which they aspired.

In its earliest formulation, what would crystallize after the Great War as this "modern youth problem" focused on poor urban youth, boys in particular, whose situation was regarded as symptomatic of the evils of the new industrial order. From very tender ages, they crowded city streets in barely respectable occupations and pastimes—hawking wares, selling newspapers, delivering messages and commodities, smoking, lounging about billiard halls and penny theatres, apprenticing in petty criminality.[52] The idea that such hapless children should be saved from their own instincts and from negligent or exploitative families, employers, and predators led to the adoption of such late-nineteenth-century legislation as the children's protection acts of Ontario and Manitoba, which specifically prohibited those under sixteen from "loitering in public places" after nine o'clock at night, and in the changes to the Criminal Code raising the age of consent for women to fourteen years.[53] Adolescents were not yet a separate legal category; those over sixteen were classified "adults." Nor had they yet, in generational terms, earned the classification of "social problem."

By the eve of the Great War, every public discussion about boys—at times bordering on moral panic, at times crossing that border—was replicated in one about girls. But troublesome adolescent worker-lads never lost centrality, because it was this group that was considered to be contributing disproportionately to rising crime rates. Much of the rise can be explained by the more careful application of the sweeping federal Juvenile Delinquents Act of 1908. With the legal codification of crime labelled "juvenile" and the creation of a related judicial machinery to deal with it, there was a corresponding rise in arrests, more often for age-related status offences such as truancy, loitering, curfew violation, and sexual promiscuity than for actual crime. Interpreted as a direct increase in adolescent criminality, however, the statistics fuelled public alarm and encouraged a culture of fear that focused on the young. The 1925 criminal court data that showed 8,064 convictions for boys and 675 convictions for girls also represented "a tremendous waste of money and happiness."[54] Whatever the relationship between the number of prosecutions and actual crime levels, law and order were served by clearing the streets of problem youth, thereby demonstrating to them the preferability of alternative forms of recreation.[55]

While giving special attention to the under-sixteens, the 1908 Act did not address the real problem of youth criminality: the sixteen to under-twenty-one age group showed a much higher crime rate than the younger group and also had the highest rate within the larger sector of the seven to twenty-one age group.[56] Many argued that not enough was being done to ensure that boys in this older group stayed out of trouble, both morally and legally. The director of the three-hundred-member Halifax Boys' Club contended that "far too large a proportion" of this older adolescent group could be "found abroad at a late hour." Their public rowdiness and mischief, easily observable, compromised not only the boys' welfare but "the citizen's welfare as well."[57] In Toronto, hundreds of boys, many "barely 16 years old" frequented "cheap shows," and it was evident to all observers that the late hours, "nervous excitement," and "moral deterioration" resulting from this practice were "injurious to character." Along with dime novels and cigarettes, such habitual pastimes prevented boys from "settling down to a trade or to regular employment" and all too often led to "idleness, theft and vicious habits."[58]

Shortly before the Great War, the Big Brothers associations began their work of providing surrogate fathers for boys of all ages, the vast majority of whom came from poor families whose domestic relations were considered most in need of supervision and regulation. In 1920, the Toronto Big Brothers Association, with 180 registered male adult volunteers at the ready, reported an unprecedented case load of 429 boys, many of these the orphaned, neglected, or deserted children of deceased or incapacitated war veterans. The most common crimes within this group were theft and disorderliness, with truancy, vagrancy, trespassing, and house-breaking next in order.[59] The new family courts established in most provinces by this time also testify to the perceived need for an institutional apparatus to deal with wayward youth within a specialized setting that would combine legal regulation and social casework to the best remedial effect. While the ideal was probation rather than incarceration or punishment, actual practice tended to blend modern ways with the more traditional: for example, Montreal's juvenile court, established in 1912, almost doubled its reform-school contingent during its first eight years of operation.[60] Although probation was the more common response by the early 1920s, it did not wholly replace incarceration or even corporal punishment. In 1920, a sixteen-year-old "bandit" who had participated in a "reign of terror" involving auto theft was sentenced to three years in Kingston Penitentiary "coupled with one whipping of five slaps with a strap." On his first court appearance, "the young desperado was disposed to treat the whole affair as a joke"; upon sentencing and the immediate delivery of the strapping, "in marked contrast to his former appearance, he... seemed cowed and broken-spirited."[61]

As possibilities for urban "girl labour" expanded, there was a corresponding (partial) redirection of public concern to the "girl problem." The focus was "moral purity" rather more than the incipient criminality associated with the boy problem. Where girls were concerned, immorality was in fact delinquency. Language, clothing, hairstyles, defiant attitudes, and behaviour narrowed the gender gap in the code of social convention, making girls their own distinct challenge to authority.[62] In some ways, girls appeared more openly and frighteningly modern, especially in their seeming ambition to emulate boys. One Montreal social worker claimed to have personally counted, on a single week night in the summer of 1922, 125 girls under sixteen "out unattended, promenading up and down" at the corner of St. Laurent and Ste. Catherine streets. The general secretary of the Big Sisters Association also deplored "the pitiable position in which many girls, young and eager for pleasure and diversion" found themselves, due to poor working conditions, overcrowded lodgings, and "other troubles which drive them out to seek amusement from commercialized sources."[63] Such institutions as the Interprovincial Home for Young Women, founded in Albert County, New Brunswick, in 1923, testified to the growth of establishments to reform the troublesome, the "fallen," and even those who merely challenged adult authority, as in the case of "one who was almost ruined through having her own way and making doormats of her parents." This particular inmate, as the residents were called, evidently "came to herself in this Home... and went out a capable, sweet young woman."[64]

The "girl runaway" was a hot subject in the press during the 1920s, fuelling public worries about the seemingly new propensity for dangerous adventuring among young women. In 1925, the *Globe's* regular Homemaker Page featured a detailed interview with Mary E. Hamilton, "New York's best-known police-woman," who estimated that some five thousand girls "disappeared" in the United States every year.[65] Hamilton's view of the girl runaway situation was true to Hall's theories: she believed that the young were "apt to go to extremes, emotionally and mentally," simply because of the fragile condition that was adolescence. Hurt feelings, a desire to be alone, rebellion against authority, boredom, love of adventure, and a "desire to see the world" were the primary motivations. Not dismissing parental responsibility, Hamilton considered that "a father's extreme severity figure[d] all too frequently" in prompting girls to take to the road; another "prominent" reason was "the claiming by parents of their children's hard-earned money."[66] Some parents felt the need to turn in their seemingly intractable offspring when they felt unable to deal with them, at times sparking serial escape attempts by those confined against their will. Such was the case of sixteen-year-old Kathleen, committed to the Orillia, Ontario, industrial refuge by her father, who reportedly was sure that a year's confinement would "cure his daughter of all her waywardness." After her first successful escape, she spent the months from May to September in "the north," where she was taken in by a sympathetic family. Something appears to have gone awry in that arrangement, because she was soon sent to live with an aunt; the aunt quickly asked to have her recommitted because she had run away to Buffalo and "was not doing at all well." The hapless Kathleen once again fled the refuge within days of her involuntary return but was located two days later, suffering from exposure.[67]

Running away was the ultimate show of adolescent rebellion, the most extreme form of self-individuation. In one reported instance, two fifteen-year-old Toronto girls left home to "be in the movies." One of the girls claimed to have two sisters who were actresses, and "to this influence the police ascribe(d) the determination of the two girls to leave home." They were ultimately tracked down by police, after several days' search, at the Metropole Hotel in Detroit.[68] The flight across the border is common enough in these escape stories to qualify as a trope. Another pair of girls, aged fourteen and fifteen, escaped from the Ursuline Academy in Chatham, Ontario, only to be "picked up" by police after a few nights in Windsor and returned to their school. The runaways confessed to have been "looking for adventure, which they expected to find in Detroit." Penniless and hungry when found, the girls said that they would go back to Chatham gladly.[69]

As applied to the young, *deviance* and *delinquency* were interchangeable terms. What history shows to have been emergent cultural trends or even simply matters of generational style, the two, often overlapping, were read as signs of expanding youthful licentiousness and criminality.[70] The growing interest in the girl problem was more pointedly about adolescent or young unmarried women than about children. Taking public discourses out of the encompassing child-protection arena made adolescents a unique concern whose problems posed different threats and required different remedial approaches.[71] Adolescent angst became the all-inclusive basis of both perceived deviance—the diverse ways in which "flaming youth" flouted convention and "flamed"—and the legal classification of delinquency.

The media discussion of the youth problem in the 1920s also consistently reveals a strong sense that "hectic modern youth" were failing to match the standards of preceding generations, especially of those who came of age in wartime. It was undecided whether this was the fault of the new generation itself or whether the older generation, especially parents, with their newly sanctified responsibilities to child and nation, were most to blame. The "modern home" usually topped the list of contributory factors. Its apparent moral vacuum explained a great deal of the "extravagance" of youth. Toronto's chief of police attributed "the prevalent lawlessness" directly to the breakdown of authority in the family. Modern parents were oblivious to how their children spent their time outside of home and school, and did not even know who their children's companions were. The modern home functioned as a mere "parking place between shows and dances."[72] More specifically emphasizing "the lawlessness among the young men of today," a family court judge warned that "the present serious condition" exposed "a not very healthy condition of affairs... when parents allow their children to be out until 3 or 4 o'clock on the Sabbath morning drinking and planning mischief.... We have worse than heathen right in our own community, for the youthful criminals of today are more efficient than the darkened criminals we have been used to.... Something must be done to stamp out this kind of thing."[73] An anonymous juvenile court judge writing in *Chatelaine* magazine's inaugural issue in 1928 insisted that the state "must train and if necessary force parents to carry the responsibility for the support of the children they have invited into the world"—the parents of those prosecuted for misdemeanours should automatically be charged with failure to properly care for and train them. While recognized to be drastic, it was felt that such legislation would do more than any other single influence to reduce the number of juvenile offences.[74]

The interwar years saw unprecedented attention to the pressures exerted by the peer group, another of Hall's fixations: the supposedly inevitable loosening of the parent-child bond was also a hallmark of modern adolescence. According to theory, the adolescent was biologically impelled to work toward self-individuation and independence, achieving these by means of emotional and eventual physical separation from parents and a simultaneous intensification of peer-group attachments. The peer group's socializing functions became qualitatively more important than those of parents.[75] Peers' role in helping the adolescent achieve self-sufficient adulthood, however, was intrinsically problematic, giving rise to worries about the nefarious effects of the group gone bad, as manifested in the street gang. By the 1920s, the gang's role in juvenile delinquency (hence in the youth problem) was a significant source of public alarm, reinforced by the popularization of Hall-inspired psychology. Thus, a series of "juvenile purse-snatchings" culminating in a botched drugstore robbery that led to the arrest of two fifteen-year-old Toronto boys was explained by the boys' membership in "a gang of juveniles who have been for some time travelling along the road to serious crime." According to police, the duo kept company with "a dozen or so lads who have been reading dime novels and recently some of them have been found carrying dangerous weapons."[76] It seemed but a short step from trashy reading to armed robbery.

Youth workers and commentators understood why the gang, with "its social spirit, its power of suggestion, its mob psychology, its scope for leadership and hero worship, its spirit of adventure and method of spreading responsibility upon many shoulders," appealed to the adolescent boy.[77] But "young hoodlums" were becoming "a nuisance" and even a menace, especially in urban areas. One man returning to his Toronto home after work in the late afternoon was confronted by such a gang, "who rolled him about the road, and, after some further horse-play, ran off." When his wife ran out into the street in response to her husband's shouts, she was "driven back into her home with a torrent of abuse." The Claremont Street neighbourhood, according to local police, was "infested with gangs of young rowdies who have no respect for the law." The law came down hard, with orders that any boys found loitering on street corners would face summary arrest. Undeterred, the boys responded in kind: "a crowd of fifty" followed a constable who attempted to carry out the orders by arresting one of their number; they threatened to attack him, further alarming the public.[78]

As noted, the sociology of the interwar years was characterized by an ecological understanding of the relationship between modernization and social disintegration. The University of Chicago sociologists who pioneered the approach also stressed the correlation between youth gangs and adult lawbreaking. Their theories about gangs, however, were contested by psychologists who, following Hall, adopted the biological model that depicted delinquency as "necessarily the product of particular personality patterns," many of which characterized adolescence itself. Softening the determinism of their interpretation in view of the fact that not all adolescents were delinquent, experts maintained that delinquency was not so much an adolescent trait as it was "a perversion of the normal psychological patterns of adolescence."[79]

Yet the "normal" psychological patterns of adolescence were themselves abnormal in reference to the only standard that mattered, that of the mature "evolved" adult, with the adult male standing tall at the evolutionary pinnacle. Dr. C.K. Clarke, psychologist, founder of the Canadian Mental Hygiene Association, and dean of the University of Toronto medical faculty, addressed eight hundred teachers in 1920 on the "deplorable depravity" of Canadian youth, reminding his audience that "upon them fell the duty of saving the race from juvenile delinquency." He had personally discovered girls as young as thirteen suffering from venereal diseases, some becoming unmarried mothers, others "commencing lives of shame," with not much to tell the difference between their shameful lots. Clarke had also seen boys who had acquired habits associated with "only the most hardened moral perverts." In his view, the source was organic: the "moral depravity" underlying youth delinquency was largely attributable to "feeblemindedness." He might as well have said "race," as he theorized that feeblemindedness disproportionately affected immigrants.[80]

The characterizations of dangerous youth shared the racialized profile that showed through so many of the period's discourses of anxiety. Not only were the foreign-born felt to be more inclined to deviance at all ages but "aliens" provided the settings most conducive to it. The *Toronto World* reported in 1918 that "aliens" owned most of the city's licensed poolrooms: a reporter who visited fourteen pool-rooms in the Queen-Bathurst district "found himself as in a strange country...a stranger among the elect.... No one spoke either French or English." Worst of all, "the preponderance of youth was noticeable."[81] The fear that such places might contaminate the children of respectable "Canadians" was matched by a dread of what "foreign" youth might be capable of in their own regard. Moreover, the immigrant neighbourhoods, with their crowding and poor housing, harboured any number of "crime-producing tendencies." They could scarcely shelter their inhabitants in safety and security. Young people inevitably strove to "escape as often as possible from their cramped quarters": "They drift to sidewalks, to gatherings under street lights, or to shops and dance-halls, anywhere where they may find space and light, and if the weather is cold, warmth." Although they rightly went out to seek light and warmth and companionship, they invariably found "opportunity for mischief that sometimes degenerates into serious misdemeanour."[82]

Despite their prevalence in the media, contemporary data did not support such racialized interpretations of the youth problem. Sociologist Charles Young's mid-Depression study of the Ukrainian settlements across Canada, primarily in the west, found their communities to be "particularly free of crimes of a serious nature." According to the 1921 census data, of some 25,000 Ukrainian residents between the ages of ten and twenty years, not one was found to be in a reformatory. But rather than trouncing the stereotype of dangerous foreign youth, Young questioned the veracity of this statistical portrayal of their respect for the law. He claimed to have personally observed much fighting in the settlements, most of it resulting from "the capers of the young males" and usually touched off by drinking. The situation was decidedly worse for Ukrainians in urban areas, where he thought he saw definite signs of the breakdown of parental authority and "misbehaviour among large numbers of the younger generation." The young men in particular, "surer of foot, more accustomed to the ways of the new world and slightly contemptuous of the old," had "gone their own way," in many instances making "a sorry mess of things." Their gangs and wild parties were largely responsible for incidents of disorder in the Ukrainian communities. Settlement teachers reported that "the imperfectly assimilated adolescent," who knew little English and lacked "character training" opportunities, all the while "shut off" to the traditional prohibitions of the older generation, was becoming "a serious menace." According to Young, national duty demanded that "inclusive programmes" be implemented to prevent the social disorganization that immigrant communities were evidently suffering due to the generational clash and the youthful (male) propensity for inflammatory action.[83]

Inter-ethnic animosity was also fuelled by youth gangs that preyed on their peers. Growing up during the 1930s in a Jewish family on Beatrice Street, in the College-Grace-Crawford area of Toronto, Fred Sharf and his friends were terrorized by the notorious anti-Semitic youth of the Pits Gang. The gang's activities led to the 1933 Christie Pits riot, in which a baseball game between a non-Jewish and a largely Jewish team ended in open gang warfare. In Sharf's recollections, though, most of the neighbourhood gangs were relatively benign, made up of "tough guys and bullies." While territorial in the manner of gangs that marked their turf carefully, they were not anti-Semitic and "if one guy in our gang knew one guy in the Bellwoods gang then we could safely walk through "their" territory." The Pits Gang, on the other hand, based its membership on a pledge of anti-Semitism, and actively sought out Jews to attack. For the youth who lived there, the Christie Pits area was "a war zone" throughout the 1930s and into the war years. One day in 1941, Sharf and his friends, by then sixteen and seventeen years old, lingered too long after watching a baseball game at Bickford Park and were predictably attacked by the Pits Gang as they left the deserted field. Although they were badly beaten and police arrived on the scene before the perpetrators—including one in a Canadian army uniform—had finished, the police "did nothing."[84]

The peer group became pathologized to the extent that the conceptualization of the gang as a criminal breeding ground took on the nature of "a scientific postulate" between 1920 and 1950.[85] Fixation on the gang menace frequently revolved around its distinctly non-middle-class ideal of manliness, the "typical" street gang usually consisting of urban working-class boys, often of immigrant background or otherwise racialized.[86] Such was the appeal of the gang theory as integral to the "modern youth problem" that even the much more benign evidence from the period's ubiquitous field surveys did little to shake it. Contemporary research often suggested that gang activities were more protective than criminal, especially in the case of young people in ethnic communities, for whom membership functioned as a social network and a cushion against the sometimes hostile host culture. Moreover, the racial mix in most urban ethnic neighbourhoods at times meant that gang identity was defined more by age and neighbourhood than by race. The boys in Fred Sharf's gang were "the best friends anyone could have..., playing together and protecting each other" against the city's prejudices.[87] Some recognition was given to these more fraternalistic gang functions, but most of it was rhetorical, hinting that the concern was more about peer influence than about gang influence in itself, the street gang serving as a convincing, visible object of that concern.

Sustaining the theories about youth and gangs was the idea that class, gender, and even race, while contributory, were now being superseded by age as a factor in delinquency. Troublemaking was quite simply becoming an age-based, often group-based inclination, mitigated somewhat—largely by the diligence of the adults in individuals' lives—yet deeply ingrained in the adolescent psyche. Could there be any question that supervision, containment, and regulation were needed? Sympathetic noises were made about how youthful criminality might be caused by "feelings of rejection, inferiority, or insecurity, directed by juvenile gang interest due to a lack of adequate social and recreational guidance." Conversion of these "instincts" and associations into healthy sports and club activities would remedy even the gang's criminal potential, "for most of its wrong-doings are traceable to the play instinct."[88] Such views permitted more active and optimistic intervention than simply cracking down through the police and the courts, though that too was advocated, especially in times when fear was transformed into moral panic and the young delinquent into the legendary folk devil.[89]

Crisis, real and imagined, must have appeared unrelenting to Canadians during this scant half-century punctuated by two global wars and the Great Depression. It is hardly surprising that anxieties about the future should have coalesced over the heads of modern youth, the future personified. While there were continuities in theme and content through these years, however, there were also changes that reflected and addressed the particular historical context of each generation, loosely defined: During the Roaring Twenties, both "flaming youth" and their negligent parents—some too unashamedly keen to be young moderns themselves—were soundly reproached for their failures, most of which arose from the gauntlet of moral traps that represented a questionable modernity. During the 1930s, youth-watchers carped about the "idleness" that predisposed the young to sin and lawlessness and inverted gender conventions, permitting the employment of women while demoralizing and emasculating single young men and married breadwinners alike.

The Depression left its impress on the generational consciousness and experience of young Canadians, who figured strongly in the ranks of the unemployed and the marginalized. Among youth aged fourteen to twenty throughout the 1930s, even the unreliable statistics of the time indicate an unemployment rate surpassing that of any other category of the employable (officially, those fourteen years and over). Despite much government and public attention to the plight of single unemployed men, young women in the same group often fared even worse, as the lines were hardened regarding the male breadwinner's foremost right to work.[90] Those who studied their situation worried about the "abnormal directions" that might be taken if "youthful zeal" were denied its "normal outlet" in wage labour. Among those under twenty-one, burglary and house-breaking charges rose more than 130 per cent between 1926 and 1936; there was an increase of almost 45 per cent in robbery.[91] Many feared that, with "hundreds of our young men and even our young women" taking to the road as a "palliative to their growing discontent," there could be little doubt that a good number would remain "homeless drifters and eventually confirmed tramps."[92]

What economist Harry Cassidy described as the "transiency of indigents" or the "aimless movement of homeless men" hit crisis proportions in the summer of 1931 and 1932. Tens of thousands of men were on the road, among them boys fifteen and sixteen years old, including many farm hands who had lost their jobs and farmers' sons who were looking to escape from the hopelessness of their rural homes. "Girl hobos" were reportedly encountered frequently, although the press rarely discussed their situation. As a teenager in Regina at the time, living on the North Side close to the railway tracks, one woman recalled that her mother always gave the boxcar riders, who were "just youngsters really," whatever she had in the way of food when they came begging at back doors, because they were so "obviously starving."[93] By 1932, the situation was being decried as "a national scandal."[94]

In May 1933, a conference of social workers and relief officials under the auspices of the Council on Child and Family Welfare decided that the federal government should assume complete responsibility for unemployed homeless men: the much-documented work camps operated by the Department of National Defence were the solution espoused until 1936.[95] The relief workers, or Royal Twenty-Centers as they called themselves in recognition of their twenty-cent daily wage, expressed their dissatisfaction with this approach in the On to Ottawa trek of that year, which ended in violence. Many of the camp inmates who participated in the trek were boys who moved to pity even those who condemned their exercise; one of the eight "leaders" arrested in Regina was a handicapped fifteen year old. These, "our sons and nephews," had "not known the love of a family or the warmth of a home for many years," in addition to not knowing the opportunity to work for their own support: "the effects of this cannot be the regeneration of the ideals of youth, but their degeneration."[96] The merciless leisure imposed by economic crisis came to be seen as symptomatic of a social necrosis that might well eat away all hope for the future—especially the hope that the young represented. The mad dark world of anarchy, sexual depravity, racial degeneration, and criminality, only hinted at during the flaming 1920s, now appeared truly imminent. Previously subtextual, fear of the future was palpably conveyed in Depression-era discourses on the youth problem.

The Depression seems to have further widened the generational divide remarked upon by earlier commentators. Many of the adolescents of the 1930s, whatever their families' social standing, were born into optimism and relative affluence only to come of age in a time of deprivation and diminished opportunity. Many would not find employment until the Depression ended, the first waves among them obliged to postpone striking out on their own, marrying, and starting families. Among these, as well as among those who, although employed, never knew the security necessary to make such plans, it was especially galling that the older generation should now be moralizing about "idle youth." Contiguous with the 1920s discussions of the youth problem is the older generation's veering between compassion and castigation, at times blaming their own generation for the nation's predicament, at other times blaming the "rising generation." More than before, however, this rising generation was becoming politicized and issuing its own warnings about the "rumble of an approaching storm" that would "surely destroy the order which is." Refusing to be forever oppressed

ON-TO-OTTAWA TREKKERS ARRESTED ON JULY 1st, 1935

The On-to-Ottawa trekkers, City of Regina Archives Photograph Collection, 1 July 1935, CORA-RPL-B-108. Reprinted with permission of the City of Regina Archives.

This composite photograph is a sympathetic depiction of the "On-To-Ottawa" relief camp protesters who were arrested in Regina on 1 July 1935. The heading "For Youth and Democracy" emphasizes the Depression's particular toll on the young and inexperienced. The youngest trekker arrested was fifteen years old.

"by the weight of a dead hand in politics, religion, business, education, amusement, conduct of private and public affairs," young people were demanding "the right to make a world" to their own satisfaction. Declaring that "our sense of values is slipping," one young woman wondered—much as had her predecessors in the context of a world stirring from the embers of war—whether "a complete revolt against old traditions" might be in order.[97] Canadians, prominent among them members of "the new generation" of the 1920s that was now taking its turn on the other side of the generational fence, were forced to concede that "it is an appalling price we are paying for folly and youth has borne and is bearing the heaviest brunt of it all."[98] Some nonetheless contended that the young were capitalizing on their historical misfortune because, in view of the "regular" adolescent state of upheaval, the crisis gave them leave to lie about, "inert, immature and inclined to indolent theorising." As "flaming youth" had done, it was their age and generation, not the system's failures, that made them "lazy and indifferent at a time when our national life needs everything we have to give."[99]

In 1938, a sit-down strike by two thousand "hungry, destitute, jobless youths from all parts of Canada" in the Vancouver General Post Office galvanized "responsible citizens" to pay attention to the fact that "tens of thousands of our young people are facing a hopeless outlook." According to a *Maclean's* reporter, the strike served warning that continued unemployment would "bolshevize many of this vast army of frustrated youth, and divert an increasing number into the ranks of the criminal underworld." As noted, the records of lawbreaking suggest that the latter trend was already being realized: in 1936 there were 3,140 young people, the majority of these under the age of eighteen years, in Canadian reformatories, and 317 boys under twenty serving sentences in penitentiaries. The Report of the Royal Commission on Penitentiaries revealed that 77 per cent of those under twenty were repeat offenders; one-third of these had first been convicted under the age of sixteen, 37 per cent before the age of eighteen.[100]

Having attained the threshold of adulthood in this time of international crisis that so deeply affected an immature industrial nation, young Canadians were forced to confront a "wall of blank negation that can neither be climbed nor cast down."[101] The problem of idle youth thus subsumed that of flaming youth during the Depression. With this notion of their idleness in the forefront, representations of youth and their associated "problems" continued to emphasize the issue of pleasures and pastimes. Commentaries on the subject, consequently, also continued to suggest that immorality, defined as "a loosening of moral fibre in respect to sex relationships," was more an issue for redress than was poverty itself.[102] Despite all the fretting about the thwarting of youthful ambitions and the decline of youth morality, some regarded the Depression as a necessary antidote—perhaps a necessary atonement—for the excesses and extravagances of the flaming youth who, like the mythical Icarus, had flown too close to the burning sun of commercialism, consumerism, materialism, even hedonism. Deprivation was a harsh but perhaps necessary lesson in sober responsibility, bringing them back to earth and to their duties as responsible citizens in the making.[103] And some of those who were attaining adulthood as the Depression commenced shared that view. A rural Ontario girl, who had spent much of her adolescence enjoying the flapper lifestyle of 1920s Toronto, where she had worked at various factory jobs from the age of fifteen, eventually surmised that "the shock of the Depression had a settling effect on my generation. I was soon married and raising a family, much to the relief of my parents who thought the carefree climate of the twenties was destroying my values."[104]

When World War II began in September 1939, public discourses on the youth problem reverberated with the concerns that had characterized them during the "war to end wars" barely a generation earlier. Young Canadians were called upon to sacrifice for the nation and the wider cause of victory. They were applauded, even glorified, for any such sacrifice, an implicit recognition of the modern version of adolescence as a moratorium from adult responsibilities. It was acknowledged that, just as Depression youth had paid a steep generational price in deferred ambitions for a "normal" life, so would those who came of age during wartime, some of whom might pay in life itself. Even those not directly involved in the war's prosecution stood to have their welfare undermined in these extraordinary times: there were now any number of "latchkey" children obliged to fend for themselves after school, as mothers increasingly worked in war industries. The spectre of spiralling juvenile delinquency due to the absence of both mothers and fathers manifested itself again, though it can hardly be said to have been truly vanquished at any time since the Great War.[105] By World War II, an "even bigger challenge" in generational conditions and relations had risen, "as the children of a depression and its handicaps are now the adolescents of another war era and the hazards that accompany it." In 1940, Toronto Big Sisters added 963 girls to its roster, with 322 more renewing contact. As the organization reported, these "were not really 'problem girls' as many seem to think, but girls with problems—some of which were the result of the long years of depression and the growing complexity of family life and which were further complicated in many cases by conditions arising from the war."[106]

Among these conditions was one that might have been greeted as an enormous improvement: the war ended the unemployment crisis and brought new opportunities for young people. Yet these opportunities were frequently interpreted as part of the "youth problem" in its particular 1940s configuration. Girls with better job prospects, for example, declined to take on work as domestics, leading to upward pressure on the wages of household workers—a good thing for the workers, but not for their middle-class employers. Others, male and female alike, were tempted to leave high school early to fill well-paying jobs in war industries.[107] Still others fared no better psychologically than their older siblings, the adolescents of the 1930s, in that they shared a similar insecurity about their prospects. The Toronto YWCA reported in 1943 that, when young people were encouraged to discuss their problems with counsellors, "the uncertainty of the future often looms large." After the war, there was a "a great increase" in the demand for counselling, "due to the unsettled conditions of the post-war world."[108]

Most feared were the spread of venereal diseases and a rise in prostitution and unwed maternity. Employing the language of war, venereal diseases were understood to be the "internal enemies of any nation," and every effort had to be extended to "enlist every responsible citizen in the war against this unseen but dangerous enemy."[109] Dr. K.J. Backman, director of venereal disease control for Manitoba, noted the "alarming fact" that the increase was chiefly in the younger age group, many sufferers only in their teens. These were the "khaki kids" who "[hung] around barracks and railway stations or [went] soldier hunting in juke joints and dance halls," caught up in "the vast social dislocation of a country at

"They enlisted straight out of school." Glenbow Museum and Archives Collection, Edson, AB, 1941. NA-3240-84. Reprinted with permission of the Glenbow Museum, Calgary, AB.

These young men from the rural Alberta town of Edson went straight from the classroom to the armed services.

war and without any organised constructive part to play in that country's war effort." When Backman and other concerned observers spoke of these young people, they were primarily, if not exclusively, discussing young women. A Winnipeg juvenile court judge reported that girls ranging in age from twelve to seventeen were "regular hangers-on at military camps or railway stations, picking up soldiers and spending day or night at one of the hotels." There was evidently a "serious increase" in the numbers aged thirteen to fifteen reported missing from home, while the proportion of infected girls in the fourteen to seventeen age range had apparently risen 50 per cent over the year 1941–42. In Victoria, British Columbia, a municipal welfare officer announced that the number of unmarried mothers had increased from seventy in 1941 to 114 in 1942; forty-nine of the latter were under twenty-one, the youngest a child of twelve. Youth-watchers inflamed a new wave of moral panic about the wartime degeneration of the younger generation, especially the girls, whose participation in the rising delinquency was consistently related to sexual misdemeanours.[110]

Under the pressures of war, governments became more inclined to take up the cause of youth, "to assure the mental and physical health of the next generation."[111] The National Physical Fitness Act (1943) proposed to extend physical education in schools, universities, the workplace, and other institutions and to co-ordinate sports nationwide. In promoting healthy recreation, loyalty, and

High School Students
WANTED!

CANADA'S New Mechanized Army offers attractive opportunities to high school and college students to serve their country in the fighting branch best suited to their talents. While serving they will be studying—taking up the theory and practice of mechanized warfare. And by their education and "yen" for leadership they will quickly qualify for promotion. Moreover, they will be aided by maintenance grants to resume their studies upon their return.

INFANTRY—Here you will be trained as signallers, mortar-men, machine-gunners, wireless operators, armorers, drivers, motor mechanics.

ARMORED CORPS — Highly skilled drivers, gunners, wireless operators and motor mechanics all form part of the tank crews.

ARTILLERY—Still another group of specialists is required for anti-aircraft, anti-tank, field, medium and survey regiments.

HOW TO ENLIST

Apply to any of these Recruiting Stations: Halifax (Cogswell St. next Hospital), Yarmouth, Kentville, Truro, New Glasgow, Sydney, Charlottetown. Or mark service selected, sign and mail this coupon to District Recruiting Officer, M.D. 6, Halifax, N.S., for free booklet.

Name .... Service ....

Street .... Address ....

Summerside Journal 27 May 1943

"High School Students Wanted," advertisement, *The Summerside Journal*, 11 January 1943, Summerside, PE. MSCH Digital Collection. www.wyattheritage.com

By 1943, the Canadian Forces were actively and directly targeting teenage boys for enlistment, as seen in this Prince Edward Island newspaper advertisement.

co-operation, the Act was integral to a home-front campaign that called upon each citizen to accept the "prime duty" of "an all-out effort to win the war" and to "get himself in good physical condition."[112] For practical purposes, the school-age population was most amenable to this sort of intervention, constituting a ready laboratory for measurement, regulation, and training. Even more important was the federal government's initiative in the interests of consulting with young Canadians to plan for the postwar world. The Canadian Youth Commission, established by the Mackenzie King Liberal government in 1940, was the first concerted, official attempt by the state to include young Canadians as active participants in developing ideals for a modern citizenship, rather than merely as subjects of adult projects toward that end.

During the early years of the twentieth century, ideas, expert and "popular," about the supposedly "natural" and "eternal" conflict between generations helped to redefine cultural categories, both in regard to the proper roles and relations of young and old and in regard to the relations of family and state, citizen and nation.[113] The result was a striking paradox. Given the nature and volume of criticism levelled against them by their elders, and even by some of their peers, it is remarkable that youth should have emerged as the shining icon of the new day. By mid-century, to be deemed "youthful" in appearance or ideas or world view or personal "style," regardless of actual chronological age, was the new cultural ideal. The "young" nations among the Western allies were now the guiding lights of the brave new world arising from the destruction of two global wars and a crushing economic crisis. Reverence for age and tradition was outmoded—youth would carry the young nation forward to lay its rightful claim to Canada's Century. At the same time, often even within the same commentary, youth as an age group came to signify a whole new problem, a modern problem that pointed to a steadily rising number of social evils and ill portents.

2

In the Home

Intergenerational Relations

It has come to the point where youth demands a voice in its own destiny and will no longer submit to the doctrine of implicit wisdom in authority or in age....Youth is at present sitting in judgment upon the older generation....High handedness simply no longer passes....You cannot conquer youth; it must be conciliated.

— *Chatelaine*, 1928

Where human relationships are concerned, there is an infinite number of possibilities between the poles of conciliation and conquest. The lines distinguishing generations are at once horizontally and vertically drawn. For most people, the central relationship of the formative, dependent, pre-adult years operates in both directions: families are hierarchically and generationally ordered even while they foster the face-to-face relations of love as well as governance. None of this is new, much less "modern." Most Canadians, for at least part of their personal histories, live in families or in some kind of familial setting. Families make up the structures of everyday life and social organization. They are also the primary site of social reproduction in its broadest sense: the locus of childhood socialization, of the generational transmission of values, mores, and culture, and of the formation of the self that constitutes the process of individuation, or growing up.

During the years considered here, what came to be remarked upon for its "newness"—its modernity—was a perceived generational divide of such breadth that it made children and parents, young and old, more estranged and "alien" in their relations than had been any previous generations. Meanwhile, the intra-generational and extrafamilial relations embodied in the peer group became increasingly influential in adolescent socialization. Much to the consternation of youth-watchers, modern youth appeared intent to dismiss the greater wisdom and experience of parents, grandparents and other kin and community members of the older generation in favour of the folly and frivolity of their own. As Mannheim theorized, the intense social change taking place during these years, much reinforced by public anxieties about the future, lent substance to the notion of oppositional "generation units."[1]

This chapter explores the relations of family and generation within the context of related demographic and socio-cultural changes. Despite the impassioned rhetoric about generational conflict that so pervaded the period's discourses on youth, the picture that emerges is not quite so stark. As the theorists surmised, differences between generations did become more apparent as the young became "modern," and as the peer group took on a new importance in the lives of modern youth. Fears about a deepening generational alienation, however, refer back to the observers' own larger anxieties more than they reflect the real experiences of most Canadian youth and their families. The period's foremost demographic trend—the prolongation of adolescent familial dependency—may have increased the potential for generational conflict, as the young remained longer in the parental home and parents were obliged to extend their tour of duty in response. But it may also have mitigated that potential in the larger interests of domestic peace and harmony.[2] While material needs were important in keeping adolescents from leaving home, they were not the only factor: changing experiences of youth affected both young and old, and it is conceivable that parenting, too, was modified as growing up became a modern experience. While public discourses as well as historical trends influence private lives, the bonds between family members—parents and children, old and young—do not inevitably correspond directly to what happens in the outside world. Private relations continue to depend, to a degree only guessed at, on personal and familial choices.

The so-called crisis in the family that appeared unrelenting through the first half of the twentieth century effectively foregrounded the modern youth problem. That crisis, however, is not altogether borne out by the period's demographic data. The continued decline in the crude birth rate, which dropped 14.4 per cent between the census years of 1921 and 1931, was the source of persistent fears about "race suicide." The modern Canadian family averaged three children instead of the customary five of Victorian Canada. By the 1920s it was also less common for women over thirty to give birth, a pattern typically found when marital fertility declines. Nonetheless, the 1921 census revealed a greater number of married Canadians than at any previous time on record. And before the Depression could take a visible toll on family formation, the 1931 census showed Canada's family population in relation to its total population (10,376,786) to be 86.6 per cent, not far from the 88.3 per cent mark that was later attained in 1966—an all-time high.[3]

In 1921, the proportion of non-adults (under twenty-one years) to adults was close, with 57 per cent in the adult category. Approximately 435 of every 1,000 Canadians, native-born or otherwise, were under the age of twenty years; there were 405,000 young men and roughly 400,000 young women aged fifteen to nineteen. More than three-quarters of a million Canadians, then, were in their high school years, regardless of where they actually spent their time.[4] The largest number was located in Ontario, with Quebec a close second. (See table 3.1.) The numbers would rise slowly: in 1931, of 10.4 million Canadians, about 1.1 million (of both sexes) were in the fifteen-to-nineteen age group; in 1941, of 11.6 million, 1.2 million were fifteen to nineteen. Both history and demography made Canada a young Dominion.

Table 3.1. Number of Juveniles of Each Sex in the Population
by Provinces, 1921

	14 Years		15 Years		16-17 Years	
	Male	Female	Male	Female	Male	Female
PEI	1,018	933	932	838	1,850	1,800
Nova Scotia	5,906	5,565	5,112	5,301	11,021	10,658
New Brunswick	4,322	4,209	3,911	3,971	8,089	7,854
Quebec	26,858	26,534	25,078	25,543	49,534	50,610
Ontario	27,081	26,186	25,583	25,211	52,250	51,637
Manitoba	6,445	6,102	5,726	5,508	11,216	11,133
Saskatchewan	7,869	7,473	6,733	6,485	13,360	12,471
Alberta	5,554	5,157	5,190	4,989	10,116	9,519
British Columbia	4,334	4,241	3,932	3,834	7,816	7,418
Canada	89,387	86,400	82,197	81,686	165,252	163,100

Source: Canada, Department of Labour, *Employment of Children and Young Persons* (Ottawa: King's Printer, 1930), 26.

The changing size of Canadian families prompted corresponding changes in the dynamics of familial relations. The modern trend of having fewer children, however, did not lighten parental duty. According to modern family experts, smaller families allowed parents unprecedented opportunities to devote themselves to their offsprings' proper upbringing. Coupled with the trend toward prolonged dependence, this effectively meant prolonged parenting, with all the emotional and financial investment thus entailed.[5] Though the former is immeasurable, contemporaries managed to estimate the budgetary impact: in 1931 dollars, the approximate total cost of raising a child to the age of eighteen— the point of theoretical financial independence—was $5,750; 77 per cent ($4,350) of this sum was thought necessary to meet the basic needs of life, 13 per cent would go to the educational costs of secondary schooling, and 10 per cent would go to combined health and recreation and social costs.[6] The last assumed continued good health and is likely too low, considering that the fee-for-service health care system could take a considerable bite out of an unfortunate family's budget. Because the statistics also point to the expansion and aging of the dependent child population, it is evident that parental investment in children was steadily growing during these years. By 1941, within the census category of young adults (aged fifteen to twenty-four, unmarried) over four-fifths lived in the parental home.[7] Although this is partly explained by the Depression, severe economic conditions did not create the phenomenon of youth dependency: these figures had been relatively stable, persistent, and high since the opening years of the century. The process would accelerate after the Great War, declining only during the 1960s as the baby boomers came of age. Put simply, the numbers signal a historic change in the dimensions of youth and the relations of family and generation.

Earlier generations of young Canadians had often migrated to find work. Young Quebeckers and Maritimers left their families in considerable numbers during the late nineteenth century as they took up jobs in New England factories, usually boarding with families from their home town, who were often kin. While many others did not venture so far afield, they frequently left their parents' hearth to "live in" with other local families in order to work (and thereby train) as domestic and farm labour; boys also apprenticed in the trades or entered into business or the professions in this manner. During a time when secondary schooling was an elite experience often restricted to boys, this extrafamilial interlude was considered important to the young person's socialization and skill training—education in its most expansive sense. At the same time, it conceivably permitted some respite from familial pressures and from generational clashes for parents and adolescent children alike. Colonial youth and those of the early years of the new Dominion commonly experienced a transit point on the passage to adulthood that presaged the protected aspects of modern adolescence. This stage of extrafamilial semi-autonomy bridged childhood dependency and the adult independence denoted by "coming into one's own" outside the parental home, most commonly through full-time wage labour, marriage, and family formation.[8]

By the last quarter of the nineteenth century, the custom of "sending out" was being undermined by such demographic and structural shifts as the decline in family size, the contraction of available land, and the expansion of urban and industrial opportunities for youth. Of particular importance was the decreasing economic value of pre-adolescent children, who now spent more hours at school, thanks to compulsory education laws in every province but Quebec and to new legislation aimed specifically at restricting child labour for those under fourteen. As younger children became more of a drag on the family economy, the paid and unpaid labour of adolescents rose in importance. The wider structural changes affecting families also meant that parents—fathers, by and large—were no longer as readily able to establish their children (more commonly their sons) on the land or in a generationally passed on trade, profession, or family business. This development contributed both to prolonged adolescent dependency and to the decline of paternal authority, the latter another of the qualitative changes characterizing the modern family.[9] The dislocations accompanying the uneven industrialization of those years meant that even older adolescents faced limited options for the kind of wage-earning that would allow for economic independence. In Canning, Nova Scotia, lack of opportunity compelled many young men to stay in school until they were aged sixteen to eighteen, while a significant number were unable to establish separate households until they were twenty-six or twenty-seven years old. Given the near-impossibility of their own financial independence, Canning's young women lived with their families of origin until they married, on average at the relatively early age of twenty-one or twenty-two.[10] Writer Mazo de la Roche recalled that, even in rapidly industrializing Ontario during those "hard years," many middle-class young men were unable to marry much earlier than the age of thirty.[11]

In the aftermath of the Great War, new or intensifying socio-economic developments consolidated this emergent pattern of youth dependency. The most important of these developments were the high cost of living, the low wages offered to untrained and inexperienced adolescents, the decline of apprenticeship and domestic service, the expansion in part-time and casual labour markets just as promising entry-level jobs were increasingly difficult to find, and the growing social value placed upon secondary schooling. Also an undeniable factor was the rise of a consumer economy that fuelled materialistic ambitions, with new products, services, and advertising urging the younger generation on to something better than what their parents had. These modernizing trends reinforced the more traditional ones that had historically worked to keep some young Canadians at home until marriage. These include the continuing demands of the working-class and farm family economy, as well as cross-class expectations that the young would make some contribution toward the family's quality of life and that respectable young women, especially in immigrant communities, would remain safely in the parental home until married.[12] Among families striving to further themselves, whether native-born or immigrant, the wages of the young were critical to collective plans to improve their material condition by buying land or a house or through education.

The same ideas that defined a modern youth problem also made containment in the family home, and increasingly in the school, a high priority for the purposes of regulating the young. Most provinces raised the age of school-leaving to fifteen or sixteen during the 1920s, keeping the majority of young Canadians within the school's confines at least during the critical formative years of early adolescence. By the 1920s, therefore, prolonged youth dependency had already become a defining trait of adolescence. Closely tied with prolonged schooling, it is perhaps more accurately classified as semi-dependency, in view of the wages earned by many young people even while they remained in school and at home.[13] Contrary to earlier notions that independence should be fostered once the teen years were entered—that "coming into one's own" was the precise point of childhood's end—modern parents were strongly advised to hold on to their young until the "dangerous" years of adolescence had been safely negotiated. A new familial status for the adolescent child and a new type of parent-child relationship were often the outcome.

This new semi-dependency of the young was featured in many of the anxious discussions about modern youth throughout the period. Much of the rhetoric, moral judgement, admonition, and advice, as well as many of the plans for the regulation of youth, sustained a theory that the potential for generational conflict grew in proportion to the time that adolescents remained in the parental home. The issue was not so much that the young were residing longer with their parents; many commentators viewed this positively, regarding lack of adult supervision as a large part of the youth problem. The issue was that many of these young people worked at full- or part-time jobs and had money to call their own, without the significant outlay required of independent adults. This could lead to tensions between parents who wanted both authority and a contribution to the family economy and children who saw themselves as wage-earning adults and wanted to keep their own hours and most of their wage packet. It is possible that a certain peace was arrived at, as parents adapted to the generational changes taking place. As economic times improved for many Canadian families, older children who contributed either unpaid labour or a portion of wages, or at least paid their own way, appear to have enjoyed a larger measure of personal freedom than had earlier generations who left home or had to relinquish more of their wages. They often earned just enough to buy themselves—in accordance with the culture and internal dynamics of their particular families—some latitude in their activities. For those who arrived as young children, and especially for the first generations born in Canada, this adolescent condition of semi-dependency also signalled acculturation. They were no longer bound by old-culture family patterns that supported paternal authority and made family needs and goals the overriding concerns for all members, especially in regard to control of filial earnings.[14]

As historical circumstances made early independence increasingly problematic, contemporaries became so uneasy about the familial and social implications of this thoroughly modern trend that the federal government commissioned an in-depth census analysis on the subject. In his comparative study of the decennial censuses of 1911, 1921, and 1931, Dominion statistician J.E. Robbins discovered that the "average young person" of twenty years in 1911 had earned twice as much as his or her counterpart of 1931. In 1911, the average accumulated earnings of an individual's teen years equalled approximately two years of the earnings of an adult male; in 1921, approximately 1.4 years; in 1931, slightly less than one year's earnings.[15] While the Depression accounts for some of the differential, both earlier census years had been years of economic recession and high unemployment. Robbins concluded that working adolescents were financially independent on reaching the age of sixteen in 1911, seventeen in 1921, and eighteen in 1931. The average annual earnings of $240 for an eighteen-year-old in 1931 permitted at best "a precarious independence" for those who lived away from home. Since the majority continued to reside at home at that age, however, even such low wages were "probably sufficient to keep them from being a drain on the family purse." As the author discovered, with some regret, "the young people of today" were enjoying "probably less than half" the economic independence of the prewar generation, conceivably that of their own parents.[16] Doubtless echoing many of his contemporaries, he contended that delayed independence was a key component of the modern youth problem, the root of many difficulties "in the home, in the community, and in the lives of the individual boys and girls that are only incidentally economic."[17] Noting that the Depression was encouraging adolescents to stay in school even longer than the 1931 census had revealed, he warned with some prescience that "if the tendency continues unchecked, young people will in a few years be dependent on parents at the age of 20."[18]

Informing Robbins's analysis is the assumption that the young were remaining longer in the family home solely because they could not earn enough to support themselves. While this is a reasonable explanation, there are other possibilities. Many families continued to need some manner of additional wages to supplement those of the male breadwinner. Most working-class families enjoyed their greatest material comfort when one or more children reached the age of paid employment, a characteristic of the traditional pre-industrial family economy that persisted through the first half of the twentieth century. Despite overall expanding prosperity during the 1920s, wages did not keep pace with the rising cost of living, nor did those years "roar" at quite the same tenor across social and regional divisions. In 1925, 69 per cent of men and 82 per cent of women earned less than $1,000 per year, considerably less than the $1,400 estimated to be the bare minimum of subsistence for a family of four. For families headed by single mothers—accounting for approximately one in six households and not including those with incapacitated husbands, whose ranks were swollen by the Great War—adolescent wages were undoubtedly critical. The son of one widow in rural eastern Ontario recalled that, by the age of thirteen, "I was turning my hand to any job that offered. In the summer of 1921 I was proud of two things: I rated second among the couple of hundred pupils who wrote their high school entrance examinations in our town and I earned more than $100 that year," with a milk route and odd jobs.[19]

Though the male breadwinner ideal was consolidated in the 1920s, its realization remained just slightly more likely than it had at the turn of the century. Until World War II, only a minority actually achieved it. An important proportion of Canadian families continued to rely on more than one wage packet, most likely adding those of adolescent children. Certainly the anecdotal evidence of the time supports this: many young Canadians worked full-time as early as fourteen years of age, or did "odd jobs" or worked part-time while continuing school, because of familial necessity. In 1918, at the age of fifteen, Elsie Freeman left her parents' struggling farm near Acton, Ontario, to take the train to a job as a domestic in Toronto. She returned home when her father asked for her help on the farm, but would head to a factory job in the city when she was seventeen.[20] In another family, when their Polish immigrant father died suddenly at the age of forty-four in 1939, Betty and her sister Rose, both Winnipeg high school students at the time, worked at part-time jobs while their mother took in boarders; they managed to stay in school long enough to earn senior matriculation.[21] Among Native youth, the stakes were higher still. Basil Johnston returned to the Cape Croker reserve in 1945, having completed only part of his first high school year at Regiopolis College in Kingston, Ontario. With his father's departure for the lumber camps, he was "left in sole possession and proprietorship" of the family home, and "survival—mine—became my first and only object in the sixteenth year of my life." His attempts at hunting and trapping frequently took him forty kilometres on foot, "often for nothing."[22]

Although much less amenable to documentation, another possible factor contributing to the deferral of youth independence involves the changing ideas about family, and especially about parent-child relations, that indicate an early-twentieth-century cultural shift. The history of parent-child relations in the modern Western world lends itself to a certain periodization. The traditional pre-industrial relationship that demanded filial piety, deference, and obedience in the face of parental (especially paternal) authority gave way with the warming trend that sustained the Victorian cult of domesticity, and thawed further in the embrace of the "egalitarian" family of the early twentieth century, melting away almost entirely during the baby boom of the post–World War II years. All of these trends capture the idealized form of "the family" rather than the lived experience of many real families. In family relations as in the wider society, who held the upper hand—parent or child, elder or youth—depended on the family's own circumstances (where and how it was situated in its internal history) as much as or even more than on the role constructions and familial ideals prevailing at any moment.

Where youthful autonomy is concerned, what needs more consideration is the influence of changing ideas about the status of young people within and outside the family circle. The Victorian warming trend reasonably contributed to a recasting of the adolescent's familial position, but more emphasis needs to be placed on the growing independence of the young relative to parental authority, regardless of their actual material dependence.[23] By the 1920s, the depiction of adolescence as a crucial stage of citizen formation gave the teen years a more distinctly in-between colouration than ever before—a more common preparatory function than had previously been enjoyed or endured by most adolescents. Modern notions about the relations of citizen and state and of family and state decreed that the rights-based definition of family would move away from the emphasis on parental rights toward recognition of the rights of children. The latter, once established for young children, could only rationally be seen as expanding with age and responsibility, even before the attainment of legal adulthood on the twenty-first birthday. These ideas about youth and family gradually permitted the resident young both a greater share of their own earnings and more voice in their own activities and destinies. These same ideas might also help to explain—perhaps as much as prolonged schooling, later marriage, and rising costs of living—why young people remained at home for a greater part of their adolescence as the century unfolded. A confluence of historical circumstances—material, cultural, national, and international—allowed them to score a better deal than had earlier generations of youth.

Were parents taking to heart the ideal of the egalitarian family, increasingly touted as a "refreshing modern alternative" to outmoded, patriarchal, authoritarian, "traditional" domestic arrangements? In 1928, the popular women's magazine *Chatelaine* carried an intriguing editorial essay on "the spirit of the strike and its application to the family." Remarking that "you cannot pick up a Canadian newspaper these days without some reference to a strike," the author argued that this collective form of class dissent was infiltrating "what a few years ago one might have considered strike-proof territory—the training grounds of youth": the family. She then described the case of four daughters, aged twelve to eighteen, who walked out of their home in London, Ontario, to protest "what, in their opinion, was uncalled-for coercion of the youngest girl." No mention is made of their mother; their father, evidently the perpetrator of this unexplained coercion, was rendered helpless in the face of "a concerted generational revolt which, justified or not, taught him that he could no longer hold unquestioned sway over a family, however young." The writer admired the sisters' bold stand, seeing in it a watershed both for the status of youth and for modern family relations.[24]

Whatever their veracity, stories such as this one form a continuing thread in the period's mass-circulating publications, suggesting that there was at least some sense of change afoot in generational relations, most readily located in changing familial relations. In this particular scenario, the girls are "courageous" while the father is "helpless," inverting the traditional patriarchal role and the father-daughter relationship, in which gender as well as the authority bestowed by age and familial position had once ensured the father's greater power. In the eyes of many observers, of course, this type of domestic modernization heralded societal crisis, but some supported what they interpreted as a counterforce to precisely such perils. Essential to this idealized modern family were its middle-class material basis, its gendered role definitions, and its adoption by both English- and French-speaking Canadians, with only slight cultural modification, for specific "national" ends. At its iconic heart was a concept of companionate marriage that made husband and wife at once best friends, a romantic couple, and business partners in the enterprise of family. Just as the modern marriage was founded on the couple's shared rights and responsibilities, so relations between parents and children were expected to be close, affectionate, and chummy in their openness and responsiveness. "Good" modern parents were supposed to be aware of socio-cultural currents insofar as they affected the younger generation and to take a stand neither prohibitive nor unquestioningly accepting. Modern parents were informed, educated, and above all amenable to expert advice. Properly raised children would co-operate with their model parents to form a strong and healthy self-identity, to maintain family harmony, to uphold social order, and to advance the national interest.[25]

The egalitarian family model was hailed by many of the period's experts as one of the most positive manifestations of modernity. An adaptive mechanism that would address the concerns at the basis of the family crisis, it was "a new and fundamental social invention as significant for the twentieth century as political democracy was for the nineteenth."[26] It corresponded more effectively and efficiently with the needs and aspirations of family members in modern times, both individually and collectively. The rise in the social position of women and children necessitated the father's transformation into "a less heroic figure than the totalitarian paternal overlord," but this was all to the good. Each family member enjoyed both duties and rights, on an equal basis, for, "ideally at least, the freedom of association and of choice, the arrangements for consultation and for free expression of opinion, the joint and deliberative decisions and the mutual trust and affection characteristic of the equalitarian family" practically eliminated the risk of exploitation.[27] Ultimately, the family played the foremost role in the transmission of democratic principles: "The democracy practised by a nation is only as strong and permanent as the measure of intelligent democratic living within the home," as premised upon "the right to self-expression and individual development."[28]

Like all previous ideals of family life, this one, with its focus on gender and generational equality as well as on self-individuation, probably presented challenges even for the families best positioned to work toward it. Poised to find evidence of the negative impact of modernization on their own construct of the family, social scientists observed that some immigrant groups were far from meeting modern "Canadian" standards of domestic life.[29] For many of the recently arrived, the post–World War I years featured family resettlement, as the target migration that had characterized earlier immigration collapsed with the outbreak of war. The time that elapsed between the sojourners' arrival and that of wives and children would create a discrepancy in their rates of acculturation and adaptation, as well as a certain emotional distance caused by separation. While their own adaptation would help that of their newly arrived families, it might also make family members feel "strange" in regards to each other, especially older children who had grown accustomed to increased responsibility—hence authority and autonomy—in their father's absence. It would be difficult for such adolescents, sons in particular, to revert to a traditional filial piety in a new-world setting where their Canadian-born peers and those of shared ethnic background who had emigrated earlier did not subscribe so closely to old-world familial customs. One young woman from Naples, only a year old when her father departed for Montreal, emigrated with her mother and siblings seven years later. By the age of thirteen, she was working ten hours a day in a macaroni factory. As she remembered, "I was often very sad. All I seemed to do was eat, work and sleep.... It was a fight every time I wanted to go out." She and her sisters were occasionally permitted to attend a movie, always chaperoned by other family members, but never a dance, at a time when dancing was the primary pastime of youth.[30]

A number of surveys during the interwar years gave considerable attention to adolescents in immigrant families, acknowledging their vital intermediary position between old-world customs and those of the new land, between tradition and modernity. In 1931, the immigration division of the Canadian National Committee for Mental Hygiene published a highly subjective study on a number of Ukrainian Canadian communities, mostly in the west. The study, under the direction of pioneering McGill sociologist Carl Dawson, was based on responses to eight hundred questionnaires circulated by his student Charles H. Young. The Ukrainians were selected because their communities across Canada were seen to afford an opportunity to examine the effects of "the change of habit and environment" across two or three generations, allowing comparison of the different age groups "along health and educational lines," as well as comparison with other ethnic groups.[31]

While noting a great many adaptive changes in family relations that he regarded as positive, Young emphasized what he saw as a breakdown in parental authority and the resultant destabilization and "demoralisation" of the younger generation, an increasing proportion of whom were Canadian-born:

> The effects of the transition from the old world culture to the new are nowhere more evident than in the family, and in no members of that institution so much as in the children. For the Ukrainian-Canadian family is the arena in which the conflicting attitudes and customs of the two cultures meet; the old as embodied in the parents with their habits formed in an entirely different society, the new as found in the children, who live in two worlds at the same time and who are rather ill at ease in both. The situation involves maladjustment for both old and young.[32]

Young's depiction of the Ukrainian Canadian adolescent's life as "in two worlds at the same time" unwittingly captures the youth experience across class, cultural, gender, and regional differences: not children yet not adults, young people in general straddled two life stages, two lifestyles, two cultures and forms of existence. But the children of immigrants faced special challenges. Simply by acquiring the language and other "aspects of our culture," some of which even the Canadian-born had to acknowledge as "not always the best," this young generation was already leaving the old behind.[33]

Dawson's own study similarly concluded that traditional controls were weakening among young Mennonites in Manitoba, especially among the young men. Patterns of family life were modernizing and (seen to be much the same thing) Canadianizing. Within the "essentially patriarchal" Mennonite family, girls married young—often while still in their teens—spent their lives occupied by childrearing and homemaking, and eschewed public participation. Boys left school early to work on the parental farm; they too were expected to marry at a relatively young age, often settling on neighbouring farms with their fathers' assistance. Parental control over adolescents was maintained by "the ordering and forbidding technique," by means of which the young person was simply denied permission to attend a dance or movie or party. According to Dawson, the young people, "whatever their secret heartburnings, have as yet made little protest; there are not enough young peoples' organizations...to crystallize the 'gang spirit' into opposition of the parents." Few had been sufficiently exposed to the "outside world and its ways" to support their determination to "be different" by rejecting their parents'—and consequently the community's—expectations of its young.[34] In the urban colonies of Winnipeg, Montreal, and Toronto, by contrast, the generational assimilative process was accelerated by closer interaction with the mainstream culture. The young were observed to be taking greater interest in dances, movies, and other commercialized amusements. Even those forbidden to take part, or who chose not to, were "influenced by the presence of these attractions," as they stood about the streets "looking rather wistfully at the non-Mennonite young people as they pass[ed] by to places of amusement."[35] The "almost continuous" contact with "Canadian ways" could make the gap between generations so great that it culminated "only too frequently in disasters to family and social relations."[36]

The sociologists' findings very much reflect their own social position and their training in theories that correlated modernization with family dysfunction, as well as those that emphasized intergenerational alienation, not to mention the prejudices of their class and time. The "experiential chasm" that they found between generations, however, is supported by the life experiences of immigrant families, where the young frequently turned to their peers as their parents proved inadequate or unable to orient them to their new social environment.[37] Opportunities for mixing with Canadian-born youth, both within and outside their own ethnic groups, in the rapidly spreading commercial venues for amusement, in youth organizations, and especially in high schools intensified conflicting loyalties and perhaps made more apparent the tension between personal autonomy and familial expectations of conformity to the larger plan. Needless to say, flappers and their male counterparts caused much consternation in the homes of immigrants with strong religious backgrounds and devotion to the concept of filial obedience. The demeanour and behaviour of daughters, whose personal morality represented family honour and reputation, were a special concern.[38] "Our parents," commented an Italian-born girl, "believe that the girl who stays at home is the best girl and has the best chance of getting married. We think that the more a girl knows, the better, and that she should go out and meet people."[39] A Canadian-born daughter of Ukrainians living in rural Manitoba vividly recalled her mother's disciplinary actions when she and her sister disobeyed:

The ethnic people really hung on to their children. They made them obey, they made them listen. We wouldn't dare speak out to our mother if she was ever chastising us. If you ever went out, you had to be back at a certain time. I remember once in Gilbert Plains, when I was a teenager, I went to a dance at Venlaw.... I came back later than my mother told me. She locked us out and she wouldn't let us in the house. We slept in the hayloft. We thought we'd put up the ladder and get up to the bedroom but she heard us putting that ladder up and told us, "I told you to be in at such and such a time, and unless you learn to listen to me, then you'll not sleep in the house." So we grabbed some old blankets in the summer kitchen and went up and slept in the hayloft.[40]

Personal memories such as these also point to the changing status of immigrant mothers, which was noted by the social scientists who visited and observed these families in day-to-day interactions. With many immigrant fathers now at work in urban factories rather than fields, arriving home late and retiring early, mothers took on more of the new-world role of manager and disciplinarian, even while ultimate authority was still at least nominally the father's.[41] Charles Young observed that young women, having long held "a notoriously inferior position in the home, even in Canada," appeared to be making gains in attaining more say in the household and in their own lives. While Ukrainian boys continued to be "the favourites," as a result of "knowledge gained through contacts with other racial groups," the girls would no longer simply submit to their parents' expectations, especially where marriage was concerned. Young attributed the improvement in the Ukrainian families' "standard of living"—by which he seems to have meant quality of life—to its adolescent members. In addition to being "in the more plastic age," the young also served as "the media through which the individuals of Ukrainian-Canadian society have contact with the community about them."[42]

This Canadianization of their children may have had certain negative effects for immigrant family relations, but it worked well in the interests of assimilation and nation building. Whatever the costs of intergenerational alienation, Canadianization was the whole point of the matter. Especially individuated were those young men from the countryside who, like so many others of their age group in rural areas across the nation, abandoned farming and found work in town. Two such exemplars, encountered by Young in Hague, Manitoba, were each nineteen years old. One, a bank clerk, owned both a sport roadster and a radio, enjoyed western novels, and slept with a gun under his pillow, for reasons unexplained. The other, employed in a grain elevator, had been prompted to leave his father's farm because of his father's "narrow-minded attitude" toward dancing: "I worked from 4 in the morning to 7 at night. Then when I wanted to lay off to clean up for a dance, he would tell me to stay and work till 10. I just told him to go chase himself."[43]

Another Dawson student from McGill University, C.M. Bayley, spent fifteen months in Montreal's Italian community and seven among the city's

Ukrainians, between 1935 and 1937. His findings, not surprisingly, echoed those of his mentor and of Young. Bayley contended that the act of immigration had "dislodged" the patriarchs from their traditional household post, yet, at least theoretically, their familial status was maintained even as it was redefined in the urban-industrial setting. Immigrants were raising children who were "culture and attitude hybrids," making fairly certain some generational tension.[44] The most common form of conflict took place between fathers and sons, the latter more easily "Canadianized" because of the greater opportunity and freedom they were permitted as boys. In both Italian and Ukrainian communities, there was "a sharp division between the sexes" in terms of parental expectations and surveillance. Boys were "mobile and independent" and actively participated in commercial recreation without much interference from their parents. This did not mean, however, that parents were indifferent to their activities. As one Italian father commented about his sixteen-year-old son, "He goes out and plays all night for a dollar or so at some night club and look at the kinds of people he meets. I bet he knows more at 16 than I do at 50. But he never says anything; he doesn't open his mouth. I ask him where he has been or where he is going and he won't say. It's no use beating him, because if you do he will run away as the others do." From the point of view of another son, with respect to his Ukrainian immigrant father, the animosity was mutual: "He shouts at me and threatens to put me out of the house. I don't say anything because it isn't any use, but I go all tense."[45]

While neither group in Bayley's study gave girls as much freedom as boys, daughters of Ukrainian families generally enjoyed a little more choice in recreation than those of Italian families, who were "expected to center their actions at home, visiting, walking, chaperoned by a sister or cousin." One Canadian-born nineteen-year-old daughter of Italian parents considered them "old-fashioned" and unable to understand "Canadian ways." Probably like many of her peers in similar family situations, while she had difficulty accepting their views, she nonetheless wanted to "act in accordance with her parents' wishes." According to Bayley, the young of both communities "complain emphatically and consistently about the backwardness of parents."[46]

In addition to the matter of youth pastimes, which preoccupied the critics of modern youth of all origins, the most common trigger of generational opposition in immigrant families was found in clashing expectations about the financial contribution of working children. The "Canadian" notion of paying board was not common among European immigrants, who "generally...demand that sons and daughters hand over their whole cheque and receive back spending money." Some of the young workers submitted and others "[found] solutions through deception," while a good number, as relief investigators and social workers discovered, "absolutely refuse[d] to surrender any of their wages." One adolescent son of Italian immigrants declared, "I won't give the old man any of my wages. Once in awhile I give my mother five or ten dollars but I won't pay board; it's not worth it." When one Italian-born labourer lost his job he felt he had no recourse but to plead for a community agency's intervention to persuade his reluctant eighteen-year-old son, a tailor's apprentice, to increase his contributions. The father understood his son's desire to spend his wages "to swagger before girls and let them think he is a big fellow," and did not want to coerce him or otherwise cause trouble within the family. Daughters appear to have been somewhat more compliant in this regard. One young stenographer who earned sixty dollars per month got forty dollars back in "spending money" from her father.[47]

From the point of view of the adolescents affected, parents were frequently domineering, repressive, exploitative, and—perhaps the worst indictment of all—hopelessly "old-fashioned." Yet clearly the tenor of the relationship between parents and children varied, both within and across immigrant communities, as all others. Culture, the length of time elapsed since arrival, rural versus urban setting, family finances, level of education and of "assimilation" of the parents, and the gender of the adolescent child all worked to condition the parental response to adolescent behaviour, as well as the reverse. Helen Gregory MacGill, a Vancouver family court judge and juvenile delinquency expert, commented on the "dissimilarity of the family attitude of the Oriental and that of the white immigrant": "The ugly hostility between parents and children which, in the case of white nationalities, breaks out in court in bitter reproaches and fierce recriminations is unknown in Oriental cases here.... Every relative to the remotest degree feels responsibility for the welfare of the younger members. The lives of these people center around their children." Interestingly, MacGill predicted that the "Canadianizing" of Asian children would see their delinquency rates more closely approximate those of "white" youth.[48]

Well might the experts comment ominously on the schism that had developed between generations in this modern world, given the very different social contexts of their parents' youth, especially of those who had grown up in other cultures. Most emphasized the centrality of family in any effective strategy to address generational conflict and what they saw as its likely outcome: youthful dissipation and delinquency. Since boys were considered a particular problem, it was important to make the home the "one safe harbour." Many parents, it seemed, "fail[ed] altogether to catch the boy's point of view.... They want him to be a grown man at 14 which is impossible. They make a home for him but they do their best to drive him out of it." The ideal relationship was "one of mutual confidence... where the boy can live his boyhood happily and in tune with his times.... The boy should learn from his parents what friendship really is; the parents should learn from the boy what the requirements of modern boyhood are."[49]

Despite the mother-focus—and mother-blame—of "scientific" childrearing advice, the experts insisted that adolescence was an opportune moment for a new intimacy between fathers and children. Once sons and daughters were past the age when they needed to be fussed over in motherly fashion, men were more comfortable relating to them as "chums." Where the modern father's role was concerned—"taken seriously," as one father maintained—it "tended to produce in

a man a state of normalcy essential to a thorough understanding of and sympathy with young people." Wise fathers would "keep pace with the freshness and
buoyancy of outlook of these young people" and would "give some heed to their
viewpoints and judgments."[50] The modern father-son relationship, as in traditional fashion, was still seen to be chiefly about transmitting the ideas and behaviour that constituted manliness. Such associations as the Trail Rangers and the
Tuxis, newly established in the early 1920s, devoted much of their program to
father-son activities.[51] Also attending to new ideas about the parent-child relationship, especially those concerning spending, the advertisers of goods and services urged fathers to note the vital fact that "Your Boy is Growing Up!" One
insurance company drew on the image of a father's pride in his maturing son's
interests and on his own necessary role in assuring that the boy's needs were met.
Thus the "genuine, typical near-man" was "keen in mind. Keen in appetite.
Knows what he wants.... Check his up-to-the-minute clothes, his ambitions,
and opinions regarding questions of the day. It costs a little more for him to get
around now because he's learning new buying habits. This means it costs dad
more, but dad hasn't forgotten his own teen-age."[52] Writer-broadcaster Harry
Boyle fondly recalled his farmer father's insistence, despite the family's
Depression-induced poverty, that his son had to have a good razor when he began
to shave, as something "every man ought to have."[53] Fathers evidently guided
their sons through the typical milestones of adolescence by "providing," as was
their manly duty.

A series of "Letters from a Schoolmaster" published in *Maclean's* in 1938
elaborates on this man-to-man theme, as an "old teacher" outlines paternal duty
in the making of a modern young gentleman. First, all fathers should enforce "to
the utmost limits of disciplinary requirements" the rules of "unfailing courtesy
to ladies, to his elders and to servants." In order to become friends "instead of
just father and son," they should play together, "for the athletic ideal cannot be
overemphasized for boys." The father should never lose his temper or his
patience with his son's questions, lest the son lose confidence in his conviction
that his father is "the fount of all things, knowledge included."[54] The schoolmaster also suggests occasional teasing, though "not too seriously or too sarcas-
tically." If the son appears unable to "take it," the father should teach him that
he must learn "to take whatever happens and to play the game."[55] While the
father in need of counsel is portrayed as a modern father, eager to avoid mistakes
and to be guided by an expert, the advice itself conjures traditional masculine
images: the stoic, the protector, the fair-minded judge, the disciplinarian, the
father as final authority.

The modern father, ostensible head of the modern egalitarian family, was
the day's ideal more than it was an attained reality—advisory sources represent an ideology in the making rather than an established value system.
However fixed the media images of the modern father, mother, and family
were, there were, of course, many configurations of these relationships in reality, shifting with time and context, replacing older images or harkening back

to them nostalgically, even coexisting in unacknowledged contradiction. Poet and socialist Dorothy Livesay grew up in a home that probably came closer to that ideal than most, largely by virtue of her father's unconventional views. Jack Livesay, journalist and founder of the Canadian Press, was described by one of his daughter's closest childhood friends as "a neurotic character" who was also "a very brilliant man," a "born iconoclast" who supported his daughter's youthful literary and political pursuits much more than did her more conservative, traditional mother.[56] He was "terribly interested in the girls"—Dorothy and her sister—and their friends, "and he used to treat us all like grown-ups and invite us to lunch at the Royal York.... When you're fourteen and you're taken out to lunch by a real grown-up man, it is a tremendous thing."[57] In her memoirs, Livesay commented that her adult character combined the "inhibitions implanted by my mother and so many ideas of freedom urged by my father," with whom she used to openly "talk about all sorts of things" during her adolescent years.[58] Yet the teenaged Dorothy also recorded in her diary how oppressive she had come to find the family setting: at the age of eighteen, she wrote, "this depression is unshakeable for it cannot be seized.... At such times it is terribly necessary for me to be away from my family—for I feel that the root of it all lies there. I am too old, suddenly to live with people."[59]

Other evidence suggests that old-fashioned roles and relations prevailed despite the calls for modernized parenting and the egalitarian family. The period's chief social welfare tribunal, the Council on Child and Family Welfare, charged that "in the average home, the fathers contribute too little to the family life, the mothers too much" and claimed that this was not "a healthy or desirable arrangement for the family."[60] *Maclean's* magazine advised men to allow at least one hour per week to "give entirely" to their sons: "An hour a week does not seem much, but how many fathers there are who have imperceptibly become so involved in the web of their daily occupations that even this hour is forgotten or put off or in some way neglected."[61] Sociologists noted that even well-meaning, sober and industrious working-class fathers were frequently too tired to "bother with children" when they returned home after a day's heavy labour, retiring early and often limiting their involvement to administering punishment.[62] One man who grew up in Halifax during the 1930s recalled that his father left too much work and responsibility to his mother, who did "all the worrying," while her husband thought it "sufficient to supply the money to keep the home together."[63] But middle-class fathers did little better. "Absorbed with business," one Montreal father of seven children, the youngest fourteen years old, was observed to act as the patriarch "too pressed to discuss trivial household matters and whose word must be obeyed." His seventeen-year-old daughter was evidently "finding the family group of little aid in the solution of her problems.... It is not surprising that [she] confides in others outside the family group and seeks an outlet for her desire for recognition and response among others of her own age."[64] Mary Peate's journalist father died after a long illness when she was seventeen; she considered that "it was probably true that he hadn't been very conscientious about fatherhood.... Perhaps he did spend too many hours in that chair, reading. Maybe it was because I came along when he was fifty, and he thought the fathering phase of his life was behind him." Yet her father's "addiction" to reading became the legacy that would ultimately inspire her own writing career.[65]

As noted earlier in this chapter, the daughters of immigrants were most likely to struggle against the tyranny of traditional paternal authority. A Macedonian girl growing up in Toronto recalled that "we were so scared of my dad that we would wait two weeks before we had enough nerve to ask him if we could go to a movie. We could never do anything... always had to be with our parents." She believed that her parents just "didn't seem to know that in Canada you don't have to act that way with your kids."[66] Another Toronto woman characterized her father as a "tyrant" toward his three daughters, especially when they were teenagers: "We literally couldn't move outside the home unless we lied about where we were going." Another girl, who grew up in rural Ontario, described her farmer father as "a very dominating man.... None of us ever felt we could go and talk to him the way we did with mother.... What he said was law and that was that."[67] A Nova Scotia man recalled the frightening "explosions" of his father on the domestic scene, especially when he lost his office job during the Depression; his mother's reassurances that her husband "was only letting off steam" protected both father and son, so that the outbursts, while worrying to the adolescent, "never made me lose respect for my father."[68] Despite fears about the decline of the traditional paterfamilias, and despite much praise for and even a few signs of the evolution of a new fatherhood, the gender- and age-defined familial hierarchy continued to sustain male dominance, both in the home and outside it.

Any number of examples from the historical record suggest that, however much young people may have balked at parental authority and regulation, their rebellion was generally as contingent and ephemeral as the life stage itself. Especially where mothers are concerned, even accounting for the nostalgia, forgotten detail, and selective recall that typify the process of remembering a life, memoirs and reminiscences suggest a general closeness in mother-child relations during the "turbulent" adolescent years. They also hint at the hidden authority of mothers within traditional families, suggesting that even children well en route to adult independence were more likely both to seek out their mothers' assistance for their plans and to be subjected to their disciplinary measures. Not surprisingly, the mother-daughter relationship was probably more intimate in this regard, as adolescence was the acknowledged critical stage for gender-role modelling. Writer Edna Jaques marvelled at her mother's "wonderful spirit," despite the hardships of homesteading in Saskatchewan and the challenges of raising three adolescent daughters: "No matter what crazy thing we tried to do, she helped whenever she could. She never had much money. Dad saw to that, and kept the purse strings tightly tied.... She would go into her little cubby hole under the stairs, dig down in a trunk and come up with the money we needed."[69] Claire Wodlinger, who grew up in Regina, also recalled her mother's consistent loving support for her every endeavour: "She encouraged me whenever she could.... She invariably told me I was pretty, even let me wear her lovely dresses until I grew out of them!... I never consciously resented her; truly I adored her."[70] The awe with which many remembered their mothers "stretching" and "making do" is a familiar theme, especially for those who came of age during the 1930s. Harry Boyle pronounced his mother "a true magician" for her ability to put together "banquets" seemingly out of thin air during his Depression youth in rural Ontario. One Winnipeg woman, thirteen years old when the Depression began, remembered many families in which "the wives really had to pull the cart to keep food on the table."[71] Others recalled the Depression experience—and their mothers' role—for the more painful marks left on their own self-development. While acknowledging her family's precarious financial situation, one young woman could not forget what she saw as her mother's undue interference when she was invited to her first high school party: "As we were very hard up I could not get a party dress and mother said I would have to wear my inevitable middy and skirt. I refused to go but my mother telephoned my friend's mother and told her why. She said she would have her daughter wear a middy too and the party was spoiled for both of us.... Any confidence I had in myself socially disappeared and was not restored for years. I do believe that matters would have been helped if mother had dressed me properly."[72]

The *Toronto Star*'s syndicated advice columnist of the 1940s, George Antheil, showed little sympathy for a young female letter writer who signed herself "Bereft," because, as she put it, "If ever there was a henpecked husband I am a henpecked daughter." Her mother was "continually ragging" at her "for no good reason." She helped with housework but could not go out with boys: "I'm no baby and yet I know I'm not grown up. I am 17.... I don't think she is at all fair with me. I am working and need a little pleasure.... My dad is swell about everything. He wouldn't mind me going out once in a while." Antheil did not feel that her letter "rang quite true." He advised her to "try some strategy" by being "honestly nice and considerate" to her mother and also by enlisting her father "in your campaign for a little more freedom."[73] To a fourteen-year-old boy who attended Scouts meetings on Friday nights and went "out with the boys" every other Saturday but wanted to go out more, he suggested that he "talk it over man to man with your dad."[74] A national tour of youth clubs in 1945 led a YWCA National Council director to conclude that "one of the most discussed topics among 'teenagers is home life.... They are most concerned... about the growing breach between themselves and their parents. Many of them claim that their parents fail to acknowledge they have grown up." "One day my mother treats me like a child, and the next day like a grown-up," one girl had told her.[75]

One of the vital sparks of generational conflict in the 1920s could be found in popular culture, and especially in what Mannheim called the *entelechy*—the particular culturally and historically specific generational style of the young. Among the many such trends that affected family relations was the rise of the flapper, the "girl of the new day." The flapper represented a singular affront to middle-class domestic ideals, marking a new epoch in generational relations in which, more than ever before, the young would differentiate themselves from their elders by means of a self-consciously adopted youth style. One Regina woman had an older sister who was "only about 14, but she was a flapper. She'd wear short skirts and big long beads. And high heels if she could get them. And she'd listen to cowboy music. All the girls her age were trying to be flappers."[76] With its somewhat androgynous, even boyish form replacing the large-breasted, wide-hipped, maternal feminine ideal of the Victorian age, the flapper look lent credence to public worries about the masculinization of modern girls and women. Introduced in the waning months of the Great War and quickly becoming in vogue in its aftermath, hair cut short, or "bobbed," also made a sensational impact, filling the media with jokes, cartoons, letters to editors for and against, enraged critiques, songs, theatrical skits, and short films. In rural Ontario, A.W. Currie remembered that the "quite audacious" bobbing trend "provoked a long debate on the morals of such a fashion.... To make things worse a few women began to use rouge and lipstick—the painted jezebels—and to wear low-cut dresses."[77]

By the 1920s, working-class girls and low-paid clerks in offices and stores, with new access to cheap, up-to-date mass-produced clothing and accessories, could be as modern in their appearance as their more affluent peers. Indeed, their adoption of the current vogue met with even greater disapproval from middle-class critics, who wondered at their frivolous spending, the wantonness suggested by their "cheap and gaudy" attire, what they might be doing to afford it, and, quite possibly, the blurring of class distinction that "fashion for all" suggested.[78] For the daughters of immigrants, the stakes were higher still: their devotion to modern fashion represented both a certain rebellion against traditional parents and a desire to be modern and Canadian. As a Canadian-born girl from an Italian family described the situation, "I have very different views from my mother.... She doesn't approve of evening clothes, bathing suits, shoes or going without stockings, and she won't allow me to go off for a weekend with other young girls and men.... We are Canadian-born and are not different from others."[79] Nor was the flapper merely an urban phenomenon. On the beach at Port Stanley, Ontario, an observer noted "the last word in flappers," sporting lipstick, "heels like stilts," skirts "bobbed several inches above the knee," and hair "the vivid blonde that comes from a bottle." Assuming that she was an American import, he was assured by his companion—a local resident—that "she's home-grown. I know her people. They live on a farm not many miles away. I could show you a thousand farm flappers just like her."[80]

The great public to-do over the flapper provoked a much-cited response in the American popular magazine *Outlook* in 1922. In "A Flapper's Appeal to Parents," eighteen-year-old author and self-professed flapper Ellen Welles Page admitted to having adopted the badges of flapperhood, as she called them: bobbed hair, face powder, fringed skirts, bright sweaters and scarves, low-heeled "finale hopper" shoes. She confessed her "adoration" of dancing, and how much she loved to "spend a large amount of time in automobiles." Yet she carefully positioned herself in the flapper spectrum as a "very moderate flapper" who eschewed rouge, lipstick, dramatic eyebrow-plucking, smoking, drinking, and petting, evidently all of a category where the evils of flapperhood were concerned. Her published appeal to the older generation was inspired by the "destructive public condemnation and denunciation" of the ways of modern youth. In fact, she professed that these "modern ways," entirely the outcome of historical changes, amounted to "a tremendous problem" for the young themselves: "The war tore away our spiritual foundations and challenged our faith. We are struggling to regain our equilibrium. The times have made us older and more experienced than you were at our age. It must be so with each succeeding generation if it is to keep pace with the rapidly advancing and mighty tide of civilization....There is no one to turn to—no one but the rest of Youth, which is as perplexed and troubled with its problems as ourselves.[81] The remainder of the young flapper's manifesto repeats much of what the older generation was also conceding, hinting that the generational divide was perhaps not as wide as envisioned from either side. Welles Page urged that parents "study" their children if they hoped to "become acquainted" with them and to relate to them not so much as offspring but as modern youth, as "the new generation." Mothers should aim to "be the understanding, loving, happy comrades of your daughter," to be their son's "chum," to "be young with him." Fathers must strive to "find out what is within the minds and hearts and souls of your children," to become their "best pal," to encourage their children "to formulate a workable philosophy of life." Above all, the older generation was obliged to "remember that we are the parents of the future."[82]

It is tempting to read this public appeal as little more than a reflection of what adults wanted to believe about young people and about idealized generational relations and the ideal modern family. Certainly its language is mimetic, echoing that of contemporary child study and the concerns that pervaded public discussions about youth. Was the "flapper's appeal to parents" genuine, its words and tone simply acknowledging the cultural changes young people were internalizing much more quickly than their disapproving elders? Intriguing though the question is for what the truth would indicate about adolescents' own views—so rarely inscribed unmediated and uncensored in the historical record—even at face value the flapper's appeal discloses much about understandings of modern youth and generational relations. If the experiential gap between the generations, especially between parents and their adolescent children, appeared to widen while that within generations narrowed, thanks to such developments as high schools and commercial recreation, the outcome was not so much a greater generational antagonism as it was a reinforced generational consciousness. More than simply an individual, biologically determined, age-delimited life stage, adolescence became a collective, historical, generational experience, a shared experience of modernity.

By the World War II years, the resurgent panic about juvenile delinquency prompted a matching wave of public attention to the importance of familial and social stability and the training of healthy, upright young citizens, both for a successful war effort and for postwar reconstruction. Despite the now-familiar discourses about "wild youth" getting wilder in times of war, specialized advice literature, newspaper columns, popular magazines, and professional and academic journals all began to feature theories, stories, and studies that countered the idea of inevitable and universal adolescent angst and generational opposition. Thanks to the moment's concerns, to growing public attention regarding the youth problem since the previous war, to the experts' expanding interest in adolescence, and—probably most of all—to parents' own experiences of coming of age in the 1920s and 1930s, parents of the 1940s were urged all the more to make studied attempts (as reflected in the title of a pamphlet aimed at them) at "understanding your teenager." Armed with up-to-date information about adolescence, parents could effectively take charge and ease their children through the inevitable—but not inevitably disastrous—upheavals of this life stage. As they were assured, during the adolescent years "it is only natural to expect a certain amount of confusion and a good deal of change and adjustment." Advisers considered that adolescence was not "the teen-ager's problem alone," however, but "part of the total family picture," requiring "adjustments" by all family members.[83] Lest they feel like "failures," parents were consoled that "with patience, sympathetic understanding, and the ability to see the humorous along with the serious side of things, you'll make out very well. And so will your teenager!"[84]

Contrary to the Hall model of generational conflict, early 1950s studies by McGill sociologists Frederick Elkin and William Westley found many instances, in the insular white middle-class suburban communities that exemplified the domestic ideal, where parental supervision operated as an effective regulatory device over adolescent behaviour. In Montreal's anglophone "Suburbantown" community, at any given moment, mothers were at home and able to keep an eye on the doings of their offspring. The community, through its high school, extracurricular activities, church, and local organizations, had built an elaborate, interconnected network of surveillance. In these "contained" surroundings, parents (or mothers, at least) were likely to know where their children were, what they were doing, and which company they were keeping—the latter, by and large, consisting of teenagers from families much like their own. As one mother described the situation, "you're lucky [here]. . . . All the activities have a religious basis and are under competent people. You don't have to worry about the children getting into trouble. All of John's friends are just impeccable."[85]

The young people under the microscope were expected to keep their parents informed of their plans: parents made "a point of knowing," and often colluded with other parents to make certain that all were aware of their children's whereabouts, activities, and behaviour. Neighbourhood parents collectively decided on the amount to dole out in allowances, the number of dates permitted per week, the activities allowed, the curfew hour, and whether "steady" relationships should be encouraged. One fifteen-year-old girl, explaining why she never went out on a weeknight, volunteered that "last year our parents thought we were going out too much. They got together and they all decided that we were. Then they said we could go out one night every week-end and we had to be in by twelve." In such productivity-oriented middle-class enclaves, young people were given little opportunity to "hang around" or involve themselves in unsupervised or "inappropriate" activities. As the observing sociologists concluded, within the "protective environment" of middle-class suburbia, young people had—at least at the moment of surveillance—effectively internalized the values and behaviours of their parents, thereby precluding "any overt rebellion or any negative contrast with other patterns."[86] A comparative study in a working-class sector of Montreal, however, suggested "sharp class differences" in this regard: working-class children evidently reported few details of their activities to their parents, and were "not expected to do so."[87] Thus, while the 1950s consolidated the notion of adolescence as a moratorium from adult responsibilities, it appears to have been a relatively more sheltered experience for those young Canadians from families whose socio-economic position could better facilitate such protection from "the outside."

Where generational relations are concerned, most specifically those within the family circle, the private nature of family life and the personal, individualized experience of growing up—in the past as in the present—get in the way of confident conclusions. But personal testimonies and memories, juxtaposed and layered with records and writings generated by experts, in the media, and otherwise belonging to the public domain, allow at least a strong sense of the changes that were taking place, alongside the more "traditional" elements of generational interaction that persisted. During these years, within the context of intensive socio-cultural change and the anxiety and questioning that accompany crisis—whether war, the difficult postwar adjustments, or economic depression—ideas about the relationships of young and old, parent and adolescent child, both within and outside the family circle, were being reconfigured. While much of this took place on the levels of expert theorizing, the public debates as disseminated through the print media, along with evidence from the more intimate, personal, mysterious side of the historical picture, suggest that, at least for the sector of largely Canadian-born middle-class families, parents were increasingly interested in taking measures to modernize their relationships with their children. Because their adolescent offspring were at the supposedly critical stage of self-formation, during which such integral building blocks of character and determinants of future success as sexual ethics, gender-role ascriptions, and democratic ideals of citizenship and service were being laid, it stands to reason that parents would pay attention to the burgeoning advice literature about "new and improved" family models and parent-child interaction. Many of these parents had already become familiar with that path at an earlier stage of their children's development, when they were introduced to the modern, scientific childrearing advice literature that circulated in vast quantities during these years.

New ideas about adolescence, inspired by Stanley Hall and his contemporaries at the century's start and reinforced on popular, official, and scholarly levels with particular force after the Great War, were certainly making an impact in the family circle by the 1950s. It is nonetheless safe to say that, as is often the case where theory and practice, ideas and reality are concerned, the public outcry about the generational conflict elements of the youth problem was based more on apprehension than on what was actually happening. What made the problem so real to youth-watchers is the unquestionable fact that, starting with the inaugural generation of "flaming youth" in the 1920s, the young were indeed a different species than their parents and elders. Of course, this had forever been the case in some measure, but in a modernizing society, as change rather than conservation, the novel rather than the traditional, became valued personal and societal objectives, youth were more generationally distinct than they had ever been. By mid-century, within a postwar setting of domestic renewal, as "flaming youth" themselves became the parents of adolescents, as the latter's schooling and economic dependency lengthened, and as "reconstruction" and stability after decades of upheaval became key national objectives, ever more active, interventionist roles in the lives of young Canadians were indicated for parents and other adult authorities. Concerns about the youth problem continued to flare into panic periodically, but the experts, with the help of state initiatives, had by then carefully scrutinized and reported on its various elements to the extent that few adults could be unaware of what was required in "understanding your teenager." And the younger generation, too, had much more information, advice, and options than their parents and grandparents had enjoyed, as a result of the steps already taken toward a modern adolescence.

3

In Love

Dating and Mating

Just put it down in your little black book that there must be some-
thing wrong if boys in high school don't try to date you. Be honest in
your self-scrutiny and maybe you'll find some flaws. Besides, don't
stick together too much. Hunt your males separately. Boys like it
that way.

— George Antheil, *Toronto Star*, 1941

Where adolescent peer relations are concerned, the most important are
undoubtedly those involving the opposite sex. The revolution in morals thought
to characterize the immediate post–World War I years was a defining trait of the
"new generation," thus a core element of the modern youth problem, if not its
very core. Certainly the tone, nature, and frequency of public discourse on adolescent sexuality point to an intensifying preoccupation, at times building
toward panic. Insofar as practices can be assessed historically, they did change,
most notably in the structures of courtship. For a number of Canadians, the
Great War served to expose traditional middle-class attitudes toward sexuality as
sham and hypocrisy. Waiting for marriage seemed ridiculous to young people
who had seen how quickly the promise of "forever" could be shattered. One man,
an Ontario high school student during the war, later remembered "a lot of horse-
play.... The girls were more free, permissive, the men more daring.... Life had
changed so much."[1]

With little variation, however, modern youth were held to relatively "old-
fashioned" moral standards and to heterosexual gender conventions where
courtship and sex were concerned. The ideals, instruction, and prescriptive

advice surrounding romantic relationships remained fairly consistent with long-standing middle-class conventions, despite the language of modern science, medicine, and psychology so frequently employed in discussion. This chapter considers some of the changes in gender roles and relations and in ideas about romance, sexuality, and marriage that transformed courtship practices into the modern phenomenon known as "dating." The new rituals of youthful mating, though much remarked upon and subjected to study, had the same end in view as those of traditional courtship: to head off premarital sexual experimentation while guiding the young toward prudent choices in marriage, which was expected to take place by one's mid-twenties, marking the final and most important of the gateways to adult citizenship.

A candid account by three teenage girls in *Maclean's* in 1922 must have shocked the magazine's middle-class readership with its off-handed detailing of "fussing parties." These popular gatherings evidently involved "just jazz and love-making," accompanied by smoking and drinking, all of which were thought—and hoped—to characterize a demi-monde of adult decadence far removed from wholesome adolescent socializing.[2] The so-called new morality was greatly influenced by the onslaught of mass culture. Movies, advertising, and mass-circulation magazines, many of them American in origin, promoted a seldom-questioned sense of a new era slamming the door on outmoded tradition, even at the fundamental levels of love and sex. By creating such cultural icons as the Sheik in a smouldering Rudolph Valentino and the Vamp in an equally seductive Theda Bara—not incidentally "racialized" as well as sexualized—Hollywood challenged the accepted standards of manliness, femininity, and respectable sexuality. Young female moviegoers seemed especially vulnerable to celebrity worship and imitation, much as the youth-watchers feared. In 1920s Winnipeg, one teenage girl being raised by a forbidding widowed father recorded in her diary that her introduction to Valentino and Clara Bow—another of the leading "It" girls of the 1920s—"changed everything" about her childish notions of physical attraction and "sex appeal": "Life was never to be the same again," she declared.[3] An Italian-born girl growing up in Montreal during the Depression years insisted that "all the Italian girls" wanted to emulate Greta Garbo: "I love Greta, yes, I love her.... [We] try to copy the actress's way of make-up, dress and style, as well as *beaucoup de snobiness*...and remember all the little jokes."[4] Looking back on adolescent outings during the World War II years, another Montreal woman recalled how her friend, nicknamed "Wooly," was adept at attracting young men because of her resemblance to a certain pin-up girl of the day: "By the summer of 1943, it was *vieux chapeau* for Wooly to have her looks compared to Rita Hayworth's. It was just coincidence that Wooly happened to wear her hair in the same style....Or so she claimed."[5] Boys were not immune to such pressures, either. As one mother complained about her sixteen-year-old daughter's "boorish" boyfriend, "He tells her that he doesn't have enough money to take her out, yet spends $15 on himself trying to look like a second Sinatra."[6]

Although boys worried about their physical appearance and "sex appeal," traditional and unwavering constructions of manliness allowed them some reprieve from the intense social pressures presented by idealized feminine beauty to girls of the period. Promoted ever more forcefully and rigidly, thanks to the flourishing of the cinema, the fan magazine, and the beauty industry, the standards that dictated a particular look at a particular time became applicable to adolescent girls as much as to their sisters of "marrying age." Social scientists noted the adverse psychological effects, placing much significance on the impact of "the idea that she is unattractive" on the adolescent girl's social development during those critical years, causing a loss of "social confidence" if, as a result of real or imagined unattractiveness, she "finds herself unpopular or merely neglected socially." When Anne grew to be the tallest girl in her class in early puberty, she became very self-conscious, avoiding peer interaction by studying, which allowed her "recognition from her elders but not her peers.... She was not one of them."[7] Another girl remembered that she "began to notice the boys particularly" when she was in third form, but also noticed that "the other girls all seemed to be liked much better by them than I was," which she blamed on her physical awkwardness and her lack of the social skills that appealed to the young, because her Methodist parents disapproved of dancing, card playing, and moviegoing.[8] Doubtless sharing the feelings of many a young woman, Lillian Allen also compared herself unfavourably to her more "developed" friends: "I was very embarrassed about my body, because I was taller and thinner than most of my friends, and my breasts didn't keep pace with my growth. My friends were beautifully rounded.... I wanted to be alluring too.... My body seemed to be contourless. For one interested in clothes this was frustrating.... So I began to have feelings of rejection and shame. Now no one would ever look at me. I didn't want to be seen in a bathing suit.... There seemed to be no one close to whom I could turn."[9]

Needless to say, much advice poured forth from regular columns and special features in newspapers and magazines, aimed precisely at encouraging young women to make the most of their appearance, as well as in the advertisements for beauty products of all kinds and in the advice literature produced to help them through their "difficult" phase. Girls were reassured that Hollywood-style beauty was not a requirement for popularity but, at the same time, were told the "natural" self could be improved upon by means of the right products and some personal effort: "Any girl can improve her looks tremendously by good grooming and the intelligent use of her best points...and simple clothes.... Girls, you don't know what a comfort such a girl can be to a boy.... He will say she is good looking because she looks good to him and he isn't worrying whether her nose is perfect.... What he wants in a girl is a whole ensemble of good looks and the funny part of it is almost any girl can achieve that."[10]

Within the tense space where traditional ideas about adolescent heterosexual relations contended—and not infrequently conflicted—with emergent ones, new courtship patterns gradually replaced the traditional form that saw young men "calling on" young women, usually in the family home and under familial supervision.[11] Modern "dating" generally entailed "going out," often in groups, often to participate in commercial amusements such as movies and dances, and usually without adult chaperones. For unhappy observers of the youth scene, the "decay of the moral structure" after the war was encouraging "thrill-seeking and exploitative relationships" that featured "dancing, petting, necking, the automobile, the amusement park, and a whole range of [related modern] institutions and practices." Modern ways of mating and commercialized recreation were undermining the sanctity of male-female relationships, making courtship little more than "an amusement and a release of organic tensions." Contemporary dating was not the "true courtship" whose objective was marriage, but "a sort of dalliance relationship" that was "largely dominated by the quest of the thrill."[12] As one sociologist declared in 1937, "the apparent change in the last decade is great; sex is no longer news."[13] By the 1940s, young Canadians were not only aware that there was "much discussion" among the older generation about the "frankness" of modern youth, they had come to take for granted this "openness" that characterized their generation: "Our parents seem to think there is too much free talk among the boys and girls; but we teenagers don't mean to be rugged; we are sincere; it just comes natural."[14]

Much as they used immigrant communities as behavioural laboratories, so contemporary social scientists eagerly applied survey techniques to the ideas and practices of young people, generally college students in their late teens and early twenties who provided a convenient, delimited, homogeneous sample. These surveys were a scientific means of acquiring "ample confirmation of increased tolerance toward previously disapproved behaviours in the area of sex and marriage," most particularly in the area of "sex freedom."[15] Yet contradictions abound. The much-cited American surveys undertaken during the late 1930s indicated that there was "less extreme petting on first or early acquaintance" among Depression-era youth but at the same time "more steady dating with fewer inhibitions as to sex intimacy following long acquaintance." The renowned "Middletown" studies of 1929 and 1937 reported that 44 per cent of boys and 34 per cent of girls of high school age had taken part in "petting parties." The later study uncovered "a sense of sharp, free behaviour between the sexes." More alarming to the older generation, the results also suggested that the growing adoption of what the younger generation saw as "sophisticated manners" in boy-girl relations was reaching down to younger and younger children.[16]

Such "scientific" findings were usually published in academic journals with a limited, largely professional readership. The subject matter was so integral to the modern youth problem, however, that they were frequently discussed in the popular press, furthering a view common among experts and increasingly among the general reading public that the younger generation had undergone a "considerable change in attitude" about sexuality, a change that encompassed "a definite trend toward relaxing disapprovals of premarital sex experience." At the same time, the experts reassured worried adults that "repeated allegations" about the adolescent sexual excesses of the 1920s were "greatly exaggerated": even as traditional strictures against premarital sex appeared to be weakening, there seemed to be "less social compulsion upon the young to go as far as they dare." That compulsion, a form of peer-group pressure, was believed to be the motivating force behind the "new morality." While both sexes were known to discuss and "rate" their dates, and although "shopping around" was legitimate for both, young women were still expected to "settle down" and "go steady" sooner than were their suitors, in large part because of continued concerns about "what boys say about them" and consequently about their own reputation.[17]

In the west, the frontier nature of settlement put a premium on romance. Because there were few young women in the predominantly Polish mining community of Coleman, Alberta, "about 20 young men" met regularly in the Catholic hall, where two others, "said to be from the United States," taught them to dance the waltz, the foxtrot, and "other dances of the day" with each other. The "great demand" for women in this society of young bachelors—where women were as important for their domestic labour as for companionship and sex—led many girls to marry young. One woman, seventeen years old when she arrived from Poland in 1923, married the same year; another, born in Coleman to an immigrant family, married at the age of sixteen in 1931.[18] The notoriety of such alleged practices caused the native-born to look askance at the "depravity" of Eastern Europeans, not only for what they did within their own communities but even more for the threat they might pose to "Canadian girls."[19] Torontonians were shocked when a twenty-five-year-old "Russian Pole" was tried in Police Court for perjury, having sworn, in attempting to get a marriage licence, that the fourteen-year-old who had "met and married him in one day" was actually nineteen. They were likely even more dismayed when the crown attorney asked the "Canadian" girl why she had married him and she replied blithely, "Because he asked me to."[20] Western Canadian women's groups lobbied their provincial governments for legislation establishing a minimum age for marriage, because it was seen to be "no uncommon thing among the non-British for girls of 13 years of age to get married to men of 40 or over." The Saskatchewan Council of Women and the Women's Section of the Grain Growers Association, for example, petitioned the provincial government to raise the age of marriage to sixteen years. In 1924, the Marriage Act was amended, as it was in Alberta, to prohibit those "15 years and under" from marrying; if either party were under eighteen, the consent of a parent or guardian was required.[21]

Obviously, it was not only "depraved foreigners" who were keen for romance in western settlements that were without a sufficient supply of either women or men of courting age. Writer Edna Jaques, who grew up in rural Saskatchewan just after the Great War, recalled that the most exciting effect of the railway's arrival for the town's young women was the "new men and boys who wore white shirts every day of the week and Sunday suits and who tipped their hats to us as they went by." Their isolated village was suddenly "overflowing with men": "You might be going with a bank boy one night, and the kid from the next farm the next night, or someone entirely new who had caught your eye for the time being."[22] The smallness of the community meant that gossip could still play an effective regulatory role, allowing for a measure of adult surveillance over the mixed-sex gatherings of the young. In fact, these gatherings were often carried out within the safe auspices of church or school, the "natural" social centres and meeting places of rural and small-town Canada.[23]

In Jaques's rural town, the young gathered in the schoolhouse on Sunday evenings to "talk and laugh together" and to participate in a short religious service. The rest of the evening was spent "getting acquainted with each other, as this was the only way we could ever meet any young people. Dad used to call it a courting school, but if it was, where could you find a better place to meet a nice, decent boy, look him over, and make your choice.... Many nice loving marriages were started here." Looking back, she professed to have been "always in love" during her teen years but "blithely went with one and another as the days went by....As long as they could dance without walking on my feet, I loved them all, or thought I did."[24]

While such "safe" venues as churches, schools, and clubs remained popular for adolescent meeting and pairing off, commercial venues kept pace; by 1950, they were in all likelihood overtaking the adult-approved spots. The young men of Garnier High School, near the town of Spanish in northern Ontario, were "on occasion" permitted to go to Gignac's, unescorted, "to congregate around the jukebox and to play pool." In Basil Johnston's memory, "many of the village girls began to patronize Gignac's.... They would arrive a few minutes after we did. They must have had an efficient 'village telegraph' to enable them to synchronize their movements with our own. All the girls were attractive, which provided us with a strong incentive to return to Gignac's as often as possible....Many romances waxed and waned between the young Indian swains and the white girls."[25] On the whole, however, Johnston notes, these were youthful and short-lived courtships. Most young people were strongly discouraged from becoming romantically involved with those who were not from their community in every sense—not of their class, religion, and especially race.

Community and cultural boundaries not only affected attitudes toward premarital sex, and consequently the behaviour of youth, but also restricted the selection process from its earliest stages. When a Protestant boy asked her out, one Catholic girl seeking her father's permission was advised, "It's easier not to start." She declined the invitation, despite her admitted attraction to the young man, and he "understood" the reasons and did not pursue her.[26] Among Italian immigrants in Montreal, those who arrived young or were Canadian-born often agreed with their elders that staying within the community was the best hope of a sound marriage. At the same time, this endogamy was very confining where casual dating was concerned. One young woman, while admitting that she preferred to go out with Italian boys and wanted to marry one, also acknowledged that "the Italian girls, too, are going out with other nationalities.... They prefer to be like the English, for the English are more refined, dress nicely and choose better things."[27] Sociologist C.M. Bayley found that by the mid-1930s, marriages were no longer commonly the result of familial matchmaking but were much more dependent upon "fortuitous circumstances" and mutual affection; there was also a small but significant movement toward intermarriage with other groups among both Italians and Ukrainians in Montreal.[28]

The children of immigrants complained that their parents were "out of step with urban trial and error courtship." Because boys were generally permitted more social freedom than their sisters, many dated French Canadian girls despite parental disapproval. They felt especially constrained by the old-world customs that dictated that "after a fellow has been to a girl's house once or twice a week for a month, the father will put his hand on his hip and say, well, what are you coming here for?" As a young mechanic explained the practice common among his Italian Canadian peers,

> We go out with French Canadian girls until we are ready to get married and then we look for an Italian girl that we would like. But this is how we must go about it.... Supposing I think I would like to take out L., I would visit the house several nights a week for quite a while to see how we get along. Then I would tell Mr.... that I have great pleasure in telling him that I like his daughter and would like to take her out. He would say that he would ask her opinion. If that is alright, then I take her out. I must take her oldest sister along or her brother; if she hasn't either, the mother or father has to come.[29]

These young men actually carried out a hybrid form of courtship, dating the "Canadian" way with girls outside their community and adopting the time-honoured old-world way with those within it, about whom they had—or at least were strongly expected to have—serious intentions for marriage.

While Edna Jaques and the eligible young women of the western settlements had an abundant selection of suitors at hand, others had to contend with a scarcity brought about by such events and problems as war and unemployment. In early 1920s Winnipeg, adolescent girls lamented that many eligible young men had to leave for the east to find work, while, as one explained the aggravated gender imbalance, "a whole generation of young men about eight or ten years older than we had lost their lives in the Great War. There went the husbands of me and many of my friends."[30] By 1943, Mary Peate recalled, "the disappearance of boys and young men" from the streets and venues of Montreal made her feel "as if an invisible Pied Piper had traversed the land, spiriting them away." The Catholic schoolgirls of her acquaintance took to praying to St. Ann, whom they believed was the patron of single girls, with a certain mock sincerity: "Dear Saint Ann / get me a man / quick as you can."[31] Adult observers worried publicly that young women were taking up with less than suitable men as a result of the war, because, "now that dates are at a premium, girls feel that they must take what they can get and not be too choosy."[32] Girls were inclined to lament the absence of eligible men even as the war ended, as reflected in one such plaint from Toronto's Northern Vocational High School yearbook, thought to be so revealing of the sad situation of teenage girls that it was reprinted in the *Star*:

> From nine a.m. til half past twelve we're penned up in a room,
> it's not the air that stifles us, dear reader, it's the gloom.
> And then for precious minutes as about our lunch we toy,
> we gaze with hungry eyes upon the nearest Northern boy.
> The war of wars is over and our boys are coming back.
> The bands they play, the people shout but we poor girls—alack,
> are lonely still and smitten by the scarcity of males.
> For thirty-two poor Northern girls the shortage still prevails.[33]

Whatever the extent of modern freedom in the romantic realm, parents cannot be said to have relinquished attempts to exert some control over the mating habits of their young, especially if testimony of their protectiveness over daughters is any indication. Writing to advice columnist "Miss Rosalind" in 1921, one young woman of eighteen related that her parents objected to her keeping company—at all—with young men. There were two prospective suitors in the wings, both "of good families," who were paying "a great deal of attention" to her. Naturally, she was tempted to "go with one of them regardless of my parents' wishes." Miss Rosalind cautioned against this approach, falling back on the well-worn advice that she "have a real heart-to-heart talk with [her] mom and dad."[34] In Winnipeg during the early 1920s, Lillian Allen had to face her religious widower-father's disapproval of dancing as well as of dating: "Meeting and going on dates with boys was complicated by the fact that I had not the courage to stand up to Father about going to dances. Boys were fearful of this problem and didn't want to get involved."[35]

In rural areas where modern courtship still bore some resemblance to the old-fashioned kind (partly due to fewer opportunities to "go out"), being "called on" at home remained popular even as dating became the modern practice. When Edna Jaques took up with Jimmy, who worked in a bank, he would join her family for dinner at her home; the young couple were then discreetly left alone together in the kitchen or parlour.[36] Of course, there were some who took undue advantage of this familial discretion. In Fenn, Alberta, a hired hand, whose girlfriend lived about fifteen kilometres from the farm where he was employed, bought a car to facilitate the courtship. When her father ordered him to go home at ten o'clock one evening, he dutifully put on his hat and coat and made to leave—but then, "pretty sure that the girl's father had retired," he resumed his visit in the parlour. At two in the morning, when he was actually ready to depart, he found that his car was out of gas and he was obliged to get the girl's father out of bed for the key to the farm's gas tank. It was "a long time" before he was permitted to call again.[37]

Chaperonage and community vigilance over adolescence may have loosened in varying degrees during this period, but this still remained the custom in various traditional societies, such as in rural Catholic Quebec, in francophone settlements outside Quebec, and certainly within immigrant communities, rural and urban, across the nation.[38] Young women were kept under strict watch, and protracted courtship was strongly discouraged. The familial form of courtship, culminating with the young man formally asking the young woman's father for her hand in marriage, remained very much the custom during the 1930s and into the 1940s. Yet hurried marriages were not unheard of in this environment, "even in respectable families," although townspeople typically believed that these were largely confined to the most lowly families. In some areas, berry-picking season had the "particular reputation" of offering stolen moments to the young.[39] In Montreal, meanwhile, since adolescents often started full-time wage labour at the age of fourteen, the young had ample opportunity to meet and court on the job. Nonetheless, girls were generally not allowed to entertain suitors in the evening before the age of sixteen or even eighteen. Most continued to meet their suitors within their own communities, through family and friends, and the young couple was usually accompanied on outings by a chaperone, most often a sibling or older family member. Strong religious and cultural sanctions helped to ensure that even when left unsupervised, the young couple behaved "properly."[40]

But even the most diligent parents ultimately could not stay apprised of everything their adolescent children got up to. In late-1920s Regina, as Claire Wodlinger remembered, "Necking was the 'in' thing with my age group and I thought it was exciting. It meant equal numbers of boys and girls would find a secluded place, indoors or out, where they would pair off and the boy would put his arm around the girl.... Sometimes the boy would try "petting."... The boys were as nervous as the girls so, although they persisted, it was a half-hearted effort and easily discouraged."[41]

Peer pressure, increasingly acknowledged as a vital factor in the modern youth problem, also drew the young into experimentation. One Toronto woman distinctly recalled a particular escapade in her last year of high school (fifth form) during the late 1930s, in confessing to "playing with fire." She had befriended a Barnardo girl two years her senior who worked as a domestic in her neighbourhood:

> She and I started to go out for walks up over the bridge and the boys up there said smart things about us. We thought it was great fun. Grandma overheard some of our conversations and gave me a long lecture, saying that I should not go where these boys were and that she knew girls whose lives had been ruined in that manner. Well, I didn't listen to her. We kept going out and soon picked up with a couple of fellows. We went for a walk one very cold night and then went and sat under the bridge where it was warmer. Before long the fellow I was with began feeling up my legs. I got scared and tore myself away from him. I got mad and made him take me home at once.... I didn't go out with him anymore.[42]

The more timid—or more "obedient," as one girl from a strict rural Catholic family put it—"knew how we were expected to behave" and internalized enough of the familial and community moral strictures against "impropriety" to act accordingly.[43] If nothing else, fear of pregnancy, in a time where it was almost entirely left to the girl and her family to deal with, certainly helped set limits on risky behaviour.

It is impossible to determine whether premarital sex was increasing at a rate to keep pace with the nervous discussions by the older generation in newspapers, magazines, and scholarly journals. In matters of a broader knowledge about sexuality, here, too, there is an intriguing ambivalence in many Canadians' memories. The notions underlying the "flaming youth" construct were built upon a scaffolding of socio-cultural modernization that extended even to sexuality. In light of new ideas about sex, many of these attributed to Freud, to the "sex appeal" sold by Hollywood and the "glossies," to generational unease about the future, and possibly to more opportunity to "get away with it" thanks to new courtship practices—as well as to the alleged new "frankness" of the young—youth-watchers might well assume that premarital sexual experimentation was the new, "modern" norm. Yet even if the young really did differ radically from their elders in their supposedly modern outlook and know-how, memories of adolescence experiences between the Great War and 1950 regularly bring back feelings of embarrassment, ignorance, shame, and even fear about sexual matters. Some remember entering their teen years "not knowing a thing about it" and learning the basic physiology and "hygiene" of sex only in gender-segregated high school classes.[44] Others learned about it in science courses, such as was the case for one Toronto woman who started high school in 1921: "I took up botany in first form and one day I was telling Tom [her older brother] about pollenization. Then he told me where babies came from. He had found out from the boy across the street, and he in turn had found out from some twins [girls] and they had been told by their mother. I was kind of shocked but interested.[45]

In Catholic schools, the matter of sex education was even more overwrought, often delivered in church or during regular religious instruction in school. Basil Johnston's male schoolmates were subjected to a special retreat, along with the senior girls from their sister school, during which a sixty- or sixty-five-year-old "very nervous" priest addressed them about sex in an oblique and unenlightening manner.[46] At the Shubenacadie residential school in Nova Scotia, Isabelle Knockwood remembered, the nuns' only version of sex education amounted to the principle that "all bodily functions are dirty." In the absence of real information, the girls "came up with our own strange notions of how anyone got pregnant."[47]

Most parents probably made some attempt to inform their adolescent offspring about "the facts of life," especially their daughters, who were expected to be more innocent than their sons but who were clearly more vulnerable to possible negative repercussions. One Toronto woman's mother did more than most in educating her daughters about sex, "always answering my many and very frank questions with equal directness." For all that, she professed herself "amazingly unconscious of sex problems." When she went to boarding school at age fifteen, one of the head girls gave her "some little blue books," probably those issued by the federal health department. Although these "gave correct sex information in a very scientific manner," they also left her "rather scared." Her sister, meanwhile, was "educated" in sexual matters through another traditional outlet, an older friend. Belying the supposed frankness and openness of modern youth about sexuality, she also claimed that "never once do I remember sex coming up for discussion, smutty or otherwise, in all the crowds of boys with whom I played or fought, nor was it mentioned by the girls in grade or high school."[48]

Claire Wodlinger worried that she would get pregnant by kissing: "I didn't have sense enough to discuss it with him [her much older boyfriend] or any of my girlfriends."[49] Women recall their misunderstanding of the actual process of reproduction even to the point of "not knowing where the baby was coming from" at the time of their first delivery after marriage. Lillian Allen attributes the ignorance of her group of friends to class and culture: "At this time our bodies were changing and boys seemed to want to touch us....We were indescribably ignorant of sex. I think those who grew up in the North End [the immigrant ward of Winnipeg] were exposed to life much earlier than we Anglo-Saxons in Crescentwood."[50] One Ontario woman who started dating in the late 1930s found that "going out in cars" caused her parents some consternation about the necessity of approaching the subject of sex: "One day I was up in my mother's room and heard her downstairs saying, 'she's going out in a car.' 'She's what?' my father said. 'She's going out in a car. With a boy. I think you'd better talk to her.' He said, 'Anne, you'd better talk to her...' All mother said was 'I guess you could tell me more than I could tell you.'...They didn't know how to tell us."[51]

Men who grew up during this time likewise remember their adolescent wonderment at "what it all meant...when they used to speak of 'secret places' and of a common phenomenon that every boy knows about—wet dreams and nightly emissions and so on—as sapping the strength and loss of virility....The panacea...was cold baths, a great deal of strenuous exercise."[52] When he came of age on the eve of World War II, writer Robert Collins confesses, he was a "sexual ignoramus" and he contends that this classification likely applied to his contemporaries in general. In Wolfville, Nova Scotia, one man recalled, his naiveté made him find it "exciting just to hold a girl's hand."[53] Hugh Garner's Depression memories of "riding the rods" in his late teens evoke his feeling that there was more empty bragging about sex than actual indulgence: "Sex on the road has become part of the hobo legend but it was largely imaginary....Most of us were too broke to buy it and too dirty and lousy most of the time to attract it."[54] "Going out" to public amusements or even to find some privacy was a complicated matter for the young unemployed and for those whose meagre wages had to go into the family pot. As one man remembered, "the times were hard on the young people. Courting, I mean, getting to know each other. It was called spooning, and about the best in the winter that a young couple could hope for was for the fellow to go over to her house and the old people to go visiting, and yet again that wasn't so hot either."[55] Writer Hugh MacLennan contended that social proscriptions remained potent for many young people of the time: "In the Thirties so much love had to be denied, indeed, was expected to be denied. For then it was largely expected that sexual fulfilment could be found only in marriage, and if marriage had to be delayed for economic reasons, the psychic tensions were very serious even for young people who went to bed with one another without benefit of clergy."[56]

The modern dating scene probably allowed for somewhat more physical affection and preliminary sexual experimentation than the older version of "visiting" under chaperone, but it is also likely that young Canadians who engaged in premarital sex were following the historical pattern of doing so within the bounds of certain traditional expectations. For most couples, sex usually took place within "steady" and exclusive relationships where there was often a tacit promise of marriage—or at least an assumption that this was the objective. For young women, sexual freedom still carried a high price. Regardless of their class or ethnic background, loss of "reputation," with or without pregnancy, brought dishonour to women and their families. While views on the gravity of the "sin" differed slightly, no organized religion tolerated sex outside marriage. In the years between the wars, in a predominantly and vigorously Catholic community, Montreal's Hôpital de la Miséricorde admitted at least 560 unwed mothers annually, evidence of the penalty that women continued to pay in the absence of effective and accessible contraception.[57] The simple understanding that she would "get thrown out of the house" if it happened to her was one young woman's "main reason that I'd never do it before marriage," despite pressure from her soldier-boyfriend, who, for his part, argued that "if I didn't give myself to him and he was torpedoed, he would die before he'd even had a chance to live."[58] Oral testimony suggests that "most everyone" at least "knew of" some young woman who had "gotten in trouble" or had "a bun in the oven" before marriage. Despite the taboos against premarital sex that persisted even while the "new morality" preoccupied youth-watchers, "there was a lot done that wasn't admitted, because there were a few illegitimate births around too," as one rural Ontario man remembered of the 1920s; "but wherever those occurred, the mother was treated as an outcast or next thing to it."[59] Across the nation, the measures taken to hide a premarital pregnancy usually required that the young woman leave home, enter an institution, and relinquish the infant for adoption.

Although the causes of the increase remain largely unaccounted for, the number of births outside marriage was definitely on the rise during these years from 1920 to 1950. Changing birth registration practices may have been a factor, given the tighter federal laws as of 1921. At the same time, the number of hospital births (to all women) increased at a historic rate, representing the majority of all births across Canada by 1938. Previously easier to keep off the record, illegitimate births were increasingly likely to be attended to institutionally and thus also registered; this development alone would have contributed to a larger statistical increase after 1931, relative to the scarce data available before that year, than was probably the case in real numbers. To some degree, however, the climbing numbers must also reflect the increase in premarital sexual relations that typically accompanies a rise in the age of marriage. In 1921, the total number of illegitimate births in English Canada was estimated at 3,334; in 1931, there were 8,365 illegitimate births recorded; the numbers rose to 10,101 in 1941, representing the highest decanal rise ever recorded in this category.[60] (See table 3.1.) In a larger context, however, between 1921 and 1941, the percentage of illegitimate births in Canada varied little, sitting between 3 and 4 per cent. With 39.3 in 1,000 live births being illegitimate in 1940, Canada followed slightly behind the United States (40.4) and England (43.0).[61]

Table 3.1: Illegitimate Births as a Percentage of Total Live Births

Year	Percentage	Year	Percentage	Year	Percentage
1921	1.97	1931	3.46	1941	4.00
1922	2.05	1932	3.57	1942	4.10
1923	2.17	1933	3.77	1943	4.10
1924	2.34	1934	3.65	1944	4.20
1925	2.60	1935	3.74	1945	4.50
1926	2.63	1936	3.90	1946	4.10
1927	2.85	1937	3.90	1947	4.00
1928	3.06	1938	4.00	1948	4.30
1929	3.17	1939	3.90	1949	3.90
1930	3.30	1940	3.90		

The statistics are derived from *Historical Statistics of Canada*, Series B1, Vital Statistics and Health, R.D. Fraser: "Live Births, Crude Birth Rate, Age-Specific Fertility Rates, Gross Reproduction Rate, and Percentage of Births in Hospitals in Canada, 1921–1974"; http://www.statcan.ca.

Just as troubling to many Canadians as youth unemployment and transience was the fact that the Great Depression saw many young people "obliged to forego those personal functions which should be the right of every normal individual, namely, marriage, the rearing of children, and the establishment of a home." Among the more serious consequences of deferred marriage were premarital sexual relationships, a rise in illegitimacy, and "a general lowering of the moral standards of youth," all of which were considered to be statistically demonstrated trends right across the nation.[62] The marriage rate declined nationally at a steady rate between 1930 and 1933—the "bottom" of the Depression—at which point an incremental upward trend began. A contemporary survey by the Ontario Young Men's Council of the YMCA found that 164 of 180 respondents (all under the age of twenty-eight) believed their income to be "insufficient for marriage"; more than half of these were without a steady income of any kind. Even more disconcerting to contemporaries, when the surveyors posed the question "Judging by the young people of your acquaintance, would you say that irregular sex relations are on the increase at the present time?" eighty-five said yes. A majority also "strongly" agreed that there was a "general lowering of the traditional standards of sexual morality."[63] The rise in illegitimacy figures between 1926 and 1936 thus seem to provide clear supporting evidence. There were "marked increases," from 6,121 in 1926 to 8,633 in 1936—a rise of more than 40 per cent over the ten-year period, although it was (and remains) "quite impossible to determine to what extent youth alone were responsible for this alarming increase."[64]

During this entire period, the population of unmarried women in Canada continued to rise, also contributing to the upward trend in illegitimate births. What is most interesting is the fact that, contrary to the fears and assumptions of youth-watchers about heightened adolescent sexual activity as a modern behavioural pattern, the highest illegitimate birth rate was found in the twenty-to-twenty-four age group (see table 3.2).[65] Social scientists also tended to attribute "illicit sex relations" to working-class, immigrant, and rural families, so that science, in effect, supported long-standing class and race-based views about the superior morality of the middle class and Anglo-Saxons. As a young woman travelling across Ontario with the Young Communist League during the Depression, poet and social worker Dorothy Livesay came to the conclusion that the most severe sanctions against premarital sex and illegitimate births were found not among middle-class circles, where, she believed, they were secretly acknowledged, but among the working and farm people who had less access to or knowledge of contraception.[66] Since fairly youthful marriages served as a pre-emptive measure, even the Depression did not deter them in all quarters. When she was sixteen, Anne Woywitka met her future husband, Bill, at a dance in their rural Alberta town, and "it wasn't long before we were being recognized as a couple, talking about marriage. Being in love, neither of us stopped to consider what life would be like. We were into the third year of the Great Depression with no end in sight." The Woywitkas married in 1932 when she was seventeen and he was twenty-two. They went to live in his parents' home with nine other family members, adding a baby of their own within a year.[67]

Reinforcing the likelihood that they would internalize at least some of the sex taboos of the moment, young Canadians had to contend more and more with the experts, whose advice on "normal" sexuality was increasingly disseminated through government agencies, churches, high schools, and youth organizations. Although many doctors and psychologists gave a passing nod to Freudian theory, the majority focused on the dark side of the "sex impulse" among youth. Because of the adolescent's emotionality, impulsiveness, and overwhelming "sex consciousness," as meticulously described by Stanley Hall, many feared that making sex at this life stage "normal"—giving it expert sanction, as it were—might promote a widespread moral degeneration that could lead only to individual breakdown and to generational and social disintegration, all summed up in the concept of the "new morality." Girls continued to draw the larger part of the warnings about sexual danger, but boys were also seen to be threatened by sex outside of lawful, heterosexual, and, by definition, adult marriage. And even though sexual awakening was biologically determined, and consequently in and of itself not only normal but necessary, the times held that modernity presented the young with an incredible range of sexual "traps." Again pointing to the decline of "the race," the venereal-disease panic occasioned by the Great War also had a definite impact on ideas about adolescent sexuality: these scourges represented both "the greatest single public health problem of modern times" and "foul and sinister manifestations of our failure to attend to the organized study and care of our growing young people."[68]

Employed by the Ontario education department as "lecturer on eugenics and personal hygiene," the infamous Arthur Beall used hyperbole, melodrama, foreboding and even terror tactics to deliver his fundamentally anti-sex message to great numbers of adolescent boys across the province during the first three decades of the twentieth century. As many of his contemporaries agreed, these boys were "ceaselessly face to face with a carnival of nastiness, a miasma of unclean and malignant influences, which attenuate the mind, pollute the imagination and disintegrate the soul—all because they atrophy and penalise the will." This miasma included "the deadly cigarette, degrading dime novels, unclean moving pictures, indecent dances."[69] Understated by comparison, prominent educator and social hygiene reformer Peter Sandiford warned a Hamilton, Ontario, audience in 1922 to pay attention to "all that society holds out to the boy and girl of the later 'teens—the beauties and the dangers of the dance—the use and abuse of card games—and of the cigarette craze."[70]

Table 3.2. Age-Specific Illegitimate Birth Rates, 1921–1951

	Ages 15–19	Ages 20–24
1921	4.9	8.5
1931	4.7	13.0
1941	5.8	12.7
1951	9.1	19.9
1956	11.1	23.9
1961	12.7	20.7

The statistics are derived from *Historical Statistics of Canada*, Series B1, Vital Statistics and Health, R.D. Fraser: "Live Births, Crude Birth Rate, Age-Specific Fertility Rates, Gross Reproduction Rate, and Percentage of Births in Hospitals in Canada, 1921–1974"; http://www.statcan.ca.

"Modern trends" were clearly implicated in this modern predicament. The "revolutionary nature of the change in attitude to sex" was attributed to changing gender ideals among the young. Such time-honoured concepts as manly chivalry, protectiveness toward women, and gentlemanly behaviour were being subverted. Still, the modern boy would not demand more from a girl "than he is given reason to believe he can get." Just as had generations before them, girls had to accept the responsibility of understanding "where harmless relationships leave off and practices leading to sexual intercourse begin."[71] Thus, the double standard that demanded sexual purity and self-control of women while making them the sirens at the root of many a man's downfall remained unmodified within the proposed model of modern heterosexual relations. Experts continued to worry that "for the most part, our girls remain in ignorance of their danger, from the shrinking on the part of the parents from talking frankly to them."[72] On the critical subject of sexuality, as on many others pertaining to the youth problem, parental intervention appeared to be a viable means of breaching an intergenerational gap made all the wider by the very different adolescent experiences of parents and their children.

The "revolution in morals" was so closely associated with the flaming youth of the 1920s that, in keeping with long-standing gender conventions that made "fallen" women the symbol of moral decay, the hapless flapper came to be its emblem. American psychologist W.I. Thomas was one of many experts who stirred controversy on the subject of the sexual proclivities of modern young women, in his "shocking" 1923 study, *The Unadjusted Girl, with Cases and Standpoint for Behavior Analysis*. Thomas discussed the adolescent girl's "lack of adjustment"—also proclaimed to be outright "demoralization"—primarily in terms of a "sexual delinquency" linked directly and unequivocally to "today's unrest."[73] Echoing Hall and ignoring Freud, he insisted that "the sex passion" played an insignificant role in female sexual delinquency. He claimed to have three thousand documented cases revealing that girls had "usually become wild before the development of sexual desire, and their casual sexual relations do not usually awaken sex feeling." It appeared instead that these "demoralized" young women, "unadjusted" to society's expectations of womanhood, deployed sexuality as "their capital," as "a condition of the realization of other wishes."[74]

The subtext of any number of similar contemporary studies suggests that this aspect of the modern youth problem did not concern female psychosexual maladjustment so much as it did a fear that modern young women were adjusting all too well to a new moral order. Women, especially the young, had little beyond marriage and motherhood that might serve as capital to ensure their social status and economic well-being. If sexuality without marriage and potential maternity were transformed into coin, so to speak—not a modern phenomenon either, but one inherent to patriarchy—it was feared that this capital might become increasingly honoured within the context of the new morality. These young women stood to gain by deliberately flouting established moral standards, gender conventions, and traditional values. Thus, the modern female adolescent was not a newly liberated sexual being but a strangely asexual temptress who used her body as the means to an end—a female archetype as old as Eve. The discussion of female sexuality in terms of "capital" is the modern twist, implying the commodification of the body itself in modern culture. Put simply, the sexuality of adolescent girls was pathological. The modern girl, the flapper, was dangerously "unadjusted."

Adolescents of both sexes who did not learn sexual self-control were also well "on the road to becoming sexual perverts."[75] As young people were warned by another psychologist, Dr. David Thom, heterosexuality quite simply had to be "accomplished" during those critical years or it would "never be accomplished in a normal way" but only by means of "some technical interference ... only after much conflict, failure and illness."[76] The medical author of the popular early-twentieth-century manual *What a Young Girl Ought to Know* warned about "fondling and gushing" between girls that might lead to a "weakening of moral fibre" and to the dissolution of same-sex affection into "a species of self-abuse." Much-cited contemporary studies such as *Factors in the Sex Life of Twenty-Two Hundred Women* (1929), by American sociologist and penal reformer Katherine Bement Davis, supported such concerns with extensive data. In Davis's study group of 1,200 unmarried American college women, 50 per cent admitted to "intense emotional relations with women after puberty," while 26 per cent engaged in "overt practices." Most worrisome, 37 per cent of those self-identifying as "overt homosexuals" had begun the practice in early adolescence.[77]

The ubiquitous warnings against same-sex adolescent attractions suggest that those attractions were fairly commonplace. Where they might once have been tolerated with a sense that they would be "outgrown" by adulthood, new research on homosexuality as well as on adolescence, along with the intense public interest in the sex lives of the young, now made such "crushes" one of the more "dangerous" elements of growing up. By the end of her high school years in the early 1930s, one Toronto woman had developed a "most desperate crush" on an older female schoolmate: "It was the only real crush I ever had on a girl and it made me very unhappy most of the time. I was always feeling slighted and never could do anything to become wonderful in her eyes.... She seemed to break down all the reticence I had and my emotional outlook was very rocky and unstable. I used to daydream magnificent dreams about the two of us.... It was a most unhealthy state.... My mind kept churning around her and never doing any useful creative work." When the object of the "crush" did not reciprocate her feelings and started going steady with a boy, she gave it up and promptly followed suit.[78]

In a twist on the unattainable opposite-sex crush, girls might also indulge in idealizing the girlfriends of the boys they desired. When she reached the age of fifteen, one girl who was "beginning to be boy crazy" focused her affections on a friend's brother, a senior on the football and basketball teams, and "a very ancient 17 years old." She was obliged to "worship from the background," however, as he had a girlfriend his own age: "I thought she was pretty wonderful too and wrote her a poem and sent her a rose as a token of my esteem."[79] At the furthest end of the spectrum, precocious sexual initiation could well happen among friends of the same sex, an occurrence probably unmentioned and unrecorded more than it was unusual. When Lillian Allen's father took her camping at Lake of the Woods with her brother and her close friend Charlotte, she and Charlotte shared a bed in their cottage. Frightened by a storm during the night, she found herself in Charlotte's comforting embrace. As Allen recorded, with surprising candour, "Then she began to finger me....It was a marvellous sensation, and before I knew what was happening, I took a sort of spasm. I found later from the book that this was an orgasm. It went right through me and then came a delicious relaxation and I drifted off to sleep."[80]

As youth-watchers feared, not all who experienced same-sex attractions in adolescence were able to "recover" quickly. One fifteen-year-old girl who developed a "devotedness" to a "special friend"—an older girl at her high school who felt the same way about her—used to wait to walk home after school with her and would get to school early in the morning "so that I could see her a few minutes before class." She even tried to adopt her friend's mannerisms. Her mother "sensed what was happening" and explained to her that it was "a natural thing to happen for a girl to love another girl—but that it was bad if carried too far—because love of that nature is really meant for two people of the opposite sex." When she told the other girl of her mother's concerns, the latter "confessed she had known there was something wrong" and was "glad to know the real reason." They resolved to stay away from each other, but she was "caught in a dreadful remorseful mood and feeling as though...I always did wrong things—that I would never be able to get married."[81] A married woman, alienated from her mother during her youth, who still "harboured" lesbian "tendencies," felt strongly that constant maternal disapproval had led her in that direction: "Mother always had a horror of Betty [her sister] or me getting boy-crazy and she always made us feel it wasn't a nice thing to do to go out with boys....I had always hated being a girl, I told mother I hated being a woman and she told me I was a wicked unnatural little girl. She said God's highest plan was for women and that I ought to look forward to having children and making a home. These talks usually ended in stony silence on my part with a secret vow never to get married or have babies or a home."[82]

In the end, these nervous discussions about adolescent sexuality were fundamentally about "normal" adult sexuality, which would be seriously compromised if the young were not taught to control—really, to repress—the "sex impulse" in favour of abstinence until they could be safely married off at an appropriate age. There was nothing modern about this strategy as applied to youth, but "the times" made it especially salient, as the young seemed to flaunt openly what previous generations had perhaps attempted to carry off discreetly. By the end of the interwar years, as sociologist Kingsley Davis argued, "a constellation of cultural conditions" was "oppos[ing] the sex standards of different groups and generations, leaving impulse only chaotically controlled."[83] Young

Canadians needed a "definite training" in sex hygiene in order to become "not only citizens who are longer lived and who are free from disease, but contented, happy units in a well balanced state."[84] Given the magnitude and intensity of public anxiety about adolescent sexuality, the sexual regulation of the young was easily the issue that drew the most attention from youth-watchers during the first half of the twentieth century, a constant and remarkably consistent theme despite changing generational and historical contexts.[85]

Supporters of school-based sex education, among whom doctors were a significant component, acknowledged that physiological principles should be the starting point. They stressed above all a "sound training in right habits and proper attitudes" and the cultivation of "ideals of purity [and], reverence for parents and parenthood."[86] In its modern scientific form and delivery, sex education would be as much about traditional moral standards as about modern standards of physical and mental hygiene. Although the discussion was ostensibly scientific, the language and tone were homiletic, expressing the experts' concern for the young with a combination of moral judgement and scientific rhetoric that underlined their authority. In Beall's adolescent male universe, the "mighty resolve" shown by "hundreds of adolescent boys" who were pledged not to indulge in any form of sexual practice before holy matrimony was "the noblest work, the most heroic, the most patriotic, in truth the most God-like work a boy can ever aim at." The results would manifest themselves gloriously upon "unborn generations of Canadians," ensuring that they, in turn, would become "citizens ennobling their country."[87]

With an eye to the prevention of what pessimists deemed "the inevitable slide" into degeneration, social-hygiene activists insisted that teachers and parents must emphasize, even more than the biological facts, "the tremendous importance of right choices in marriage."[88] Again, the arguments imitated those of the wider scientific childrearing campaign: not only was the present "health of the nation" at stake, so also was that of a future Canada. Parents were urged to start by educating themselves, or, even better, to rush their children to properly trained experts lest they do inestimable harm by "conducting their own campaign."[89] Yet most who pronounced on the sexual aspects of the youth problem insisted that "the proper teacher" was the parent, "especially the mother." They were equally convinced that the home had, as in so many other matters, "fallen down in this task" and that the burden had consequently shifted to the school.[90] Their recommended simple and direct school-based approach to sex education, however, would never be that simple, nor would it be readily accomplished. Such goals were not transformed into regular sex instruction for students of any age, on any systematic basis, during this entire period.

While family and school were providing inadequately for the sex training of the young, the media attempted to make up some of the lack. By the 1930s, film was increasingly touted as one of the most efficient modern means of educating the masses. The Social Hygiene Council of Canada produced *The End of the Road* in 1932, purportedly "one of the most powerful and graphic educational pictures ever to be filmed." Shown to more than five thousand Torontonians at Massey Hall, in women's-only and men's-only viewings, the film depicted "the ultimate retribution that overtakes those who indulge in the social indiscretions of youth." Intended to benefit parents and any other adults "entrusted with the guidance of a younger and less responsible generation," it told the story of two young women dealing with "the problems that beset practically all of modern youth"—those concerning premarital sex. The moral is made abundantly clear: the girl with an informed and involved modern mother escapes both sex and tragedy; her friend, let down by a flighty and ignorant mother, is ruined forevermore.[91]

The modern age, as we have noted, was not only the cinematic age but also that of mass-produced advice literature. By no means a modern genre, advice literature was nonetheless published and disseminated in far greater numbers after the Great War than at any earlier time, much of it through widely read "family" magazines, both American and Canadian. Medical and mental health professionals, along with any number of state and voluntary agencies, clubs and associations, professional groups, journalists, clergy, and teachers, contributed to the swelling chorus of advice intended to promote the self-improvement of the young and the improved parenting technique of adults. The literature was reasonably most popular with middle-class, fairly informed readers keen on "modern" ways of doing things, but its very range and distribution suggest that it likely found its way into less affluent homes as well.

Also increasingly popular was a new species of newspaper advice columnist who appeared on a weekly, sometimes daily, basis in the "women's pages," many of them lending a sympathetic ear specifically to adolescents, mostly girls. A postage stamp would permit young readers to address their darkest secrets and deepest worries to these comfortably distant and anonymous mentors, just as anonymously and without shame. Advice columnists could bridge the rift between generations, providing the counsel that youth could not comfortably seek from parents, teachers, clergy, or other adults in their lives. The publication of their letters must have provided a secret thrill of acknowledgement as well—of being "understood" by an influential adult for the seriousness of their situation—while their peer-readers could identify with the predicament detailed and also reasonably gain from the advice offered. Many of these advisers were syndicated, mostly American, columnists; others were "home-grown"; all took on a tone of wise but worldly guidance to teenagers in distress, mostly in regard to their relations with parents, with peers, and especially with the other sex. Dorothy Dix, the most famous of the advisers until her death in 1951, produced a daily column that was read by an estimated sixty million people in North America and Great Britain. In Canada, "Dear Dorothy" appeared in the women's pages of newspapers ranging from the small-town *Guelph Daily Mercury* to the *Montreal Daily Gazette*. Dix took an even-handed, reasonable tone in advising both parents and adolescents: "It is a time for driving with a light rein," she told one mother of teenaged girls; "Parents should seek to guide rather than drive at that period."[92]

"In the Know" advertisement, Kotex feminine hygiene products, from *Good Housekeeping*, November 1948; also featured in *Chatelaine*. Reprinted with permission of the Museum of Menstruation and Women's Health, www.mum.org.

This Kotex campaign featured a series of different multiple-choice "self-testing" ads depicting common teenage social scenarios, mostly about the dating scene. A list of options to check allowed the reader to assess whether she was effectively "in the know" about contemporary etiquette.

The adolescent advice-seekers sent the usual queries, mostly concerned with their attractiveness to boys and how best to conduct romantic relationships while avoiding parental disapproval and the perils of sex. One sixteen year old declared an unusual problem: she was simply "too attractive to the opposite sex" and sought to understand "the reason why a girl is too attractive," as her would-be suitors were having "some bitter disputes" over her. As she told it, "it is not because I am more than particular with my toilet or anything but manners and grammar." She did not "care for the boys any more than to be sociable with all and to have a good chum when I go out," and signed herself "Yours in Bewilderment—Cutie." The columnist, Miss Rosalind, determined that "the reason some people are more attractive than others is—personality!" While she found herself unable to explain precisely what was meant by that concept—"nor have I ever found any person who could explain"—she asserted that "it is something to be thankful for because it gives a girl such a blessed privilege to be a help and inspiration to all who come in contact with her." In sum, the worried "Cutie" should resign herself to her at times "bewildering" blessing, while other girl readers should make note of the importance of cultivating "personality."

Breaking with the female adviser mode was a daily syndicated column, "A Man Talks to Women," written by George Antheil, that debuted in the women's pages of the *Toronto Star* in 1939. Antheil's purpose was to "tell women readers the male side of a great many questions" in a "breezy, new, different" way that was also "filled with sound reasoning."[93] A writer, a modernist composer of international repute, and a self-professed "student of applied psychology," Antheil was described as being "as modern as the young people of today." Reserving one column each week expressly for "teen problems," he adopted an avuncular tone toward the "nieces and nephews" who often addressed their letters to "Dear Uncle George." Again, most were written by young women aged fifteen to seventeen; most sought guidance to become more popular in general and especially with the opposite sex; many complained about the rigidity and unfairness of old-fashioned parents.

By far the most common question raised by young advice-seekers concerned kissing and other such romantic activities. "Rosalie" asked, "When and where should a girl allow a boy to kiss her?"—apparently a common query among "other teenagers up against that puzzling question of kissing."[94] It was not that boys did not bother about the subject: one who signed his letter "An Abject Thing" reported that he had offended a girl he had asked for a goodnight kiss and that "she is still mad," while he was becoming "more abject every day."[95] Antheil acknowledged that he had discussed this problem many times before, and that he expected "to be answering it as long as I write a column." He also contended that "every youngster who writes to me knows the answer but either they want to have me confirm it or else they think that the peculiar circumstances of their case makes it different." His response was similar to that of women columnists, reflecting the dominant understandings of gender and sexuality as well as ideas about adolescence. Women tended to take the matter of kissing "rather seriously," while men did not "as a rule." "Rosalie" had confessed that when a "nice boy" had tried to kiss her at her door at the close of their first date, she had "politely said no" and he had "got peeved and left," promising to call "some time"—and she had not heard from him since. Her questions were rhetorical: "Why can't a boy take a girl out without expecting to kiss her? Why is it that a boy gets peeved when she refuses to park?"[96] In similar fashion, another female writer lamented that her date thought she was "a flat tire and not a bit human" when she would not kiss him, and she also wondered, "Why does a girl have to pay with a lot of petting just because he paid for her soda? Does a girl have to pet to be popular?" Antheil advised both girls—and many others over the years—that they should not kiss unless willing, whether "on the first or tenth date." But he also fell back on the biological argument about gendered differences in sex drive: "As long as boys are boys they are always going to ask you for a kiss or try to kiss you....I agree it shouldn't be a promiscuous habit. But laugh it off, kid them out of it."[97] It was up to women to stay in control, seeing as men could not help being men.

Antheil's turn as resident adviser for the *Toronto Star* was followed in 1945 by Mary Starr's column "If You Take My Advice," which would run daily for more than twenty years.[98] The matter of teen relationships, and especially "how far to go" with the opposite sex, remained paramount. One young female reader believed that she recognized another ("Blue Eyes") who had previously written for advice about "necking," and responded in an outrage: "I also live in a small town and this girl, who believes that one has to neck to be popular with the stronger sex, is known to all and has not such a good reputation as would be described by others. Most of her ex-boyfriends, especially one, quit her for girls who take an interest in other things, such as dancing, sport, etc." "Blue Eyes herself" had evidently informed her high school acquaintances that she had written "the disgusting letter," whereupon they decided to "avoid" her, "and let her know what we thought of such cheap, common ideas." With a vow to "endeavour through our loyalty to you and to our standards of living to give it to her one way or another," the writer's strong words point to the power of gossip and peer ostracism as regulating mechanisms within the social group. Starr certainly recognized the damaging potential of this harsh stance, assuring the writer that the girl had been "punished sufficiently," and suggesting a different collective approach: "Don't you think you could take her into your crowd, get her interested in sports and dancing and then, by showing her it is possible to have a far better time this way, to get her to change her views and her way of life?" Shunning and isolation, Starr insisted, would "only force her into choosing the wrong kind of companions and might bring her very real harm."[99]

The ambivalence of teenage girls about their own developing sexuality, intensified by the mixed messages concerning sex that informed the period's gender-delimited constructions and moral expectations about "normal" sexual behaviour as well as normal adolescent behaviour, reverberates in the assumptions of both advice-seekers and advisers. One young woman, "Seventeen," was "reluctant to ask [her] parents" whether it was " wrong to like necking." As she explained herself, "It is hard to admit such a thing because I sound bold and cheap, but until this year I had never kissed a boy really so as to make me feel all queer and emotional inside. I didn't allow the boy to see that I liked it. On the contrary, I am considered the slow 'nice girl' type—a doubtful honour! But after going around with a super lad from a different school I have discovered my skeleton-in-a-closet. I don't know whether to feel guilty or accept it as part of growing up." Starr found this "a delicate question and one that is difficult to deal with in a newspaper column." She advised "Seventeen" to get counselling at the YWCA, but she did make the effort to "at least put your mind at rest—you have no cause for alarm—no skeleton in your closet." While this was "the most natural feeling in the world" and "love is a natural and beautiful emotion," there was no doubt to be entertained about the "wrongness" of "the promiscuous necking, petting, smooching of this generation, the 'spooning' of the last."[100] The adolescent writer did not mention love, but the equation of heterosexual love with the "rightness" of sexual relations is presumed, the link between "wrongness"—youthful promiscuity—and premarital sex embedded in the language and tone as much as in the advice itself.

The new body of advice literature, directed at young readers rather than at their parents, inspired an expanding range of publications produced and circulated by youth clubs and associations, church-affiliated groups, federal and provincial health departments, provincial education departments, and such agencies as the Canadian Council on Child Welfare and the Social Hygiene Council of Canada. Among the earliest were the high-circulation volumes of the infamous *Sex and Self* series, the bestselling sex information literature in Canada between 1900 and 1915, written and distributed by doctors and Protestant clergy. In addition, Canadian youth were often treated to British and American publications, as well as to Canadian imitations of these. Much of the literature was gender-exclusive, aimed at either boys or girls, with such titles as *The Wonderful Story of Life: A Mother Talks with Her Daughter Regarding Life and Reproduction* (1921), *The Story of Life: As Told to His Sons and as Told to Her Daughters* (1922), *What Every Lad Should Know about Sex* (1935), and *Ourselves: A Few Facts for Young Men* (1935).

By the 1940s, as high schools started to incorporate some careful sex-and-relationship information into their health curricula, pamphlets such as the American-produced *Dating Days* (1949) came in themselves to signify a certain rite of passage. Speaking directly to teenagers about their presumed "dating problems"—making adolescent relationships, like adolescence itself, inherently problematic—the authors emphasized how "boy-girl relationships do have a bearing on marriage." To that traditional, socially sanctioned end, they urged a modern, active approach to dating, once again defined as "a process of trial and error," because "if you are not friendly with a number of different persons, you really won't be the best possible judge of what you want in your ideal person, and dating, of course, is one of the ways in which you can make these judgments."[101] If a take-charge approach was advocated, it was nonetheless advised that in "the normal dating situation...it's best for the girl to wait until she's asked." While this might seem "a bit hard" for girls, they could reassure themselves that "a fellow tends to shy away from a girl who seems to be pushing herself"; just as important, "it happens to be the prevailing social custom." Likewise, it was "the accepted social pattern that boys pay the way," and any offer to contribute to the cost of entertainment might risk making a young man feel "a blow to his masculine pride." Also important was the ubiquitous warning that, "generally speaking," a girl who allowed a kiss on a first date might well leave "a mistaken impression." Those who had "not been successful" in the dating game were encouraged to ask for help from parents, teachers, the school counsellor, "or some other trusted adult adviser."[102]

Youth associations produced their own titles, which repeated many of these same time-honoured maxims, reconfigured, though superficially, to fit the modern dating situation. The Girl Guides of Canada's *Checklist on Looks, "Poise-onality," Social Habits, Health, and a Serious Note on Tolerance* served up "Dating Data" in poetic form:

> It is really fun to dance,
> But I'm sure to watch my stance.
> When all the rest begin to neck,
> Can I keep myself in check?
> Being ready and waiting for him to arrive,
> Is something for which I always strive.
> I try to be interesting in all I say,
> So he will call another day,
> But when he wants to talk to me,
> I listen attentively as can be.
> Lots of friends mean lots of fun.
> Til I meet my only one.[103]

The message to young women was traditional: they were to be chaste and wait for the "only one"—a passive pose but also a strong one in the face of peer pressure to engage in necking and other such "questionable" activity. But such feminine passivity belied the active measures that could be—in fact, advisedly should be—taken to attract "the one" by being interesting, "attentive," and "a good listener," and by having fun with "lots of friends," thereby circulating socially to increase the chances of locating him.

With public concerns about reproduction—social and biological—magnified against a background of global warfare, World War II intensified attention to teenage sexuality. The usual anxieties about widespread "immorality" that are historically associated with war, especially then, in light of the Great War's recent experience and its generational impact, prompted warnings about "waiting" that associated sexual self-control—especially for young woman, also as usual—with patriotism and victory. The *Toronto Star*'s George Antheil observed that "the more patriotic the boys become ... the more romantic the womenfolk of the land become.... The young people are carried away with this talk of war and bravery." Two young women jointly beseeched "Uncle George" for counsel about their relationships: "What in the world will we do if war should take the world's two most wonderful boys away from us?... There's the horrible feeling that they might not come back to us." Antheil advised, "Don't rush things, girls... War or no war, just remember that it is best for the girl to wait for the boy to say the magic words that will make her joyous."[104] For the generation of young Canadians who came of age during World War II—both the young men who enlisted while in their teens and the girls whom they "left behind"—history pre-empted what was by the 1940s becoming the typical—or at least normative—experience of modern adolescence.

In the mid-to-late 1940s, since reconstruction was foremost in the minds of Canadians, the topic of healthy adolescent relationships became more than ever the subject of regular discussion and expert consultation. Young Canadians also had their say in the matter, thanks to the federal government's funding of the Canadian Youth Commission and of that commission's national surveys, one of which was entirely dedicated to the subject of marriage and family. The commission fretted about the effect of "wartime attitudes on sex and morals," as young women took up with older men and as the "general feeling of strain and excitement" and the "relaxed sex and moral codes" made for "freer and temporary relationships." Because values had slackened, parents and youth leaders had to make every effort to help young people to "work through their confusion and to arrive at a sense of values which has vital meaning for them," especially where marriage and family were concerned.

The vast majority of briefs submitted by youth groups across the country cited the need for more sex information, both at school and at home, for marriage clinics, and for doctors, nurses, and psychologists "trained to instruct and advise about sex problems."[105] It was also agreed that "too many young people... feel that they embark upon marriage quite unprepared." Only 18 per cent of the polled high school students believed that their schools prepared them adequately for family life; within this group, 59 per cent of francophone youth were satisfied with the efforts of their schools, but only a scant 12 per cent of those in English-speaking schools across Canada were. Across the land, the home economics curriculum, exclusively for girls, was seen to make the "most significant contribution" to education for family living. Ontario now included family living and "wholesome relationships between boys and girls" in all its grade 11 physical and health education courses. Other provinces were approaching these all-important areas "in piecemeal fashion."[106] In addition to the Catholic Church's extensive efforts in Quebec, the YM-YWCA was found to be doing the most on behalf of preparation for marriage and family living, including sex education and counselling."[107]

By 1950, the YMCA was sponsoring a Toronto imprint of a popular American manual for teenagers written by psychologist Evelyn Mills Duvall, *Facts of Life and Love for Teen-Agers*. Sales were so swift that the book, an inexpensive paperback, was in its fifth printing by 1953. In a straightforward style, carefully balancing "scientific" detail and mainstream morality, Duvall insisted that parents were the "natural" sources for sex information but that, where this source was somehow lacking—and there was again a tacit understanding that most parents, and, for that matter, most adolescents, were not up to "frank" dialogue about sex—expert advice would fill in the blanks. Adolescents needed such information because "dating, courtship and being in love are not all fun." Echoing Stanley Hall nearly a half-century before, Duvall asserted that "growing up has never been easy," but that it was newly challenging "in the complex world of today." At bottom, the teen years were a "complex of bewilderments" in which the young could "easily get lost" and enter the "confused mental state" that presages a troubled adulthood.[108]

In a chapter specifically addressing "Sex Troubles and Worries," young readers learned that their developing sexuality carried the potential for untold personal difficulties—the premise of all modern adolescent advice literature. Because youth had "far more freedom than in former years," they were now "frequently exposed" to danger. Although Duvall emphasized the consequences of unwed pregnancy for young women, seemingly the only outcome of premarital sexuality, she also contended that boys suffer from "premature" sexual relations because "sowing wild oats so often means the harvest of a crop of thistles." Contraception is mentioned as "a personal, a social and a medical question," but no information is provided apart from a warning that doctors must be consulted. The manual concludes with "Your Sex Life Is Yours to Choose," but the message conveyed is that there is but one choice sanctioned by mutually supportive systems of social convention, middle-class values, traditional gender constructions, and Christian morality. The closing section, "Heading Toward Marriage," reminds young readers that this "tie that binds" is their ultimate goal, ensuring their health and wholeness as well as those of society and nation, and that appropriate attitudes and behaviour in regard to sexuality are basic qualities of citizenship.[109]

Chatelaine's 1948 feature on the subject, written expressly for teenage girls, also made use of an American "marriage and family living" expert to discuss the presumed central issue for that age group: "How good are you at romance?" As the author explained, despite the fact that boys were "still expected to take the lead in courtship," young women could "do a lot to promote and encourage it." The (male) authority surmised, in fact, that "maybe she always has done the priming and we're just beginning to be frank enough to admit it." Thus the "basic elements of a past age" remained: girls all knew that it was hard to meet "eligible boys," to "gain the attention of the one you want," and especially to "create so much interest that a date will follow." His advice on the subject ultimately amounts to a discussion of traditional feminine wiles and their value in attracting and influencing relationships leading to "success" in marriage. Girls are not to initiate conversations with boys because "our customs still dictate that the man should be the pursuer and the girl the pursued, even though she may catch him in the end." The best move for a girl, therefore, is to "subtly arouse a desire in him to take the initiative." The expert's "method" was encapsulated in the acronym AIDA. Originally devised as an advertising formula, the letters stood for "attention, interest, desire and action," meant to outline how to "sell anything—including yourself." Feminine subservience was the key to victory, in that young women were to let men decide where to go on dates, let them do most of the talking, and make them feel popular and successful and manly by telling them that "you adore them...over and over again."[110]

Although it was a women's magazine, *Chatelaine* also gave attention to the boys' perspective, at least in regard to what they thought about the girls they dated—or avoided. In "Ten Strings to Your Beau," regular columnist Lotta Dempsey sought to solve "the mystery of the soundless telephone and the unused porch swing at the house of the attractive girl they date once and then sign off." Dempsey enlisted the assistance of a number of "Tall, Dark and Helpfuls," who produced a handy list of "ten pointers," featuring such advice as "Don't be the lily who thinks money grows in pockets like moth-holes, or the 'my family are droops' type who complains about her family, or the 'yatata-yata-ta—chatterbox.'" The boys also let on that "every boy who takes you out is subconsciously rating you, away in the back of his head, as a possible permanent partner." Consequently, girls were to be "sure of one angle": "He wants to feel that the shine hasn't been rubbed off you in other ways too."[111]

Not surprisingly, young people themselves adopted stances that, for all the alleged frankness and modern outlook of their generation about romance and sex, reflected and reinforced tenacious social constructions of gender and sexuality. Young men continued to be portrayed and to represent themselves as the frequent dupes of manipulative women. Male sexuality—the biological imperative that dominated the adolescent experience for boys and girls alike—rendered boys all too vulnerable to the equally biologically driven snares set out by their female peers. Young men declared themselves "fooled into following and then trapped by the clever methods of the ferocious female," who seemed to be "over-anxious for the kill." Young women plotted, conspired, calculated, and set out to trap young men; thus, the latter were cautioned by their peers that "in the spring a young man's thoughts turn to what the girls have been thinking about all winter.... Watch your step with the opposite sex and don't get caught."[112] The mock trepidation of the "stalked" male was also matched in a certain bitterness and anger associated with the supposed callousness of women. Possibly as a creative exercise in humour but also possibly in reference to personal heartbreak, one young poet expressed himself in distinctly misogynistic rhyme:

> The reddish lustre of your hair ·
> Resembles mouldy must,.I think...
> Your crimson lips do me inspire
> With thoughts of my beloved cow
> ...your teeth remind me of the pearls
> that cost a nickel or a dime
> You super-smoocher of all girls
> Why do I waste my time?

> Some day when I become mature,
> and lessons I learn from past mistakes
> I know that I will be quite sure
> you really haven't what it takes.[113]

Advice columnists were also inclined to support the standard view of the predatory female. "Two Bewildered Lads" of eighteen jointly asked *Toronto Star* adviser George Antheil what to do about their predicament: they were "in love" with the same sixteen-year-old girl. She seemed to enjoy alternating between them, going out with each a few weeks at a time: "She won't choose between us. We decided to get together about this instead of fighting." Antheil was straightforward in his "manly" assessment of the situation, responding that "the little girl is having fun.... She gets double 'allowance entertainment' when she goes out with two guys.... One or the other boy ought to get another girl and break up her game."[114]

By the 1950s, dating and "going steady" were no longer simply modern trends but mainstream adolescent practices. Yet the residual, historical elements of these practices remained influential even among that generation. In suburban anglo-Montreal, teenage courtship was generally conducted under adult supervision and within established middle-class gender conventions. Going steady had become so institutionalized that it had taken on the qualities of practicality in providing the benefits of a reliable partner for teenagers' social events. One sixteen-year-old boy expressed his desire to "play the field" until he neared the end of fourth form and his high school career the subsequent year; at that point, in his view, "it's a good idea to start going steady so you can be sure to go to all the important dances, like the graduation dance." Interestingly, as going steady became another anticipated "normal" adolescent phase, young people became less inclined to think of their "steadies" as potential partners for life. As one young woman explained, "going steady is all right, but it's silly to think of marriage at our age. You just stay clear of the subject.... You know that you have to break up one day but you just hope that day will never come." Parents concurred; one mother discussed her son's "steady" relationship with his girlfriend's mother because she did not "think it was a good idea," a viewpoint shared by the other mother. They did not intervene, but, most fortuitously for all concerned, "all the kids in the group stopped going steady and he stopped too."[115]

What was new about the "new morality" that surfaced in the early post–World War I years and that was met with a near-constant outpouring of adult dread, outrage, admonition, and advice throughout this period? The focus on adolescent sexuality was nothing "modern," seeing as sexual maturation is integral to the life stage. G. Stanley Hall did not invent (though he certainly reinforced) the connections between biological puberty and the many and varied elements of the larger process of growing to adulthood. More important, those connections between the sexuality of youth and an idealized citizenship were new and modern, in that the ideal had traditionally spoken to moral/religious rectitude and social respectability. In a young nation striving to forge a clear and glorious path in a changing world order and in the midst of its own growing pains, the regulation of youth, and especially of youth's troubling sexual proclivities, amounted to a modern problem worth the attention and effort of all reasoning adults who would be modern and Canadian. Yet the residual strains are evident, as modern adolescence and modern citizenship alike were framed within older notions about gender, race, class, and generation as markers of identity and status.

Was there new participation in sexual activity among young Canadians as a result of the new morality? Certainly an effective means of measurement is lacking where actual sex is concerned, though the attention paid to that very notion can be summed up as extensive. Where memory and memoir offer some crucial insights, they suggest that adolescents growing up within this historical context tasted the ambivalence that is associated with the new, the transitional, and the liminal, whether culturally or personally, and probably most often both. Parental involvement in the courtship choices of the young also continued to vary with ethnic and religious background, as might be expected. The adolescent offspring of immigrant families were likely subject to the most social pressure to make their selections within the community and to stay within its strictures concerning sex, as well as experiencing more familial involvement in the actual process, as in French Canadian Catholic families.[116] Interfaith courtship and marriage remained rare, and relationships crossing the rigid boundaries of race rarer still— or just as hidden as those same-sex relationships regarded as "inverse" or "perverse." Dating likely provided more opportunity for physical affection and preliminary sexual experimentation, but it appears likely that, just as familial, religious, and community values reined in the young, so too did the not-unwarranted fear of unwed pregnancy in a time when it spelled ruin for many young women, "illegitimacy" for their children, and a trap for young men pressured into marriage. The first small steps toward sexual revolution were taken, but the persistence of such "traditional" considerations managed to ground enough of the "flaming" youth and the succeeding generations to hold it off until the 1960s. The new morality that slowly took shape during this earlier period was real, but not so much realized, at least not among most adolescents.

4

At School

The Culture of "Modern High"

Your training has given you a strong bias towards what is right.
Faults of the intellect such as prejudice, unfairness and loose
thinking are inexcusable in high school graduates. Moral faults
are unthinkable.

— E.A. Munro, principal, Magee High School, 1944

*T*he central institution of modern adolescence was undoubtedly the high
school. Its primary function was to "sort and develop" those on the verge of
adulthood—"the most valuable raw material of which the country is pos-
sessed"—to ensure that young Canadians would attain their "maximum useful-
ness in building up and enriching our national structure." The high school experience, moreover, would foster community spirit as "could never be [done]
through church, home or press" by also training the young for productive community service.[1] Underlying the favoured rhetoric were widely drawn, related
economic objectives concerning national investment, youth as capital, and productivity as the "ultimate and essential qualification" of a modern citizenship "of
the highest order possible."[2] In the ideal modern high school, those who were
experiencing the "most formative and creative period of their lives" would be led
to "the truest culture" through a citizenship training that prepared them for "a
career of material and social helpfulness."[3]

By World War I, public commitment to progressive schooling as a means to
"uplift" the masses, a number of whom were only recently arrived, had sharpened
the view that schools had to offer more than the customary academic subjects in

order to benefit the largest number of children. Despite the prevailing opinion that the young were "made or marred" before reaching their sixteenth birthdays, as popularized by Stanley Hall and his followers, the high school held much promise as a preventive, or at least remedial, influence that could be brought to bear on the youth problem. This chapter considers how high schools developed as the principal instrument for containing and regulating modern youth and its problems. In gathering together more young people for longer periods than ever before, and by means of a number of curricular and extracurricular modifications that both reflected and expanded upon developing theories about adolescence, the modern high school assisted greatly in the making of distinctively modern generational styles and experiences during the years considered here.

Secondary schooling was a nineteenth-century phenomenon, but the high school's historical moment, manifesting in "the second great transformation" of Canadian education, arrived in the years immediately following the Great War.[4] The 1920s marked the first time that the majority of Canadian adolescents passed through high school doors, to remain there for a longer time than had any previous cohort. Without downplaying the continuing middle-class and Anglo-Celtic predominance of the student body, its class, gender, and ethnic mix was also wider than ever before.[5] By the 1930s, compulsory school attendance laws were in effect in all provinces but New Brunswick and Quebec. In the latter province, attendance was mandated in 1943, and the age of school-leaving was then fixed at fourteen.[6] The statutory school-leaving age varied provincially: thirteen years in Prince Edward Island, fourteen in the rural districts of Nova Scotia and in Manitoba, fifteen in Alberta, British Columbia, and Saskatchewan, and sixteen across Ontario and in Nova Scotia's towns and cities. Even within provinces, it could also vary according to the urban/rural divide: in all provinces but British Columbia, pupils could legitimately absent themselves from school, usually for not more than six weeks of a single term, if their services were deemed necessary for their own maintenance or that of others, usually family members. In Prince Edward Island, attendance was required in rural districts for only 60 per cent of the school term, apart from the larger towns of Charlottetown and Summerside. Except for Prince Edward Island and British Columbia, however, the law prohibited the employment of school-age children during regular school hours unless they were officially exempt from attendance. Those over thirteen in Nova Scotia and over fourteen in Ontario could apply for special employment certificates that freed them from any obligation to attend school.[7]

Despite the various legislative allowances to accommodate for family need that continued to keep a fair proportion of adolescents out of the expanding high schools, the national trend showed that more students were attending high school well into their adolescent years, and for longer periods overall. The near-universal abolition of high school entrance examinations as well as of tuition and matriculation fees made accessibility and affordability lesser concerns than before for many working-class and farm families, both Canadian-born and

immigrant. Structural economic change meant fewer job opportunities for adolescent workers, especially of the entry-level variety that offered some prospects
to the untrained and inexperienced young.[8] Also of growing importance by the
interwar years was what historian Robert Stamp has called "the intangible
desire" on the part of more parents that their children surpass them in educational attainment, and consequently in occupation and social class. This conver-
gence of historical developments permitted the high school's influence to be exercised more widely than formerly.[9]

Not only was the high school integral to the formation of a modern generational culture (entelechy), it was also important to the postwar nation-building
project that was premised on Anglo-conformity, traditional middle-class values
and the efficiency and productivity that were modern industry's catchwords.
The 1931 Dominion census showed that some 50,000 young people left school
before age thirteen—28,000 of these in Quebec alone—but the larger number
now entered the labour market between the ages of fifteen and eighteen, usually after some attendance at high school or technical or business school. About
half of all young Canadians were at school at the age of sixteen; after the seventeenth birthday, however, only a small proportion were engaged in any form of
schooling.[10] There were now slightly more girls between the ages of fifteen and
seventeen than boys of that age group at school, reflecting their slightly larger
number within that age category in the wider population. Men continued to far
outnumber women in postsecondary programs. By the 1920s, high school was no
longer the privileged enclave of the academically oriented middle class, and by
the start of World War II, some measure of high school attendance had become
the common experience of Canadian youth, even while the majority still entered
the working world before the age of eighteen.[11]

Ontario, the most populous and industrialized province, took the lead in
this postwar pattern of educational growth. In 1919, the Conservative government of Howard Ferguson passed the Adolescent School Attendance Act, which
was implemented in January 1921. Serving as a model for other provincial governments, the Act raised the age of school-leaving to sixteen. Its intentions were
explicit: the high school would upgrade the academic training of the young, but
it would also supervise, direct, and police their activities. Those who had spent
their childhood and early youth in "unnecessary employments" or in "actual
idleness" would henceforth be subjected to the school's "systematic training and
discipline."[12] The population of Ontario's high schools quadrupled during the
1920s and grew at an overall rate of 325 per cent between 1918 and 1938.[13] Every
annual report of the provincial education department noted this rising crest,
which characterized the rural areas serviced only by so-called continuation
schools as well as the towns and cities. The cornerstone for the new Jarvis Street
Collegiate Institute, which had grown out of the Toronto High School (1871),
was laid in 1922.[14] Meanwhile, the city's Riverdale Collegiate Institute saw its
numbers more than double between 1918 (448 students) and 1923 (962), reaching a pre–World War II high of 1,194 in 1933.[15]

Nor was this pattern of growth limited to Ontario, as a massive construction boom took place across the nation to house the new high school contingent. At Canada's oldest anglophone secondary school, New Brunswick's Fredericton High School, a new building accommodating 425 students was opened in 1925; by 1931, unrelenting enrolment pressures had necessitated the construction of an annex consisting of five classrooms and a garage.[16]

While the expansion affected each province, the pattern of schooling that developed was by no means uniform. By 1950, Ontario had set up a network of technical, commercial, and vocational schools alongside the more traditional high schools and collegiates. Quebec had maintained its system of classical colleges, with little provision made for vocational and technical education. In British Columbia, junior high schools had been established for grades 7 to 9, after which students would proceed to a vocational or academic high school according to their perceived needs, abilities, and ambitions. The matriculation course—generally five years of study—was a necessary prerequisite for both university education and entry into such business professions as banking and accountancy.[17]

Although class patterns in attendance persisted well past World War II, secondary schooling was becoming a viable option for more of the young members of working-class families during these years. The modern high school was idealized as "the school of the common people," where "the rich and the poor, the high and the low, the Protestant and the Roman Catholic, mingle together and work together in the spirit of amity and equality, regardless of distinctions of class or creed." In the northern Ontario mining town of Timmins, the high school that opened in September 1923 was already filled to capacity a year later; plans were being made for more incoming students, "many of them with foreign names but with loyal Canadian hearts."[18] In the industrial city of Hamilton, Ontario, despite the strain on working-class family budgets caused by the forfeited wages of teenage children, the high school population from this sector doubled in the collegiates and exploded in the new technical schools, from 206 in 1921 to over 1,400 in 1930. A similar process was at work in London's secondary schools.[19] The extension of secondary schooling brought immigrant and working-class youth somewhat closer to an adolescence of the kind that traditionally belonged to their native-born and more affluent peers. For the generations coming of age between the Great War and mid-century, adolescence would be characterized by schooling and its related social and cultural activities. The development of the modern high school signified a historic modification of the very structures and meanings of adolescence.[20]

Historian Paula Fass has noted that the expansion of immigrant communities in American cities, especially as the first generations of the American-born reached adolescence, contributed in no small way to public valuation of the high school, leading eventually to a new common school era. In the process, the high school's socialization functions also acquired new scope and importance.[21] Certainly this was the express objective of schooling for the offspring of the "new Canadians." As one educator argued, "there is an important duty to perform in seeing that the children of these newcomers are given every opportunity to receive proper training for intelligent citizenship." The first Canadian-born generations, as well as those who arrived while still young, had to be acknowledged as "the material upon which Canadians as nation-builders must work."[22] Reform leader J.S. Woodsworth contended that school would help to bridge "the widening gap between the parent and child." It was also expected to be a salutary means of resolving the matter of a supposed "social disorganisation of the younger generation" in immigrant communities. The alleged "deficiency in moral responsibility" of Ukrainian Canadian youth, sociologist Charles Young believed, could best be corrected in the high school.[23]

As in the United States, Canadian surveys suggested that the children of immigrants were slowly beginning to attend high school in growing numbers by the 1930s. Although, in Young's view, the Ukrainians in prewar prairie settlements had initially "refused to cooperate," resulting in a high rate of illiteracy in the first Canadian-born generation, he did observe signs of improvement. Manitoba's Department of Education was commenting on increased attendance by Ukrainian Canadians as early as 1920, while still concluding that "even yet the number is few comparatively." The high school in Vita, Manitoba, had only one Ukrainian Canadian student in 1924, but twenty-two by 1927. Due to the size of families and their usual financial limitations, parents often worked toward giving one member the opportunity, "with the usual hope of making a lawyer or teacher of that one."[24] In western Mennonite communities, more rural elementary schools were providing grade 8 by the mid-1920s, thereby enabling more pupils—about two hundred in Manitoba's West Reserve, most of them located in or near the towns—to continue into high school.[25] That the schooling of at least one adolescent child in a family was an important collective goal is witnessed in recorded instances of "whole families" in Manitoba earning extra money by digging seneca root in order "to keep one of the boys or girls, usually the former, in high school." In Alberta, approximately 15 per cent of immigrant or first-generation youth attended high school.[26] Young himself interviewed a farmer who had six sons, two of whom had graduated from the University of Alberta, two of whom were "well on" in their courses at that university, and the remaining two of whom were about to enter, "and the farm had been mortgaged to send them there!"[27] But it was not necessarily the case that sons were favoured over daughters in immigrant families. The 1936 census of the Prairie provinces showed that young working women had attained a much higher level of schooling than their male counterparts, with over 60 per cent of the Manitoba sample having some form of education or training beyond the elementary level. Across ethnic categories, young women predominated among the "educational crop of the improved schooling of recent years."[28]

Immigrant children in cities tended to fare better educationally than their rural cousins, just as urban youth of any background were better situated to take advantage of the new high schools. A survey of the immigrant working-class community in Winnipeg's North End found that "a good proportion" of its young residents reached high school, some continuing on to university. The same was found to characterize the experience of immigrant youth in other Canadian cities.[29] In 1922, Sadhu Singh Dhami, "a turbaned teenager" newly arrived in Vancouver from the Punjab, was one of only sixteen East Indian students at any level of the British Columbia school system. He remembered his high school experiences in a very positive light, despite the prejudices that his community encountered regularly: "My most meaningful introduction to the new world began in the John Oliver High School, South Vancouver. The first Sikh boy with long hair and turban to be seen in the area, I was received with a warmth of feeling which masked curiosity. If the teachers' encouragement made learning easier, the gay, youthful atmosphere made life most enjoyable; only the inordinate attention of the girls embarrassed me."[30] Others had the "benefit" of being Canadian-born but were still unable to fit in with their schoolmates because of the race and poverty that marked them out. One woman, born in Venlaw, Manitoba, to recent Ukrainian immigrants, recalled her own disheartening experience during the 1920s thus: "I had three years of high school...then it got to where I just couldn't continue because my father couldn't provide. My mother used to do day work and she used to get discarded clothing from people. Sometimes she'd remake it for us and sometimes not. Sometimes just as it was, we'd put it on. And then there was another thing that was bad! They'd recognize this clothing that belonged to other people and they'd call out, 'You've got Mrs. Leper's dress on! You've got Mrs. Morrison's coat on!'...When you got to be sixteen, seventeen, you begin to notice that. And I left school and I went to work in a hotel."[31]

By the 1940s, the offspring of first-generation Canadians were increasingly continuing on to some secondary-school training. At Toronto's Jarvis Collegiate, as remembered by a Toronto-born woman who attended at the time, "Many of the students, although they came from inner city homes, were the children of first generation immigrants, a large number of them Chinese, who were determined that their children should succeed in the new world, and education was the obvious route."[32]

Aboriginal adolescents felt the special challenges that had so long worked against their schooling at any but the most truly elementary level. When the residential school in Spanish, Ontario, was expanded to inaugurate a high school for boys in 1946, there was some skepticism on the reserves: "Some elders found the idea that sixteen- to twenty-year-old men were still attending school somewhat hard to believe and accept....Not a few had some doubts as to the motives inspiring youth to remain in school. Still others doubted the intelligence of the students. They could not understand why a boy or girl needed four or five extra years to learn to read, write and count."[33] Most of the prejudice, however, came from the community outside. As a young girl, Isabelle Knockwood was "rewarded" for good behaviour at the Shubenacadie Residential School in Nova Scotia by being chosen, along with a male student, to attend a public high school: "We walked to and from Shubie village on opposite sides of the road, afraid to speak or even to look at each other. For two long lonely years I walked with my head down from the 'Resi' to the high school in Shubie.... I had the feeling that eyes were always watching from the windows of the school to make sure I did not talk to any of the villagers or go into any of their homes or stores." Despite the fact that she passed her years there "in complete social isolation as the only Mi'kmaw girl in the school," considered herself academically "far behind the other students," and continued to be subjected to humiliation and even physical abuse at the hands of the teachers, Knockwood persisted. For her, the public high school represented "a door ajar": "I began to be excited for the first time at the whole idea of learning things."[34]

Most immigrants to the Sangudo area of Alberta were of British and American origins, but within a radius of twenty-five kilometres could be found "truly a melting pot of nationalities," including families of Ukrainian, Greek, Scandinavian, Polish, German, and Hungarian backgrounds. Commenting on the multi-ethnic composition of the Sangudo High School, the yearbook editor remarked that "the spirit of cooperation and friendship is excellent. We do not think of ourselves as people of various nationalities but as Canadians."[35] During World War II, another student contended that, although it was "only natural" that the recently arrived "still love the land of their birth," the enlistment of their sons, many of them from the high school or recent graduates, showed "an unflinching loyalty to Canada."[36] But the situation was far from ideal for such minority-group students. A delegate from "one of Toronto's largest high schools," to the 1941 United Church regional youth conference reported that there were many cases of anti-Semitism at his school. One student was actually barred from a position on the playground staff for racial reasons. Some were advised to change their names in order to pass examinations. There was evidently a case of a Jewish girl who had received First Class Honours all year "being failed by five marks in one subject and thus not graduating." As many as 90 per cent of young people from "coloured" families did not complete elementary school, and the numbers finishing high school were "so small that we may consider that number a non-entity."[37] After two hundred years of settlement in Nova Scotia, by 1949 only three Canadian-born blacks had graduated from postsecondary institutions.[38]

All too often, even those young people from minority groups who successfully finished high school found their ambitions thwarted. One young black man recalled being told by the principal of his school that there was no chance of his getting a job in business because of his race.[39] In 1940, a Japanese Canadian high school student observed that, "despite the fact that we have been born and educated in Canada, we are aliens in the land of our birth.... We have been trained to become Canadian citizens and yet citizenship is refused to us." She felt strongly that it was the duty of the second generation to become educated but conceded that "in the business world our hopes and ambitions are cruelly shattered by Canada's refusal to accept us."[40] Similarly, a Chinese Canadian student contended that, among his group, "there is little desire in many cases to study hard, because if a person intends to stay in ths country, the amount of education received will not decide the type of work one will get." He characterized their situation as "a state of shattered hopes and ambitions" that resulted in "a submissive fatalistic group of young people."[41]

Even as the 1930s closed, and despite the clear inroads made, many working-class families still could not afford much in the way of secondary schooling for adolescent offspring whose wages were needed at home. A national sample taken in 1936 indicated that only 27.2 per cent of children fifteen years and older were in school. The class basis of that school population is evident: nearly 50 per cent of the children of the managerial class were in school, while fewer than 20 per cent of those of unskilled workers attended.[42] Inadequate family income was the "dominating influence" in determining the age of school-leaving throughout this entire period. Because the average cost of four years of high school was an estimated $550 (1929–39), a high school education was assuredly "hard to fit" into a family budget of less than $1,500 that had to meet the needs of several children.[43] Nonetheless, both adults and adolescents surveyed thought that "to get a better job" was the most important reason to attend high school.[44] The type of schooling available took "little cognizance of the aims and ambitions of the poor man's child who would become a carpenter, mechanic or clerk," thereby favouring the traditional high school contingent: the offspring of reasonably affluent families who were intended for postsecondary education or for administrative and professional employment.[45]

Extension of formal schooling was consequently seen as only a partial solution to the youth problem. It was effective mainly in holding the very youth who would likely have attended even in the absence of legislative compulsion—those thought to pose little in the way of a social menace in the first place. For the presumedly more problematic adolescents from working-class and immigrant homes, the law provided ways to evade or circumvent compulsory schooling. Recognizing both the primacy of parental authority and the continued need for supplementary wages in many families, "home permits" that sanctioned release from school for the purposes of household, farm, or paid labour were "freely granted" to fourteen and fifteen year olds. There were cases, especially in the nation's farming and fishing districts, in which familial reliance on the labour of even the youngest members persisted, and where, consequently, even those under fourteen could receive permits.[46] In Montreal, the provincial labour department insisted that all boys and girls under sixteen show a certificate of education in order to earn reprieve and as evidence of their ability to read and write.[47] The labour department's new office was "swamped by a crowd of several hundred" boys and girls on its first morning offering this option, "all eager to get the educational certificates which will entitle them to work although under the age of 16."[48] New Brunswick had the highest rate of illiteracy in all Canada according to the 1931 census, a large number of boys and girls having left school by the age of twelve years "with so little advancement that they soon come to the point of classifying themselves as not able to read and write." Ten years later, the loss of students between first grade and the fourth year of high school was close to 82 per cent.[49]

It was also reasoned that a large proportion of the estimated 70 to 90 per cent leaving school at fifteen did not do so because of economic pressure: not being academically inclined, they succumbed to the "innate restlessness" of adolescence.[50] In Nova Scotia, school board reports of the time resound with truancy cases. One sixteen-year-old boy skipped nearly two weeks over the course of the academic year, was tardy "at least once a day," was caught smoking on school grounds, and was "generally indolent in his work" and "most annoying during school hours, doing smart stunts to make the others laugh" behind the teacher's back. A fourteen-year-old boy had a "most exasperating" manner, as his teacher complained: "When I tell him to go to work he just sits and grins at me." Another fourteen-year-old boy went "absent without leave" for eight days; having stayed out after recess to smoke on school grounds, he fled home "in preference to taking a strapping" as his just reward.[51] Girls also took their turn. Near the end of fifth form at Jarvis Collegiate in Toronto, Mildred Young "had a lovely time wandering through the Don Valley" with two other girls on a bright spring morning, rather than going on to school. Although they arrived at noon "quite content with the indolent morning," there had been "great consternation" at their apparent disappearance, and "everyone was furious."[52] Truancy and running away were regular occurrences at the Shubenacadie residential school, also in Nova Scotia, despite the harsh punishment they entailed. At the age of fifteen, Isabelle Knockwood and an older girl snuck out a bathroom window to attend a Tarzan movie; Knockwood was terrified of being caught or reported on, since the townspeople knew that the girls were not permitted to leave the school after dark.[53] Young people found ways to resist, whether through "smart stunts" or simple non-participation. Despite the strict behavioural regulations, the vigilance of faculty, and the persistence of corporal punishment, there are memories of "lively pranks" that took place on "the sacred precincts" of high schools, some of which "passed into the category of myth and legend" as part of school lore.[54]

Concerns about the continued high dropout rate, truancy, and the general unruliness of the adolescent student body, as well as about the irrelevance of a classical academic curriculum for many of the new students at its desks, led to concerted attempts to offer other streams—technical, commercial, and otherwise vocational. These employment-focused courses, it was argued, would capture the interest and ensure the practical training of young men and women heading for the workforce as soon as possible after the age of school-leaving. The decline in formal apprenticeship since the nineteenth century, much lamented by social observers and much studied by governments, was a loss that could be remedied through the improved and expanded vocational training that increasingly began to be offered in high schools during the interwar years.[55] These courses, primarily aimed at boys, were matched by parallel streams of "business" or "commercial" training, mostly to prepare young women for new opportunities in office and retail work. In 1930, Ontario's six commercial high schools were all predominantly female in enrolment, with young women making up over three-quarters of their 6,721 students: at Toronto's High School of Commerce, young women outnumbered men by a ratio of three to one. Commercial training was now preferred over the domestic science or "practical arts" training that had come into vogue for future wives and mothers just before the Great War.[56] Like most others, St. John Vocational High School in New Brunswick developed a separate Department of Practical Arts for its girls, in the interests of meeting "one of the arresting challenges to society to properly educate the girls." As "practical workers, homemakers and voters," this and succeeding generations of young women would have "a determining influence upon our future."[57]

The new vocational or practical programs were inspired by the recommendations of the 1908 Royal Commission on Industrial Training and Technical Education (the Macdonald-Robertson Commission). Pre-empted by war, these recommendations were finally addressed in the 1919 Act for the Promotion of Technical Education in Canada. At the provincial level, the groundwork was laid in Ontario's Industrial Education Act of 1911, which provided provincial funding for technical education for adolescents beyond the school-leaving age of fourteen.[58] By 1920, general industrial schools had been established in Brantford, Hamilton, London, and Toronto, along with a variety of specialized trade schools, technical high schools, and new technical departments within existing schools across the province. This trend was captured in the addition of "Vocational Institute" to the traditional "Collegiate" name at this time, more accurately reflecting the high schools' curricular as well as physical expansion. More than one-quarter of all Ontario high school students were studying in the vocational programs offered by forty-two high schools on the eve of the Depression.[59]

Also established at this time were co-operative industrial training courses for apprentices and for those in day schools needing practical instruction, as well as evening classes in industrial, technical, and art schools for students who worked during the day. Most of the provincial department's efforts were directed at these evening classes. Despite the intention to serve adolescents, these classes were largely filled by mature men and women, perhaps because parents, as it was argued, were "indifferent or antipathetic to instruction calculated to fit directly for work in the shop or at the bench."[60] Certainly organized labour objected to this type of education, seeing it as a thinly veiled form of class discrimination. The access to schooling that working-class parents wanted for their children did not necessarily amount to supporting "streaming" into the kind of wage labour that characterized their own lives. For working-class girls, a few years of commercial courses could lead to office work, and thereby to upward mobility; rarely did it lead beyond high school matriculation. For boys, the leap out of the working class was even less likely to occur as a result of time spent in high school, given the specialized vocational orientation of their schooling. What is important about the vocational-education movement is that it aimed to impart marketable skills at no expense to employers. It also trained young people in the attitudes appropriate to modern industry, its production still ordered along the lines of class, race, gender, and age, but now also according to scientific-management concepts that emphasized stop-watch efficiency. And the efficient modern worker was also the efficient modern citizen.

Vocational training did not equalize opportunity so much as it relocated job training from the factory or shop to the school.[61] Advocates of the approach argued that social peace and integration would be served through achievement of "a common social purpose" by having all kinds of students mix in the same building, thus permitting the high school to "infuse a common cultural background" and "a common social tradition for all."[62] But despite such hopes, distinctions in status and cultural capital would be maintained through largely exclusive curricular streams. The outcome was not merely more relevant education or more practical education, but the widespread adoption of a separate and specialized curriculum for some students, one that ostensibly respected the democratic principle of public schooling while maintaining gender, race, and class inequalities.[63] For example, the London Technical School, which opened in 1912 as the London Industrial School, could not overcome its public image as "an institution for less desirable students." Even teachers at the school remembered a "general feeling... that you were rather an inferior type" for attending the school, that it was intended "for the people who just didn't have the ability or didn't belong to the right class of people [or] if your family was poor."[64]

By 1931, the St. John Vocational School in New Brunswick boasted its highest enrolment ever, with seven hundred students, a measure of the success of the new educational approach. That same year, however, would see its provincial funding slashed in half due to Depression exigencies. This fate befell vocational programs and schools across the nation as the foundational federal Act for the Promotion of Technical Education was suspended indefinitely.[65] Despite the financial setbacks, the socio-economic dislocations of that decade reinforced the perceived need for vocational training while also supporting certain national goals through both the curriculum and the developing extracurriculum. As high school attendance continued to rise through the 1930s, in part because employment avenues were closed to many young workers, the emphasis on citizenship training that had imbued educational rhetoric during the expansionist 1920s gained new life despite—or because of—the straitened circumstances of the time.[66]

Notwithstanding the vocational education campaign, the continuing lack of articulation between modern schooling and the modern labour market remained an issue for educators, employers, and youth-watchers in general. The curricular transformations of the 1920s still saw regular high school offerings heavily weighted toward the tiny minority who would go on to university. Meanwhile, the number of students who dropped out at the earliest opportunity, with only one or two years of secondary education behind them, remained "far too high."[67] A study of Montreal high schools carried out at different points during the 1930s showed that only one in ten high school entrants actually graduated. The Depression's length and severity demonstrated beyond doubt how the "deficiencies" in education and vocational planning negatively affected an estimated two-thirds of the annual group of school- leavers. The effects of this youthful misdirection were seen to be cumulative and far-reaching, and "the sorry harvest of impaired faculties and initiative which has been laid up for the future [was] not measured solely by the relief rolls."[68]

With the coming of World War II, the diversion of funds and government energies to the war effort after many years of Depression-induced cost-cutting would make their impact felt on the nation's high schools. As teachers enlisted, courses were cut, facilities became crowded, and classes grew bigger. By 1941, the Ontario government had implemented the Easter Scheme, which granted students their full year's credit if they left school in the spring to assist farmers; at least six thousand students took up the offer that year.[69] War entered the classroom, as technical courses were frequently "slanted . . . to the grim necessities of today," with lessons based on war production needs. At the Ford of Canada Trade School in Windsor, Ontario, high school–age male apprentices, the "craftsmen of tomorrow," acquired skills seen as essential to the "growing strength" of Canada and the empire.[70] At Toronto's Central Tech, seven hundred students were being trained for war industry in special evening and night shifts.[71] Forty thousand boys in high schools across Canada worked on the production of scale models of ninety different fighting aircraft, both of the Allied nations and of the Axis; fifty thousand of these models were urgently needed for training pilots, observers, and gunners in the British Commonwealth Air Training Plan to identify planes instantly from any angle. Meanwhile, among high school girls, "knitting was once supposed to be the chief wartime occupation," but that was before the "all-out slacks and bandannas of this war." In some schools, girls had "ganged up" and insisted that they too be admitted into the Commonwealth model airplane plan: "In these cases the knitting needles are idle while the young ladies cut patterns and paint up the finished models," their participation staying within the domain of traditional feminine skills. Every boy who completed an acceptable model as part of his war effort earned an official certificate from the RCAF; no mention is made of recognition for the girls' efforts.[72]

The socio-economic differences between urban and rural communities figured significantly in high school attendance. In 1921, rural youth between the ages of fifteen and nineteen accounted for 30.3 per cent of school attendants, urban youth for 41.2 per cent; a decade later, 19.8 per cent and 25.4 per cent of rural and urban youth respectively were in high school. The farm family budget, the need for the labour of children on the farm, and problems of geographic distance help to explain the differentials. High school attendance often involved considerable expense for the many rural youth who had to board in towns and cities in order to have access to education beyond the primary level.[73] Growing up in the small rural town of Jolicure, New Brunswick, during the 1920s, where the local school had one room and nine grades, required of one young man that he board with a farm family in Sackville in order to attend high school; he found it "harder" living away from home—"far different"—and he had to do such "odd jobs" as delivering milk to help cover his board.[74] Sisters Lorna and Frances Hood, from Magaguadavic, New Brunswick, stayed together at Mrs. Green's boarding house across the street from Fredericton High School until matriculation.[75] On the other coast, in Prince George, British Columbia, Hazel Huckvale started high school in 1925, "and, sad to say, we had to go ten miles to high school, which in those days, meant we had to stay away from Monday to Friday. It was quite a lonely time for me. I don't look back on my high school days as great years of jolly living. It was quite a lonely time to go away from home every Monday and back on Friday. Those two days of the weekend were very special."[76]

Not only was the expense an obstacle to many parents, the idea of sending off their adolescent children to live away from home caused much anxiety. As one mother contended, "this is often a disastrous procedure so far as their progress and training are concerned. The lack of parental supervision and discipline, and atmosphere of home and the lure of town life with its facilities for amusements, often proves too much for a young girl or lad and they end up unsuccessful."[77]

Rural parents complained about the hardships endured by high school students who attempted to commute to distant schools. One father from Loggieville, New Brunswick, described how his son and other local youth, attending the Chatham high school because the local school went only to tenth grade, were obliged to do a daily four-hour return trip. His son barely had time to eat dinner, study, and fall into bed exhausted before starting the process again at six in the morning. The young man and his friends persisted, because, as his father explained, "this has been going on for years but there never was so many attending the Chatham schools from here before, I think the reason can be accounted for because of present conditions here, there is absolutely no work for young people here and there [sic] mind are turned to a better education, to make them better fitted for the battle of living."[78] By the end of the 1930s, New Brunswick had opened its first rural high school, in Northumberland County, and was hoping to establish "modern composite high schools" with both academic and vocational streams, intended to be "within reach of all" by bus or dormitory residence. A correspondence division was also set up to "bring high school advantages by mail" to those living in remote parts of the province.[79] Correspondence increasingly became the solution to both financial and geographic complications: during the Depression, Irene Rigler's family, in Sylvan Glade, British Columbia, could not afford to let her board to attend Baron Byng High School in Prince George, so she and several friends tackled high school by correspondence.[80]

Secondary school education was increasingly important to rural families for its own sake, but the rural high school was also believed to be an effective means of "upgrading" the quality of life in rural communities and keeping the young from joining the ongoing exodus to the city. Dalhousie University education professor Alexander Mowat wrote frequently on these matters during the 1940s. Mowat argued that young people raised in the country enjoyed certain natural "advantages" over their city cousins. They understood "the meaning of hard work" and, lacking the "distracting" urban influences, were able to "develop a more stable and well balanced personality" as a result. The rural high school would go far to ensure that the young would stay and "raise the whole tenor of rural or coastal life." Yet even Mowat acknowledged the paradox: by providing a glimpse of other possibilities, rural high schools might defeat their own purpose and encourage the young to seek their fortunes elsewhere.[81] Instead of "adjusting them to their environment," the high schools often reinforced the message that the rural environment was not "a congenial one," and frequently functioned "only as a means of escape from the farm."[82] To offset this "urbanizing" influence, agriculture and home economics courses were designed to promote "a truly rural philosophy" through the curriculum, one that would enable rural high school students to understand the advantages of remaining in the community.[83]

The modern high school also provided a newly structured and increasingly important extracurriculum. This "school outside of school hours" was designed with a specific citizen-making objective: to provide safe, adult-approved, and supervised alternatives to the commercial, unsupervised, and unregulated leisure activities that were luring both city and country youth into danger. The extracurriculum delivered essential lessons about values and behaviour that equated loyalty to the school with national duty and patriotism. As much as did specific civics lessons taught in the classroom, these helped to preserve and reproduce the values of a "Canadian" middle class intent on stabilizing itself amidst jarring socio-cultural change, including generational insubordination. In his annual report of 1920, an Ontario high school inspector reported a "pretty general complaint among teachers" about how, since the war's end, their students were "unsettled by the general spirit of unrest that is prevalent throughout the province." It was agreed that "the allurements of the automobile and the movies and the craze for dancing" were "seriously interfering" with their attention to their studies. The situation in some high schools had evidently deteriorated to the point that several principals had "protested publicly," feeling compelled to warn parents that "the moral fibre of the young is being weakened and their success in life endangered by their pursuit of pleasure."[84] A balanced and ordered regimen of school, work, and play was the only effective approach. As Stanley Hall himself remonstrated, "we are progressively forgetting that for the complete apprenticeship to life, youth needs repose, leisure, art, legends, romance, idealization, and in a word, humanism, if it is to enter the kingdom of man well-equipped for man's highest work in the world."[85]

By the 1920s, unprecedented high school enrolments, increasingly regular attendance, and rising graduation rates allowed a significant age cohort to make its way collectively through high school. This demographic watershed provided the basis for an institutionalized, teacher-supervised peer-group culture, which largely replaced the less formal traditional framework of student clubs and teams. With sufficient numbers to support a network of peer societies, the cultural system of the modern high school took more definite form in such mixed-sex activities as student government, clubs, journalism, and the newly important (though certainly not new) expressions of identity signified by traditional school colours, school songs and cheers, and gender-segregated athletic teams.[86] A sampling of

high school yearbooks suggests the degree to which the extracurriculum imparted convention and conformity. However much—or little—they reflect majority
experience, these publications self-consciously promoted ideas and behaviour representing the official institutional culture—as they could not help but do, seeing
as they were hardly unmediated expressions of adolescent views. Despite their
obvious limitations in disclosing the voices of youth, these student-generated
sources uncover the normative culture, and thus the measures that the young
were taught to motivate themselves and to assess their own "progress" against
certain benchmarks as they matured.

Extracurricular activities for boys were designed to reinforce contemporary
ideals of manliness, guiding them toward becoming all-round productive men in
both work and play.[87] It was especially important that planned activities be
directed to that end in the modern high school, where "a noticeable feature" of
the student body was that girls generally outnumbered boys. It was surmised
that "through personal desire or for family reasons," boys were impatient to be
free of school and out earning their own living. The new attendance legislation
and the revised curriculum were important approaches to the problem of keeping boys in school, but a strong case was also made in favour of larger playgrounds and "a more general encouragement" of games, sports, and other school-
related but non-academic pastimes. "All work and no play" would never appeal
to "the average boy," but "the chance of getting a place on the school's baseball,
hockey or basketball team, or taking part in the school's literary society, dramatic or debating club," educators contended, would give him "an entirely different
view of the high school."[88]

The persistent controversy over cadet training for high school boys during
the interwar years also underlines prevailing ideas about how best to prepare
boys for their future roles as providers, protectors, defenders, and leaders. The
cadet movement originated with the late-nineteenth-century English Canadian
brand of imperialist nationalism that promoted militarism as vital to membership in nation and empire, as well as to a superior type of manliness. In 1896,
Ontario legislation permitted any high school board to instigate military instruction for boys and provided a fifty-dollar annual grant to that purpose. By 1900,
cadet training was taking place in thirty-three Ontario high schools. The movement really took off after 1909, however, when the British high commissioner to
Canada, Sir Donald Gordon Smith, Lord Strathcona, set up a half-million-dollar
trust fund to promote it. Under the auspices of the federal militia, funds were
distributed to any high school that could bring together at least twenty boys to
perform military exercises. The Strathcona Fund's objective was "to improve the
physical and intellectual capabilities of children, by inculcating habits of alert-
ness, orderliness and prompt obedience," but equally "to bring up the boys to
patriotism and to a realisation that the first duty of a free citizen is to be prepared to defend his country." While the founder intended that physical training
and elementary drill be encouraged for boys and girls alike, "especial importance"
was given to the teaching of military drill to all high school boys.[89] The 1911

appointment of Sam Hughes, an avid supporter of cadet training, as minister of the militia, along with Canadian participation in the Great War, greatly strengthened public support for this program.[90] The 1915 annual report of the Ontario education department remarked that "it is manifest everywhere that the boys for the first time feel that military drill is worthwhile, and that it may have for them and their country a momentous value."[91] Even as the war ended, the number of cadet corps in the province continued to grow, from 168 in 1918 to 248 in 1919.[92]

Interest in cadet training in high schools across the nation continued through most of the 1920s. As the war's enormous toll sank in, however, agitation arose against what a substantial number of Canadians now saw as an inappropriate use of school time and facilities to promote the kind of militarism that had led to the catastrophic "war to end wars."[93] The Edmonton, Alberta, public school board decided in 1927 to continue cadet training only with parental approval for each participant and with the provision of alternative physical instruction for the sons of parents who objected, as an increasing number were doing.[94] Many school boards in Ontario, including the largest, Toronto, had suspended cadet training by the early 1930s; others, such as Barrie, Ontario, saw their high school cadet corps thrive during the Depression.[95] By the time war once again appeared imminent, many boards across Canada were in the process of reviving cadet training. Those who supported its reinstitution argued that "the state owes to each boy that he be instructed mentally, morally and physically, that he may be fitted to compete in the business world for a livelihood and bear his share of the burdens of the state." Thus, military drill was important not only for reasons of national defence, but also because it protected boys against effeminacy: "Without drill or [physical] culture, the first thing that we will be seeing in Canada will be afternoon classes for boys in crochet work and knitting."[96] As might be expected, World War II finished the debate. The Royal Canadian Navy sponsored Sea Cadets, and the Air Cadet League of Canada, formed in 1940, raised its first squadrons in 1941. An estimated 230,000 former sea, army, and air cadets served during World War II.[97]

Girls also participated actively in many extracurricular activities, new and traditional, but the leadership positions usually went to boys, especially in student government and school publications. When girls aspired to leadership roles, their ambitions were considered by their peers to be so unusual as to call for justification. At southwestern Ontario's Kitchener Collegiate Institute, the first-ever female student council president was elected in 1931; the student newspaper editorialized that "undoubtedly a girl would have emerged victorious earlier had she succeeded in securing the votes of her own sex," among whom, in the view of this male commentator, "competition seems to be more vital.... Evidently they hesitate to concede victory to their own sex."[98] Thus, her triumph was explained as a deviation from the usual scheme of things, in which "typical" feminine jealousy and rivalry kept young women from such "male" achievements. In a remarkably similar tone, the failure of the lone female candidate to win the presidency in the 1930 school council election at Fort William Collegiate and Technical Institute in Ontario was explained by the male victor as a matter of "the fickleness of the gentler sex." Having backed her at first, the female students unexpectedly "turned" the ballot toward him, thus preventing her from becoming "the first girl to handle the business of this school."[99]

The expanding roster of organized activities that made up the new extracurriculum served to legitimize the peer group as a socializing agency, giving it an acknowledged role in the process of cultural transmission. It was "in common activity with his compeers" that the adolescent learned "the responsibilities of social living which no adult can teach him."[100] This focus on peer-based learning within the setting of school-based socializing obscured the fact that much of what was imparted came from the teachers who organized and supervised the activities. The lessons had to do with progressive middle-class goals that supported both competition and teamwork, both commitment to the community and individual initiative, as well as the personal success denoted as "popularity." Young Canadians were introduced to select ideals of adult behaviour that would help them define a self-identity within certain acceptable parameters, while they were also getting some of the requisite training for adulthood.[101] Faculty were quick to correlate successful extracurricular programs with "exceptional capacity in achievement" and, significantly, with "the charm manifested in the personalities of the leaders," a feature of high school culture thought to be "quite striking."[102]

Social and citizenship skills were encapsulated in the concept of "school spirit," the very premise of the extracurriculum. During the 1920s, "school spirit" became the rallying call and emblematic expression of modern high school culture. Although representing "the fun and comradeship of school-days," the larger purpose of school spirit, as noted by students themselves, was the teaching of loyalty, co-operation, and fairness. During a time when theories about adolescent angst held sway, school spirit was believed to "invariably cheer those pupils who are prone to pitch their tents on the north side of life"; their "morbid outlook" would be conquered by "enthusiasm, loyalty and friendliness." Special exercises were undertaken during regular school hours to foster this spirit, which was also promoted in student publications, student government, clubs, and teams. At Ottawa Collegiate, as in many other high schools, an assembly was held each morning in the auditorium to ensure "a happy ushering in of the school day" through a sing-a-long accompanied by the school orchestra, an opening prayer, the national anthem, and announcements.[103] Alexandra High School in Medicine Hat, Alberta, held regular assemblies and pep rallies that featured the collective performance of such popular inspirational songs as "You Gotta Accentuate the Positive," followed by pep talks from the principal and vice-principal about the importance of attendance at school sports events.[104] The auditorium was thought to be the "central feature" of the modern high school, home to these daily assemblies that did so much to nurture a healthy school spirit and "to train the pupils in public speaking, in self control, in orderly habits, in consideration for others and in respect for authority."[105] Most important, school spirit could not be confined within school walls. One young yearbook editor proclaimed that it lent a tone of "vivacity" to the entire community while preparing students "for the greater field of activity than our school environment, the field where mistakes are not so kindly overlooked—life."[106]

As high schools made gyms and assembly halls integral parts of their functioning physical space and strove to provide organized recreational programs under trained leadership, the trend was lauded as one of the "more progressive signs in modern education." A new understanding of high school as preparation for a healthy, wholesome, well-rounded adulthood brought about an emphasis on the balancing of intellectual achievement with the development of social and citizenship skills. High school was to be valued as much for the cultural education that it provided through peer-group activity as for its more traditional learning experiences. In fact, social activities would enhance both scholarship and mental and physical health by replenishing the essential energy expended in book study. As one principal pointed out, "It should not be forgotten that our young people are also preparing for future leisure...and the mind well stored with interesting knowledge...does not have to go abroad for entertainment. The entertainment of such a student is self-contained."[107] Self-containment was the implicit purpose of the extracurriculum. It would build effectively on the entire school program—and on generational relationships, both internally (between students) and between students and teachers.

Most Canadian high schools of this time adopted at least a limited form of student self-government. Student government not only encouraged the young to take a greater interest in their school, but was also seen to provide excellent citizenship training by fostering collective responsibility and, it was theorized, reducing the need for adult intervention in student affairs. By means of their elected peer representatives, students would take care of their own disciplinary issues, interacting with both peers and authorities in resolving them.[108] As in many other schools, the student council of Toronto's Northern Vocational High School was responsible for the management of social and athletic events, the morning assembly, and minor disciplinary problems that involved smoking, bad language, and "unbecoming conduct" on the school premises. At Fort William Collegiate and Technical Institute, commencing in 1921, each form elected two representatives to the new Student Administrative Council, which was supposed to take charge of "anything and everything that was done in the school except study."[109] Student governments were designed to be mechanisms for self-policing, but they also taught adolescents an appropriate code of conduct within an ethical context that could effectively use peer pressure to ensure conformity.[110]

High school athletics became increasingly institutionalized during these years, coming to represent, as never before, both the motivating force of school spirit and its ultimate measure. Since life was supposed to be based on fair play— "the knowledge of how to win and how to lose"—it was obvious that nothing would help to develop "a better, more noble character" than sports.[111] In this manner, sports became an important instrument for the socialization of immigrant children, promoting a "Canadianism" based on the physical discipline, fair play, and teamwork thought to characterize British culture. Even while styles of play changed historically, it was argued, the gold standard would ever be "the desirable citizen of the future." If the school and its playing fields were made "the centre and servant of a satisfying community life," youth would easily find an attractive alternative to the streets, the dance halls and billiard halls and speakeasies, and countless other unhealthy and immoral pursuits in the name of fun. "Well-conducted" physical exercises, gymnastics, and games were not only means of keeping the body fit, but also of "training the characteristics essential to a virile manhood and womanhood." School boards were duly empowered by law to set aside annual funds to support athletics and other school games.[112]

Records indicate that by 1920, almost every high school had its athletic societies, often considered to "have the most to do with extracurriculars."[113] Interform and interscholastic matches provided opportunities for healthy competition and camaraderie, even for romance, all under the watchful eye of teachers and coaches. At tiny Oak Bay High School in Victoria, British Columbia, which had barely one hundred students in the early 1920s, basketball, rugby, cricket, and girls' basketball and field hockey teams were enthusiastically supported.[114] Among the Native male students at the impoverished Garnier Residential School in Spanish, Ontario, hockey "was earnestly observed and followed, and dominated all aspects of life." The stars of their senior team "had fulfilled dreams and ambitions nurtured since they had come to the school seven, eight and nine years before."[115] Regular physical education classes often became auditions for the singling out of prospective athletic stars. As one man recalled about his experiences at Vancouver's John Oliver High School during the 1940s, "after the potential track and field and basketball stars were sorted out for special treatment, much of the time the rest of us were put to a sort of PE busy work."[116]

Operating at once as activity, spectacle, and ultimate manifestation of school spirit, the modern sports regime also offered up a new set of adolescent heroes. The muscular Christianity of the Victorian age, with its correlation of moral integrity and manly strength and endurance, was being eclipsed by an emphasis on physique and physical achievement as yardsticks of both manliness and of the newly coined "sex appeal" that the period's advertisers sold alongside new consumer products. While never named explicitly in student publications, sex appeal—obliquely referred to as "It"—was certainly important to young people. The common scenario at matches was an all-boy game with a mixed audience, whose participation was encouraged by the newly organized and feminized extracurricular activity of cheerleading, which was becoming both a sport in itself and a badge of social success for teenage girls. The school's "reputation" was considered to be upheld not by victory alone, but by the intensity of its members' support. In fact, the "rooters" themselves were often part of the competition, their school spirit judged for its cheering, horns, and "snake-walks," and, of course, for the size of its crowd.[117] Annual field days, even in small towns, could draw as many as three hundred spectators. The Guelph Collegiate yearbook reported in 1926 that "everyone seems to be taking more interest in sports than hitherto, and many were eager to help in any way, even if they could not play the games themselves," with "the girls in particular showing more than their usual interest."[118] Sports prowess for both boys and girls and personal connection to high school sports heroes for girls provided entry into the hierarchy of popularity within the age group—just as their absence could as readily spell social failure. All this physical energy and enthusiasm was just the sort of "pep" that 1920s popular culture applauded.

In fact, the 1920s brought about a new peak for girls' high school athletics, with extracurricular opportunities expanding and intramural leagues growing rapidly. Basketball, invented in 1891 by Ontario native James Naismith, was especially popular, as noted in the Renfrew Collegiate yearbook for 1922: "Every year basketball becomes more and more the real game among the collegiate girls and is played not only by the favoured few on the regular team but by nearly every girl in the school." At one memorable game between Guelph Collegiate and Galt Collegiate girls, one of the players felt her bloomers slipping, at which point "in the extremity all the other girls of both teams formed a circle around her while repairs were made—we men all seated or standing around the hall, a few hundred of us, quite fascinated by this unforeseen development."[119] But girls' athletic clubs often served up more than sports activities, with yearbook references indicating that recitations, songs, and dancing demonstrations were common components of meetings. In late-1920s Toronto, Jarvis, Harbord, and Parkdale collegiates all chose to discontinue their Girls' Athletic Associations in favour of the new Hi-Y Clubs, which were school-based but organized under the auspices of the YMCA and YWCA. The new clubs still featured sports, but they also included drama and art in their programs, in an effort to broaden their appeal and bring into the safety of the group the young women who were not athletically inclined.[120]

High schools also began to formalize their identity markers—the colours, cheers, crests, mottos, and songs that had traditionally indicated exclusive private-school membership. At Arnprior High School in Ontario, principal A.H.D. Ross made one of his first projects upon his appointment in 1919 the search for a suitable motto and crest for the school. After consulting with his staff (but not students) and after considering 120 mottos, the choice was the Latin phrase *Hodie non cras*, meaning "today, not tomorrow," a motto that "constantly holds before us the idea of making the best possible use of present opportunities." The crest, it was decided, "should be as elegant and chaste as possible," the chosen one boasting an hourglass, a "lamp of knowledge," and an open book. Noting that "the outstanding characteristics of college and school yells which have stood the test of time are the frequent repetition of the name of the institution, the introduction of some startling foreign word or phrase, and the reiteration of an unalterable determination to overcome all opposition and finally achieve victory," the principal personally composed the official school cheer: "Arnprior High School!! Rah, rah, rah!! On the field and in the class—*hodie non cras*!! Our colours are the red and white for which we'll fight with all our might!! Arnprior High School!! Rah, rah rah!!"[121] At Guelph Collegiate, the rallying cry was a simple and, it was

Montreal high school girls' first basketball team, 1926. Wm. Notman and Son, II-270769, McCord Museum. Reprinted with permission of the McCord Museum, Montreal, QC.

Although physical education and extracurricular sports remained strictly gender-segregated, young women were increasingly involved in high school team activities during the 1920s, especially basketball, as reflected in this team portrait from the anglophone Montreal High School.

hoped, infectious: "Chee hee! Chee haw! Chee haw! Haw! Haw! Collegiate, Collegiate, Rah! Rah! Rah!"[122]

This formula was followed across the nation, reflecting both the new importance ascribed to school spirit that such emblems signified and the active involvement of principals and teaching staff in their creation. At times, students were encouraged to participate: at Ontario's Fergus High School, the school motto, *Per ardua ad astra*, was the direct result of a student contest held in 1930.[123] The winner of Alexandra High School's song competition was its yearbook editor, who conjured up both words and piano accompaniment for his anthem celebrating the school's values and the democratic principles for which World War II was then being waged: "The green and white of Alexandra High / Are symbols of a modern institution. / They stand for freedom, truth, democracy, / The essence of our union constitution."[124] At Kitchener Collegiate, on the other hand, the faculty-initiated campaign to replace the old school song "O Fair Ontario" with a new student composition was sadly "unconsummated" after several years' effort, inciting much lamenting by student leaders about the embarrassing lack of school spirit.[125] Ultimately, school spirit was primarily an adult project, its various pieces designed, manufactured, and distributed by means of the relationship between faculty and the acknowledged student leaders. Students who recognized this were at times motivated to complain about such things as the "feeble" nature and effect of student government, "practically a dead issue" at some schools; despite the promise to empower students to manage the school's extracurriculum, in reality student councils were "overrun by staff supervision."[126]

The gendered nature of the curriculum and the strict practice at most high schools of keeping boys and girls physically separated in hallways and classrooms—girls on one side, boys on the other—and often with separate entrances and playgrounds meant that, as one man remembered about his Vancouver high school during the 1940s, "the school environment then was not conducive to close relations with girls on site, as it were."[127] At the Catholic Notre-Dame-de-Grace high school in Montreal, the boys' and girls' sections were "hermetically sealed off from one another like two separate schools"; boys and girls ate lunch separately and had different exit times so that they would not "even catch a glimpse of each other, let alone meet."[128] Perhaps the most important of all extracurricular activities, therefore, in their obvious appeal to the young and in their increasing frequency, were the "socials." Usually emphasizing music and often dancing, socials allowed young men and women opportunities to meet and get to know each other, the primary purpose of adolescent socializing. As dating became the modern custom, these school-supervised activities appeared to be a safe alternative to the unsupervised public spaces where "spooning" and even "necking and petting" might otherwise take place undeterred.

Capitalizing on (or perhaps co-opting) the "modern dance rage," school dances became the highlight of the extracurriculum. As one man recalled, "They were great occasions. Much competition amongst the boys to invite the popular girls, the girls dressing in 'formals,' and the boys in their best suit, their 'Sunday' or 'Church' suit."[129] At Guelph Collegiate in Ontario, "tea dances," so-called because they were held between four and six o'clock in the afternoon in the school auditorium, were given "splendid" support by the lower-form students for whom they were intended. Although the Depression limited the number of dances, the school's 1933 yearbook described end-of-term festivities in a manner that suggests anything but austerity, the auditorium fitted out in streamers from skylight to balcony, an awning made of multicoloured balloons, and the green collegiate crest "in sharp relief upon each pillar" against a background in "futuristic design" that "brought into prominence the orchestral stand at the front." Jean's Night-Hawks provided "all that could be desired in the way of dance rhythm." The varied program included an "extraordinary rose-dance," in which young men tossed rosebuds over the balcony and then danced with the young women who caught them, combining romance with a bit of competition and probably no small amount of disappointment for the less nimble. There was also little sign of Depression restraint in Kitchener, Ontario, where the KCI

Girls in sports gear. Glenbow Museum and Archives Collection, ND 3-3213, Edmonton, AB, 1926. Reprinted with permission of the Glenbow Museum, Calgary, AB.

Exemplifying the "girl of the new day," these young Edmonton women lean casually against a car, fresh from the sports field and modelling what would have been regarded—in the very recent past—as inappropriate, even shocking attire, and bobbed hair.

Christmas dance in 1937 had "young ladies and escorts" entering the gymnasium through a "snow-laden cottage" created for the occasion.[130]

Neither did World War II dampen the spirit of Alexandra High School students in Medicine Hat, Alberta. Their 1944 Sadie Hawkins dance—for which gender conventions were deliberately inverted, young women issuing invitations to young men—was a "howling success": a "grand time" was had by 175 students enjoying doughnuts and pop and an orchestra doing some "solid sending."[131] Vancouver's John Oliver High School held a "grade 9 mixer" in 1945 to welcome new students and launch extracurricular activities for the new academic year. The freshmen were reportedly "all 'in the groove' on the floor that night—of course we know this was due to the lessons received at noon hours from the Mixer Committee," which evidently took the youngsters in hand to prepare them for their high school inauguration.[132] The boys at the Garnier Residential School in Spanish, Ontario, were obliged to learn how to dance under the tutelage of their priest and principal, practising "foxtrots, quadrilles, tangos, two-steps, polkas and flings" with each other until they were sufficiently instructed to participate in heavily chaperoned Saturday night dances with the girls from St. Joseph's School across the road.[133] Dances also did duty for the war effort. At Sangudo High School, in Sangudo, Alberta, the winners of the "spot dance" for "most romantic couple" were subjected to a "mock wedding," with the principal playing the piano while "the bride carried a beautiful bouquet of war savings stamps."[134]

Some critics wondered at the schools' place in encouraging these activities, for all that this was preferable to many of the commercial alternatives. The Toronto Board of Education, echoed by other boards in the province, considered that more attention was being paid to such "frills" as dancing and swimming than to "really necessary studies."[135] Along these lines, an Ottawa Collegiate "scandal" of 1927 struck such nervous chords among parents, teachers, and other worried adults that a provincial Royal Commission was established to investigate the allegations of immorality levelled against the school. The scandal began with the *Ottawa Evening Citizen's* front-page publication, under the sensational headline, "Charges Unspeakable Conditions at O.C.I. Dances," of a litany of accusations by a local Presbyterian minister.[136] The clergyman even declared that his statement about Ottawa Collegiate Institute was meant as a "blanket condemnation" of the entire coeducational high school system in the province. As he saw it, modern high schools were the hazardous grounds of "children with the freedom and licence of adults but lacking the experience and balance." His only supporting evidence, however, consisted of stories that parents had told him about "petting parties" and "drinking parties" in connection with school events, not actually on school premises. Nonetheless, a woman with a daughter and two sons attending the school testified that she never permitted them to go to any school dances because of the "rumours" about "looseness of morality" involving "hip flasks and hasty marriages."[137]

Testifying for the other side, a senior collegiate student who had never missed a dance in the previous four years maintained that he had seen "nothing he would classify as objectionable," as well he might. The principal himself insisted that "insubordination did not exist as a general thing" and that boys and girls were kept strictly segregated in both playground and classroom arrangements. The

Students of Castor High School. Glenbow Museum and Archives Collection, ND 3-3213, Castor, AB, 1926. Reprinted with permission of the Glenbow Museum, Calgary, AB.
    This group photograph of students from Castor High School shows how secondary education was increasingly the nation-wide trend, even in small rural towns such as Castor.

commission concluded that there was ."no reason to believe any of the conditions [the minister] alleged as rendering it unsafe for parents to send children to Ottawa Collegiate Institute exist at all."[138] Whatever adolescents were engaging in off the premises, official extracurricular activities were evidently above reproach. Yet one of the Ottawa commissioners "could not help" advising parental accompaniment for youth attending dances, especially girls, because "modern conditions are such that they have to be met in some such way." Despite the evidence—or its absence, in this case—the unease of adults concerning "modern conditions" heightened an intergenerational suspicion that was itself an emergent modern cultural trait.

    The Depression had mixed effects on the culture of the modern high school. The financial constraints facing school boards put a halt to some key extracurricular activities. Student publications were among the first to be axed, as the community businesses that underwrote their costs through advertising withdrew support. But the Depression also strengthened a common perception of the critical role of such activities in the lives of young people, who now had ever fewer prospects for "healthy" socializing with their peers.[139] Hard times also contributed greatly to the expansion of the high school population. The Ontario Ministry of Education consistently reported a "considerable increase" in "congestion" and "serious overcrowding" in high schools throughout the province

because of "enforced economies" on the part of municipalities and, more specifically, because more young people were staying in school or returning due to
unemployment.[140] Many adolescents were embarrassed and ashamed as their
deteriorating family circumstances compelled them to attend in ever-shabbier
attire at a moment in their lives when appearance counted for so much.[141] Other
young people, less fortunate or perhaps less patient than these, took to the
streets and to the rails, collectively embodying the archetypal "lost generation"
that attained the threshold of adulthood in this time of international crisis. The
citizenship arguments that justified the high school's primacy in the adolescent
world took on new power in the crisis atmosphere of the Great Depression:
"Now, more than ever before, [the young person] is a social being, a citizen of the
world, he must develop a social consciousness. . . . It is to make good citizens that
the modern school must bend its energies."[142]

Recognizing the importance of keeping up morale under these circumstances, teachers were reportedly devoting much time to non-academic activities, with music a high priority. Glee clubs, which featured chorus singing and
were frequently dominated by girls, were thought to be especially motivation-
al, but the important point was the "advantage found in working together for a
common end." The extracurriculum became even more organized and formalized with the creation of leagues to ensure "high standards of efficiency" in
extracurricular activities, to encourage "a fine sense of honour in interschool
competitions," and to maintain, "as in athletics, a proper balance between the
physical and the intellectual."[143] Students themselves, however, noted the overall "seriousness" of tone, the deadening of "school spirit" wrought by the
Depression: "In fact, depression seem[ed] rampant in the school, as much in
esprit de corps as in anything else." In some schools, participation in extracurricular activities dropped markedly. At Guelph Collegiate, a drama club production
of *Julius Caesar* was "sadly handicapped" by students who either did not appear
at practices or withdrew the day before the play's opening. There was also difficulty in getting members of the school sports teams, especially the senior
teams, out to practice.[144]

World War II placed its own restraints on high school extracurriculars, especially as a number of the older boys enlisted, leaving a vacuum in senior male
leadership and athletic participation and creating a shortage of eligible "older"
boys for mixed-sex social activities. Citizenship and national objectives were
even more strongly emphasized in light of the international crisis. "We must not
think of ourselves as merely onlookers in the tremendous drama which unfolds
itself from day to day," one principal admonished his students. Employing recreational metaphors creatively, he declared that

> We are participants and a realisation of this is very important. Spectators
> have no responsibility in the way a game is played; the players have. The
> tumult of the tanks, bursting bombs from warring aircraft and all the
> other awful machinery of war is not a part of a show presented for our

entertainment....We must feel that we are a part of these events; that in the shaping of the future, the much heralded post war world, we have a much greater share of responsibility than we realize at present.[145]

Montreal High School students produced a show, featuring student talent, to raise money for a mobile canteen to send overseas, while the city's teenage girls joined such groups as Hilda Galt's Dance for Defence and the Evans Sisters Revue, travelling to camps on buses in the evenings and on weekends to entertain servicemen.[146] At Magee High School in Vancouver, the student council held weekly Stamp Days and collected salvage. Girls were "given their choice of two of the following: knitting, sewing, rivet sorting, home nursing and cadets." The last, revived for boys in 1940, started organizing young women for the first time in 1942. The school's female Air Cadets—at times called "cadet-ettes"—were trained by a senior male cadet and were said to be "trying their best...to bring their standards up to those that the boys have set." On the national scene, in 1943 the Canadian Auxilliary Service Corps organized a new cadet corps for girls twelve years old and over.[147]

Compulsory school attendance to age sixteen effectively made high school the common adolescent occupation during the years from the Great War to 1950. It was not, however, a universal, homogeneous experience for those outside the Canadian-born middle class. Across the nation at mid-century, the school dropout rate continued to be as closely associated with social class as it had ever been: the extra wage earners in low-income families were children in their teen years. The fathers who occupied the higher professions (doctors, lawyers, and so on) had almost three-quarters of their children aged fourteen to twenty-four in school; fathers who worked as unskilled manual labourers, by comparison, had a little over one-third of their children in school, and these children were also more likely to drop out earlier. Of the farm population fourteen years of age and over in 1951, a mere 29.6 per cent had nine years of schooling, compared to 55.1 per cent of the urban population.[148] Among disadvantaged youth of Aboriginal heritage, there was much rejoicing about rising high school attendance, with 834 Native students attending classes above eighth grade in 1950. This was "a considerable increase" over the 661 recorded the previous year, a "splendid record" that not only indicated "more classrooms and improved teaching methods," but also demonstrated "the fact that the Indian youth is taking greater interest in his own education."[149]

The modern high school reinforced class, ethnic, and gender distinctions in significant ways—not only through particular types of schooling, but also by making more apparent the contrasts between high school culture and the outside lives of less favoured students. The peer society at the basis of the extracurriculum contributed to the construction of a behavioural code: it disciplined, usually by exclusion, those who did not conform to recognized group standards. This allowed for a status hierarchy of in and out, good and bad, increasingly expressed in the political terminology of "popular" and "unpopular." Those who did not, or could not fit in, either reconstructed a group identity among others like themselves, suffered alone, or left. Living in Toronto's working-class Cabbagetown neighbour-hood, the young Depression-era protagonist of Hugh Garner's autobiographical novel *Cabbagetown* attends the "Tech" in the hope that "somehow the school would release him from his shabby district and even shabbier home, and make him a belonging part of its friendliness and comradeship and happier life." He finds, instead, that socio-economic divisions are "of fine complexity but nevertheless clearly marked," given away by such things as after-school jobs and shabby clothes that prevent young people from participating in extracurricular socializing. The fictional hero, in common with many of his real historical counterparts, remains "an outsider from the cliques revolving around athletics, the school magazine, the auditorium stage, the possession of a Model T Ford."[150]

For every student able to declare "I have been having a very enjoyable time at high school....I think high school days must be the best in one's life," there were those like Dorothy Livesay, who would look back wistfully on her high school years at the Toronto private girls' school Glen Mawr:

> By the time I entered the Fifth Form I was aware of "not belonging" to the socialite Sixth Form circle of girls who came from Toronto's "best" families. They were well-to-do, good at basketball and skating, rigorous in their lady-like behaviour patterns—vying with each other for a dance with the Prince of Wales. Whereas I was an unathletic "frump"...a freck-led girl with glasses who always "came first" when the monthly reports were read aloud at Prayers by the Principal....Undoubtedly in self-pro-tection, I sought out other isolates who at heart were rebels also, against authority and "proper" behaviour.[151]

Young people did not simply "take" whatever form of social activity that adults deemed was good for them. They were quite capable of subverting attempts to train them by setting up alternative, "secret" societies or by participating in exist-ing clubs only to the degree and in the measure that they chose, as well as by sim-ply refusing any involvement. Yet by the 1950s, peer-group socialization by means of school-based extracurricular activities had been successfully institu-tionalized. As one young man expressed it, "a guy should know how to dance and be in on the sports. Sports is very important."[152] The high school provided the necessary "lessons."

Even in public high schools exhibiting an unprecedented class, ethnic, and gender mix, and even with a new roster of academic and social opportunities, many young people could not measure up against the cultural capital inherited by their better-established peers.[153] Those from affluent families continued to enjoy certain advantages in shaping the clubs and their activities and, in turn, derived special class-specific benefits through their participation. As a student and later a teacher at St. John High School in New Brunswick during the inter-war years, Murray Sargent recalled that "there were youngsters coming out of Fredericton who were always, almost always, winning the Governor General's medal for [high school achievement]....They were always in the top, or well within the first five...but they were coddled kids!"[154] In high school as in other institutional cultures, the axiom that "nothing succeeds like success" held true: the same student, usually male, often occupied several official extracurricular positions. At the same school, the 1940 valedictorian was also president of the Hi-Y Club, treasurer of the student council, secretary-treasurer of the badminton club, advertising manager of the school newspaper, manager of the basketball team, sergeant in the cadet corp and, "in spite of all this," the student newspaper marvelled, "he has some time for sports."[155]

As Pierre Bourdieu points out, the school functions "in the manner of a huge classificatory machine which inscribes changes within the purview of the structure," effectively helping "to make and to impose the legitimate exclusions and inclusions which form the basis of the social order." What Bourdieu's research has shown is an altogether unsurprising "very close statistical relationship" between achievement and ascription, the latter referring to social origins and status. Cloaked with the democratic rhetoric of equality and merit, schools perpetuate and legitimate social hierarchies as well as the values and goals of the dominant class; there is a greater investment in the cultural capital of some types of students, generally those better placed socially to begin with, than in others.[156] The extracurriculum, an increasingly integral part of the pedagogic action pertaining to modern secondary education, plays a vital role in this selection process. The new high school thus established the peer group as the chief agent of adolescent socialization through promotion of its students' membership in and identification with the school. In some ways, high school was a levelling element in the diversifying adolescent social environment. As a member of the graduating class of 1945, whose schooling ended along with the war, one woman remembered her peers' strong sense that "the traditional system was not to be challenged and we were not conflicted by value choices....We saw ourselves as 'decent people.' We were not trained for uncertainty....Succeeding within the system was approved and the unconventional or the strivers were viewed as interlopers."[157]

Before public schooling, restricted admission ensured the reproduction of existing social relations. In the twentieth-century educational system, and especially in the modern high school, the schools themselves replicated the differentiating structures of the larger society.[158] By gathering together a sector of the population whose primary collective identification was age, the high school also reinforced generational consciousness. Its evolving culture imprinted particular generational styles that, while retaining significant continuities, nonetheless changed in keeping with the historical circumstances of each succeeding cohort. Reinforced by growing attendance, the apparently universal nature of the high school experience allowed for a measure of generational cohesion and reassuring uniformity during a time when, especially given the amorphous nature of an "adolescent" national identity, a sense of clearly delineated national objectives was of tremendous importance. As high schools began to serve a wider community, their socializing functions changed as much as their population and curriculum. The extracurriculum reflected and projected the new social meanings ascribed to adolescence and consequently to the high school as the key formative institution in the lives of young Canadians.

The expansion of secondary schooling during the years considered here was important in the making of a modern adolescence in Canada. Adolescents came to identify and to be identified more with school and leisure than with paid labour. But even a stronger generational identification did not obliterate hierarchies within that generation. The developing culture of the modern high school, newly institutionalized in the peer societies of the extracurriculum by the 1920s, accommodated and promoted status cliques and exclusionary divides even within generations. School assists the home and the community in transmitting and consolidating the class, race and gender identities integral to the formation of the self. Young people learn what is expected of them, both in their day-to-day behaviour and in terms of how they will make their way as adults. These expectations are shaped by socio-economic status and familial position as well as by contemporary ideals about what constitutes "success" and full membership in adult society. They are further developed through the type of schooling that is delivered and, more to the point, through individual and group experiences of the school's institutional culture. More so than either home or community, the school performs these functions within an explicit generational framework, through age grading and the development of distinct levels of schooling, each with its own age-specific extracurriculum as well as the customary curriculum, and—increasingly the case in the modern public education system—each within its own physical space.

5

On the Job

Training and Earning

There is a coming of age for work as well as for voting, and for the great part of Canadian youth it comes long before the age of enfranchisement.

— Blodwen Davies, *Youth Speaks Its Mind*, 1948

*M*odern industrial Canada needed to cultivate a certain type of labourer. The efficiency ideologues of the Great War years, whose influence continued into the interwar period, stressed the need for careful training from early childhood. This would ensure productivity, in its broadest sense: in the workplace, in government, in society at large, and even in the home, where the necessary management regimen was ideally initiated in infancy.[1] Not surprisingly, public discussions about youth labour emphasized training, not merely in terms of job-related skills, but just as much in terms of character formation, self-management, and citizenship, the latter encompassing these other individual traits in their most expansive—productive—sense. Canada's youth held the key to its national prosperity and to its international standing among the new century's industrial leaders.

This chapter considers the economic contours of modern adolescence, with a view to understanding the changing nature and relations of the youth labour market and how these changes, in turn, affected the culture of adolescence, as well as the family economy. As discussed, the 1920s marked a steady upward trend in both the participation rate in secondary schooling and in the ages of those attending. Despite the significance of this dawning of the "age of high school," there remained an equally important proportion of young Canadians between the ages of thirteen and nineteen who left school for work, many of them before matriculation. While many worked part-time during their high school stay, the first full-time paying job constituted a major point of transition. It was a threshold to a figurative adulthood, which was, in reality, almost a suspended state: a good number of adolescents who were "earning their keep" were at least semi-dependent on parents and living in the family home. Meant to be both responsive and formative at once, in that they addressed the youth problem while also promoting a particular ideal of citizenship, public discussions and state initiatives respecting youth labour were integral to the experience of coming of age in early twentieth-century Canada.

By the 1920s, the effects of the late-Victorian outcry against child labour had been realized in the restriction or prohibition of the paid labour of those under fourteen years. The notion of who was too young to work, at least in certain occupations, had gradually expanded to include young adolescents in the fourteen- to-sixteen age group, the most common point of labour-force entry for young Canadians. Growing concern about the health and welfare, as well as the morality, of these young workers drew attention to the nature of work for all those under the age of majority, especially as most were finished with formal schooling by age sixteen. As the previous chapter indicates, there were escalating arguments for vocational guidance and relevant in-class and on-the-job training so that the young could be steered clear of the dreaded "blind-alley" job.[2] Such discussions reached a peak during the Depression years, when the youth problem essentially became the "problem of idle youth." The labour shortages occasioned by war production, however, did not end anxieties about "dead-enders": Canadians were inspired to worry that the young were shortchanging themselves and effectively mortgaging their futures by leaving school precipitously to fill high-paying but temporary jobs in war industry and in the armed forces.

The period's youth employment data present a paradox. As discussed, the statistics point unequivocally to the lengthening familial dependency of young Canadians, a trend important enough to be one of the primary modern characteristics of the youth experience. A number of labour-market changes that affected youth—and consequently their prospects for coming "into their own"—were apparent by the 1920s; the 1930s would at once consolidate these trends and take them temporarily off course. The number of Canadians under the age of fifteen who worked full-time for wages was clearly declining by 1921. This downward shift reflected a process that had begun with the previous century's protective labour laws, now being furthered by compulsory education and extended school-leaving legislation, as well as by important changes in the nature of production. Evidence from both private and public sources, however, suggests that a significant proportion of these under-fifteens were still earning wages on a part-time basis, the extent of their labour obscured because casual, after-school, and weekend employment rarely showed up on official records.[3] Also significant is the fact that, by the 1920s, even as fewer of those between fifteen and nineteen earned sufficient wages to leave the family home, more members of this age group enjoyed a more active participation in the developing consumer economy than ever before. At least a few decades before the supposed "invention" of the "teenage market" in the 1950s, this age group was taking substantial steps toward defining a youth market presence that would be another hallmark of modernity, the increasingly entwining consumer and popular cultures.[4]

The late-nineteenth-century laws proscribing child labour and establishing mandatory schooling to age fourteen defined childhood's end, or at least the end of a period that was publically acknowledged and officially protected under the name of childhood. These laws were the earliest official demarcation of two distinct life stages before adulthood: those between fourteen and eighteen were neither children nor full-fledged adult citizens.[5] The labour legislation of the early twentieth century extended the state's protective capacity in regard to the working young. Regulations on minimum wages for girls were issued in Manitoba, Saskatchewan, and British Columbia before 1921, and in Alberta and Ontario shortly afterward. In 1923, British Columbia raised the minimum age of factory employment for boys to fifteen. There were any number of attempts to regulate the types, conditions, and hours of employment for youth, the maximum protected age ranging from fourteen years for New Brunswick boys to sixteen in most of the other provinces; in Quebec, the upper limit was eighteen years. Reflecting the continued belief that young women were in need of special protection, similar laws were effected for girls under eighteen in all the provinces by the 1930s. On the whole, it appears that restrictions on hours had little impact on workday realities for the young. Since the original factory legislation of the 1880s, hours for women of all ages and for youth under fourteen were limited to ten a day and sixty weekly in Ontario and the provinces to the east; the statutory limits in Manitoba and Alberta were nine hours a day and fifty-four weekly; in Saskatchewan and British Columbia, eight hours a day and forty-eight weekly.[6] Many young workers, male and female, continued to face a long and arduous day's labour.

That work, not high school, was the main activity of older adolescents is indicated in any cursory glance at the ages and numbers of employed youth during this period. The number of young Canadians aged ten to fifteen gainfully employed "for the greater part of their time" in 1921 was 73,000, or 6.8 per cent of this age group. But the total nearly doubled for those aged sixteen and seventeen, with 154,345 gainfully employed on a full-time basis.[7] While agriculture remained the chief employer of youth, the manufacturing sector ranked second and was a particularly important source of employment for those over fifteen— 14,268 juveniles ten to fifteen years of age, 1.3 per cent of that age group, worked in factories in 1921; more than twice that number (34,185) were in the fifteen-to-eighteen age group. Over 14,000 of these, from both groups, were employed in Ontario factories.[8] In sum, the 1921 census data reveal that the total number of young Canadians working for wages before reaching their eighteenth birthdays was 227,553. Of every one hundred boys, then, more than ten were working for wages or on the family farm, while nearly three in every one hundred girls were also working. Quebec's youth employment was indisputably the highest in Canada, with 49.6 percent of fourteen-year-old boys in that province employed.[9] The 1931 census showed that males under twenty continued to outnumber females in waged employment, although young women were definitely gaining. About 56 per cent of all male Canadians in this age group worked, while the corresponding proportion for girls was less than half that number.[10] (See table 5.1.)

Table 5.1: Number of Persons of All Ages and of Juveniles of Certain Ages Employed in Factories in Canada and Each Province in 1921

	all ages	13 years	14 years	15 years	16 years	16-17
Prince Edward Island	1,267	15	14	31	60	95
Nova Scotia	20,066	40	70	194	304	1,165
New Brunswick	17,210	38	115	244	397	1,098
Quebec	147,902	462	1,909	4,226	6,597	13,503
Ontario	229,132	109	1,467	4,559	6,135	15,463
Manitoba	16,789	6	56	246	308	1,099
Saskatchewan	5,133	1	17	50	68	235
Alberta	8,592	—	9	83	92	425
British Columbia	29,429	9	71	227	307	1,102
Canada	475,520	680	3,728	9,860	14,268	34,185

Source: *Department of Labour, The Employment of Children and Young Persons in Canada* (Ottawa: King's Printer, 1930), 40.

By the mid-1920s, with the western wheat boom fuelling the economy and assembly-line production systems increasingly being adopted in industry, employment opportunities for untrained, unskilled workers in the older adolescent group increased, even while the laws protecting the under-fifteens were often breached.[11] The rapid expansion of commercial amusements and services introduced many new jobs of a menial, casual nature that could be performed by older children and young adolescents on a part-time basis, after school, during the evening, and on weekends. In 1925, boys as young as eleven were found working until midnight and later in bowling alleys, or as "runners" for local cinemas, delivering films to the railway station after the evening shows.[12] The relative affluence of those who kept their jobs during the Great Depression allowed for growth in such middle-class and largely male leisure activities as bowling and golf, which also led to employment opportunities for youth, many of whom had acquired the "family breadwinner" title by default.[13]

Intensifying concerns about juvenile delinquency and an increasing correlation between delinquency and street trades incited a number of provincial statutes that enabled municipal councils to make strict bylaws regulating the employment of children under sixteen as messengers or vendors of newspapers and small wares. Street-sellers under eighteen were now commonly reclassified as neglected children, making them subject to being taken into custody by children's aid societies. Any person "causing a child to be neglected" in this manner could be fined.[14] Already in 1913, the Ontario Children's Protection Act had been amended so that no girl under sixteen and no boy under twelve could "engage or be licensed or permitted to engage" in any street trade or occupation. The first direct and specific statutory prohibition of street trades in Canada, this Act was again amended in 1919 to raise the age of boys to fourteen, and in 1922 to prohibit boys under sixteen from engaging in any street trade or occupation between ten o'clock in the evening and six in the morning.[15] The British Columbia legislature passed the Night Employment of Young Persons Act in 1921, adopting the recommendations of the 1919 Convention of the International Labour Organization, under the auspices of the League of Nations, which prohibited employment of persons under eighteen years between eight in the evening and seven in the morning.[16]

Contemporary studies indicate that such legislative tightening was not sufficient to stop children and young adolescents from working on the city streets. When University of Toronto sociologist F.C. Jackson investigated the Hamilton, Ontario, street trades in 1932, his conclusions likely surprised few Canadians. Jackson argued that children who worked on the streets during or after regular school hours were deprived of "wholesome recreation, regular meal hours or home training." Echoing long-standing concerns, newsboys were singled out for their "comparatively high delinquency rate," evidence that "the moral influences surrounding the work are bound to leave their mark upon such impressionable material." The intensive competition in the trade, where boys were held financially responsible for their unsold newspapers, was a "strong incentive to late nights and shady practices." Sensationalist newspaper accounts about a "crime wave of fair proportions" involving Toronto messenger and errand boys who victimized "many city stores" reinforced the links between particular types of youth employment and incipient criminality.[17] Jackson ultimately concluded that the street-trades problem was rooted in the slack enforcement of the Children's Protection Act and corresponding city bylaws because of the "lack of recognition of their importance on the part of the public."[18] Yet he, like numerous commentators, overlooked the fact that these working children and adolescents made important contributions to their families' upkeep. At the depths of the Depression and in an industrial city such as Hamilton, the subjects of his study could well have been the principal or sole breadwinners. Strict enforcement of protective legislation was certainly intended "for their own good," but it might easily have pushed these young workers and their families into destitution.[19]

A great many concerns were voiced about young workers' "lack of general education and of vocational training, and their physical and mental immaturity, with consequent susceptibility to the diseases, accidents and moral hazards of the working world," especially in view of the manner in which "all such effects on the individual react on society."[20] The sixteen-year-old daughter of a Hull, Quebec, policeman, for example, suffered serious scalp wounds at an Ottawa factory when, catching her hair in some shafting, she was whirled around the belt twice before the electrical current could be turned off and her hair cut to release her.[21] Contemporary studies acknowledged the greater susceptibility of adolescents to industrial diseases and especially to industrial poisons, as well as to accidents, most notably those resulting in permanent disability. There are no age-differentiated data, however, to show to what extent young workers were affected by such dangers. When the Great War's pressing home-front needs prompted state interest in the correlates of worker health, productivity, and "national efficiency," some forays were made into "industrial hygiene," with various provinces establishing divisions within their health departments. Some industrial centres, starting with Ontario, instigated factory medical inspections that included physical examinations for workers. However, there is no suggestion that the age of workers was a specific concern, nor that the particular health problems of adolescent workers were given special consideration.[22]

American and British studies from the period reveal that the humid environment necessary in cotton manufacture and the dust that arose in the process, were conducive to the "excessive incidence" of respiratory disease, including tuberculosis, among its workers. A large proportion of these were under twenty and female. Those who worked with non-ferrous metals, as in printing, engraving, and metal-polishing, were at high risk of exposure to poisonous fumes and dusts. The health repercussions of nicotine and tobacco dust in factories producing cigarettes and of vegetable dusts in the biscuit and confectionary industries were also recognized as being "more or less harmful." Sawmills and other woodworking places, pulp and paper mills, the metal trades and industries using power-driven machinery all had high accident rates that were believed to involve a disproportionate number of young workers; it was known that, of the eighty-four fatal industrial accidents in 1927, twenty-eight of the victims were under eighteen years of age. Lumbering accounted for the highest number of fatal accidents to workers under eighteen, as well as to those eighteen to twenty-one, with manufacturing in second place.[23] The effect of farm work on the health of the young was even more difficult to trace, but it was thought that "ill effects from overwork" belied the "common belief . . . that farm work is the certain road to good physical development and health."[24]

Especially as compared with Britain and some of the American states, provincial governments—even those with active industrial hygiene divisions and workers' compensation programs—offered little to regulate the employment of young persons in dangerous trades, especially those such as the electrical apparatus and rubber industries, which saw rapid development during the interwar years.[25] A Montreal health survey conducted in 1928 recommended that no one under eighteen be employed without a medical examination by health department physicians and an official certificate permitting "employment at certain work." No action was taken on the recommendation. By the 1930s, all provincial statutes stipulated that young persons were not to be employed in work where their health was "liable to be injured." Such an imprecise directive, however, left great scope for interpretation and especially for neglect. None of the provincial factory laws required that industrial establishments be regularly inspected by physicians or medical officers of health.[26]

The medical profession, despite its dominant role in the period's campaigns to regulate child health and education, and despite its growing interest in adolescence, was decidedly vague about the relationships between health, class, age, and the nature of work: "The damage done to the child from excessive work may be difficult to detect until he has been engaged at it for a period of years." Consistent with the larger "expert" discourse on adolescence, medical concerns that were explicitly tied to the life stage of these young workers referred to emotional or psychological more than to physical problems. Thus doctors worried about the "striking phenomenon" of youth's "rebellion against authority," a phenomenon otherwise regarded as "normal" among adolescents. For young workers, some contended, "monotony in this period of life will kill the best instincts of the future citizen, and very often leads to Bolshevistic tendencies, or sometimes to the vicious characters so often encountered in city life." Young workers might, moreover, embrace views "sufficiently warped to drag down hundreds or even thousands."[27] Where young women were concerned, doctors worried about the impact of fatigue and other work-related health threats on the fragile physical and nervous systems of this "delicate" group, considering that they might lead to "permanent derangement of health and difficulty in childbearing." The "fundamental fact" determining women's place in industry was simply that "nearly every woman is a potential mother." Young working women were believed to be even more prone to all manner of "breakdowns" than were their more affluent sisters. Such concerns about the health of young workers and worker efficiency were closely connected, often masking anxieties about production with those about reproduction.[28]

As this discussion of work-related risks suggests, much of the evidence about youth labour in the past is patchy, often anecdotal and autobiographical. A significant part of young people's work defied easy measurement because of its marginality and even invisibility in the formal labour market. Yet there is enough evidence to sustain the notion of its persistence and its continued importance to families, and also to show that social convention and familial expectations upheld a certain filial duty in this regard, especially but not exclusively in immigrant households. One young woman who had left Naples for Montreal as a child was obliged to take on full-time factory labour at the age of thirteen: "This was hard work. I used to get up at five o'clock as it took an hour to reach work on the street car. We worked from 7 to 5 and though I was supposed to weigh macaroni in the boxes, I had to do much other work and this was very hard."[29] Despite the steady chorus of worries about child and youth labour, it was also the general wisdom that some sort of part-time, after-school, or weekend job would convey critical lessons in self-discipline, money management, thrift, and the importance of earning one's keep through honest toil. *Chatelaine* magazine promoted sales by regularly exhorting its (largely female) readership to "help your boy or girl to help him or herself" by "showing them" the opportunity to sell subscriptions door to door. Fathers were urged to "give your boy or girl an early start in training for business" in this manner.[30]

A great many young adolescents held part-time jobs, a pattern that seems to have been the norm even in fairly well-off middle-class families during this period. For some families, of course, the need was entirely economic. A.W. Currie remembered the intensive labour that his part-time job—necessary support for his widowed mother in small-town Ontario in the 1920s—demanded of him:

> My big break came when I was 15 for I got a job in the town's largest grocery store after school on Saturdays and during the summer holidays. From some points of view it was hard work.... I had to help fill shelves from stock in the basement; put the proper weight of white or brown sugar, salt and such in bags for subsequent sale; do the same for anything from tumeric to prunes and coffee on customers' order..., write out orders given by customers across the counter or over the telephone; remember the correct price of every article including what was on sale that weekend, for only a few prices were displayed within the store..., clean, get accustomed to wearing a long apron and "remain pleasant all day."[31]

Currie worked after school from four to six o'clock, Monday to Friday. On Saturdays he worked from six in the morning until eight in the evening— "at full clip" during the final four or five of these fourteen hours, in order to fill all orders before the store closed. For this he received four dollars per week and, during summer vacation, seven dollars for six full days' work.

Opportunity for part-time work also reflected gender conventions that were often reinforced by the nature of the local economy. In the Cariboo-Chilcotin region of central interior British Columbia—the so-called hub of the Cariboo, with its important lumbering and service sectors—the nature of the local economy meant that few adolescent girls worked part-time while still in school during the 1940s and early 1950s. Boys, on the other hand, easily found "some kind of little job" in stores, garages, or with tradespeople.[32] Parents in an affluent anglophone Montreal suburb in the 1950s agreed that their teenagers learned "proper" economic values through after-school jobs that would impress upon them the virtues of work and saving. As one mother described it, "I've always encouraged the boys to take any stray jobs—cutting the grass of neighbours, putting up storm windows, even baby-sitting.... It's not the money. They should learn that you just don't get money, you work for it. It develops a sense of responsibility." Part-time work was the norm for adolescent boys in the community, and increasingly common for girls.[33]

The meticulous analyses undertaken by the McGill School of Social Research during the 1930s, especially those of Leonard Marsh, help to fill out the historical picture on youth labour. Marsh's close examination of the 1931 census, supplemented by additional data from 1936, reveals that the largest workforce ever attained in Canada to that date was recorded in 1929–30, at around 2.8 million.[34] While immigration accounted for some of this expanded labour supply, the data suggest that recruitment from domestic sources was greater than ever before. Also important is the fact that large shifts in the occupational structure occurred during the years 1925–29, particularly among the least specialized workers, a category dominated by women and those under twenty. Domestic sources, including the pool of youth leaving school, supplied about 40 per cent of the new labour that fed the industrial growth of the late 1920s. The bulk of this growing labour force was absorbed by industry, trade, and service, which employed from 54 to 60 per cent of the working population over age fourteen.[35]

Looking more closely at the type of work performed by young Canadians at this time, the numbers bear out the age- and gender-defined limits of the jobs available to them. The plurality of young men under twenty worked in low-skilled service (20 per cent), with the second and third highest sectors close behind: unskilled/manual accounted for 19 per cent, while the clerical and semi-skilled categories were about even at 15 per cent each. Gender and age characterized the industrial apprenticeship category, which was entirely male and counted fully 80 per cent of its members in their teen years. Also notable are the similarities between the work of office and store clerks insofar as age and gender distribution are concerned. A large proportion of junior clerks and sales clerks, the majority of the latter male, were employed in these areas. More than half (55 per cent) of clerical workers were under twenty-five, with 20 per cent of this group in their teens. Particularly striking is the youthful character of female employment. With 20 per cent of all working women under twenty—in contrast to only 10 per cent of working men—and another 30 per cent under twenty-five, half of all working women were under twenty-five, compared to less than one-quarter of working men. The youngest group of all was the unskilled workers in factories and stores, together with those listed as farm workers: of these all together, nearly three-quarters were under twenty-five. Marsh also noted the "indications of impermanence" in the job categories dominated by the under-twenties, male and female. The service sector was markedly "transitional" in that it was an entry point for many young people. In this category were the "typical youths' occupations," such as those of messenger, delivery boy, and female domestic. Finally, the farm remained the chief employer of youth labour: nearly 60 per cent of all farm workers were under twenty-five.[36]

Reflecting the nature of the Depression as a crisis of male breadwinners, the 1931 census saw a definite increase in the cheaper employment of young women, with 25 per cent of those aged fourteen to twenty gainfully employed by comparison to 16 per cent in 1921. The figures show the significance of manufacturing as "women's work": females under eighteen constituted 19.4 per cent of all women factory operatives, while only 7.6 per cent of male factory workers belonged to that age group. Textiles was the most important of all manufacturing sectors for these girls, and also for boys in the ten-to-fifteen age group. As was the case historically, the bulk of this youth labour was employed in cotton manufacture, among the first industries and still (at this time) the principal industry employing the young.[37] It is also evident that many of the jobs filled by women were in industries offering employment primarily to younger workers, the cohort most likely to contain large numbers of women, who otherwise sowed "a very heavy employment mortality...almost as soon as the 'teen ages are passed." Few commentators, including Marsh, recognized the confusion of cause and effect underlying both their own explanations and the female career path itself. Young women left wage labour upon marriage, but jobs were offered to them entirely on that expectation, thereby normalizing and institutionalizing their low wages, limited prospects, and high "employment mortality."[38]

Although feminization of clerical work was proceeding rapidly, men and women were employed in this category in the proportion of about four to three. The smaller total number of wage-earning women, however, made clerical work proportionately much more important for them, accounting for 18 per cent of total female employment for all age groups. As stenographers, junior clerks and cashiers, girls definitely outnumbered boys.[39] Among girls, the most obvious changes occurred in the area of service occupations, especially in the expanding leisure and beauty industries. The number of waitresses, cooks, and other female restaurant workers doubled (from 6,400 to 12,800) in this decade, while the number of female workers in laundries and cleaning establishments more than doubled. The rapid growth of the beauty industry is demonstrated by the fact that the number of hairdressers, manicurists, and beauty parlour operators increased from a few hundred in 1921 to over 6,400 by 1931. While there was certainly a net increase in the number of salesgirls—a little under 10,000, or 28 per cent overall—this was relatively small in comparison to the other service categories, and also remarkably smaller than the growth in the clerical category.[40]

The employment data indicate that age—as much as and sometimes more than the usual variables of class, gender, race, education, and location—determined the type of work available to job-seekers. It is also clear that in every province, and in the nation as a whole, significant numbers of young people between the ages of fourteen and twenty were working. Many of these were engaged in full-time unwaged labour. In 1931, with the Great Depression already pushing down the numbers, about 56 per cent of all male Canadians in the fourteen-to-twenty age group were employed; slightly less than half that percentage of young women were working.[41] The proportion of young workers of both sexes was about equal in Ontario and Quebec, the most industrialized provinces. In Ontario, however, more of this group earned wages (43,000 gainfully employed, 23,000 wage earners), while a larger proportion of young Quebeckers were unwaged workers, in majority farmers' children and other unpaid household workers (57,000 gainfully employed, 25,000 wage earners).

Quebec's age distribution of younger workers—with more of the fourteen-to-twenty group employed than in Ontario—was closer to that of the country as a whole.[42]

The 1930s data underline a number of important points about youth labour that would hold consistently true over the entire period. The first is the primacy of farm workers in the youth labour force; the second is the fact that much youth labour was unpaid, at least in monetary terms, and not only among young farm help. Nearly half of all young men in their teens, and an actual majority at every age until the age of eighteen, worked in agriculture, but only about 30 per cent of male farm workers under twenty earned wages.[43] As could be expected, given its unpaid and predominantly familial nature, this was a transitory feature of the youth labour market, with most workers in this category moving out of it by their early twenties and only a few ultimately becoming farmers themselves.[44] Unpaid adolescent labour, however, was also far from unknown in urban areas. Among young male workers alone, there were about twelve thousand known adolescent boys working without wages in stores, in other small family businesses, and as "outworkers" and apprentices, a number that is probably lower than the reality. Everywhere in Canada, unpaid workers were disproportionately located at the younger end of the age range, as opportunities for paid employment as well as personal choice and autonomy from family rose incrementally with age.[45] Older children and younger adolescents often laboured without wages at home, on the farm, in family businesses, or in the household, while their elder siblings were more likely to have paid employment, within or outside the family circle. The bulk of the unpaid were in two strikingly gender-defined and traditional occupational groups. Boys predominated in agricultural labour and girls in domestic service, both mostly on the family farm or in the home.[46]

A considerable proportion of waged work for urban youth was temporary, casual, or stopgap. Also significant are the recruitment patterns that characterized different occupational classes. For each employment category—again clearly showing the workings of age in terms of rank and status—the youngest workers were relegated to the bottom-most levels. Young managers, for example, could be found in charge of small stores, boarding houses, and roadside refreshment counters. A majority in the commercial category worked as canvassers and collectors on a commission basis. The youngest clerical workers were office boys, while the most junior in the skilled trades were apprentices.[47] Excluding the young farmhands, nearly 67,000 workers under twenty were employed at unskilled jobs in various industrial and service fields, constituting about one-eighth of the non-rural unskilled group. The numbers troubled youth-watchers because these were the "blind-alley" or "dead-end" jobs that offered no guarantee of regular employment, training, or skill development, and little in the way of "prospects" or future options, and therefore were "a matter of eminent social concern." By the 1940s, social scientists and educators were unanimous in emphasizing the direct correlation between early school-leaving and dead-end work.[48] Such work might even be conducive to immorality and criminality: a special committee investigating child and youth labour in Toronto put much weight on its discovery that "half the men in our prisons had...never learned a trade."[49] Beyond representing an ample and consequently cheap youth labour supply, the numbers spoke to "a social problem spread over many industries."[50]

Figure 5.1. Workers Aged up to 21 as Percentages of All Gainfully Employed in Each Class

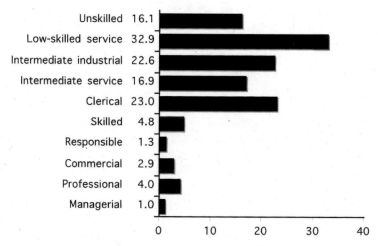

Source: Leonard Marsh, *Canadians in and out of Work* (Toronto: Oxford University Press, 1940), 223.

Despite the strength of gender ideologies in Catholic Quebec, the reality belied the ideal. In Montreal and Quebec City, the proportion of wage-earning women aged fourteen to twenty was larger than in Ontario and Canada as a whole.[51] Again, the gendered nature of the youth labour force necessarily reflected the type of industry that predominated: the so-called light industry and textiles that took the lead in Quebec were traditional employers of young women and continued to be a vital source for that sector throughout these years. Across the nation, this generation of daughters was growing in importance as contributors to the family economy beyond the level of household help, often serving as the secondary breadwinners, especially in cases where brothers were kept in school to further family objectives or when fathers and brothers were under- or unemployed. Elsie Freeman went to work in a textile plant in Toronto in 1920, at seventeen years of age. She slept on her newly married uncle's sofa and worked forty-four hours a week for seventeen cents an hour. Yet she recalled being "happy as a lark as all the other workers were young girls like myself."[52] In 1937, at the age of eighteen, Shirley B. arrived in Winnipeg from impoverished eastern Poland with her mother and six younger siblings. Her father, who had preceded them by five years, had arms "like a lump" from cutting wood for a dollar a day. She was fortunate to find work for five dollars a week, sewing caps by machine; her father allowed her fifty cents from her pay packet, "and the rest I gave it to him because he had to pay for our tickets."[53] The textile industries were, in fact, the most important of all manufacturing employers for girls under eighteen, and also for boys in the younger ten-to-fifteen age group.[54]

During the 1920s, as the wheat boom and western settlement continued apace, even the large numbers of young Canadian-born, immigrant, and first-generation farmhands in the country did not appear to meet the need. The result was the creation of an ill-considered program of juvenile immigration from Great Britain, an updated version of the equally fraught late-nineteenth-century scheme involving the "Home" or "Barnardo" children—the deserted, orphaned, or simply poor British children effectively transported to Canada to be "adopted" into farm families.[55] The Empire Settlement Act, passed by the British parliament in 1922, was intended to supply agricultural and household help and to be "limited to children suitable for that purpose." From the Canadian perspective, the migration of "desirable types of British young people" was seen as a "hopeful and constructive solution to Canada's need for increased population." The two governments would jointly cover the eighty-dollar passage for each young immigrant.[56] The first contingent of sixty teenagers, mostly boys brought to Canada under the care of the Salvation Army, reached Winnipeg in mid-March of 1923. The majority were to be "distributed" to farm families in the Brandon area, where they would learn "Canadian farming methods" in the interests of fitting them to become "future farmers."[57]

Reports of deprivation, overwork, and physical, emotional, and sexual abuse, as well as several cases of suicide, led to increasing restriction of the program over the six years of its official implementation.[58] The inquest into the 1923 suicide by hanging of sixteen-year-old Charles Bulpitt, a British farmhand sent to Goderich, Ontario, saw a courtroom filled to capacity as well as detailed press coverage. It was felt that this publicity did "more to make Canada safe for small British and European immigrants than all the welfare organizations that have been working on the questions."[59] Bulpitt's case struck terror in those concerned about youth in general and about juvenile immigration in particular. The tragic chain of circumstances that led to his death started with his "misplacing" on a farm instead of in an office, "for which his education and desire fitted him": "The loneliness among strangers, the unaccustomed and uncongenial work, and the unwarranted punishment he received for misconduct all combined to prompt him to take his life." Testimony revealed that he had twice tried to run away. He was whipped for insubordination and "telling lies" and was given no recreational opportunities outside of Sunday school. The thirty-three-year-old farmer who had been his employer, after admitting to having whipped the boy "not daily" but "frequently," was sentenced to two months in a Goderich jail.[60]

Ontarians were shocked again when, within days of young Bulpitt's death, John Payne, another juvenile immigrant working on a farm in Emily Township in eastern Ontario, also killed himself, by ingesting the common household poison Paris Green, which brought about a slow and agonizing death. It was felt that the Bulpitt case had inspired Payne to consider suicide. There was no clear evidence of mistreatment by the farmer and his wife, although she admitted that she had "threatened to return him to the Barnardo home if he did not mend his ways" and that he had seemed "unreasonably affected" by this threat.[61]

In 1925, as a result of these cases and many other troubling reports across the nation, the federal government revised the original agreement to provide only for the emigration of boys between fourteen and nineteen years of age, and girls of fourteen to seventeen years; unaccompanied juveniles under fourteen were prohibited from applying to the program. It was finally abandoned amidst public controversy on both sides of the Atlantic. The main movement of juvenile emigrants had ended by 1928, but not before some 90,000 young labourers had arrived, of whom 23,799 were girls intended for domestic service.[62] According to the Canadian Council on Child and Family Welfare, the Salvation Army, which had supervised the emigration of these young people, "had given very little aftercare to any classes of its immigrants and had not been very conscientious in its selections with the result that, even with the training centres and hostels, large numbers of immigrants brought under these auspices were early found on the poverty line or contributing to our dependents."[63] But in 1931, as the gates of the Depression-wracked nation were closing on virtually all immigrants, some 2,190 juveniles were again admitted to Canada under the scheme.[64]

In the Ukrainian communities of the west, meanwhile, "with rare exceptions," young men were leaving the family farm to avoid the "economic and social suicide" represented in the impoverished "rural swamps" settled by their parents. Although Winnipeg was their primary destination, many of the first generation of Canadian-born migrated to American cities, just as had young Maritimers and Quebeckers in earlier years.[65] The majority of the communities' young women continued to work the fields, but a growing number of these were also leaving home for employment. In the area around Elphinstone, Manitoba, many girls went into domestic work "in Anglosaxon districts," a fact interpreted as a sure means to making their own homes cleaner and "more nearly" approaching "the Canadian standard." Others preferred to go to the cities, where they "drifted to the third-class restaurants," many of which were considered to be "places of questionable repute." The more fortunate were those who, settling in Toronto, had found employment in packing plants, mostly in dairy and hog-casing departments. With wages averaging twelve to fourteen dollars weekly, these jobs provided a healthy paycheque for young, unskilled female workers, especially during the 1930s.[66]

The experience of young immigrant workers tended to be harder than that of their "Canadian" peers—not surprising in view of the marginalization entailed by both age and race. Both prior to and after the Exclusion Act of 1923, which barred further Asian immigration and severely restricted the lives of those already in the country until 1947, most Chinese immigrants were offered only those jobs in domestic service, laundries, and restaurants that were otherwise dominated by low-paid female labour and that featured menial work, long hours, poor conditions and wages, and little security.[67] One woman who arrived in Saskatchewan from Kwangtung province in 1918 at the age of eighteen recalled, "We were very poor at home. People came here to look for money. My uncle was here then, and he applied for me to come. He paid the $500 head tax for me... so I came and went to wash dishes."[68]

Since most adolescents remained at home until at least the age of eighteen, even while earning wages, the number of young women who constituted the seemingly pervasive "girl problem" of the day—those who left small-town and rural homes for city employment—was actually very small. As is true overall of the enormous "modern youth problem," the extent of concern about the dangers that this "girl migration" represented was far out of proportion to the reality.[69] Yet "moral health," to youth-watchers, was the common problem of working girls in the city: at the typical wage rate of seven dollars per week or less, overstepping the bounds into casual prostitution appeared the menace that stood to make working girls the "social wreckage" of the nation.[70] And it was not only the traditional women's organizations, such as the National Council of Women of Canada and the rural Women's Institutes, that were worried. Even as modern, urban, and professional a group as the Canadian Business Women's Club urged that this "problem" be addressed in order to "stay the tide or the influx of girls between the ages of 15 and 20 from the smaller places to our larger cities, by providing suitable occupation for those girls in their home towns." The conviction that rural areas and small towns were somehow "safer" for the virtuous young, especially women, allowed even the mostly unmarried and thoroughly modern business women to wonder, "why should the girl of 'teen age be so misguided... in making such a choice when comparing her home life and its valuable associations with the poor recompense as offered by the city?" As the club's representative Marjorie McMahon commented in 1921, the city offered inexperienced working girls only "cheap meals, drab lodgings and chance acquaintances, at an age when the most important friendships of her life are formed." McMahon claimed personal knowledge of girls "in the asylum," their sad fate brought about by the conditions of city life. She asserted, however, that "it is not the work they do that kills but the absence of home surroundings."[71]

Contemporary social scientists were especially interested in the characteristics of youth employment because of what these portended for the future of the Canadian labour force in terms of supply, distribution, education, training, and, not least important, citizenship. Thus, Leonard Marsh saw the entry point into employment as "the most strategically important stage of all" in the life cycle.[72] By age seventeen, when only about one-quarter of the nation's potentially employable youths were still in school, the labour market dominated these young lives. The choice between "learning and earning" was often made for young people once they reached the age when class, familial expectations, and cultural values placed a premium on paid labour over schooling. Whether the result of individual choice or family strategy, the outcome, Marsh acknowledged, was essentially a matter of class: "It is different for the farmer's son at twelve, the artisan's son at fourteen, the son of a clerk at sixteen, the son of the professional man at eighteen or twenty."[73]

If the historical trend was an overall lengthening of youth dependency, the end of adolescence was materially designated: it simply accorded with the family's economic situation, which, by and large, determined the options available to the young. Growing up in British Columbia, Jim's experience during the late 1920s was not uncommon. His family's financial needs prompted him to leave school at fourteen, when his father took him to Cranbrook Sawmills to find work: "I got a job as a bull cook first, then I was on the slab saw and then I worked as a flunky in the kitchen, and . . . what they call the green chain, on the pond, had to wear cork boots and run around on the floating logs on the pond. Push them into the green chain with a pike pole and got into the mill then. . . . The wages were forty dollars a month and board. Six day week, ten hour days."[74]

Contemporaries recognized that most adolescents left school to join the workforce because the contributions of wage-earning children remained important to many families. In 1931, half of all male heads of families earned between $500 and $1,500 per year. About two-thirds earned less than $1,200, while more than 40 per cent earned less than $500, or less than $10 weekly based on an entire year's consistent employment. The typical married wage-earner was unlikely to earn more than $100 a month.[75] The minimum standard for a decent standard of living would have to be $1,500, at a time when 40 per cent of skilled workers earned $1,000 or less. Even this, however, was not an income granting "any sure access to the amenities of modern civilized life, apart altogether from the wider freedom of education, social intercourse and cultivated leisure." Even at "the most frugal calculation," the minimum necessary annual income for that would have to be about $2,000, characteristic only of the managerial, professional, and "higher grade commercial and clerical" families that constituted the upper 15 per cent of wage and salary earners. At a "generous estimate," this was no more than a quarter of all Canadian families.[76]

The average income of all male family heads in 1931 was $1,185, while the average family income was somewhat higher, at $1,366. The wages of other family members were evidently supplementing those of the primary breadwinner, a custom of long standing in working-class families.[77] The usual order of supplementation in terms of financial importance was that of sons, then daughters, and finally wives.[78] The "low skilled service group," which included janitors, laundry workers, messengers, elevator tenders, and office cleaners, revealed the largest proportion of earning children, as "partly by choice but probably more by necessity," few in this group continued at school beyond age fourteen.[79] The families of industrial workers lived very close to "precarious margins," while the families of the semi-skilled and unskilled were "almost wholly below the margin if they [had] to rely on the father's earnings."

The earnings of their adolescent members kept many families above the subsistence level. For the greater proportion of this occupational class (300,000 families, or 40 per cent of wage-earner families in 1931), however, the combined resources of breadwinners and other working family members were inadequate. The number of farm families with "no certainty of a bare living income," according to Marsh, amounted to about one-fifth of the total.[80] Yet, at least insofar as their contributions were measurable in wages, the children and wives of the poorest families contributed, in round numbers, only two hundred dollars per year. Even accounting for other means of supplementing the family income, including unwaged labour and unmeasured wage labour, the result suggests a smaller contribution than might be assumed, implying also that working children kept a good part of their income for their own use. As members of modernizing families, their chief contribution could possibly have entailed attending to their own needs while continuing to live at home in a state most accurately described as semi-dependency. If working children were relatively self-supporting within the family, this would benefit the family overall without greatly affecting its total income.[81] Where adolescent offspring contributed significant amounts from their wages—as many would have been obliged to do when the chief breadwinner was unemployed—the "family cycle of dependency and 'son-and-daughter-income'" usually permitted only short-lived gains in family living standards: sons reached marriage age before reaching their maximum earning period, and daughters attained both within a few years of each other. Fully earning adults, Marsh concluded, were probably found in "broken families" more often than in "normal" ones.[82]

While the majority of young working Canadians had been financially unable to leave the parental home even during prosperous times, the Depression very quickly reinforced the formidable obstacles before them. Already in 1930, it was estimated that fully 70 per cent of the unemployed were single men and youths; many of the latter were the first of the Depression school-leavers—a cohort that would not secure regular full-time employment until the decade's end.[83] Among those who did manage to find or retain work, age was a telling factor in wages earned. In Montreal, young men under twenty earned even less, with an average weekly pay of $9.88, than did adult women, historically the lowest-paid of adult workers. Young women made the least of all groups: earning about $8.40 per week, they averaged about 85 per cent of the earnings of their male peers.[84] Among the younger earners, the gendered wage differential was much lower, the greatest gap being the one that separated age groups. Young men garnered 38 per cent of what adult males earned and 73 per cent of adult female earnings; young women, at the very bottom, made 32 per cent of adult male earnings and 62 per cent of adult female earnings. Both were a long way from the wages of the iconic adult male breadwinner.[85]

The prime justifications for the low wage rates of workers under twenty were their "green" status as unskilled, inexperienced labourers and the necessity that employers spend time and money providing some modicum of training. The immediate post–World War I years saw a number of joint business-government initiatives to revive and modernize apprenticeship, the traditional contractual relationship that assured (mostly) young men, usually at a very low rate of pay, on-the-job skills training. The Royal Commission on Industrial Training and Technical Education (the Macdonald-Robertson Commission), reporting in 1913, had stressed that a modern industrial nation such as Canada was in great need of skilled workers, that there was a shortage of these in the land, and that Canadian businesses, on the whole, were reluctant to take on the responsibility and cost of training their own, much preferring to look to immigration to fill the need.[86] The commissioners found that there was "practically unanimity" among those who testified that the federal government should promote industrial training and technical education through financial assistance of secondary school and night school programs and through expansion of the existing facilities.[87] Such state involvement was critical within the context of a rapidly changing economy, with its consequences for youth labour, especially in regard to preparing the young to become efficient and productive adult workers. Postponed by the war, the outcome was the federal Technical Education Act of 1919.

On the wane since the late nineteenth century, the traditional form of apprenticeship did not disappear entirely during these years, although it was much modified. In the printing trades, apprenticeship under written contract remained the recognized gateway, at least in larger establishments. A number of other trades operated under a looser form of contractual relationship, whereby a young worker would begin training under an informal, usually verbal agreement, "in accordance with known conditions obtaining in the plant"; the car shops of the railway companies were notable examples of this sort of training commitment.[88] On the whole, however, the development of industry and the demand for labour were leading to the abandonment of the traditional apprenticeship system, which restricted jobs to those who had completed a fairly lengthy formal training. Mechanization, especially assembly-line production, had cut into the need for specialized skills in a number of areas, creating a demand instead for machine tenders, who would quickly pick up the skills necessary to work a particular machine in some part of the production process. In many trades, therefore, adolescents working alongside adults could be taught enough knowledge of the necessary operations to carry them out without any apprenticeship-like contractual obligation, either on the part of the employer to train them or on the part of the young worker to become an all-round craftsman. It was argued that the burgeoning of this type of specialized work, which held out the prospect of high initial earnings, encouraged impatient youth to forsake the future for short-term gain.[89]

Because of such public concerns, and by means of the assistance allocated to the provinces under the 1919 Technical Education Act, some progress was made in reviving formal apprenticeship in the early postwar years, particularly in the building trades, where mechanization had made fewer inroads. In 1921, the manufacturing industries had 1,790 formal apprentices in the under-sixteen age group; the majority (5,232) came from the sixteen-to-seventeen age group. Of these totals, 614 were females fourteen to fifteen years old, and 1,796 were females fifteen to seventeen. Most of the young women were training as dressmakers and seamstresses. The only significant overlap between young women and men was in the printing and bookbinding trades, but even there, men greatly outnumbered women: there were 416 under-sixteen boys in these trades by comparison to 162 girls, and 1,032 young men over sixteen to 407 young women. The other significant areas for female apprenticeship were the traditional feminine crafts of tailoring (635) and millinery (499), but here the term *apprentice* meant little more than "beginner." In these trades, where women again were classified as temporary workers, there were seldom formal agreements, but there was an implicit understanding that young women would be trained on the job and would receive commensurate pay.[90]

As discussed, the cornerstone of the modern apprenticeship system was the technical school. A small number of these predated the Great War. The Toronto Technical School opened with much fanfare in 1913, its "national and industrial importance" matched by its "importance as a factor in the development of the human race"; its very architecture was proclaimed "a monument in honour of the dignity of labour."[91] In 1925, the new Hamilton Technical School would come to play a central role in that city's industrial training. Arrangements were made with the building trades employers for carpentry and bricklaying apprentices to attend classes in related drafting and practical work. The courses of study were jointly arranged by the participating businesses and the school. Employers were held responsible for the attendance, remuneration, and discipline of the apprentices, while the school co-ordinated their instruction and living arrangements. The attainment of journeyman ranking required that the apprentice successfully complete a series of examinations as well as the employment contract. At the request of Hamilton employers, the plan was quickly extended to make similar provision for plastering, plumbing, sheet metal, electrical installation, and painting apprentices. The plan appeared to work: from fewer than fifty industrial apprentices, all from one company, in 1923, attendance had tripled to over 150 apprentices from fifteen of the city's leading industries by 1929.[92]

Hamilton's encouraging results lent support to the passage of the Ontario Apprenticeship Act in 1928. Modelled on this training scheme, the Act was intended to bring about a modern, state-regulated form of apprenticeship. All contracts were registered with a provincial inspector of apprenticeship under the auspices of the labour department. Apprentices were to be no younger than sixteen years and no older than eighteen at the start of their four-year training, and were required to have successfully completed the work of the junior fourth book in order to be accepted into the program. The act also fixed the ratio of apprentices to journeymen in each trade and established guidelines for the terms of apprenticeship, the wages to be paid, and the nature of shop-floor and in-class training. Apprentices attended special day classes for eight weeks, with five eight-hour days or 320 class hours in total, during each of their first and second years. Weekly allowances were paid to them while they were in school and, if necessary, they were provided with railway fares to the nearest town where these special classes were held. Third- and fourth-year apprentices were required to attend evening classes twice weekly from October to March, with fees paid by the apprentice.[93]

In October 1930, the Ontario Apprenticeship Act registered 1,386 apprentices; the plurality (432) were in plumbing, with the next highest number (210) in electrical installation. The smallest number (12) was in masonry, among the most traditional of the trades. Without any possibility of foreseeing the duration and depth of the economic crisis at hand, the success of the joint Hamilton Technical School/employer program prompted A.W. Crawford, inspector of apprenticeship, to announce the expansion of training classes to vocational-technical high schools in Toronto, London, Windsor, and Ottawa. Where the number of apprentices in any particular trade at any centre did not justify local classes, apprentices would be sent to another centre. During attendance at these eight-week in-class sessions, which were directed by the provincial education department, each apprentice received a living allowance of ten dollars per week in lieu of wages. Money for this purpose and for necessary railway fares was provided from the Assessment Fund, into which employers in the designated trades contributed one-eighth of 1 per cent of their annual payroll. The tuition fees and all costs of instruction were shared by the municipalities and the provincial government.[94] Ontario's inspector of apprenticeship reported how "gratifying" it was that the apprentices who had attended classes were, "with very few exceptions, eager to receive further instruction" and that visitors to the classes were "astonished at the excellence of the work done and somewhat surprised at the keen interest of the apprentices." Even employers initially critical of the scheme, he declared, were "compelled, after visiting the classes, to admit that at least this branch of the work is well worth while."[95]

But just as the Ontario plan was really taking off, it was derailed by Depression cutbacks in both industrial production and state expenditure. Lack of money impeded the establishment of classes in a number of centres during the winter of 1932. Apprentices from all parts of the province had to attend the session at the Hamilton Technical School, contributing to the problem of ready accessibility that was considered to be the most worrisome of "our troubles in developing this new system of apprenticeship." Hamilton was chosen because of the "splendid facilities" offered by its new technical school, but also because the vocational-technical high schools in other cities were becoming crowded as more young people stayed in school or returned to it for lack of employment options. Ontario Apprenticeship Branch reports through the remainder of the 1930s lament the disastrous effect of economic decline on the number of apprenticeship positions. Apprentices already indentured faced unsteady employment and layoffs, as employers could not provide for them without "laying off old employees, married men with families, whom they felt had the first claim to any work available." It was becoming increasingly difficult to collect the fees that constituted the employers' share of the cost of in-class time. By 1932, the labour department decided to suspend assessment rather than impose any additional expense on employers. At the Depression's worst in 1933, with unemployment at an all-time high, the Apprenticeship Branch found it "impractical" to carry out many of the requirements of the Act. Employers were simply asked to do their best for apprentices, and many temporary transfers were effected in an effort to keep the young men—eight hundred contracts in all—employed. It was clearly inadvisable to encourage the registration of new apprentices until conditions improved.[96]

Provinces with similar plans followed suit.[97] The Vancouver Apprenticeship Council had to amend its own regulations requiring contractors to retain indentured apprentices with full pay regardless of the work available. The council consented to the layoff of indentured apprentices during slack seasons because of the "unusual conditions now existing." Youth unemployment was quite simply the "worst feature" of the ongoing depression, not only for its noteworthy current effects, but also because "many of the boys growing up today in idleness will be too old to learn a trade when business picks up."[98] By the winter of 1934, the number of apprentices had so declined that the Ontario board could not justify the expense of holding special classes for them.[99] Finally, in mid-1936, the chief inspector was obliged to pronounce the Apprenticeship Act "dormant." The number of active contracts in the nine designated trades was now only 319.[100]

The national opinion surveys of youth (aged 15 to 24) conducted by the Canadian Youth Commission during World War II stressed the value of apprenticeship to ease the transition from school to full-time wage-earning. At the same time, however, the CYC interviews uncovered a common view that "in the modern shop with its clearly defined jobs, there [was] little place for the youthful learner," who was regarded as "more of a nuisance than anything else." Young Canadians considered existing apprenticeship systems "inadequate and usually not attractive," mainly because of low wages and insecurity. Consequently, the young—almost exclusively young men—were "apt to take on any good job that turn[ed] up rather than wait on the chances of learnership."[101] This problem was considered to be anything but "a simple one": in the mid-1940s, there were more than a million young Canadians aged sixteen to twenty, and "except in periods of full employment, private industry has difficulty in making room for all the beginning workers in search of jobs."[102]

The unemployment crisis of the 1930s assailed the young, especially those just leaving school, with particular fury. The period's statistics are known to underplay the true extent of joblessness, but a sense of the desperate situation for youth seeking work is nonetheless conveyed by the numbers available. During the worst years, 1931 to 1933, some 300,000 workers over the age of fourteen were unemployed.[103] Using supplementary census data, contemporary analysts accounted for at least 200,000 of these displaced wage earners. The largest proportion of them—more than half the total (105,000)—were classified as "new entrants, 17 and under, unabsorbed by wage employment." Another 14,000 were "urban adolescents reaching the ages of 18 to 24." Approximately 79,000 of this group, of whom an important sector were likely in this same age range, were farmers' sons returning from their now-obliterated city jobs and displacing hired farm labour.[104] The statistics also suggest that about two-thirds of each year's "crop" of young men leaving school was consistently without gainful employment, implying an average two years of idleness for all non-farm boys. The number of girls in the same category was estimated to be about one-third as large, although it is here that the numbers most likely underestimate the true extent of joblessness. Young dependent women were more likely to give up their job search or to perform unpaid and unaccounted-for labour in the family home, under societal pressure to leave jobs to male breadwinners. The available data, rough edges and all, indicate a proportion of youth unemployment during the darkest years that amounted to about one-fifth of the total Canadian workforce. In the Prairie provinces, one of the foremost effects was a net decline in population, the exodus consisting largely of single men; the migration from Saskatchewan was of such scope that it actually depleted the existing ranks of youth labour.[105] As Marsh surmised, "even on the minimum basis of estimate...the youth problem is serious enough."[106]

Local studies of youth unemployment bear out the estimates derived from the aggregate census data. A 1934 YMCA survey of nine hundred Montreal boys who had left high school between 1931 and that year found only 44.4 per cent of their number employed in some capacity, and not necessarily full-time. Excluding those who had returned to school primarily because they could not find work, the unemployment rate was approximately 30 per cent. The survey committee urged more community interest in "the whole problem of the plight of youth," now clearly "a matter of national importance."[107] Among Toronto public school, collegiate, and technical/commercial students who left school in 1936, 20 per cent of young men and 30 per cent of young women reported themselves unemployed a year later, a proportion the surveyors conceded would likely have been "far greater" had they tracked down the "unknown" 20 per cent.[108] A 1937 Halifax survey found that adolescent males "directly or indirectly dependent upon material aid" had reached the "startling total" of 1,100, yet those on relief represented "only a small part of the total number of unemployed juveniles," because most would be in the care of their families and therefore not separately listed on the municipal rolls.[109]

Nowhere was the condition of youth worse than on the nation's impoverished Native reserves. As a professional social worker and committed socialist, Dorothy Livesay was horrified by what she found on those that she visited during the Depression, which had rendered life for the young even more fraught than usual:

Nearly the whole island [of Caughnawaugha, in Quebec] is on relief....
And what of the youth? In the winter they face complete idleness. In the summer, the canning factories at St Hilaire, twenty miles away, open

their doors to Caughnawaugha. The bus fare there and back takes twenty five cents out of the day's pay. The girls arrive in the morning at seven. They are paid seventy-five cents for every hundred pounds of vegetables, but two hundred pounds is the limit for a good day. Most days are much poorer and involve a great deal of waiting which goes unpaid for. It is a common thing for a girl to come home at six at night with only thirty five cents in her pocket—the rest of the days' earnings having been paid out in bus fare. Under conditions like these, the youth is called "degenerate."[110]

One Dumfries, New Brunswick, boy, at the age of fourteen, worked for a farmer for a dollar a day: "I did all his farming; pitching on sixty five loads of hay, nineteen loads of straw, and plowing for him that fall.... The next year I worked for [another farmer] for 135 days earning $1.00 a day." By the time he was sixteen, the Depression had deepened; with some friends, he found work cutting hardwood at a logging camp, but "we couldn't make a dollar a day so we quit and came home." He then chopped cord wood for fifty cents a day, a job he kept "for the next two or three winters" because "times were hard.... You did well to get enough to eat."[111] Ironically, young women were in some ways better positioned to find work, because of the nature of the work they were expected to do and because they were paid less than men. But these very reasons, along with the strong public belief that work should go to men, meant that they also faced serious difficulties. In Saskatchewan, probably the worst hit of all the provinces, Vida Richard was eighteen years old when the Depression began: "I was trying to get my first job. Things were sure rough. Sometimes I used to clean a woman's house once a week for my room. I would babysit for her, twenty-five cents a night. Then I got a job as a cashier in the evening in a little café, two nights a week, twenty-five cents an hour.... During the Depression they used to tell you, if you can't do this for this price, we'll get someone who can.[112] As late as mid-1939, it was estimated that there were still some 250,000 young people "who had never had a real job in their lives." Among employed youth, many were working only part-time, with inadequate wages, approaching "near destitution in agriculture."[113]

The dispensability of youth labour in hard times made for rough conditions both in finding employment and on the job but did not entirely quell the spirit of youth to resist their employers' attempts to exploit them. The burgeoning leisure industries of the 1920s still attracted enough better-off participants during the "Dirty Thirties" to employ young men, frequently younger adolescents (thirteen to sixteen), at times in competition with married men who could not find other work. But wages and working conditions were often unsatisfactory—and easily justified thanks to the all-too-ready surplus of available labour. Caddies and "pinboys" at bowling alleys were particularly hard-pressed. By organizing and striking, they managed to defy those people, starting with their employers, who argued that they should be grateful to have paying jobs at all and that they were working merely for pocket money. In confronting both work-related issues and the public notions that made the young into disposable labour because of their age and familial dependency, they earned their badges as "the only groups of youthful workers who consistently struck during the Great Depression."[114]

As was historically their lot, the inexperienced and untrained young were relegated to the unskilled, undervalued labour that was insecure and poorly paid at the best of times; now this too became a highly competitive sector. The young were also the lowest-ranked in the hierarchy of the "deserving," especially young women. A certain moralism about the youth problem thus continued after the Depression's effective extinguishing of "flaming youth." Even such sympathetic social scientists as Marsh and his McGill associates contended that young people—and their parents—must shoulder some part of the responsibility for youth unemployment. Employers complained that young people were unwilling to "begin at the bottom," were inclined to see on-the-job learning as "meaningless apprenticeship," and seldom worked at the level of efficiency of which they were "physically and intellectually capable." The unwarranted ambitions of parents were also to blame, as they strove to "place their children in the best positions, regardless of their limitations."[115] Parents intent on upward mobility for their offspring showed a "growing disregard of the primary industries": they needed reminding that "a successful machinist has a much greater chance for happiness and presents a far more impressive spectacle than an executive failure." Most revealing in its tone of intergenerational suspicion was the idea that the young had been "spoiled" by "adherence to an abnormally high standard of living" during the prosperous times of their childhood. As one expert on youth unemployment declared, parents had "overstressed the importance of the material rewards" for work, the result being that Canadian youth had lost "what might be called for want of a better term, the 'pioneer spirit' and in its place has grown up an outlook that is undeniably materialistic."[116]

The older generation thus pointed once again to the fundamental moral flaw that was seen to typify the rising generation: an overblown materialism fuelled by the heightened expectations of the 1920s, when modernity elevated the things and pastimes that mass production was bringing within reach of more social groups. As higher living standards and educational levels made upward mobility at least a reasonable prospect, parents wanted more for their children than their own lot in life, and the young saw that "more" might be attainable. Labelled "materialistic" and therefore cast within a context of failed virtue, such optimistic goals were reinterpreted as threats to the "natural order"—especially when they belonged to a hard-hit social group during a moment of profound destabilization. Wanting—and holding out for—something "more" made youth unemployment a character flaw. For some, even helping young people to find jobs seemed "a hopeless task...for the simple reason that so many of them are seeking work and hoping they will not find it." The vestiges of an atavistic Poor Law notion that unemployment destroyed all incentive to work or even to live an "upright" life battled the more sentient view that youth's attitude to work could only be "an outgrowth of their own environment," in that continual rejection generated despondency.[117]

Among the Mackenzie King Liberal government's Depression-fighting measures was the establishment in 1935 of the National Employment Commission. The NEC's 1937 report strongly urged federal-provincial initiatives on behalf of the nation's youth, more specifically, training and apprentice courses. That year, the King government launched the Dominion-Provincial Youth Training Programme with $1,000,000 of federal money.[118] The plan initially applied to those eighteen to thirty years of age but was quickly amended to make the lower limit sixteen years.[119] Applicants were to be "without gainful employment and in necessitous circumstances," and not in school or in other training programs. The selection process, to be undertaken "without discrimination or favour in regard to racial origin, religious beliefs or political affiliations," was left to the provinces. The prime objective was to keep these young Canadians occupied and off public relief, and to place them in a position "to secure available jobs" by developing their "resourcefulness, skill and independence."[120] According to New Brunswick's director of education, "national interests" made training in citizenship and physical education "one of the most important" of the scheme's purposes. Most provinces conducted "leadership training" work through "study clubs" that used citizenship as their main theme.[121] Classifying the "youth problem" as "a permanent one," the best solution was the provision of "more freedom from discouraging, cramping or exacting work, more systematic guidance facilities and in general a better environment for Canadians in the 'teen ages, both urban and rural." Keeping the young in school or in some form of training would also relieve the pressure on the labour market "at the stage at which it is likely to do most harm" to them, thus preserving and ensuring, in better-educated and better-trained youth, "the major Canadian reserve against the future." A total of 55,457 young Canadians, of whom 32,301 were men, received training in 1,474 classes during the first year of the program's operation, though only about 14,650, male and female, finished courses "of a character to fit them for employment." Of this number, 3,282 (2,064 men and 1,218 women), or slightly over 22 per cent, found work, thus confirming the official view that "work can be found by at least some of Canada's unemployed young people provided they are equipped by training to do it."[122]

The Canadian Youth Commission, which owed its very creation in 1940 to the King government's recognition of the Depression's toll on the young, emphasized how the experience had imprinted this generation. Surveying youth organizations across the nation, the CYC "quickly discovered that no one under thirty remembered normal times. . . . So deep are the scars left upon Canadian youth from the Depression years that any of their discussions of postwar employment were prefaced . . . by reference back to what had been and what must never come again."[123] As one Quebec youth group submitted, unemployment caused more damage among young people than among adults: "It confuses them in a period of adaptation and development, undermines their confidence in life and can even destroy their latent possibilities."[124] The CYC's final report on this topic, *Youth and Jobs*, urged national responsibility for full employment. The commission wanted to see programs for youth aged sixteen to twenty-one that offered paid work "of varied kinds" as well as physical, vocational and citizenship training, the latter to ensure "the experience of democratic living."[125] Remembering the Depression's army-regulated work camps for single unemployed men, the majority of youth polled expressed their opposition to any idea of compulsory national service. Instead they called for "projects of general value" that offered "real wages," including conservation; construction of rural schools, libraries, parks, shelters, and tennis courts; and a variety of possible services to public and private agencies. The "real objective" of the plan would be the development of "good citizens who would find a normal place for themselves in the life of the community."[126] Like their elders, the young adopted the language of citizenship and national welfare—a language that obviously held much resonance for Canadians of this time—to promote their generational ends.

By 1940, three broad youth-employment trends had become evident. First, not surprisingly, the wide-open field of unskilled and semi-skilled labour remained the predominant employer of the youngest among the under-twenties; second, white-collar vocations, represented by the clerical and professional occupations, did not recruit substantial numbers until the ages of seventeen or eighteen; third, the level "distinguished either by seniority and experience or extended education" recruited hardly at all before the age of twenty-one and often long after that age. Recruitment to the skilled trades among workers under twenty-one was relatively small-scale, although, as discussed, it had been showing some signs of growth before the crash of 1929.[127] For urban youths, the largest occupational fields appeared to "wax and then wane" in rhythm with their stage of adolescence, some very early and others toward the end. The lowest service category, comprising store delivery boys, messengers, bellboys, and predominantly female domestic servants, lost members rapidly as early as the age of seventeen, a "mortality" that characterized the so-called blind-alley or stopgap occupation. While some young Canadians moved on of their own accord, with a "noticeable influx" to the intermediate manual groups at the ages of seventeen and eighteen, these were lines of work where younger employees were actually most in demand. By the age of seventeen, "boys' rates" had to be raised, making it more profitable for employers to replace the maturing delivery boy from a younger and cheaper reserve. Likewise, the intermediate service sector, although open slightly longer, was fairly closed to persons over twenty-one years old. The largest category open to the under-twenties, therefore, was unskilled industrial work, mainly light factory jobs. Yet the ephemeral nature of work in this area is revealed in the fact that it also accounted for the largest number of the unemployed.[128]

Published on the eve of World War II, Leonard Marsh's employment study concluded on an ominous note where jobs for Canadian adolescents, most particularly future male breadwinners, were concerned: "The narrowing of opportunity on the very threshold of manhood thus backs up on itself...a large part of the fund of labour which in the 'teens may seem to have wide scope." Some young workers might feel the pressure after their first job, at fifteen or sixteen;

others experienced it at nineteen or twenty, when the supply of unskilled labour was enlarged by migrants from the farm and overseas, who tended to be somewhat older, and when learner posts were much harder to find, with most provinces adhering to an upper age limit of twenty-one years for formal apprenticeship.[129] Young women encountered the restraining effects of market demand even sooner. The service category, already disproportionately composed of women, contained fewer eighteen and nineteen year olds than any other age, while the numbers of "light" factory workers among women also declined after the age of twenty. Marriage partly explains the decline, but age was also an important factor: there was more demand for younger girls in these areas, and younger girls—with little or no experience and consequently few alternatives—were also more likely to take up the jobs. Cheap female labour was typically a little younger than cheap male labour as a result. Sharing a common view, Marsh argued that young women's own attitudes and ambitions most often shaped their prospects. He conceded, however, that modern industry's growing dependence on young unskilled female labour, and the evidence of oversupply in white-collar fields, made it impossible to regard the problem of training and entry-level positions for youth "as only a male one."[130]

None of these findings about the youth labour market and the nature of employment during the interwar years is startling. By World War II, employment beyond the dead-end or blind-alley jobs was contingent on the education of the job-seeker—a fact underscored by the economic crisis just ending. Put simply, the steadier, better-paying, and more promising jobs accrued to the better-schooled—and therefore usually older—of the youth sector, especially among young men. The data call into question any notion of a "golden age" for unskilled youth employment that might have existed before schooling or specialized training, as well as maturity, were requisite. Gaining entry into the world of wage labour, especially for those who left school before age sixteen, was challenging simply because of their age. The majority of that group stepped into adulthood as cheap and dispensable labour. Nor was this simply an outcome of the Depression. Long-term structural changes in production meant that modern commerce and industry had fewer places than formerly for beginners, the vast majority of whom were under twenty. Many of the unskilled jobs customarily the lot of the young were now performed by machinery; many of the new jobs resulting from production changes required the skills, or at least the experience base, of older workers. In fact, reasoned the Canadian Youth Commission, in "a great majority" of cases, even when the work was classified "unskilled," jobs called for "a certain physical and mental maturity" and "a degree of emotional stability" that Canadian youth, "from the very fact that they are young," could not be expected to have. It was generally believed that, where under-eighteens were employed, "the usual experience" was higher costs to the employer because of age-related higher accident rates, breakage and wastage, the extra supervision required, and the higher rates of turnover.[131]

Technological advances had made increased training a prerequisite of employment. For many young Canadians, certain occupational paths were thus closed: their families lacked the means to provide for this training. This was especially the case in the category of white-collar and professional employment, the means of entrance into which were tightly class-, race-, and gender-delimited as well as age-defined. The CYC's 1943 national youth opinion survey showed that 40 per cent of young Canadians would enter the professions if they could, in stark contrast to the 5 to 6 per cent of high school students who actually went on to the university courses that the professions demanded—and the population of high school students, while steadily on the rise, still represented less than half of the public school population. Most commentators were agreed that education, including vocational guidance, was the solution. What was needed above all was "a detailed occupational outlook service for the whole school leaving population," which would allow for "constructive and scientific planning for Canadian youth."[132]

The social significance of youth labour meant that even a healthy economy did little to quell worries about what the young should appropriately be trained and employed to do. During the early years of World War II, with the economy running full-throttle and a shortage of adult male labour looming, a *Saturday Night* magazine contributor surmised that many boys and girls aged fourteen and fifteen were being permitted to leave school to do "necessary war work," despite the fact that most provinces had by then raised the age of school-leaving to sixteen.[133] Enticed by the opportunities presented by the war economy, the 30,911 teenagers who left Toronto high schools in 1943–44 immediately sought full-time work.[134] After years of "making do," "stretching," going without, and barely getting by, Canadian families were taking advantage of new opportunities to catch up and "get ahead." Those who came of age during the hard times were naturally eager to earn and to buy. Young people themselves, even while happy to "have a swell job, earning good money," as one young man described his situation, also considered the long-term repercussions: "I gave up my studies to take the job because we needed money badly and here was the chance. I know I won't have it much longer, and I won't have my education either. Maybe I was wrong to give up school. I'm not fit for any skilled work."[135] In the *Saturday Night* commentator's view, which was shared by many others, the war effort and "doing your bit" were unquestionably important, but "the future health, success and happiness of thousands of our young people, which means the future wealth of the country," demanded more serious protection.[136]

Across the nation, young people performed essential work for the war effort as adult labour, both male and female, became increasingly scarce. Girls over sixteen joined the Farmerettes Brigade of the Women's Land Army, staying in camps and performing eight to ten hours of farm work each day for twenty-four cents an hour.[137] In the cities, girls like fifteen-year-old Rita were recruited to do messenger service for various federal agencies in Ottawa. Rita was one of thirty-odd young people employed by the Consumer Branch of the federal government. Although anaemic and diabetic, she worked from 9:00 to 5:30, attended night school three nights per week to learn typing and shorthand, and "in her spare

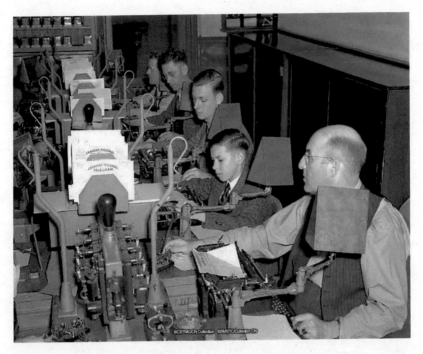

Teenage telephone operators, CN Images of Canada Gallery, CN001976. Canadian Science and Technology Museum, Ottawa. www.imagescn.technomuses.ca.

Teenagers were an important labour resource during the manpower shortage of World War II. This photograph depicts sixteen-year-old telegraph operators in the Canadian National Telegraphs office, Edmonton, AB.

time, she sings, plays the piano and tap dances." According to *Chatelaine* magazine, her hard work and energy ensured that "Rita has a future."[138] In Montreal, Mary Peate had no difficulty finding work in the typing pool, alongside many other teenage girls with minimal training and often no experience at all. At the age of sixteen, having completed a business course and one interview, she was working nine to six on weekdays, nine to one on Saturdays, for eighty-two dollars per month. She gave her widowed mother half her monthly pay for room and board, "and with the rest I'd pay for my clothes, streetcar fare, lunches, entertainment, make-up and toilet articles."[139]

The circumstances of prolonged economic crisis, followed immediately by global conflict, placed the generations coming of age during and shortly after World War II in a historically tenuous position where employment was concerned. The small prospects for youth during the 1930s, coupled with the ephemeral nature of employment "for the duration," meant that the war's end could conceivably flood the labour market with several waves of relatively inexperienced and untrained workers under the age of thirty—of whom the over-twenties would be most

Telegraph "messengerette" E. Miller, Toronto, 1942. CN Images of Canada Gallery, CN000430. Canadian Science and Technology Museum, Ottawa. www.imagescn.technomuses.ca

The exigencies of war meant that young women were also called upon to serve, many of them in such "non-traditional" occupations as bicycle courier.

likely to succeed in finding work. The National Employment Service, established by the landmark Unemployment Insurance Act of 1940, set up special youth employment depots in select urban centres across the nation. The Toronto centre, opened in February 1946, was to be the prototype. In addition to helping job-seekers aged sixteen to twenty-one years to find employment, it was intended to provide vocational guidance, including aptitude testing.[140]

Magazines gave much advice to the postwar generation of adolescent job-seekers, fresh out of school, who had "the doubtful privilege of being in the vanguard of masses of brand-new workers trying to get established." The war's end also put an end to the labour shortage that had fed "the eager acceptance" of inexperienced and, "let's face it, often irresponsible youth."[141] While there were jobs to be had for teenagers, according to *Chatelaine* magazine a number of employers had indicated that "some of you aren't hep yet to the rapid change in conditions since V-E day." Ten out of twelve teenagers recently hired at a Toronto textile plant were dropped by the end of the first month, because they "didn't bother" to come to work on time, stayed home "on the slightest pretext," or did not follow the instructions of their foreman. The magazine advised its young female readers that at any interview they would be "checked on four important points: appearance, manner, speech, [and] qualifications."[142] Realistically, they should expect that entry-level jobs would net them "around $17 to $22 a week...more likely $17." They were also advised to pay room and board to their families even if they were not asked to do so, because the practice "gets you into the habit of being self-sufficient and you'll pause before wasting your hard-earned, rationed money." Finally, young women would "do better on the old wedding-ring round-up the harder you work now, because the more successful you are the more interesting men you'll meet."[143]

For many young Canadians, the adolescence that regulatory legislation permitted them amounted to only a brief respite from adult responsibility, namely, that of earning their keep. Among farm and working-class youth, full-time labour remained the true rite of passage. The sixteenth birthday—official age of school-leaving in most provinces by the end of the 1920s—marked their obligatory entry into the adult world of work.[144] Also important is the fact that few adolescents could strike out entirely on their own even if working for full-time wages. Because the economic independence that signifies adulthood was controlled by adults in authority—whether parents demanding a share of wages, a society that increasingly pegged career prospects to higher levels of formal schooling and training, or employers who slotted the young into low-paid, casual, often part-time and ephemeral or "blind-alley" jobs—socio-economic status would remain firmly age-delimited.

6

At Play

Fads, Fashions, and Fun

It is time that the civic conscience awakened to the debauchery and degrading circumstances of the dance halls...the reeking atmosphere...the absolutely inevitable stirring of sexual passion entailed in the so-called jitney and other similar dances.
— *Guelph Daily Mercury, 1921*

*I*n October 1921 a "large gathering" reportedly collected in Guelph, Ontario, to hear a local preacher discuss the social and spiritual repercussions of the "youth dance craze." The speaker cited expert evidence, from "authorities who had no interest in the religious aspects," who proclaimed young dance hall patrons to be "failures in classroom and physical culture." It was urgent that responsible citizens "lend their influence in remedying these conditions."[1] Such an impassioned outcry against dance halls cannot be dismissed as simply clerical duty in the salvation of young souls. The small-town preacher's dismay about the antics of modern youth was replicated across a multiplicity of discourses, religious and secular, "expert" and non-expert. Its language of moral outrage and foreboding only thinly veiled the real issue: the youth autonomy symbolized by the "palaces for pleasure" that were the burgeoning commercial amusement places of the time. Whatever these places sold as entertainment, they were important bases for a modern style of recreation that was very much geared to the young consumer, a vital emergent market for producers and sellers of goods as well as mass entertainment.

By the 1920s, Canadian adolescents were spending much of their leisure time, as well as greater amounts of money in the pursuit of leisure, apart from their families and out of the home. With children at school and adults occupied by housekeeping and wage labour, truly free time was very much the dominion of the in-betweens. They were enjoying greater social freedom in the streets and public venues, and more selection in the widening array of modern amusements available as a result of technological advances and mass production. Along with their own enthusiastic participation, these factors were shaping a youth culture expressed through leisure activity, much of which involved cash transactions in commercial venues, a thoroughly modern and increasingly democratic endeavour.[2] This chapter considers how popular culture and modern adolescence became entwined in the public eye during these years, eventually coming to constitute the youth problem in essence. The matter of how the young had fun was grounded in larger issues of citizenship, national welfare, and the very nature of modernity, with its ethic of consumption and its "new" and highly questionable morality.

Consumer culture held out enticing possibilities to those who could buy. Therein, of course, could be found its contradictions. More people were being urged to buy more, and mass production meant that more people actually could. But there obviously remained very real material limits on what some, as individuals and as members of certain social groups, could reasonably buy. In this respect, age mattered as much as did class, race and gender in delimiting the extent and nature of consumer participation. Producers and advertisers of the time were finding the youth market as promising as the expanding market of wage-earning women—with much overlap between the two. The young were easily the social group most captivated by the latest and newest of all things and activities, and most likely to embrace the technologies required to make and deliver whatever manner of goods. Public understanding of this inclination fuelled much concern about unrestrained youthful hedonism and its wider national implications. But the young were constrained by the fact that, even for those who earned their own wages, their very youth necessarily impinged on the amounts that they could spend and thus on their freedom to spend, restricting them for the most part to cheap amusements. Nonetheless, young people had enough "play money" to warrant the establishment of a youth market as early as the 1920s. To those intent on delivering the goods and services of the modern age, it became apparent over this period that, as well as buying, youth sells.[3]

These "contradictions and connections between the promises and the limitations of consumer culture," as American historian Nan Enstad demonstrates, are worth exploring for what they offer about the ways in which certain social groups managed and manoeuvred their own "matrix of meanings" in daily life. More to the point, while consumer culture offered working-class women "a new range of representations, symbols, activities and spaces with which to create class, gender and ethnic identities," it is evident that adolescents likewise "embraced these new resources and created practices that were in themselves a form of politics in that they shifted the cultural terrain," in some respects at least, to address their own generational needs and interests.[4] In the process—and more visibly than in any other area of adolescent life and culture, as this chapter indicates—each of the generations studied here developed the entelechy that was its historic identity.

While industrialization did not obliterate traditional popular culture, it did hasten its fragmentation. The breakdown in skills and the advent of mass production weakened shop-floor craft culture. Remnants of preindustrial rituals and pranks, often featuring young apprentices, which had combined sociability and labour in the workplace, were suppressed under the new code of production that demanded strict attention to the task at hand under a system in which "time is money." In conjunction with this decline of a masculine work-based culture, however, young workers of both sexes attained access to more jobs, to more and freer contact at work and outside, to some money of their own, and to the consequent ability to leave work at day's end and go out to buy "fun." Urbanization, technology, and the ease of transportation afforded by cars also allowed more commercialized opportunities for fun.[5] Charles Young observed with a certain amazement that even in the recently settled immigrant communities of the prairies, "more and more the hunger for recreation and amusement is also getting satisfaction in the village, especially since the advent of the motor-car which is now in general use among the Ukrainians in the better districts." In Canora, Saskatchewan, on summer Saturday nights, "the streets thronged with the beautiful bright-eyed Ukrainian girls who, in dress and deportment, could not be distinguished from our most typical Anglo-Saxons."[6] Where fashion and amusement were concerned, age-group identification could blur ethnic boundaries.

By the 1920s, social scientists were presenting leisure as a positive social force that, by providing the necessary opportunities for human beings to recover and re-create their energies, could be martialled to reinforce the work ethic.[7] The challenge, yet again, was posed by modernizing forces. In conjunction with diminishing child labour and extended schooling, Canadian youth were confronted with unprecedented time on their hands to fill as they chose. Representing a realm of autonomy and choice, leisure held much potential for "mismanagement" by people of all ages, but by none more than adolescents. Leisure had become a complicated matter, contributing, paradoxically, to the very confusion and disorder seen to characterize modernity: "Our recreations include ten activities where [our] grandfathers knew one." Because of their "recreational illiteracy," Canadians appeared to be surrendering to "all the mechanical gadgetry in which we seek stimulation for jaded play appetites." Yet it was this very mechanized mode of living that made more important "the need to develop vocational-creative abilities," to ensure "a sort of safeguard for the soul, oppressed as it is by push buttons, levers and mass production."[8]

Ideas about modern leisure intersected and overlapped with critiques of the new consumer ethic and discussions of the all-encompassing youth problem. Such discourses shared their basis in the critics' vision of an increasingly undisciplined, even hedonistic society spawning a mass culture that was simply "consumed" in every sense and that catered only to the baser "natural" instincts, serving at once

Three young women at Mount Royal Lookout, Montreal, ca. 1924. Anonymous. Gift from Mr. and Mrs. Morley Swan, MP-1993.40.86. McCord Museum. Reprinted with permission of the McCord Museum, Montreal, QC.

The flapper style of the 1920s featured unconstructed clothing with "masculine" lines, short hems, sheer stockings, and the ubiquitous "bob."

to titillate and stupify. This "paying to be amused" enriched the loathsome pur-
veyor while doubly impoverishing the purchaser. The greatest social danger of the
day appeared to be the emergence of a "multitude of people in all classes of society with no skill they can exercise, either for their own enjoyment or other people's benefit, but with plenty of money in their pockets for the purpose of ready-
made pleasures." Work and play were ideally bound in a relationship geared
toward the shaping of an efficient modern Canada, both productive and princi-
pled: "Lack of all-round keenness in work and play is probably one of our greatest
failings in the practice of citizenship."[9] Canadians, and especially those in the critical adolescent stage, had to stop thinking about leisure "merely in terms of play
or pleasure," so that their pastimes would be at once restorative and productive.
For the young, leisure would ideally constitute an enjoyable but otherwise stringent form of preparatory training for their all-important future roles, reinforcing
ideals of bodily and mental fitness as well as citizenship goals. It was a tall order
to place in the realm of fun.

The interpretation of leisure as modern evil came to be applied consistently
to the pastimes of young people, its peculiar breeding ground. Yet the record of
the past two centuries discloses the reiterative nature of public anxieties about
what the young do to entertain themselves. In industrial societies, these worries
are largely spawned by the interaction of new technologies with popular culture.[10] During times of intensive change, direct correlation is made between
social breakdown, worrisome young people, and the popular amusements of the
age, whether the penny theatres, "penny-dreadfuls," and dime novels of the nineteenth century or the ever-widening and ever more technologically sophisticated
catalogue of youth-corrupting pastimes offered up during the past century and
into the present day. The result has invariably manifested itself in moral panic.
As British historian John Springhall warns, the latter concept contains the
assumption (on the part of historians) that the threat of the day was actually
minuscule and the response exaggerated out of all proportion, reflecting the self-
centred worries of the critics more than social reality. Such an assumption can
downplay the inflammatory effects on the public consciousness of the complex,
interlocking roles played by various pressure groups, community organizations,
and state agencies, while also neglecting the wider environment of social anomie.
Their involvement in the unique construction of the problem at hand also helps
to explain why panic is an understandable public response in specific historical
circumstances.[11]

Among present-day critics, as among those of the early twentieth century,
another common assumption is that, given the transitory nature of youth itself,
youth culture is in large part mere passing fancy—at least as long as it is perceived to be non-threatening. The ways in which young people become both
cultural producers and cultural consumers, however, is historically significant.
The unfolding of a distinctly modern popular culture had much to do with the
development of a distinctive youth culture. Taking enthusiastic advantage of a
broadening range of consumer choices, the young drew deliberate generational

boundaries around their age-defined habitus. The generations considered here were each helped along immensely in their apparent choices by the producers, advertisers, and sellers of the day, only too happy to create needs in hopes of filling them with all the new items that their money (or their parents' money) could buy. With growing intensity and focus over the period, the language of the "new," of the modern, of youth itself, became the sellers' language, as the young constituted themselves as a growing market force in consumer society. Far from simply buying, they were taking active part in shaping the trends, movements, products, and institutions that defined modern life.[12] The public perception of adolescence as a distinct stage of life with its own generational culture was correspondingly enhanced. For all the ephemeral quality of youth "fads," by the term's very definition a great many of the popular amusements and recreational activities that were principally aimed at and adopted by young people were steadily co-opted into "adult" popular culture, in everything from fashion and hairstyles through slang, music, dance, film, and any number of pastimes. In a culture that increasingly honoured the "latest," youth became the foremost trendsetters, establishing a pattern—itself a modern trend—that has far outlasted specific fads and that shows no sign of abating as twenty-first-century society continues the process of juvenilization.[13]

The specific chronology of these developments, as witnessed in what were increasingly classified as the generational fads and fancies of the day, testifies to the making of the modern teenager before that species' supposed mid-century emergence to the blare of television, rock 'n' roll and the "bad boy" genre of Hollywood cinema. Already by the 1920s, young people were on their way to becoming integral to the consumer base for modern variations on popular culture and for the new technologies that delivered them to the masses, such as the "talkie," the radio and the gramophone, the telephone and the automobile, all of which, increasingly available and affordable, enhanced and facilitated their involvement in peer-group leisure activities.[14] Many of these activities took place outside the home and away from family, in public, fee-charging venues, whether specifically geared to adolescents or "all-ages" spaces that nonetheless drew a predominantly young crowd. To a great many contemporaries, in fact, it was evident that "the idea with lots of the youth of today is what's the use of staying home if there's anywhere else you can go?"[15] And the young appeared to share this notion, as witnessed in the views of one Montreal-born son of Italian immigrants: "My parents keep after me every time I go out, they want to know why I can't stay at home but I've just got to be going somewhere.... They shout and shout but I go just the same."[16]

Early-twentieth-century changes in the organization of both work and leisure gave rise to a youth-oriented mixed-sex recreational arena, more removed than ever before from the watchful gaze of adults.[17] The abundant and varied diversions of the modern age—the dance halls, cinemas, spectator sports, automobile trips, and speakeasies—energized an emergent youth culture that would come to signify mass culture itself. By the early post–World War I years, mass culture was being identified as the modern demon animating the youth problem. Both popular culture and youth came to be demonized as a result. Increasingly, the law was applied to the problem. Seductive adolescent pastimes that took place in public spaces were legally proscribed in variations on Ontario's Minors' Protection Act of 1927: "No child under the age of 18" was permitted entry into a billiard, pool, or bagatelle room "for the purpose of loitering or to play billiards, pool or bagatelle therein." The same Act outlawed tobacco sales to those under eighteen.[18] Discussions about modern youth made constant reference to the special attraction that mass culture, actuated by modern technology, held out to the young, who were more modern than their parents could ever hope to be. Critics worried that young Canadians were being sucked into the intensely materialistic, commercialized, immoral/amoral vortex of modernity. The youthful "thirst for pleasure and luxury and money" was undermining "the qualities of mind and character that must form the foundation for a race."[19]

The movies stood unchallenged as the most potent of the new cultural forces affecting youth. Government reports, professional journals, popular magazines, the daily press, the nation's pulpits, and the House of Commons and provincial legislatures all resounded with moral indignation about the screen images that planted "wrongful notions" in young minds, the new "talkies" using dialogue to magnify the poisonous effects. The harvest sown by this filmic "evil seed" was measured in the increase in theft and violent crime among boys and "sexual immorality" among girls, upon whom Hollywood's effects were deemed "constantly and seriously demoralizing."[20] The tone and extent of the panic over movies also points to the great difficulty of dissuading Canadians, especially the young, from frequent cinema attendance. Marketing surveys of the time found that age was the single greatest factor in movie attendance.[21] A 1936 survey of one hundred adolescents in Halifax found that ninety-six regularly attended the cinema, with thirty-eight going at least once a week and roughly one-quarter at least once every two weeks; the remaining one-third attended twice a month "or more often." Murder, detective, and "thrilling pictures" were favoured by both sexes. Among the girls, collecting photographs of film stars was also the most popular hobby declared.[22] From the perspective of those who would regulate all modern pastimes, the Canadian passion for cinema-going was sadly reflected in data revealing that, while regular church attendance drew "scarcely half our people," over 90 per cent of Canadians were regular moviegoers, and fully 60 per cent of these were under the age of eighteen. Even during the Depression, most moviegoers attended once a month; in larger centres, the average attendance was twenty to thirty-five times per year.[23] Going to the movies had become an integral youth pastime. The cinema was affordable, accessible, and relatively tame as commercial amusements went. It permitted a public, safe (and dark) setting for the rituals of adolescent meeting and courtship.[24] Even the embarrassment of having to return soft drink and milk bottles, in great demand during the salvage campaigns of World War II, just to collect enough change to attend was considered worth doing for the pleasure of seeing the latest movie.[25]

If the statistics suggest that few Canadians of any age were as perturbed by the negative effects of a "filmized" popular culture as the vehement and unrelenting commentary might imply, critics—many associated with reformist organizations and state agencies devoted to the cause of child and family welfare—considered various means to contain the movie virus. Calls for regulation rose to fever pitch in the aftermath of a fire at the Laurier Palace cinema in Montreal in January 1927, in which seventy-eight children, one-third of them young teenagers between the ages of thirteen and sixteen, perished at a Sunday matinee screening of the ominously titled comedy *Gets 'Em Young*. Despite the 1919 provincial legislation prohibiting those under sixteen from attending films without adult accompaniment, and despite the owner's previous convictions under that law as well as for breaching fire regulations about crowding the aisles, the majority of the audience was both under sixteen and unaccompanied. According to the coroner's testimony at the inquiry, three-quarters were at the cinema without their parents' knowledge or permission. Most provinces subsequently tightened their regulations for licensing, inspection, and ages and hours of admission.[26] Ontario allowed no admission to any unaccompanied child under fifteen except on Saturdays between the hours of nine in the morning and six in the evening, during which time a "matron" was to be present in supervisory capacity. In addition to the usual difficulties of enforcement, even such legislation left considerable opportunity for movie attendance by children and youth. The law consequently did little to relieve adult anxieties about the dangers of overcrowding at theatres and even less in regard to the "bad influence" of the movies on budding sexual and criminal proclivities.[27]

Since controlling the age of attendance was not particularly fruitful, the other favoured option was to control what was actually shown on the screen. There were censor boards in place in most provinces by 1914, but there was seemingly little faith in their efficacy, judging by the frequency of arguments for a single national board to ensure the uniformity and consistency believed to be needed.[28] Already by the war's end, public pressure had brought about amendments to censorship regulations, making them at once more precise and more encompassing. Most provinces imitated Manitoba's sweeping provisions of 1916: that province's censor board would not approve any film depicting scenes "of an immoral or obscene nature, or which indicate or suggest lewdness or indecency or marital infidelity or showing the details of murder, robbery, or criminal assault or depicting criminals as heroic characters," or, for that matter, "any other picture" considered to be "injurious to public morals, suggestive of evil to the minds of children and young people or against the public welfare."[29] Ontario's board eliminated such scenes of depravity as that of a young woman picking up a man's watch from the floor beside her bed, and such subversive dialogue as a reference to "old Comrade God Himself."[30]

There were corresponding calls for "a true effort" to make movies the conveners of "civilized" messages that would counter the horrifying prospect of national degeneration, for "a higher type of life should be exhibited if we are not

Young staff of the Capitol Theatre, Saskatoon, SK, 1929. Image call no. PH88-982. Reprinted with permission of the Saskatoon Public Library.

The movies provided both a major source of entertainment and part-time employment for young people, as demonstrated in this photo of the young staff of the Capitol Theatre, Saskatoon. The manager and assistant manager sport military-style uniforms.

to be left behind by nations which are now regarded by us as heathens." Various rating schemes were initiated in the interests of educating a naive moviegoing public, especially parents of children and adolescents. The nation's largest social service agency, the Canadian Council on Child and Family Welfare, began publishing a "White List" of approved films for those under adult age in 1927. The Canadian Motion Picture Distributors Association collaborated in the preparation of the list, and copies were distributed to every theatre in Canada. The list also found a wider audience in family-oriented mass-circulation magazines such as *Chatelaine*. Yet the challenges posed by popular culture to the health and morality of the young loomed much larger than could be addressed by any combination of official and voluntary regulation of the movies. In 1931, Charlotte Whitton, the council's executive director, complained that even the dissemination of this bimonthly select list of motion pictures saw "little progress made . . . though existing in a field that cries out for service."[31] Attempts to slay, or at least tame, the Hollywood dragon appeared futile. These were the films that people wanted to see; film producers and cinema managers were well aware of the importance of catering to their loyal young clientele.[32] As one contemporary film critic sized up the situation, "the motion picture has grown up by appeal to the interests of childhood and youth."[33] In the modern age, this "new generation," just as unsympathetic to the way of life of its elders as those elders were to theirs, was demanding films in harmony with the life it was leading, or at least aspired to lead.[34]

By the 1920s, Hollywood had discovered modern youth as both subject and object of its productions. In his classic 1939 history of American film, Lewis Jacob described the nature of "that remarkable series of jazz-age pictures," which, reflecting "the hedonism of a nation on the wave of prosperity," was instrumental in quite literally broadcasting new styles, new living standards, new behavioural trends: "The old order now crumbled away entirely. The screen world became crowded with dancing mothers, flaming youth, jazz babies, cake eaters, flappers. Revolution in etiquette, culture, and conduct generally broke out in this new film domain."[35] The films' titles gave away their storylines: *The Wildness of Youth, The Madness of Youth, Risky Business, Reckless Youth, Our Dancing Daughters, Children of Divorce, Children of the Ritz, Modern Maidens,* and, of course, *Flaming Youth,* which gave the 1920s generation its name. Produced in 1923, this last film, the first of the so-called flapper films, was based on a novel that asked the question burning on many a youth-watcher's mind: "How far are our mothers permitting their flapper daughters to go?" It was proclaimed "The Picture Everybody Is Talking About" just before its Toronto opening at the Hippodrome in February 1924.[36]

The film's primary significance is its status at the front of a long line of imitations that featured jazz, dancing, young women in short skirts and hair, and abundant cigarette smoking and drinking from flasks. Worst of all to those who would be outraged were these films' intimations of youthful sexual immorality and disrespect for—even defiance of—adult authority. The increasingly stringent censorship regulations in Canada and the United States meant that much of the debauchery was implied or off screen, however, especially the indulgence in alcohol and sex that gave "flaming youth" their notoriety. Clara Bow, the decade's "flaming incarnation of the flapper spirit"—the "It Girl"—was never shown on screen doing anything more outrageous than waving a long cigarette holder, enjoying a midnight car ride, or participating in an impassioned but fleeting kiss. Ironically, this "wild youth" film genre reflected the nature of the youth problem itself: the alleged wildness of modern youth was also "off screen" in the sense that it was likely more implied than realized by most young Canadians. The true source of contention was not so much their antics as their style.[37]

The flapper films capitalized on contemporary ideas about modern youth and generational opposition from both sides at once. While drawing in the young crowd by portraying the fun-loving aspects that appealed to their age group, reinforcing both generational style and consciousness in the process, they also conveyed a moral lesson. This was precisely the lesson that their adult critics wanted heard, delivered through the medium most likely to get the message across. The common outcome for the films' young protagonists, usually after much debauchery and its complications, was a wisdom born of regrettable experience. The remorseful young protagonist comes to understand that temperance (in all things) is not to be disdained if adult maturity is ever to be won—or at least if adolescence is to be survived. The feckless and "flaming" young person, male or female, is usually redeemed by the loving devotion of a more conservative, more "mature" partner.[38]

For all that critics saw the movies as yet another stepping stone in the downfall of youth—and the nation—their ultimate message supported the conventional white, middle-class, Christian value system underpinning ideas about adulthood, family, social responsibility, moral behaviour, and gender relations. As Lewis Jacob commented sardonically, "the sermonizing with which such films ended was mocked by the attractiveness with which they portrayed sin."[39] But Jacob also maintained that the American films produced between 1919 and 1929, which won wide audiences in Canada and effectively eclipsed its own fledgling film industry, should be read as "eloquent social documents" because they reflect "the spirit of the decade," if not life as experienced by most.[40] Hollywood's representation of contemporary reality is not the issue. What matters is that the movies, the most popular form of modern popular culture, not only drew young audiences but projected back to them a generational style and image that helped to make these happen, all the while portraying the very things that made them a modern problem. For example, the renowned Cecil B. DeMille's first talkie, *The Godless Girl* (1929), about a high school girl delinquent who manages to redeem herself, opens with a screen title declaring its intention to expose "the insidious propaganda teaching atheism and menacing the youth of the nation."[41]

Where 1920s films had glamourized youth, the most popular Hollywood movies of the Depression decade—the gangster films—idealized the modern urban outlaw, all too often cultivated from the ranks of male juvenile delinquents. During a time when some young people might well have wondered what could be achieved by hard work and law-abiding behaviour, the criminal gangs and activities depicted in these films might have appeared heroic. At bottom, they offered non-conformism as a means of escape from Depression dreariness. Jacob believed that the "indiscriminate rebellion against moral conventions" characterizing the jazz-age films was replaced in the 1930s by "an earnest search for moral norms," resulting in both a new on-screen realism and also a "powerful and unceasing censorship." The new realism and the reinvigorated censorship crusade collided over the issue of gangster films.[42] To youth-watchers, the enthusiasm for these "shoot 'em up" movies bespoke only young lives heading downward, the nation rapidly following suit. In the United States, with every step closely followed by Canadians, organized protest against gangster movies reached new volume over the release of the 1932 Howard Hawks film *Scarface*, starring Paul Muni as the Al Capone–like central figure.[43] The outcome was the Motion Picture Production Code, or Hays Code, endorsed by the industry's own Motion Picture Producers and Distributors of America and made mandatory in 1934, as well as the formation of the policing organization known as the League of Decency.

In specific response to the gangster films, the Hays Code decreed that crime was not to be portrayed in any sympathetic light or in any way that could inspire imitation.[44] Adding additional fuel to the fire was the publication of the Payne Fund Studies, also in 1934. In eight scholarly volumes, these studies detailed research data that amply supported the links being popularly drawn between movies, the moral degeneration of youth, and rising juvenile delinquency rates.[45] When the conclusions were published in popular format as *Our Movie-Made Children*, the book quickly became an international bestseller; it served up all the "expert," "scientific," and modern testimony that might be desired in respect to the need to police the movies on behalf of the nation's children and youth.[46]

The results, again, were ambiguous and ambivalent. Gangster movies retained their draw, but the second wave, in the late 1930s, depicted even more forcefully the connection between youthful impressionability—hence the downward spiral so easily commenced—and the moral lesson that crime, or youthful transgression writ large, simply does not pay. Especially popular was the Dead End Kids series, beginning with the movie of that name in 1937. With a screenplay by Lillian Hellman, the film captured the generational cycle of despair and criminality bred in the urban slum environment, resonating with the period's escalating fears about the repercussions on the younger generation of unemployment, continued deprivation, and the frustration of legitimate youthful ambitions. The six young members of the Dead End set, purportedly "found on the streets" but actually professional teenage actors, also starred in the quick sequels, which included *Angels with Dirty Faces* and *Crime School* (1938), and *Angels Wash Their Faces* and *Hell's Kitchen* (1939). In each, the formula demanded that the young gang members duel with the forces of good and evil as represented by adult role models of both categories. The former was often a professional or a cleric, the latter a mobster of some prominence; the two usually shared the lowly slum beginnings of their young charges.[47] The link between class and racial inferiority and the youth problem was also obviously reinforced through such narrative lines.

With the Depression's end and the necessity of keeping up citizen morale during wartime—Hollywood having entered the war before the United States—movies that featured youth began to play down the flamboyance of the 1920s generation and steered away from the frustrations of the Depression generation. They now aimed to show the doings of responsible, wholesome young things, playful and perhaps a bit mischievous but sweet and decidedly unthreatening. Profiting from the late-1930s popularity of such child stars (now teenagers) as Judy Garland, Shirley Temple, and Mickey Rooney, Hollywood offered up vehicles tailor-made for these actors and geared toward a wartime family audience that wanted to see good, clean, all-American youth, and not youth problems in any form. Rooney was featured in the Andy Hardy series, in which he played a teenager struggling with "typical" adolescent problems but helped immensely by the wise, patient, loving guidance of his father, Judge Hardy. Garland teamed up with him in two of these popular films before *The Wizard of Oz* (1939), and again in *Babes in Arms* and *Babes on Broadway*.[48] Generational relations were given another spin in the 1947 film *The Bachelor and the Bobby Soxer*. The nineteen-year-old Temple, the darling of the 1930s, played a seventeen-year-old bobby soxer enduring the travails of a mad "crush" on a handsome and urbane older man, Cary Grant, largely in reaction to her "so callow" high school "jock" boyfriend. Order is regained when her older sister is matched up with the bachelor, and the now wiser bobby soxer happily returns to her own peer group.[49]

Movie-going topped the list both for young Canadians pursuing modern recreational opportunities and for the adults who strove to regulate that pursuit, but the so-called dance craze vied closely for that ranking. Dancing as a social activity was certainly nothing new. In the 1920s, however, it appeared to have "a grip on our young people such as it never had before."[50] The number of editorials, letters from irate readers, "scientific" analyses, eyewitness accounts, and clerical admonitions reported in the popular press concerning the dance phenomenon of that decade is immeasurable. It was not only the seeming dance-obsession of the young that perturbed Canadians, but even more so the style of dancing, sometimes called "whirling." Modern dance appeared to be all about sex, a stylized public mating ritual that, bad enough in its lewd and suggestive bodily contact, was made all the worse because it was performed in darkened, often packed, too often unchaperoned commercial dance halls where cigarettes burned and illicit liquor flowed. Such "fevered" dances as the foxtrot, the jitney, the Lindy hop, the bunny hug, the Charleston, and the truly heinous tango were linked with everything from juvenile delinquency through madness and "race suicide," another obsession of the age and one closely linked to the young generation, future parents that they were.[51]

As was the case in regards to the movie-mania of the young, Canadian critics of popular culture were able to turn to American experts for the necessary "science" to back their protests about the young generation's "dance-o-mania." Among the most fear-inspiring of these was a widely circulated tract by Dr. R.A. Adams, self-proclaimed "author, editor, lecturer on Higher Eugenics, Sex Hygiene Prophylactics and Social Economics." Adams declared that "the devil chose well" in making the dance "one of his surest, truest and most potent instruments of destruction...of the bodies, minds, lives and souls, of men and women." Here was an instrument that not only would ruin the present generation but, "by means of Heredity, Pre-natal Influence and Defective Environment," would pass its degenerative effects to future generations. Devoting the better part of several hundred pages to the immorality of modern dance, vehemently sustained by racist condemnation of the "Negro" origins of the "habit," he continually conflated its health repercussions with its implications for the souls of white Christian youth.[52]

Such moralizing about dancing was by no means the exclusive domain of experts and clerics. If sex were not its principal attraction to the young, asked one dance-foe from Whitby, Ontario, "why is it when the sexes are segregated, the dance, with all its supposed benefits, becomes as dead as the proverbial door nail? Eliminate the sex instinct and you strip the dance of all its thrills."[53] Commentary, both bemused and alarmed, singled out such dance fads as the codfish cuddle, "named doubtless because no one but a fish would make bold to attempt it.... It is an opportunity, hitherto undreamed of, for the transfer of rouge that would make any pale young man glow.... The til-death-do-us-part grasp is used, also mincing steps that take the dancer nowhere in particular." The "devotees" of the dance, being "in the flower of their youth," considered eccentricity their greatest triumph, and "so they [went] on dancing themselves to perdition."[54]

The fact that young dancers kept pace to the "uncivilized" and "primitive" strains and "mad rhythms" of jazz and other "Negro" music was equally objectionable to many observers. The earliest jazz musicians on the Canadian scene were American performers appearing on the vaudeville circuit in the mid- to late 1910s. Canadian musicians, as much as young music-lovers, quickly took up this cultural import. Jazz historians date the music's commercial beginnings in Canada to about 1917, at which point recordings of the music and the growth of commercial dance halls fuelled its popularity. The jazz phenomenon was further facilitated during the 1920s by radio broadcasting, the cheap cost of producing records, and rising radio and gramophone ownership.[55] Already in 1922, the American magazine *Photoplay* was reporting that the eighteen-to-thirty age group accounted for 48 per cent of all phonograph and record purchases, although making up only 23 per cent of the U.S. population.[56] In an evolutionary process hinging on youthful tastes and the youth market, the music industry increasingly responded to these with music and dance styles aimed directly at them and purposely distinguishing the new generational style from the old— jazz, the "crooners" of the late 1930s, the Big Band sound, swing jive, and ultimately the revolutionary "youth sound" of the 1950s, rock 'n' roll.

The unrestrained, free-form, highly improvised syncopated rhythms of jazz signified the music of the modern age, and consequently of modern youth. Because the Great War drew away many of the nation's seasoned musicians, the development of jazz in Canadian cities, according to musicologist Mark Miller, was accelerated as they were replaced in the dance halls by "younger men with the newer ideas of a generation maturing under the formative influence of jazz, a music that offered their youthful energies full release." Among the best known of the early Canadian jazz bands was the Winnipeg Jazz Babies, who came together during that city's tumultuous spring of 1919, amidst the General Strike. The band was composed of seven teenage boys, the oldest only eighteen. They were regular performers at the city's Manitoba and Alhambra dance halls and earned wider renown through tours across the western provinces.[57] Montreal, with a growing community of single black men, many of them Americans imported to work for the railway, became the contemporary hotbed of Canadian jazz, although many of the "white" clubs in the city, as across the continent, would not hire black or "mixed" bands.[58] The Catholic Church in Quebec railed mightily against the wicked implications of jazz and dance for a devout, traditional, francophone society.[59] The *Vancouver Sun*'s music critic called jazz and the shimmy the "twin sisters of corruption." In an even more extreme—and racist— response, one letter-writer to that newspaper pronounced it "nigger trash," exposing his resentment that this "vulgar music" was all that "the average Vancouver dancing audience...care to hear."[60]

While roused to panic over dancing, jazz, and the dance hall itself, the commentators were not, as was often the case, entirely misinterpreting the situation, even as they exaggerated the dangers to youth. During this period, the dance hall came to be a favoured stage for young people experimenting with a thrilling new generational style which served to define their own personal style—their personal "aura," as the marketers of sex appeal called it—with due attention to appearance, technique, and attraction of the opposite sex. For contemporary youth-watchers, this very style became the visual symbol of troubling emergent attitudes toward leisure, sexuality, and personal fulfilment.[61] Modern "dance hall girls" were surrendering to the odious flapper influence, and not only in their manner of dressing: more important, "the very clothing worn is an indication of the character and the ideals which are actuating our growing girls." The gauzy, strappy, short-skirted flapper costume bore witness to "a degradation in the minds of young women suggestive of a return to animal instinct and opposed to the dictates of what we are pleased to call civilization." The "risks" taken by immodestly dressed girls were quite simply "enough to make a mother's heart stop."[62] But the boyish look of the day—deliberately downplaying traditional conventions of feminine beauty, freeing up both preparation time and physical movement—was a special generational marker for young women. For the first time in history, youth was setting the fashion pace. Age, class, gender, and race, however, weighted even the flimsiest of mass-produced items of fashion with different social meanings. Along with other elements of style such as smoking, drinking, and "loose" attitudes toward fun and sex—if not necessarily loose behaviour—dress and coiffure signified the thoroughly modern girl.[63] Yet much of the flouting of gender-defined middle-class convention remained at this level of the symbolic. Very real restrictions on women's lives persisted, especially for girls still largely dependent on their families.

For the anti-dance set, the ideal was "adequate philanthropic or civic provision for the normal demand for rhythm and music in recreation." Until this noble objective was realized, public regulation of the commercial dance hall, by means of licensing to establish hours of operation and ages of admittance, was critical. But "the thing that would really alter" the situation was supervision by a chaperone who was "doing it because of her motives and not for the money entailed."[64] The chaperone would have "control of the dances" and "of correct methods of dancing," clearly intended in the moral and not the performative sense of correctness. But despite a great many determined resolutions by the Council on Child and Family Welfare and a variety of other interested groups, progress in regulating public dance halls as "a menace to the physical and moral life of youth" was slow, piecemeal, and largely ineffectual. Requiring public halls to be registered, licensed, and inspected by provincial governments at least kept them under watch, a surveillance that could be extended through municipal bylaws, which were often more stringent in their requirements.[65] In Ottawa, the two dance halls that existed in 1929 were licensed by both city and province, with the municipality prohibiting the admittance of "any unescorted woman." They were also chaperoned and obliged to close at midnight.[66] Kitchener and Galt, Ontario, each hired a policewoman expressly to keep an eye on "moral conditions" in and around the towns' dance halls. But Guelph residents lamented that no provision was made in its three dance halls "to prevent, say, a drunken man from annoying girls.... There is no paid chaperone, there is not even a 'chucker-out.'"[67]

Dance fever continued to infect the young during the "swing era" of the 1930s, notwithstanding Depression hardships—and perhaps even because of them. Helped along by radio exposure and inexpensive recordings, popular music became increasingly accessible to young Canadians. In Regina, as a young teenager when the Depression began, one woman was more fortunate than most, in that her father kept his job, though at reduced wages: "We didn't miss money that much," she remembered, "as long as we had money for the dance hall."[68] She met her future husband at a dance in the city's Trianon ballroom in 1939, when she was nineteen: "We used to have programs and you made sure your program was filled with the names of dances. There was an orchestra.... That's where Mart Kenney played a couple of times. We danced to him. The Silver Tones Seven was another orchestra that played there all the time."[69] Young people could attend on their own, but most went with friends or as part of a couple: "You could have a drink...Coke, 7 Up or Cream Soda...but no liquor. You could have chocolate bars and just dance and listen to the music really....During my era it was only the boys that were drinking, maybe at sixteen or seventeen."[70] Mart Kenney and His Western Gentlemen, who toured across the country, performed on radio, and also recorded, were among the best-known Canadian dance bands of the time. Their signature tune was the 1922 Billy Hill–Larry Yoell waltz "The West, a Nest and You, Dear," a veritable paean to nation-building as much as to youthful romance: "The West, a nest, and you dear, oh what a dream could be...a cozy little cottage beside the sunset sea...I know someday our dreams will all come true...a cradle, a baby and you dear...the West, a nest, and you."[71]

The big band sound, with its accompanying jitterbug dance style, continued into the war years, popularized in countless dance halls and high school gyms by recordings of the American Glenn Miller band and tours by Guy Lombardo and His Royal Canadians. Writer Robert Collins looked back on his youth with a certain wistful nostalgia for the music of the war years, recalling the early 1940s as

a time of young men swirling young women through the intricate weaving patterns of the jitterbug, skirts planing out like saucers with a tantalizing flash of thigh. Of music forever linked to that war, wistful ballads of love and parting: "I'll Be Seeing You" and "White Cliffs of Dover" and "When the Lights Go On Again." A thousand pianists with a single accomplishment, a nimble left hand that could coax out the rippling, rumbling eight-to-the-bar of boogie-woogie. And the World War II anthem, Glenn Miller's "In the Mood," soaring.[72]

When the news came that Miller, then director of the American Air Force Band, had gone down in an airplane during a flight from England to Paris just before Christmas 1944, Mary Peate remembered that "if somehow the Nazis had known he was on that plane and shot it down, they couldn't have struck a worse blow to our morale. . . . People felt as if they'd lost someone close to them. . . . They had been wooed, won and wed to his music."[73]

By the mid-1940s, the "jazz babies" and swing enthusiasts were evolving into a generation of "hepcats," a swelling new source of fandom for the crooners of the day. The biggest star among them was easily "The Voice," as American singer Frank Sinatra was known by his adoring fans, the majority of whom were teenage girls. By this time, dancing and the dance hall seem to have lost some of their centrality in discussions of the youth problem. Jazz, swing, bebop, and their variations in modern popular music, as well as the related dance styles, were being appropriated into mainstream popular culture, which meant that adults were indulging in rather larger numbers. This co-option removed these music and dance styles from the domain of adolescent transgression and generational style and rendered them reasonably "safe" and more truly popular. There was still occasional bemused commentary about teen "idolatry," as occasioned by The Voice in particular, and about the jive and jitterbug dance styles of the period, which required youthful agility and energy. In May 1945, the *Toronto Star* report-ed on a riot of thirteen thousand teenage Sinatra fans in Philadelphia when rumours swirled that he was attending a meeting to discuss "the problems of 'teen-agers and means of curbing juvenile delinquency."[74] When Sinatra made his only 1944 Canadian appearance in Montreal, "a wall of sound greeted him. . . . You couldn't hear a note for the shrieks and screams." "Frankie" was "the male singer to whom we would compare all others and always find them wanting."[75]

Though concerns emanated from press, pulpit, and psychologists about the effects of the Sinatra craze, with diagnoses of mass hypnotism, mass hysteria, "mass frustrated love without direction," and even "wartime degeneracy" regu-larly delivered, the hyperbole surrounding the moral, physical, "mental hygiene," and "race suicide" effects of popular music and its accompanying dance styles was actually quieting down by the war's end. [76] Like the high schools did, youth clubs and organizations incorporated dancing as a regular social activity, also mit-igating its earlier "immoral" representation. As George McKnight recalled about his dance experiences at the Alberni, British Columbia, Teen Town in the late 1940s and early 1950s,

> I was only 13 or 14 at this time and I used to stay at the Hut for the teen dances. It was a great time. . . . In those early years nobody sat on the side-lines, the dancing was too compelling. The time at the dances was just straight music and jiving. . . . Hanging out as a young kid, some of the older girls liked to get me up on the dance floor and that's where I learned to dance. That was ok with me. . . . I was too bashful to ever ask any of them for a date . . . but I had some big crushes on some of those girls.[77]

The burgeoning "teen club" or "teen town" movement went the furthest—and was possibly the most successful—of all the period's attempts at providing regulated and supervised youth havens for "wholesome" dancing and other leisure activity. Although certainly not a long time in coming, it would take the next generation's rock 'n' roll fever to bring back the full force of adult apprehension about music and dance.[78]

As had the flapper style, fashion became very much a way of defining youth's domain during these years, and consequently another source of adult disapproval. Clothing that differentiated age groups was a fairly recent development, dating from the late nineteenth century. Except for such juvenile styles as smocks for baby boys and short pants for their pre-adolescent brothers, those not yet adult generally dressed in smaller versions of their parents' apparel. As youth became the burning icon of the modern age, direct targeting of that particular demographic (even before the latter became an industry buzzword) was apparent in the advertising campaigns, specialty items, and specialized stores and sections of established department stores that catered specifically to the clothing needs and desires of adolescents. By the 1920s—considered a "golden age" of advertising as mass media delivered the message to more homes than ever before—marketers were relying on psychological studies to understand and especially to manipulate consumer behaviour. Convinced that the young represented a sizable market sector of their own, they adopted a form of generational theory that presaged current emphasis on "demographics" in buying and selling. Promoting "newness" was the key to capturing not only the young consumer, but also those who aspired to be youthful in taste, outlook, lifestyle, even physical appearance. The language of the new and the young became vital to modern sales strategies. With their "scientific" psychological models, marketers could theorize that certain spending habits and purchasing patterns were established in youth, shaping, for example, those who came of age during the Depression as a particular type of adult consumer who differed substantially from the next generation, which grew up during more prosperous times.[79]

Producers and their marketing crews also began to see that the youth market was integral to family purchasing. A number of American surveys during the 1920s gave strong evidence that adolescent members of the family influenced both the decision to buy and the final selection. It is certainly feasible that parents might consider their adolescent offspring to be more attuned to and informed about the latest modern products, regardless whether they actually followed through on the purchase itself. Already in 1922, the immensely popular American *Photoplay* magazine surveyed age-related buying to uncover the fact that the eighteen-to-thirty cohort spent more in consumer purchases relative to their actual numbers than any other age group.[80] Noted Columbia University psychologist Albert T. Poffenberger found the *Photoplay* study worthy of comment in his 1925 book on advertising: he remarked that "a greater gap than ever existed before" had grown between generations as a result of modern innovation, and that young people not only "rule[d] the market" in regard to their own purchases, but also exerted a "powerful influence" on all family purchases. The "widespread appeal" to the young manifested in contemporary advertising was easily explained by the fact that youth were less resistant than their elders to new concepts and new products.[81] Thirteen budget studies conducted in 1929 by the American advertising firm Nystrom revealed that the largest proportion of the family clothing budget, regardless of family income, was spent by daughters over fifteen, with sons over fifteen typically next in line.[82] Younger children presumably were more often clothed in hand-me-downs or home-sewn attire, while adults, especially mothers who spent more time at home, had less selection of clothing and wore their clothes for longer periods before buying new ones. Such cultural shifts as the increasing importance of in-home socializing for the young—parties, gatherings to listen to the radio, as well as dating—might well see middle-class adolescents pressure their parents to buy radios, better furniture, even cars.[83] The newly commercialized modern "beauty culture" of hairdressing salons, cosmetics, and related products also played a major role in strengthening the marketing connection between youth and attractiveness, especially feminine beauty.[84]

The classification and presentation of clothing on the basis of gender and age—childhood and adulthood—had become increasingly common features of both store display and advertising since the late nineteenth century. The sectionalization of fashion for age groups within the larger categories, however, is a post–World War I invention. The importance of the "collegiate" style was apparent to manufacturers and retailers by the mid-1920s, as more young consumers spent their days in high school classrooms and their after-school hours in the company of their peers. By the 1930s, the major North American department stores, including Robert Simpson's and such Canadian companies as Eaton's, Woodwards, Northway, and Ogilvie, were operating exclusive youth apparel departments and recognizing the new importance of the back-to-school selling season. Fashion manufacturers as well as pattern companies also began to feature "misses" and "young men's" sizes and styles at this time. At first these were modelled on adult fashions, sometimes in lighter, brighter fabrics and colours for the youth market, reflecting the perceived needs of the young for comfortable, fashionable, "fun" clothing suitable for play, parties, and dancing.[85] Northway's flagship department store, which opened in downtown Toronto in 1928, gave its entire second floor over to children's wear while highlighting a special "'Teenage Shop."[86] Local, independent clothiers did likewise. In Fort William, Ontario, the high school yearbook featured a full-page back cover advertisement for Rutledge and Jackson—known in the community as "the Big Store"—which portrayed a natty young man wearing a trench coat and cap, with knee breeches and long socks. The caption declared that "the age of specialists finds us specializing in High School Clothes, Shoes and Haberdashery.... We've outfitted Dad, Let's outfit his lad."[87]

The 1920s saw the beginnings of another new cultural trend: the equation of youth not only with the modern, but also with the aesthetic, particularly regarding fashion and standards of physical beauty. The young, fit, virile, and handsome male was idealized in the form of the "matinee idol" and "sex symbol" of the new age, notably the iconic Sheik, Rudolph Valentino, whose exotic and erotic qualities spoke to a forbidden racialized sexuality associated with a new breed of "lounge lizards," "cake-eaters," "boy flappers," and "tango pirates." Young, lascivious, and mainly foreign-born or "of foreign blood," these were dangerous men who waited to trap unsuspecting and naive white women. They were also men who danced "divinely," transgressing traditional constructions of manliness. Yet the message was decidedly mixed: eugenicists obsessing about race suicide maintained that (white) male beauty should be interpreted as "a sign of fitness for parenthood."[88]

While the film idols, both male and female, were not themselves adolescents, their "style" was sold as the style of young moderns and worthy of emulation as such. Hollywood became the new international fashion centre, a modern rival to Paris as style capital of the world, its films the ultimate means of popularizing new styles quickly and efficiently to all who could purchase a movie ticket. Especially keen to buy were the working girls whose precarious social status made shopping for up-to-date fashions a marker of identity as well as a pleasurable way to pass their time and dispense their earnings.[89] The descriptor "young-looking," with its connotations of smooth skin, up-to-date hair and clothing, and a slender body, entailed new social pressures that would escalate over the course of the century. Youth itself became a modern consumer product to be purchased in everything from cosmetics, undergarments, and hair dye to fad diets, popular beverages, new exercise regimens, and even plastic surgery.

The American soft-drink manufacturer Coca Cola was among the most effective of those companies that took up the modernity, youth, and beauty campaign. It employed young female models in calendars and advertising campaigns, commencing in earnest in the 1920s, when it also adopted youth slang in its target advertising. In turn, "Coke" culture permeated youth culture with its own language and imagery. Hallmark Cards, for example, initiated a line of "Betty Betz" greeting cards during the mid-1940s that were actively promoted as "greeting cards that speak the Coke set lingo" and as "groovy new greeting cards designed just for you [teenagers]." The "groovy" signifier was a cultural reference associated with late-1930s swing-jive musicians and their fans. By making reference to "the Coke set"—the Coca Cola company's own invention—the Hallmark advertising campaign sold a "groovy" youth subculture; the "Coke date" came to mean a non-alcoholic but still "cool" adolescent date.[90]

The movies were a prime engine of transmission for this modern association between age, personal beauty, and what came to be known as "lifestyle," as well as a boon to entire industries devoted to the battle against aging and the ugliness and decrepitude that it was coming to stand for.[91] The film industry's establishment of youth as icon received a considerable boost from the concomitant growth in mass-circulation "family" and "ladies'" magazines, and of the advertising that they conveyed. As film stars became celebrities and idols rather than mere actors, they were increasingly seen off screen endorsing products in

Smart dresses for junior misses, *Eaton's Spring and Summer Catalogue, 1926*, "Before E-Commerce: Canada's Mail Order Catalogues." www.civilization.ca/cpm/catalog. Reprinted with permission of Sears Canada.

By the 1920s, clothing manufacturers and stores were designing specifically with the teenager in mind, a modern departure from the pre-war trend that generally did not distinguish between adolescent and adult fashion.

"Soda Date," advertisement, Kotex feminine hygiene products, from *Good Housekeeping*, May 1944; also in *Chatelaine* and other Canadian "ladies' magazines." Reprinted with permission of the Museum of Menstruation and Women's Health, www.mum.org.

By the 1940s, advertisers were increasingly intent on direct marketing to teenagers, especially girls. Reflecting the era's gender ideals and working on the modern adolescent's desire for "popularity," the ads targeted "relationship" issues and advised on how to attract, entertain, and keep a boyfriend. This one depicts the typical "soda date" or "Coke date" of the day.

the magazines. When readers were told that "every woman and girl wants a Mary Pickford cap—craze of the age," the message undoubtedly left its imprint. In the early twentieth century, Canadians were not only avid consumers of American film and magazines but could increasingly turn to made-in-Canada magazines. Magazines became market-directed, increasingly reliant on advertising revenue, and increasingly oriented to light reading as an important component of modern leisure.[92] Through mass media and advertising, myriad representations of "youth as style" entered middle-class Canadian homes.[93] The new moving-picture medium, the newly popular magazine, and the burgeoning advertising industry reinforced circulating images of youth, thereby contributing to the intensity of public attention to the actual human subjects as well as to the commodification of youth as the latest product to enhance modern life— or to make it truly modern.

If slowed somewhat by Depression spending restraints, the idea of "youth fashion" (or, increasingly, "'teen-age fashion") was entrenched by World War II, as 1940s magazines and newspapers—advertisements and features alike—suggest. The bobby-soxers of the 1940s derived their name from the short rolled socks that many young women adopted in lieu of the silk or nylon stockings that wartime production regulations had more or less legislated out of being. Also popular, for casual wear at least, was clothing with writing on it, in particular the loose-fitting pullovers or "sloppy joes" of the late war years. These became the uniform of teenage girls, along with "a skirt, generally plaid, or matching the sweater, often pleated, coming to mid-knee or slightly above; pearls, or a detachable Peter Pan collar; white socks, and brown and white scuffed saddle shoes or polished loafers."[94] The war and Hollywood were also normalizing the wearing of pants by women: in 1945, the "must-have" item for adolescent girls was the plaid pedal-pusher, "not a long short but more of a short slack."[95]

Among young men, the generationally defined, countercultural, and oppositional posture adopted by the brotherhood of "zoots" or "zoot-suiters," while representing only a very small minority, caused all manner of disproportionate
panic. Using fashion to distinguish themselves as young and non-conformist,
even within their peer group, the zoot-suiters also flaunted a new variation on
masculinity, and especially masculine sexuality, that was deeply troubling to
many observers. The possibility that youthful sexuality might be a contributing
cause of the zoot-suit troubles, which culminated in street violence in Toronto
and especially in Montreal, is entirely plausible within the context of the
wartime concerns—recirculated once again from the Great War—about a loosening of sexual morality. The zoot controversy was about the seeming desire of
modern youth in general—though chiefly those who were male, urban, and
often depicted as being (if not actually) of "non-Canadian" or even "non-anglo-
phone" background—to set themselves apart in provocative subcultures.

Zoot suits made the news in the United States and Canada in the early summer of 1943. Put simply, this form of attire was adopted as a type of counter-uni-
form to the military apparel on display on the streets of wartime Canada by a
"jive-set" of young urban men also known as "the boys with the reat pleats."[96]
Many of the anti-zoot contingent were irked by the defiantly unconventional
outfit, fundamentally a caricature of respectable male business and "Sunday
best" attire—but also by their wearers' even more offensive stance in defiance of
the Wartime Prices and Trade Board, which actually prohibited the manufacture
of the suits. Zoot suits were not only immoral, they were illegal. Flustered board
officials could uncover no evidence of their being manufactured on a large scale
and surmised that "the small tailor" might be hoarding fabric and making them
for the black market, or even that "many of them were evidently imported from
the United States before our restrictions went into effect."[97]

The zoot suit comprised pants "with the ankles so tight they can hardly be
pulled over the feet" and a long "Prince Albert–type" jacket reaching to the knees
and featuring exaggerated shoulder padding. Accessories included suede shoes, a
wide-brimmed hat, usually of brown straw with a wide and "noisy" hatband,
and, "zootiest of all," a watch chain descending to the shoes in a wide loop. This
was the outfit of the urban dandy, unmanly in its various overstated details—a
suit for lolling about street corners and smoky billiard halls, for drinking and
"cutting a rug" in dance halls, but not for working or fighting or carrying out the
activities that proper adult males were supposed to carry out. Depending on the
flourishes desired, it might cost anywhere from forty-five to eighty dollars, easily a weekly pay packet, often two, for the young men who flaunted the ensemble. Some attributed its origins to Hollywood, and specifically to wartime star
Clark Gable, who, it was announced, had "exchanged his zoot suit for the uniform of the United States Army," thereby redeeming himself both as a man and
as a patriotic citizen. Others theorized that the suits originated in Harlem,
"where the negroes congregate," immediately framing the outfit within popular
understandings of racial inferiority. Thus, the zoot suit represented youthful

wantonness, frivolity, and disrespect for authority as much as had the flapper outfit of the 1920s.[98] For their part, the younger generation saw the anti-zoot campaign, backed by government, police, and military force, as "persecution of a minority," meaning "teenagers in general."[99] Wartime generational antagonism, already fuelled by public panic over juvenile delinquency, came to a head over the zoot.

By 1943, the zoot suit's presence on the American west coast, where it was identified with marginalized African and Hispanic American youth, was stirring social conflict there, as much between Mannheim's "generation units"—those belonging to the same generation but not the same youth culture—as intergenerationally. In Toronto, an adolescent zoot-suiter told a *Globe* reporter that he wore the suit because "it looks very good. It's in style, and if I want to wear it, why should I be stopped?" His five male companions, however, evidently thought him "nuts" and declared that they "wouldn't be found dead wearing one of those outfits." One expressed sympathy for the servicemen, who had "exchanged their civilian clothes for a uniform of which they are very proud. They feel a lot of these kids wearing the funny clothes should be either in the army, navy or air force." The city's tailors contended that the zoot suit's end was in sight, "not by violence but by sheer ridicule," because Canadian boys were "too conscious of their strength, they like hard fighting games too much, to go for such attire," as one tailor explained.[100]

During a time of national sacrifice, these young men in flamboyant clothing, many assumed to be "of foreign birth" or otherwise not white (as well as being "afficionados of jazz," which implied the same thing to many adults), greatly offended those whose own military uniform demonstrated maturity, patriotic duty, and a large measure of masculine heroism. In particular, the fight was on between servicemen of all ages and the "slackers" in zoot suits, a significant proportion of whom were not even of military age.[101] If the question agitating "Toronto's jive-set" was "To zoot or not to zoot," the response on the part of city-based servicemen derived from "strong feelings toward the rug-cutters." Only because Toronto police "stepped firmly on the boys with the reat pleats," according to the city's dance, pool hall and theatre managers, were the riots that plagued Los Angeles avoided.[102] Police had believed it necessary to remove jukeboxes from two popular recreational beaches, Sunnyside and Hanlan's Point, after sailors and other members of the armed forces had "heaved zoot suiters into the lake or torn the clothing from them."[103]

Although the zoot suit was primarily an urban phenomenon, neither its adoption nor the "trouble" with which its wearers were associated was confined to big cities. Through the mid-1940s, there were sporadic reports of zoot-suit wearing youths perpetrating various forms of public mischief, as in Victoria Park in Kitchener, Ontario, where a group was caught pushing young children off swings.[104] A Brantford, Ontario, family was affronted when, on their way home from the cinema, a "car full of zoot-suiters...of foreign ancestry" yelled "sarcastic remarks" at them. The same young men were later spotted "driving around wasting gas, trying to pick up girls"; their lack of success in that endeavour prompted them to call the girls "shameful names." The young woman who wrote to the *Globe* to protest their activities declared that "they are wasting material and gas for lack of which our boys are dying!"[105]

The real zoot-suit trouble seems to have centred in Montreal and environs. In late May 1943, an hour-long battle took place between "boys" from the St. Lambert suburb and other youths "said to be zoot suiters from Montreal." The street fight was claimed to have been the outcome of an effort by zoot-suiters to eject non-suit-wearing St. Lambert youths from a restaurant, and involved an estimated two hundred young rioters in total.[106] Further clashes, mostly between the standard enemy sides of zoot-suiters and servicemen, were reported through the fall of 1943 and the winter of 1944. The apex was reached almost exactly a year after the St. Lambert fracas, in late May and early June 1944, when the Montreal area was again the scene of street-fighting between zoot-suiters and servicemen, primarily sailors.[107] Initially, the city press identified the zoot-suiters as mainly of Italian background, with some francophones among them, while the soldiers and civilian non-zooters were declared to be mostly English-speaking "Canadians." In Verdun early in June, several hundred servicemen sought out zooters at nightclubs, poolrooms, and dance halls, beating them, stripping them, and shredding their despised suits. Dozens were injured, and more than forty— of whom thirty-seven were sailors—were arrested.[108]

The subject was discussed at the highest military and political levels. An inquiry ordered by the Navy produced the predictable verdict that the zooters were a "definite sect or clan of a subversive nature who aim at sabotaging the war effort by unwarranted attacks on service personnel."[109] Their alleged "Italian ancestry" was evidence of their ill will, disloyalty, and absence of patriotism; allegations that they were primarily francophone were cast in the same manner.[110] Justice Minister Louis St. Laurent announced in the House of Commons that both the RCMP and Montreal police had dismissed "racial" and political causes, and offered his own view that rivalry between servicemen and civilians over the city's young women was the true underlying cause, effectively construing the matter as one of youthful male sexuality. Whatever the ultimate explanation, what is important is that the zoot-suit riots stirred public anxiety—once again focused squarely on the youth problem—in an especially anxious time. Much as had happened in Los Angeles, the riots served, quite literally, to recapture public space for those who represented authority and the wartime necessity of civilian deference, while confirming for "deviant" and often-times "minority" youth that their own power to transgress would be carefully contained. The generational style adopted by this group of young men would not be countenanced by the generation in power at a time when national sacrifice and unity were the foremost priorities.

Slowly emerging from wartime production restrictions in 1945, Canadian garment manufacturers and fashion retailers launched right into their cultivation of a closer and more direct—increasingly without parental mediation—relationship with adolescents. A committee of three dozen teenage girls "with school books in their laps" was invited to view and critique that year's models at an unnamed Toronto department store. What they pronounced "crummy" was given "a big X" by "anxious buyers." This meeting between "hard-headed executive and wind blown bobby-soxer" was "no vagrant sampling of opinion," but "a contact carefully cultivated as a weathervane in the directing of Canada's fourth largest industry," which, to the tune of $500,000,000 for women's clothes alone, was on a par with the auto industry. Moreover, about 60 per cent of Canadian clothing designers—forty-three manufacturers in Toronto alone—were actually engaged in producing teenage fashions exclusively. Even as the war was ending, it had been established that the teenager provided "the whole style impetus." "Beyond doubt," declared the president of the Dress Manufacturers Guild of Toronto, "they are the most important factor in the industry."[111]

The reasons for such developments in the fashion retail industry had been uncovered by the marketing surveys of the 1920s: the growing purchasing power of youth, matched by the steadily growing demand on their part for selection, style, and quantity in their own wardrobes. The adolescent girl was found to have "absolutely a minimum of six dresses," while her mother had only three; without the teenager, "the industry would be practically on a housecoat basis." Large department stores began to set up "teenage councils" of their own; starting in 1938 with twelve girls, one of these closed its eighth annual meeting in 1946 with a council of thirty-six girls and thirty boys. Surveys were distributed, interviews were conducted, fashion shows and dances were staged, and the program kept two store employees fully employed for the entire year, because, put succinctly, "the teenager is definitely a business entity." Clearly this trend had gained a foothold in Canada some time before the supposed discovery of the teenager in the 1950s.

Targeted market research of this nature also persuaded Canadian clothing manufacturers and sellers that teenagers were not inclined to adopt American fashion trends outright, disliking, for example, the "loud" colours that were popular among American youth.[112] Whatever the success of attempts to encourage an indigenous Canadian teenage style, the popular magazines aimed for a regional focus in their fashion features. *Chatelaine* printed a spread on youth fashion in western Canada, a region that was itself "perpetually young in mood and action." Readers were informed that western Canadian teens were "knowledgeable about fashion." The western girls unanimously reported that they desired "all purpose" coats, "something new in sweaters," and "plaid skirts that won't make us look hippy." While they preferred going bare-headed, they wanted "a bit of veiling or a clutch of flowers on a half-hat" for date dresses and "small felt rollers" for tailored suits. In fact, there was nothing particularly, recognizably "western" in the clothes modelled by western teenagers in the photographs accompanying the article. As the writers themselves concluded, "the clothes they like to wear, and the way they wear 'em, come together in that easy, feminine, yet purposeful young look which all *Chatelaine* teen-agers, cross

Young Canada, *Eaton's Fall and Winter Catalogue, 1948–49;* "Before E-Commerce: Canada's Mail Order Catalogues." www.civilization.ca/cpm/catalog. Reprinted with permission of Sears Canada.

After World War II, teen fashion was a burgeoning sector of the garment industry, warranting more elaborate advertising campaigns and specialized sections in department stores.

country, have described as their target for fall '46."[113] At the same time that the young were working on a distinctive generational style, they were also, on the whole, giving in to style conformity as promoted by the adults who made and sold "teenage" products.

Because modern leisure was so intertwined with mass culture, it challenged the established relations of class, gender, race, and family, many of which were age-delimited, making it so fundamental and such an overwhelming part of the "problem of modern youth" that the two became essentially the same problem. Whether consideration was given to movies, dance halls, music, or clothing styles, it was the moral implications of this emergent youth culture, with its sexual overtones and its association with working-class, uncultured, and possibly "unrespectable" adolescents, that chiefly offended and challenged adult observers. The exact type of offence might change generationally, in keeping with the ephemeral nature of fads and fashions, but the tone of public discourses about them were echoed across succeeding generations.

However frivolous, morally suspect, and even "dangerous" the cultural practices of the young across the decades studied here appeared, youth managed to play an important historical role as producers, consumers, and disseminators of new aesthetic forms, new products, new practices, and new values. The modern culture that they embraced and helped to shape was in many ways their own— in the years since the Great War, the juvenilization of popular culture has been steady and unabated.[114] Yet however much, and however dangerously, adolescent independence appeared to be growing during these years, young Canadians remained largely under the governance of parents, teachers, employers, lawmakers, and other authoritative adults. Not having reached the age of majority, they had neither voice nor visibility in decision-making circles. By regulating commercial amusements through adult fiat—legislation, supervision, discipline and other forms of authority—and also by summoning up wholesome alternatives to these through school, church, and club, worried adults tried to limit the transgressive potential of youth leisure that so frightened them: an inappropriate crossing into the jealously guarded realm of adult privilege without the requisite, socially prescribed attainments that signified "maturity" and citizen status, and equally without adult sanction. Legislative and voluntary attempts to regulate cinemas, dance halls, and other public places of amusement may have helped to keep these social spaces "on the level," but they did not dissuade adolescents from frequenting them. Young people were formulating their own rites of passage into adulthood in newly important, if not altogether new, informal leisure institutions. While their critics feared the growing autonomy and market power of the young, it was, ironically, what the young lacked in power that made them focus their lives on consumption, fun, and the politics of play.[115]

7

At the Club

Youth Organizations

*No citizen of the town is over 19 and each citizen is unique in that
he is not a citizen of today but a citizen of tomorrow. Every day Teen
Town bubbles with activity.... This club has filled an important
place in their lives..., making its members more self-reliant and
better citizens.*

— W. Hicks, *Toronto Star*, 1946

*A*s the previous chapter suggests, where the young were concerned, leisure
was a veritable no-man's land, to employ the Great War imagery that saturated
the contemporary media. The youthful desire for excitement could be explained
biologically as a "natural" inclination in light of Stanley Hall's theories, but the
enticements of modern popular culture appeared to be intensifying both the natural urge and its unnatural, if not altogether deviant and dangerous, implications. Adult vigilance was required to guide youth through the maelstrom of new
temptations, although it would have to be carried out cautiously: the young
were "sensitive" to any "interference" from the adults in their lives.[1] Nonetheless,
with emerging cultural alternatives contributing so much to interpretations of
the youth problem, Canadians needed reminding that "the indices we need to
consult most carefully are moral indices."[2]

This chapter considers the development, objectives, and activities of a selection of the myriad organizations for youth that flourished during the years from
the Great War to 1950. The sorting of young Canadians into approved clubs and
activities, by capitalizing on the supposed "gang instinct" as well as on theories
about the importance of certain forms of peer-group socialization, was just as

vital to ensuring their cultivation as productive citizens as were schooling and training for work. A prime objective of the period's campaign for solutions to the youth problem and its wider issue, that of social order, was to get young people off the streets, out of the gangs, cinemas, and dance halls, and into adult-supervised, community-based, Christian-influenced, and often church-affiliated organizations that offered up "character training" and lessons in citizenship by means of wholesome recreational activities.

The first half of the twentieth century saw the elaboration of an ever-extended roster of planned, structured, and supervised recreation for youth. Organizations founded before the Great War, such as the Young Men's and Young Women's Christian Associations, the Boy Scouts, and the Girl Guides, expanded internationally, establishing a firm base in Canada by the 1920s. The immediate postwar years also witnessed new and flourishing indigenous groups, such as the Tuxis Boys and the Canadian Girls in Training. Affiliated with the Protestant churches, especially the United Church, these groups were premised on a fourfold standard derived from Christian principles and emphasizing the relationship between an activist Christianity and democratic citizenship. Moreover, as noted, the King government attempted to bring youth into the fold of postwar planning by establishing the Canadian Youth Commission in 1940. By 1950, the American-inaugurated "Teen Town" movement, with its municipal government structure that also resembled the Tuxis's "Boys' Parliament," would lend support to the joint character- and citizenship-training objectives of the earlier youth organizations.

More significant than the actual activities of all these groups, which combined community voluntarism with adult-approved, structured, peer-based recreation, was their purpose. What their adult leaders meant by "recreation" was intended literally to re-create traditional social conventions and relations, transmitting them generationally, to those most in need of being "re-created": the problematic young.[3] Supporters of "group work" emphasized the capacity of a planned and supervised leisure, braced by scientific study and professional direction, to prevent social problems stemming from the misdirection of youthful energy. The experts would steer young people into creative, fulfilling, productive, Christian pastimes, because, as we have seen, adults were preoccupied with the idea that "if no wholesome satisfaction is at hand to supply the need, something will be found that serves the purpose, but which may later lead to mental and moral indigestion."[4] In their trained hands, the result would be a "pedagogy of vigilance," a sort of newly formalized apprenticeship for citizenship under the guise of good, clean, "productive" fun, with all the inherent contradictions that this objective implies.[5]

The idea—ideal, in effect—of community was central to these plans to organize and regulate youth recreation. The community needed to formulate "constructive principles for social education" in the interests of "reaching out toward the social vision of the normal," with "normalization" meaning the same as "Canadianization" in its standard definition as the instillation of white, middle-class, Anglo-Protestant values.[6] The humane, economical, and efficient course for communities was "to make such provision as will safeguard at once the health and morals of its growing citizens." By the 1940s, modern recreation came to be seen as a community responsibility in the same manner as had public health, the two also sharing the goals of encouraging physical and mental fitness in the national interest. The concept of community signified service, obedience, respect for authority, and commitment to family and nation. In practice, the concept of community operated at every level to affirm the status quo.[7]

Also common to the sundry plans for healthy youthful pastimes was Christianity, or at least the mainstream Protestantism that was the predominant faith of middle-class English Canadians. The Protestant churches' interest in youth issues derived from the activist Christianity of the Social Gospel movement, but it was also a direct response to the threat of secularization posed by mass culture. For its part, the Roman Catholic hierarchy, interventionist especially in Quebec, found such "modern inventions" as flappers, cinema, and jazz to be not only menacing to the faith and morality of the young, but actual contraventions of Catholic doctrine. If modernity were effacing traditional Christian values, and if parents were faltering in their character-training responsibilities, the churches would have to intercede "to recover lost ground and safeguard the future by properly organized and supervised recreation."[8] In order to retain any degree of social influence, they would have to compete for the attention of modern youth with the various popular pursuits that young people were taking up so enthusiastically, because "whenever doctrines or religious customs cannot be interpreted to hold the interest of youth, the end of those doctrines and customs is in sight."[9] During a fraught moment in its own history, organized Christianity had to muster its forces to provide new options for "good Christian fun." This would prove to be a Manichean struggle that permitted only limited success to the forces of good.

The criteria for purposeful youth recreation were very much bound by dominant notions of class, gender, and race, now coalescing in new ideas about what constituted "age-appropriate" pastimes. It was feared that the working-class youth who left school in early adolescence, and who were assumed to be devoid of "any home or other training," would enter the realm of adult autonomy without the benefits of a properly regulated transition. Untrained, uncultured, and disaffected, they would reproduce all their class disadvantages, physically and morally, in future generations. The absence of proper socialization by means of healthy pastimes left working-class youth "robbed of the gift of imagination." With few prospects for making a valuable contribution to the community, they would "leave the world peopled by [their] own kind and no better than when they entered it."[10] Where immigrant youth were concerned, their "own kind" was even more in need of the "civilizing" and "Canadianizing" recreation that would ideally steer them away from "old-world" culture.

The best way for the community to meet its recreational responsibilities, consequently, was through the encouragement of youth clubs. Such "group work" would contribute much to "the team play necessary to democracy and unselfish cooperative living," from which the young would learn "the responsibilities of social living which no adult can teach [them]."[11] Outside of family, school, and church, but with their wholehearted support, clubs and organizations were the best means of conditioning youth to the community's objectives. These were the instruments through which national ideals could be most effectively reproduced in the Canadian-born and implanted in the offspring of "foreigners." Not surprisingly, then, just as gendered and racialized understandings of the youth problem and the meanings of modern citizenship informed public discussions and state initiatives, they also underlay the specific plans and structures of youth organizations.

The most influential and widespread of the non-denominational early-twentieth-century organizations were unquestionably the international Boy Scouts and Girl Guides movements. Born of British imperialist, militarist, Protestant, and essentially racist ideas that resonated deeply with many Canadians, even in a modern age that was supposed to be "Canada's Century," the scouting movement was initiated in 1908 by Boer War hero Sir Robert Baden-Powell. In Canada, the Boy Scouts officially took root in 1909. Their sister organization, under the leadership of Baden-Powell's sister Agnes and later his wife, Olave, was established the following year, as growing numbers of girls indicated their interest in scouting.[12] Scouts and Guides shared the Ten Scout Laws, which impressed upon them the ethic of Christian service as the foundation of character and citizenship, as well as the importance of personal obedience, within a quasi-military structure complete with drilling exercises, survival techniques, uniforms, and badges. They were required to promise allegiance to God and the king, to perform "good deeds," and to remain "pure in thought, word and deed."[13]

As their founder insisted, by becoming a Scout and adhering to the Ten Scout Laws, every boy would be "of use" to nation and empire.[14] Girl Guides would take up their "greatest duty in life" by learning "how to be women—self-helpful, happy, prosperous and capable of keeping good homes and of bringing up good children."[15] Through experiential learning techniques, and by their own enthusiastic community service, young people would come to exemplify the "British" ideals of manliness, womanliness, and citizenship.[16] Nowhere was this promoted more thoroughly than among those considered most in need. The federal Indian Affairs Branch reported proudly in 1942 that a "large number of senior pupils" in both day and residential schools across the nation were "displaying a keen interest" in the Girl Guides and Boy Scouts. These youth groups were considered to "provide the Indian youth with valuable lessons in the art of self-government" and to "encourage him, too, to assume responsibility for the accomplishment of tasks that he can complete better and more economically for himself than any other agency that might be designed to help him."[17]

In 1914, in light of the popularity of the Scouts in Canada and in order to promote other such "healthy" organizations for boys, the first National committee on Boys' Work was formed. The committee consisted of delegates from all Protestant denominations, appointed by the National Council of the YMCA;

it was headed by Taylor Statten, secretary of the YMCA's own Boys' Work Committee. Within a year of its establishment, it had sponsored a number of regional Leaders Training Camps and three Boys Conferences. The Great War again played no small part in inspiring such "group work." Foremost among "the greatest of all the problems of the war," it was argued, was the dire need to replace "the cream of Canada's manhood," who had answered the call to service with their own lives. Through organized recreation, the "young men of promise yet in their early youth" would be cultivated to fill the places left empty, both at the front and at home.[18] The outcome, in 1918, were the Trail Rangers program, for boys aged twelve to fourteen, and the Tuxis program for boys aged fifteen to seventeen. The basis of both was the Canadian Standard Efficiency Training program, which quickly gained a foothold across Canada.[19] By 1928, there were 2,287 registered groups in 928 communities, boasting a total enrolment of 27,921 boys. The Tuxis also inaugurated annual Boys' Parliaments, conducted in provincial legislative buildings. In these mock parliaments of representatives elected from the club membership, the Tuxis boys decided their own activities for the year. They also passed earnest resolutions condemning the use of tobacco, alcohol, and drugs and urging Sunday observance and club activity, "because youth generally fails to use his leisure time in activities that really re-create." The ultimate achievement was "complete Christian living among boys."[20]

There was no question in the minds of Tuxis leaders that "the welfare and proper training and development, mentally, morally and physically, of the teenage boys of our country, today assumes a role of national import, far greater than has ever before been known in history."[21] By the 1920s, as the street-gang menace took on increasing emphasis in both expert and public discourses, proper guidance of adolescent boys came to be seen as "so vital a need, so tremendous a task, and a problem of such compelling interest" that there were calls for the establishment of "boyology" as a legitimate subfield of psychology. Certainly, boys in "the most plastic period of their lives" needed the example and guidance of "men of calibre" to help them achieve "sterling manhood."[22] In Winnipeg, the Rotary Club financed the salary of a "boy worker" and the operation of a community-wide program for boys that featured movies on evenings and Saturdays, instruction in such useful and manly pastimes as aircraft building and Morse code, chess and checkers, special drawing classes, and "character building talks." The high proportion of low-income families in the city necessitated such provision, "which contributes so largely to character development and to the maintenance of wholesome interests and citizenship."[23] Healthy recreation, healthy masculinity, and good citizenship were a package: the Tuxis and Trail Rangers were particularly enthusiastic about father-and-son activities, as "a noble character is a father's best gift to his son."[24]

It was also during the interwar years that the oldest of the youth organizations, the Young Men's and Young Women's Christian Associations, made concerted efforts to lure more adolescents into their fold, especially those from working-class and immigrant families. The national leadership of the YMCA felt that "social education" should be the organization's principal aim: they wanted to make young people aware of "changing forces" so as to enjoin them in working toward "a more Christian Social Order."[25] Both groups conducted intensive recruiting drives that sent staff members into local factories and shops to present health talks and lectures on various social topics, and to encourage membership among young workers.[26] Taking advantage of the rapidly expanding high school population, the associations also created special ties with students through their new Hi-Y programs. Established during the heady years of high school expansion in the 1920s, the purpose of these new programs was "to create, maintain and extend throughout the school and community high standards of Christian character." Like all the extracurricular activities initiated by the schools themselves, they aimed to foster a "better school spirit" in boys and girls "of good character."[27] The Girls' Hi-Y also had the particular mission of "uniting in an effort to assist those less fortunate," usually by the girls' serving as counsellors at summer camps for underprivileged children.[28]

Ideas about the pressing need for boyology aside, the years following the Great War saw many arguments that club activities under religious or community leadership were even more critical for their sisters, especially those young women who had left school to earn wages. Because of their life circumstances, "the personality which has been cramped all day just has to have expression and attention," which, it was thought, led to dressing "in the extreme" and "being noisy on the street" to attract notice. Such girls had to be marshalled into purposeful groups, where appropriate attention could fill their needs and obviate their desires to look elsewhere for the inappropriate type.[29] Agnes Baden-Powell argued that, knowing few "restraints" after leaving school and entering employment, these girls absolutely needed the character training offered by the Girl Guides in the interests of their future motherhood.[30] Guiding offered to all Canadian girls—"and through them to the girls of generations to come"—the "firm grasp on life" that was crucial in "a great period of social change, when new ideas in business, science and education are making the most interesting world for girls that history has ever known." The group experience would equip the "future women of Canada" to meet the "responsibilities and privileges of citizenship with a spirit that will be a great influence for good in the life of our Dominion."[31]

The Great War also saw the creation of Canadian Girls in Training, a group for twelve to seventeen year olds that corresponded to the YMCA's Tuxis program for boys. CGIT's avowed purpose was "to take a united stand on personal and group standards which will make it possible for the Canadian Girls in Training as a body to influence the standards of dress, behaviour in public and in school of the girls in the community." The training aspects emphasized Christianity and citizenship within a non-competitive setting that recognized that adolescent girls' social needs were different from those of boys.[32] From its base in Ontario, the CGIT movement spread rapidly across the province and throughout eastern Canada. By 1919, CGIT was holding twenty-eight conferences annually, with four thousand girls attending.[33] When the first Maritime conference of "over 500 girls and potential leaders" was held in Halifax that spring, the *Halifax Mail* waxed eloquent about the value of such girls' organizations as well as the value of girls to the modern nation, proclaiming that "the day of the girl has come—she must have her own place in the schemes for moral, mental and physical up-building," for these were "the potential mothers of the race, the potential women of the nation."[34] In 1924, CGIT boasted an enrolment of over thirty thousand teenage girls across the nation. "Under the wing" of a friend, Mildred Young joined a group that met on Jarvis Street in Toronto during World War II: "CGIT was supposed to teach us responsibility as well as numerous other useful things that would fit us for the life we were expected to lead. Two of us would make dinner the night of the meeting.... From time to time we were given rough balls of khaki wool with which to knit socks and scarves for the soldiers.... We were also taught how to sew diapers and make babies' layettes."[35]

These church-affiliated, gender-segregated, community-based groups made a point of providing opportunities for adolescents to meet in mixed company for refreshments, talks, games, and sometimes "wholesome" films, all under "proper supervision" and within "a favourable and safe environment."[36] The activity, excitement, and association with the opposite sex "craved" by all adolescents were seen to be better met under church and community auspices than under those of commerce.[37] These events were also believed to allow for "a very natural opportunity to discuss some of the important questions of family life and home building," inasmuch as adolescents were "sure to be thinking much about these things." The "wise leadership" that recognized this interest and gave "something of the radiance and inspiration of religion" to discussions on sexuality was "doing much to guide and enrich the lives of these young people."[38] In fact, the young members of these groups were themselves instrumental in bringing about such discussions. Formally resolving at their annual parliament of 1924 that "cheap ideas of friendship with girls [were] all too common," that sex education was of "vital importance in boy life," and that much harm was being wrought "in the whole community" due to ignorance, the Tuxis boys implored their group mentors, parents, and educational authorities to ensure that "steps be taken as soon as possible" to include sex education in their programs.[39]

Just as the relationship of youth and modernity was embedded in anxieties about the youth problem, so too was the association of youth and the city, another of the themes underlying the public preoccupation with the young during these years. The city held a fatal attraction to the young: it was a trap, as Stanley Hall had earlier warned, glittering, seductive, and dangerous to those whose health and judgement could not withstand either its attractions or its dangers. Canada crossed the threshold of urbanization in 1921; worries about rural out-migration that had been escalating since the war focused even more urgent attention on ways in which rural life could be "modernized" sufficiently to keep its young. Rural advocates believed that the maintenance of country life was "necessary to the perpetuity of the nation" but feared that "strong vigorous capable men and women" were being "constantly recruited from the farms... to lead the decadent urban hosts whose lives are being burned out in the great mael-strom of activities centering in the city." One of the ways in which farm life could be made more attractive—"perhaps the most direct thing" for its promotion—was through boys' and girls' clubs.[40] A large part of the campaign for rural revitalization of these years involved the provision of suitable after-school organ-ized activities for rural youth, primarily in the form of Junior Farmers' clubs and junior versions of the Women's Institutes. By 1914, the Ontario agricultural department had organized Junior Farmers' clubs in Peel, York, and Durham coun-ties. These quickly proved so successful that they were established in every coun-ty in the province.[41] The Junior Farmers planned their own program, were "trained in Parliamentary procedure," participated in interclub public speaking and debating, and, in summer, held acre-profit and livestock-profit competitions as well as contests in livestock, seed judging, and weed identification.[42]

Rural weeklies reported ongoing activities that included joint meetings for Junior Farmers and Junior WI members, and the holding of various socials to raise money, primarily for sporting and other equipment for the boys' group. The eight Junior Women's Institutes in Peel County, Ontario, had a very full roster of literary and social programs, debates, public-speaking competitions, sewing for the home branch of the Soldiers Settlement Board, and writing letters and send-ing magazines and newspapers to "lonely families in Northern Ontario." They also held dances, with Junior Farmers "always figuring then."[43] The clubs' activ-ities were decidedly gendered along traditional lines. While the boys heard visit-ing lecturers on agricultural improvement, the need for immigrant farm labour, and the use of farm machinery, the girls heard speakers on school improvement, care of the sick, and "when a girl travels alone."[44] The Junior Farmers of Bolton, Ontario, listed plays, competitions, excursions, and parties among their 1929 activities, for which plans were simply wrought: "Boys drive, girls cater."[45]

The most concerted organization of rural youth during this period was the New Canada movement of the early 1930s, as much a response to Depression conditions in the countryside as it was another means of working against youth out-migration. Rural newspapers lent their support to this "non-political" and "purely voluntary effort on the part of a group of young farm leaders" to moti-vate the young so that they might, first, "fearlessly face the facts of 1933, the implications of the machine, and a world radically changed by scientific inven-tion and the upheaval of the war." In addition, the movement sought acknowl-edgement that the nation's future depended on agricultural prosperity, and "therefore that rural youth should take the lead in a movement to save agricul-ture and thereby save Canada." Its leaders insisted that the movement's educa-tional work be undertaken in a "scientific" manner: "Its study will start with the actual concrete problems that farmers and the country as a whole are facing today and will attempt gradually to form intelligent opinion on the basis of this study." Within a year, the organization was making some headway in addressing other youth groups such as the Tuxis, CGIT, the Junior Farmers, and a number of other church and community associations involving the young. By the beginning of 1934, twenty-two meetings had been arranged for rural Middlesex County in Ontario.[46]

By the early 1930s, there were some indications that those who aspired to direct youth through organized recreation were achieving a measure of success. Surveys of high school students suggested—to the surveyors, at least—that "everyone knows the importance of the right use of leisure," though it was considered that much more could be done through the schools to "prepare sufficiently for the best use of future leisure by the pupils." A survey of one hundred Halifax children aged ten to fourteen found that "almost exactly one third of both boys and girls are members of no clubs or other organization and play no organized games," which still left an impressive two-thirds accounted for by these "regulated" modes of recreational activity.[47] Out of anti-social gangs, reported a Winnipeg child welfare worker in 1933, the club movement had encouraged the development of "integrated social groups" through twenty-five boys' clubs and twelve girls' clubs. The boys' clubs were particularly effective, drawing 16,203 boys to meetings over the course of that year: "To many boys these clubs might be the big event of the week, and in many cases it was noticed that there was a gradual sprucing up in their clothing and the care exercised in their general appearance."[48] The Boy Scouts, Girl Guides, Tuxis, CGIT, YMCA, and YWCA had enrolled over two million adolescents across the nation by 1936. The Depression may actually have helped their cause: the Girl Guides experienced an increase of 4,722 members in 1932/33, suggesting that Guiding was providing girls with "a wonderful opportunity for interesting and wholesome recreation in these lean days, when other forms of amusement are more costly." The numbers continued to grow through the 1930s and 1940s.[49]

As the Girl Guides' annual reports observed in the early Depression years, Guiding continued "to play a large part in Canadianizing the children of our foreign settlers." Some twenty nationalities were reportedly "working happily together in one Winnipeg company," while a number of rural Saskatchewan schools were setting up Scout and Guide groups "with successful results in teaching citizenship to their foreign born pupils."[50] In Vancouver, the United Church arranged for a "Rising Sun Square" of Tuxis boys at its Japanese Mission, where its members served the immigrants and their Canadian-born children, about half of whom were not Christian. Their young leader had been in the country only a year. The group was pronounced "a fine bright lot of fellows and as full of life as any other Square in Canada."[51] Immigrant communities wanted organizations and activities that allowed for cultural transmission, and thus preservation, within the framework of a collective understanding of the extent and nature of the "Canadianization" required for the community's benefit.[52] What evidence we have of their social formation suggests that the ideas behind the campaign to structure adolescent recreation were not as "foreign" to these foreigners as their observers believed. Most immigrant groups organized their own versions of "uplifting" activities for their youth, for whom the stakes were even higher: not only did they represent the culture's future in a new land, they also had to

Boys and Girls Clubs, Chinese Presbyterian Church, Victoria, BC, 1930. Reprinted with permission of the Chinese Churches of Canada. www.chinesechurches.org

Young men and women from immigrant families also participated in the youth organization drive of the interwar years, although most of their groups remained racially segregated, as this photograph of male members of the Chinese Presbyterian Church's athletic club and CGIT girls suggests.

become "Canadian" in order for the community and its individual members to succeed.[53] The joint objective was to keep youth "contained" and on the path to successful adulthood—which demanded a certain amount of assimilation—while also maintaining attachment to the old-world culture and passing on its distinctive traits generationally.

Western Canada's immigrant communities shared many of the youth-anxieties of the "mainstream," aggravated by worries about the "contamination" that the Canadian-born generation of youth also signified for its own group, in counter-suspicion to the prejudices of their Canadian critics. The largest social institution in Alberta's Ukrainian community was the Ukrainian Labour-Farmer Temple Association. With eighty-eight branches in 1929, it also had forty branches of a Youth Section and published, among its regular newspapers, The World of Youth.[54] Starting in Saskatoon in 1923, there were attempts to organize a Society of Young Doukhobors in order to "lift the good name of Doukhoborism out of the mire and to perpetuate its high ideals." The organizers had mixed success, to the degree that "three-fourths of the young people did not know what it was all about." The most important obstacles, however, were generational: "suspicion" on the part of the older generation, along with the younger generation's evident difficulty in speaking the native language. Despite the group's intended purpose as a youth organization, about two-thirds of the regular attendance at meetings was made up of the older generation. Feeling constrained to speak "in the native tongue" due to customs of intergenerational courtesy and deference, the young soon complained that the older group took control.[55]

Similar organizations, as well as challenges, were found among Alberta's Mormon population, which counted about fifteen thousand members in the early 1930s. Each ward had its own activities for youth, including the Young Men's Mutual Improvement Association, which took in members aged twelve to twenty-one. In addition to meeting weekly on their own, the young men held regular joint meetings with the Young Ladies Mutual Improvement Association. Both groups aimed for the "self-improvement" of members through study and leisure activities, with special emphasis on reading, public speaking, dramas, athletics (especially basketball), singing, and dancing. The young men also sponsored a Boy Scout group, while the church offered its own "attractive programme" for teenage girls, known as "Beehive Work" and corresponding to the Girl Guide program.[56] In Winkler, Manitoba, "queen of the Mennonite towns," where the young evidently spoke English on the street and "almost exclusively" among themselves, as also in the town of Gretna, there were "plentiful" organizations for both athletic and social purposes offered to the young.[57]

The community service at the basis of these youth groups—new and old, international and Canadian—received extra emphasis during the Depression, when members were called upon to take active part in alleviating the suffering associated with the massive crisis of unemployment. The benefits were manifold: young people were kept occupied in useful, socially beneficial activity; their "national duty" was emphasized to them and modelled through activity; they were helping to keep social peace and bolster a faltering economic system and a faulty social welfare network through voluntary activity. The rhetoric employed by the youth groups to discuss plans for relief work belies fears of the nefarious ideologies and organizations that young Canadians might otherwise be drawn to, communism in particular. Much was at stake, therefore, in using youth groups to ward off insidious doctrines and potential social disorder. Theirs was the generation that was suffering disproportionately. Toronto mayor James Simpson, seeking ways to "rehabilitate the lost generation," remarked that the "deplorable" conditions of the time left several thousand young people with nowhere to turn. He urged that community members do "a little heart-searching" so as to understand "the evils that can arise if the problem is not dealt with."[58] As usual, the effect was considered particularly bad for young men; all those interested in the welfare of boys "must bend their efforts to preserving their morale and assisting their education until times improve."[59] One son of Italian immigrants, who came of age in Toronto during the 1930s, remembered that churches converted their basements and small gathering rooms to provide for free recreational gatherings in the evenings, with one day a week set aside for youth social activities and "a night or two" for basketball and volleyball.[60]

The young were believed to be the social group most inclined to transform any sense of alienation from the established order into plans for its radical reconstruction, perhaps even its overthrow. Community service, or "the real spirit of citizenship," inarguably had to be brought to the fore in times like these. Consequently, when Prime Minister Richard B. Bennett appealed to the nation for all to do their part to remedy the plight of the unemployed, the executive committee of the Canadian Girl Guides Association was at the ready with plans. The Guides intended to hold "relief fun entertainments" for the young unemployed; to contribute food, clothing, fuel, or money as collected by Guide and Ranger companies; and to invite unemployed girls to "occasional recreational evenings arranged especially for the visitors," helping out materially and, more important, by providing "training in the fundamentals of democracy and good citizenship, which are so greatly needed today."[61]

In the midst of raging and largely futile debates over state responsibility for the suffering masses, the only palliative offered to youth (besides postponing the date of unemployment through extended schooling) was to ensure participation in "some definite activity." After seeming progress in organizing young Canadians into purposeful clubs and pastimes, there were worrisome indications that those left to their own devices were turning to less positive outlets. As funding for both school and community recreational programs dried up, the gang appeared to be "again developing into a contaminating source of infection."[62] And by the late 1930s, the flourishing of various anti-democratic movements around the world made the young appear ever more a menace to social order, as these movements "recognized and exploited the potential power for social change which youth possesses." To counter this, social workers argued the equal importance of vocational training and recreational opportunities, especially sports and games. Any recreational activity based on "a broad social view" would represent a step toward the reintegration of alienated youth into the social mainstream.[63] Organized recreation was a form of "social education" that would demonstrate to the young "the idea of democracy involving unselfishness, his or her own worth, conventions with respect to sex, the worth of religion as a workable philosophy of life." Consequently, it was both "economical and safe to conserve a source of future good citizenship."[64] There were even some who maintained that the Depression was delivering a necessary lesson to modern youth by teaching them the benefits of active participation and community service as leisure activity while weaning them away from "the easier way of paying to be amused."[65] As one rural newspaper editorialized, "The chief criticism of youth a few years ago was that they could not be interested in public greatness or problems. They were interested only in dancing and a good time. Apparently the Jazz Age for youth is passing."[66]

Despite optimistic reports by government agencies, youth workers, recreation experts, and the media about young people's growing involvement in healthy, safe, and supervised group activity, it was also evident by the 1930s that most of the adolescents reached by the club movement resembled their own children: middle-class, Protestant, white high school students. These young Canadians were included in discussions about the overriding youth problem but were not its most worrisome components. While community and church agencies performed an outstanding service in the "modelling and shaping" of youth, and while they "touched many strata of society," surveys showed that their clubs were not reaching the underprivileged boys and girls whose recreational needs should be "first and foremost." Nothing of lasting benefit could be attained unless such clubs could gather "those who roam the streets, those who congregate in gangs, around stores, poolrooms, and other hangouts" and bring these strays into the fold. The true problem of modern youth was not being adequately addressed in the club movement. Most cities had "little or no machinery" to bring needy boys and girls into contact with the very recreational agencies designed to best serve them as well as the national interest.[67]

Heeding the call to organize "idle youth" and keep them busy, a number of community-based groups sprang up to meet the needs of, as well as Canadians' own fears about, the young people less likely to be found in the mainstream organizations. In 1937, the Vancouver police initiated the Junior G-Men of Canada, attracting three thousand members in its first year of operation. The group was formed specifically to organize adolescents who were not "in the same social and financial stratum as the majority of members in these clubs of the more or less well to do," as well as "that large class that does not go to church or attend Sunday School." The G-Men's founder, Ronald G. Everleigh, had trained for the ministry before joining the city's police force as a juvenile delinquency officer. His observations in that role had led him to "several definite conclusions" about the causes of delinquency, among which he emphasized the "lack of the ordinary privileges and opportunities which should be the heritage of every boy and girl, and particularly unsupervised leisure time." The original seventeen male members selected the group's name from the popular gangster films of the time. As was so often the scenario in these contentious films, they "wanted the world to know that they were tough guys, but their civilized sense of the fitness of things impelled them to associate themselves with the tough guys who were on the side of law and order." Or so their adult supervisors hoped. The group's charter laid out its goals as "the training of the youth of Canada for the responsibilities of citizenship," and especially "the maintenance of law and order." Every member took an oath before the host city's chief constable "to be truthful, honest, clean in speech and habits, a good sportsman and a good example to the community," but "above all else [to] honour his parents and be true to his flag." Despite the name and the male focus, within short order the G-Men's downtown Vancouver headquarters in an abandoned factory saw a mixed-sex group of about two hundred young people taking part in various gender-delineated productive activities: gymnastics, handicrafts, nursing, dramatics, and gardening classes for girls, and classes in radio, automotive, woodworking, model-airplane construction, and safe driving for boys.[68]

The Depression galvanized a variety of youth movements internationally, the most notorious of which are doubtless those associated with the fascist national revitalization campaigns of Hitler and Mussolini. While some Canadians feared the implications of an organized and politicized youth movement, others hailed the formation of the Canadian Youth Congress in Toronto in 1935 as evidence that the spirit of youth could be put to nation-building purposes—peace, employment, and education—during a bleak time.[69] Although most of its members were older youth and university students, the Canadian Youth Congress must nonetheless be acknowledged here for its attempts to translate generational consciousness and collective ideals into political action—and, just as much, for the adult trepidation that it raised because of what these signified. At the inaugural congress, delegates from 201 youth groups—primarily church-affiliated and university-based but also from the leftist ranks of the peace movement, labour organizations, and associations of the unemployed—produced a youth platform. Under the banner of "Peace, Freedom and Progress," they lobbied the King government for what was effectively a "new deal" for young Canadians. Capturing the persistent optimism of youth in the face of the Depression's ravages, one participant declared that the shared experiences and ideals of their generation must overcome all other differences that might divide Canadians of their time: "There must be, from this time in Canada, neither Jew nor Gentile, French nor English, westerner nor easterner, but a Canadian youth movement conscious of differences, indeed, but seeing in those very differences a means of developing a culture that will be worthy of the name Canadian."[70]

With twenty-seven local congresses established across the country by 1936, the Canadian Youth Congress framed a Declaration of the Rights of Canadian Youth as well as a Canadian Youth Act, which were submitted to all associated youth groups for their consideration. The intention was to present the final versions to Parliament for legislative action.[71] Committed to changing the laws of the land in order to recognize the distinct needs of young Canadians, and supported by such suspect groups as the Trades and Labour Congress, the Canadian Youth Congress was bound to rouse official suspicion. Despite the lack of any evidence of subversion, it was kept under continuous surveillance by the Royal Canadian Mounted Police. The coming of World War II made the group's generational call to arms much clearer, and undoubtedly more disconcerting to the older generation. At its fifth congress, held in Montreal in July 1940, the group reaffirmed its "allegiance to the democratic traditions of our country and of the British Commonwealth," and stated its commitment to seeing totalitarianism defeated. Yet its members protested the curtailment of civil liberties through the sweeping War Measures Act and the Defence of Canada Regulations, and called for the repeal of those measures. They also objected to the National Mobilization Registration Act, which would facilitate conscription, and declared their support for organized labour.[72] Although its members continued to meet, to promote the rights of youth in an adult-run world seemingly bent on self-destruction, to protest the spread of fascism, and to advocate for peace, in 1942 the Canadian Youth Congress was declared illegal under the Defence of Canada Regulations.[73] With the war emergency as justification, the state could readily take its stand against a generation of youth that was attempting to rally its collective consciousness to engender the kinds of socio-economic and political changes that would further its own interests.

The Canadian Youth Congress may have met with resounding state disapproval to the point of being forcibly disbanded, but Canada's entry into the war necessarily made youth a valued resource and compelled the federal government, for the first time in history, to make some gesture toward taking into account the needs and desires of the young. The King government therefore went about creating a CYC of its own. The Royal Commission on Dominion-Provincial Relations (1937–40) heard from a number of youth organizations during its sessions, many of which supported the YMCA's recommendation that a Dominion Youth Bureau be established to research the needs of youth and make policy for the "protection and development" of youth as "our most valuable national resource."[74] In 1940, ostensibly to ensure that the voice of youth was heard in plans for postwar reconstruction, the Canadian Youth Commission (rather than Congress) was created. Through a number of national surveys on jobs, health, recreation, clubs, marriage and family, and citizenship—the understood basis of all the others—the commission heard from youth groups across the land. It was not made permanent, however, and little in the way of policy actually ensued from its recommendations. Moreover, although over a thousand study groups of about a dozen members each were formed, the CYC was heavily weighted toward urban Anglo-Protestant youth participation, reflecting the membership of its constitutent groups. What is most important about this state-supported CYC is not its accomplishments but that its very existence testifies to the growing acknowledgement of age as the marker of a distinct socio-political group and a particular class of citizens. Even for its members below the age of majority, youth as a group was becoming a recognized collective force in national life.[75]

The youth clubs played a vital role in the war effort, as might be expected, seeing as they represented a ready supply of organized young people ostensibly dedicated to social service. As during the Great War, the call was answered enthusiastically by the Girl Guides, who were reminded that the "service of youth" was a "vital service for the nation." The Guides' quasi-military structure allowed for the quick development of a wartime program, which saw a stepped-up emphasis on emergency preparedness, physical fitness, homecraft, nursing, and first aid. The Guides also participated in the customary female home-front activities, "quietly but busily knitting, sewing, making bandages, acting as messengers, typists or chauffeurs and otherwise assisting local war agencies" across the land.[76] A fourteen-year-old patrol leader from Alberta reported to the *Free Press Prairie Farmer* that "the companies in our town have sent one shipment of clothes for the homeless victims in bomb-shattered Great Britain and they are busily making more." She also reminded the newspaper's young readers that "the future queen, Princess Elizabeth, is a Girl Guide."[77] The Boy Scouts followed suit: they were also active in the collection of salvage, undertook the shipping of hundreds of pounds of seeds to Britain, and promoted and grew Victory Gardens. They served as messengers, telegraph operators, and first-aid attendants, and they took part in Victory Loan campaigns.[78] As a CGIT member, Mildred Young joined other girls who sold tags on Saturday mornings "for a multitude of good causes."[79]

The delinquency panic of the World War II years saw new initiatives to involve the young themselves in finding "solutions" to this particularly frightening element of the youth problem. The solutions proposed by youth, not surprisingly, were those espoused by concerned adults all along. During the 1940s, Canada's largest delinquency prevention bureau was in Montreal. In 1947, the city's police force established Police Juvenile Clubs, the only such in Canada. The clubs claimed 50,000 members under the age of eighteen in that city alone. Forty-five thousand had signed up in the first three weeks. The police contended that these clubs were a major factor in the city's declining juvenile crime rate, down from "more than 4,000" in 1943 to 1,800 by 1948. The clubs provided sports facilities and "a healthy outlet for youth," as well as encouraging "better social attitudes" and "humanizing the police force."[80]

Shortly after the war's end, *Chatelaine* magazine sent its Edmonton 'Teen-Age Council girls to investigate that city's youth problem. The girls began by interviewing local authorities to see what clubs and organizations, sports, hobbies, church groups, and the like were available as alternatives to—and preventatives for—gangs and delinquency. This seemed a logical starting point, for, in their own words, "all of us are in Edmonteens or basketball or go to Ski Village or camp or take part in dramatics or help in the 'teen-age radio program and the 'teen-age pages in our local newspapers." The girls did not question the efficacy of either their investigative methods or the organizations themselves where the "problem" was concerned, "until the Mayor asked us how much of an effort we were making to get the 'teen-agers who really need our help into our special groups and activities." The mayor theorized that "it's mostly the lone wolves, the boys and girls who don't seem to fit in, who get into trouble. Especially in undesirable districts where, through no fault of their own, they have been allowed to grow up." In his experience, "no boy or girl attached to a really first rate athletic organization had become a problem."[81] The girls concluded that there were several pressing needs, most notably for "vital, active leadership by olders" in youth groups, for more facilities for group activities, and for "wider plans for our teen groups than just dancing."[82]

By the 1940s, the term *teenager*, in its various spellings and permutations, was part of the common vocabulary. A new level of youth organization also came about in the form of the "teen club" or "teen canteen." The teen club's function had more to do with socializing than service, but its purpose remained that of its predecessors: to operate as a safe haven for the young in a "dangerous" world of unsupervised peer activity in commercialized adult settings. In 1944, the *Toronto Star* recognized a city woman, Mrs. E. Trevor, as the "originator, planner, organizer and bulwark of Toronto's only 'teenage club," which boasted a regular membership of over one hundred high school students. As the reporter explained, "in the eccentric idiom of the high school, when she actualized her dream of a club for teenagers early in December, she was really cooking with gas, not just slapping her gums. She was hep to the dirty boogie and the all-importance of the Saturday night rat race." In her own words, Mrs. Trevor, mother of two teenage girls, "just decided that something ought to be done about providing inexpensive fun" for young people. A club of their own gave them "every opportunity to feel important and independent" at the very moment in their lives when they most needed to. Membership was restricted to high school students who could pay the two-dollar fee. Weekly Saturday-night dances, featuring local high school orchestras and also offering games, coffee, and hot dogs for a cover charge of twenty-five cents, were the "main event." The club had only two basic rules: for members, "no smoking and no drinking"; for parents, "come as often as you please but don't stay too long." Mrs. Trevor, who had come of age during the 1920s, knew from her own generation's experience that adolescents wanted to "play at being grown-ups and to feel that nobody's bossing them," and consequently she instructed the chaperones to "stay in the background and only interfere if things aren't going as they should." Also an "amateur student of psychology," the intrepid Mrs. Trevor saw the club "not only as a source of healthy and inexpensive fun, but as a means of developing youthful initiative." The young members were learning leadership traits and the democratic process, because "nothing is done unless they indicate they want it by popular vote."[83]

Most of these new teen clubs came about as a result of such voluntary private initiatives, whether by inspired individuals or by community groups. But a movement toward establishing municipally sponsored community centres, long called for by public-recreation advocates, permitted the transfer of adolescents' favourite commercial pastimes and meeting spaces to clubs specifically for their age group and associated with these new venues. The postwar community centre thus often served a dual purpose, functioning also as a youth centre: a publicly supported, officially sanctioned, and adult-supervised non-commercial alternative to the menacing sites for adolescent amusement that had so perturbed youth-watchers since the previous war. That this was a new chapter in the campaign to organize and regulate youth pastimes is given witness in a popular magazine and newspaper advertisement for Coca Cola Company, which had been identifying its products with youthful fun and games since the 1920s: "Across the land, you find youth meeting together to talk, to dance, to have fun at Youth Centres"—and, naturally, to drink Coke, the preferred beverage of youth and "a symbol of hospitality and friendliness."[84] By the end of 1946, there were twenty-two community centres in the Toronto area alone. These not only provided the young with an adult-sanctioned "something to do" but also functioned as an alternative to church-affiliated clubs, which "were doing a wonderful job but had a limited appeal" due to their denominationalism. It even appeared to some that the declining rates of juvenile delinquency could be traced directly to the growth of community centres that sponsored teen clubs.[85] One of the YWCA's directors, who undertook a national tour of established teen clubs in 1945, declared that she found "absolutely no racial or social discrimination among 'teenagers in their 'teen clubs and centres" across the land. She noted the existence of "as many as 29" clubs in one city, permitting young people to "shop around to see which one offers them most." One of the most successful was the Tac House in Saskatoon, where a professional youth worker and her board ran popular programs in handicrafts and etiquette, as well as holding the requisite dances.[86]

The favourite postwar youth organization in Canada came out of an American phenomenon known as Teen Town. Unlike many earlier youth organizations, Teen Towns were not gender-segregated, which probably helped to account for much of their appeal. Modelled on municipal councils, the Teen Towns were specifically designed to provide for peer-group socializing and, just as important, to impart citizenship training, in a more engaged and participatory manner than had most groups, by actively demonstrating to their young members their future roles as leaders and voters. With no member over the age of nineteen, each Teen Town elected its own mayor and town council from its "citizens of tomorrow."[87] Teen Town events and projects were funded by the club membership through nominal membership fees, "tag days," performances, a canteen, and regular dances. Like other youth groups, they were also sponsored and mentored by local adult organizations such as the Rotarians and the national council of the YM/YWCA. The Teen Town concept succeeded beyond all expectations: by 1949, it ranked as the top youth organization in Canada.

The first Canadian Teen Town appears to have begun in Penticton, British Columbia, in 1944. That year, under the sponsorship of the Alberni Parent-Teacher Association, and employing the high school students' council as its governing body, the Alberni District Teen Age Club was formed. Within two years, that club officially became a Teen Town, with a mayor, twelve councillors, and an adult advisory committee. By 1949, there were twelve thousand Teen Town members in British Columbia alone.[88] One of Alberni Teen Town's earliest "mayors" would remember his involvement, starting when he was in second form, with much fondness: "Lots of memories of meetings, planning events, work bees, dances, and travelling. Above all it was enjoyable and rewarding experience working with people in the Teen Town movement and the community." Following what seems to have been the common model, his council had an even gender split of six boys and six girls, with local high school teachers as their adult advisers. Another Teen Town member started his association with the group at the age of thirteen, when he took on a part-time janitorial job that paid him $1.75 per hour, far more than the $5.50 per month that he had netted from his paper route. He became a member, then a councillor, and eventually served on regional and provincial executives, learning along the way "a lot of life skills, which have served me well over the years."[89] The group's teen centre, known as the Teen Hut because it had served as an armed-forces shelter during the war, was extensively renovated by volunteers. It ultimately boasted a dance floor with a small stage, a "Coke bar" and lounge area, and an activities room where teens could play ping pong, checkers, darts, and various board games. Local bands

Maple Leaf Gardens musical show, Simpson's "Teen-Town Time" dance. City of Toronto Archives, Series 1057, Item 7184, [ca. 1946]; Alexandra Studio fonds, Series 1057.

By the period's end, corporations and institutions had "co-opted" teen dance and music as well as fashion, promoting civic interests as well as their own products and objectives. This dance concert featured Bobby Gimby, who had played with the renowned Mart Kenney, had his own CBC radio show, and would go on to compose the Centennial anthem "CA-NA-DA" nearly twenty years later.

and the members' own 78s provided music for their very popular dances. Members earned money for activities and also performed community service by taking part in such projects as handling the parking at Klondike Night celebrations and raising funds for the March of Dimes.[90] The very successful Port Alberni group fostered additional clubs in the district, at Cherry Creek and Sproat Lake, opening up opportunities for local teenagers to "attend three Teen Town dances on one weekend.... The bands liked this too."[91]

In large cities such as Toronto, any number of Teen Towns could flourish: the *Toronto Star* reported that in April 1946, two bands and 10,300 Teen-Towners from thirty-eight different Toronto and district clubs made Maple Leaf Gardens "jump and jive" on a "floor so packed that it was scarcely possible to move one foot six inches from its mate." The dancers were attired in "their favourite party costumes, the girls in skirts, sweaters and loafers; the boys in loud jackets, wild ties and trousers that came a careful four inches from their shoe tops."[92] Reports of "rowdyism" at the teen club dances held in Rolo Road School in Leaside, Ontario, brought indignant responses from its sponsors, the local Lions Club.

The dances were supervised by at least three Lions members, the school janitor, and a constable from the Leaside police force. The latter was paid by the club to "take his post on the nearest corner" after the dance ended, "to see that all the youngsters get started on their way home and that there is no loitering." Despite a membership of five hundred local teenagers, of whom about three hundred faithfully attended the weekly dances, the constable reported that he had never seen evidence of drinking or rowdyism. In fact, he declared, "the only trouble with our dances is that they are becoming too popular.... The crowds are getting bigger every week and it does make them hard to handle, but I have never seen evidence of the misconduct."[93]

As the 1940s closed, the distinctive attire, music, dance, and even "lingo" of young Canadians were no longer regularly depicted as morally offensive and even threatening. Increasingly, by this time, they were being represented as cute, clever, endearing—to be commented upon with indulgent bemusement, if not outright amusement, by adult onlookers. The change in tone and rhetoric can be accounted for by several decades' worth of adult co-optation of youth culture through organized and supervised activity, thus the "safe-making" of fearsome adolescent pastimes, as well as the reassuring passage of time that proved that successive generations of modern youth eventually grew up and became "normal" adult citizens. Perhaps more to the point, the waning of adult shock and dismay at the antics of modern youth can be explained by the normalization and institutionalization of the distinctive life stage that was modern adolescence. Teenagers were just regular everyday young Canadians by 1950, though a different species than the members of other age groups—at times disturbing, often provocative, occasionally still threatening, as attested to by the ongoing discussions about juvenile delinquency and gang subcultures in the popular and professional media. But many of the generational traits considered problematic in and of themselves were now being recognized as ephemeral, transitory, manageable—even healthy—steps along the passage to adulthood.

Because culture is a process situated within the give and take of social relationships, those with social and political influence—the dominant class, in short, and in this particular instance the older generation—can impress its views on the rest of society, both formally and informally, as the "legitimate representation of the standards to which it should aspire."[94] When the relationship is generational, in which the authority of age reinforces that of class, it is also clear that young people can be, and are, subject to a fairly coercive campaign of regulation. Yet while leisure activities affirm cultural patterns, they also serve as an arena for the articulation of different values and behaviours. With money in their pockets, time on their hands, and the desire to participate in new and interesting social activities that were increasingly age-classified, hence intrinsic to a generational entelechy, young people were not entirely powerless in the face of these adult pressures. School, club, and church provided alternative spaces and activities, but there was much overlap in membership and function between those that met

Teenage demonstration, *Canadian Tribune* photograph, Library and Archives Canada, Folder 10; 1974-264; PA-093704, Ottawa, ON, April 1950.

This photograph of Ottawa teenagers protesting the municipal Board of Control's attempts to restrict their use of local community centres for their teen clubs indicates that young Canadians were assertive in protecting the institutions that were important to their age group and generation.

with adult approval and those that did not. With the growing importance of the peer group in youth socialization, facilitated by the expansion of high school education and—ironically—the spread of youth organizations, young Canadians were able to develop a more cohesive generational style. As in their participation in the commercialized amusements of the modern age, they used organized recreational groups and activities to create an identifying youth culture that both borrowed and strove to differentiate itself from the wider mainstream (adult) culture.

Conclusion

Youth's Dominion

This is the case of a high school land, forever frozen in adolescence.
— Earle Birney, "The Case of Canada," 1948

Written as the second half of Canada's Century approached, Earle Birney's satiric verse (above) captures the purpose with which I began this study: to consider the development of a modern adolescence within the context of a nation that was suffering the "growing pains" of becoming a mature participant in the modern world order. Whether Canada had crossed that threshold by 1950 or, as the poet suggests, was still "frozen in adolescence," is a metaphorical rendering of the question of national identity that has so pervaded our history.

Examining adolescence historically does much to dispel notions of what is "natural," "inevitable," and universal about this life stage and about generational relations. At the same time, history points to the relationship, replete with contradictions, between youth, modernity, and national identity. Adolescence became a modern phenomenon, increasingly distinct, increasingly identifiable as a special state of being—and becoming—during the years between the Great War and 1950. Yet it was never the universal experience that it was made out to be by experts and non-experts alike. Being young is not the same for all young people.[1] Commonalities in age, generation, and culture do not necessarily surmount other social differences to make the young a homogeneous class. Because they occupy a subordinate stratum in the hierarchy of age (and consequently power) that orders most societies, oppression and discrimination figured in the experiences of youth in the past and continue to do so. It is nonetheless difficult to sustain any argument that young people have consistently endured the kind of group oppression or systemic discrimination affecting those singled out by class, race, gender, or sexual orientation. Nor can any strong sense of the young as a uniformly progressive, radical, "avant-garde" force be upheld, despite the fact that they are often the first to embrace social change and that youth movements have played important roles in motivating or responding to social change.

Each generation refashions the entelechy of its predecessor to reflect its own cultural-historical moment and the particular nature of the destabilizing forces that affect how its members are nurtured, schooled, trained, and employed, how they court and how they pass the time, their "inborn way of experiencing life and the world."[2] As young Canadians came of age during the Great War, the Great Depression, and World War II, not only their experience and "style" of adolescence but also their collective consciousness were necessarily shaped by these world events. As with so many of the "social problems" defined as such in the first half of the twentieth century, the modern youth problem was originally associated with working-class and immigrant families that were, in the eyes of their largely middle-class, white, Canadian-born observers, inherently problematic. The solutions promoted to contain the youth problem were fundamentally the kinds of institutions, organizations, programs, and policies that reflected their values, fears, and objectives, their very sense of what "Canadian" meant and what the nation needed. High schools, vocational courses, juvenile and family courts, state-regulated apprenticeships, the new extracurriculum, and voluntary youth associations, to name a few of the most important developments, were all firmly in the hands of adults from this social group. This is not to say that young Canadians avoided, resented, or simply ignored new opportunities for secondary school education or for participation in extracurricular activities and "outside" youth groups. The available numbers, however, as well as the autobiographical material and more impressionistic evidence, suggest that an easy majority of those who completed high school, became active in school-based extracurricular activities, and joined the approved clubs were their own children, or those least likely to be part of the youth problem.

While the high school experience of youth from immigrant, rural, and less affluent families was generally shorter or more complicated than that of their more fortunate peers, their involvement in the culture of the modern high school more passive or ephemeral, and their entry into paid labour earlier and at a lower occupational rank, these teenagers nonetheless took active part in defining their generation's moment. As popular recreation became increasingly a consumer product, dependent on a widening network of related forms of consumption—from clothing to personal grooming through the new technologies embodied in radio, telephones, and, of course, cars—young workers both bought into, and purposefully contributed to the making of a modern youth culture.[3] Earlier entry into full-time labour meant more disposable income, even taking into account the traditional contributions to the family. It was perhaps in this area more than any other that working-class adolescents could claim a space of their own. What they lacked in status and authority at school, at home, at work, and in the political system they could assert in the leisure marketplace: at the pool hall, at the dance hall, and in other commercial amusement places where, among their peers, to be seen counted as much as family name or socio-economic status. Their own recollections, in diaries, memoirs, and oral histories, show that working-class and immigrant youth, whether in school or employed, were not removed from the activities that defined generational style. In some ways, then, modern adolescence cut across boundaries of class and race, affording more young Canadians from less-privileged families at least some version of a shared generational experience.

Certain general trends are evident in the years examined here. First, and most important, the matter of youth socialization become paramount in public discussions about the problem that they constituted. Behind this preoccupation, which at times took shape in varying degrees of moral panic, was the notion that there exists an ideal socially defined role into which the adolescent can be directed and trained. Whatever the limitations on personal freedom and self-individuation, this intensely regulatory goal seemed more amenable to the common good, in present and future, than the troubling alternative of leaving the young to their own resources, possibly to form self- and collective identities that fit poorly with adult objectives. Or so was the great anxiety of the times. It was derived from fears about the efficacy of the traditional socializing agencies—family, church, school, and community—seemingly so undermined by modernity that they could not, without some modernization of their own, carry out the crucial role of making ideal modern citizens.

Thanks to the expansion of the state and its agencies and to the growing influence of medicine and psychology, all assisted by the intensified everyday impact of the modern media and mass culture, it was increasingly understood that modern citizens had to be trained to that end from infancy. It also became more and more the accepted wisdom that this training, supervision, and regulation had to be extended into the critical years when children were expected to loosen their adherence to families of origin and to make their own way, which usually required financial independence, leaving home, and marriage. If the infant and young child needed the supervision and regulation of experts, how much more so did the adolescent, with one foot out the door of home and school, thereby escaping the guidance—and policing—of adults? In light of Hall-inspired theories about the inherent irrationality of the adolescent, the in-between years were fraught with demons that would threaten society as much as individual lives. Moreover, as the peer group came to be acknowledged for its formative role during this critical life stage, the concern became even more a generational one. Adolescents as a group made much more impact on society than did individual babies or collective schoolchildren. They were potentially too "dangerous" to be left to raise each other, as modernity seemed to entail.

The modernization of society necessarily affected ideas about the family. With companionate marriage and the egalitarian family the new "modern" models, with the decline in family size and the prolongation of adolescent dependency, with the rise of consumerism and mass culture, relations within and between generations also changed. A collective consciousness, manifested in distinctive generational cultures, or the entelechy that Mannheim discussed, became more definite. After the Great War, the young were different from their parents and elders, not merely because of their age but also because of "the times." The two—youth and modernity—became entwined, signifying at once anxiety and hope. Adolescents were a "problem" because they were young and modern—but for the same reason they were also hope embodied. They were developing citizens in a developing nation, beings intent on self-formation and precious maturity in a Canada pursuing much the same goals. All that mattered, ultimately, was that the young be properly steered through a socializing process that would ensure the best outcome for the nation. For young Canadians—for young Canada—the stakes were high.

This much at least can be said for what it meant to be young and modern and "in process" in a young Canada. As adults looked to have dominion over successive generations of youth who came of age in times of internal flux and world upheaval, so the young, in turn, sought to make youth—consequently, their own generation—very much their own dominion. Reformers, experts, concerned observers, and worried parents helped to shape policies and programs enacted by the state and reflected in changes, some more theoretical than realized, to schooling, labour, leisure, and family life. Since sexual maturation and adolescence were conflated, and since sexuality, long a target area for those who sought to regulate and "purify," was also a notable component of youth's dominion, anxieties about the "new morality" rang loud and clear through the public discourses and much of the regulatory policy of these years. Related to this new morality and an equally important element of the pervasive "youth problem" was the rise of a commercialized popular culture that became increasingly associated with youth, hence with the youth problem. The key world-historical events of these years—the postwar ennui of the "lost generation" and the "roaring" and "flaming" aspects of the 1920s, the Great Depression of the 1930s, the Second World War and the "brave new world" of the 1940s, as these played themselves out in the particular conditions of Canadian life—imprinted the self-identity, generational consciousness, and collective biography of those who came of age between the Great War and 1950.

Certainly the 1950s, where this study ends, were years of tremendous public attention to the young. But that attention represents an intensification of interest (furthered by the new medium of television) and a solidification of earlier trends, rather than a break with the past or any "discovery" of teenagers. A number of structural and cultural similarities suggest why the 1920s and the 1950s shared a popular focus on adolescence, a focus that supports an earlier genesis for the modern adolescent. Both were decades of recovery and reconstruction after global wars in which Canada—a youngster in terms of nationhood, identity, and cohesion—played a major "adult" role. These national experiences understandably gave rise to perspectives that looked at once backward in sorrow at the toll on the nation's youth and forward in the hope for the future that youth intrinsically represented. Both decades saw a renewed celebration of domesticity in the name of a "normalcy" interrupted by war. Both saw the expanded participation of young people and women as enfranchised citizens, in education, and in paid labour. Both witnessed renewed economic prosperity and important technological advances, spurred by wartime exigencies, that would shape consumption and popular culture in that moment and forevermore. Between 1920 and 1950, an intertwined youth market and youth culture were established as components of a modern industrial nation. All told, the modern teenager was well on the scene by mid-twentieth century, already a visible and growing force in society and culture and—ironically, given the lack of any true political power—through those media into the realm of politics. Embedded with contradictions, youth is at once a classification of subordination and, increasingly through the twentieth century, also a powerful symbol of a desirable state of being. In modern times, youth is both a desire and the means to attain it, both objective and commodity.[4]

Philippe Ariès's judgement of the twentieth century as "the century of adolescence" raises questions about what has happened to the process and experience as entailed by that age classification since 1950. With the usual benefits of looking backward, it is evident that adolescence has been prolonged even more. A strong case can be made for the consequent infantilization of what were once termed "young adults," as well as for the overall juvenilization of culture. There can be no doubt that "the youth problem," although no longer discussed within that rather old-fashioned category, is very much a current issue. Contemporary adolescents animate a particularly dramatic version of the "youth in crisis" story that has been unfolding in these pages. Marcel Danesi's intensive study of contemporary teenage culture leads him to conclude that "today, an increasingly larger group of teenagers lives outside the traditional moral structures and value systems of the culture. . . . Like never before, the teenager of today is projected into a confused, often violent and dangerous, subculture that all too frequently extols destructiveness."[5] Another recent examination of postmodern adolescence, by a psychologist and a family physician, observes that "adults through the ages have complained about children being less respectful of their elders and more difficult to manage than preceding generations." The authors give voice to what must surely be a common question: Could it be that this time it is for real? A historically unprecedented level of peer orientation has subverted the generational transmission of knowledge and guidance, from adult to child, elder to youth; parents no longer seem to matter. Less parental direction and more state involvement, corresponding with the weakening of family and community ties, may have had the ironic effect of strengthening the peer attachment that observers have worried about since the time of G. Stanley Hall. The young relate sideways, almost exclusively, with those of their own generation, becoming ever more alienated from their elders, and consequently from their society.[6]

To historians, there is much that is familiar here. All of these experts on contemporary youth correctly observe that many have been bothered, over many years, about the condition of the young in their communities, that much of this attention has dwelt on the adverse, and that few workable, long-lasting solutions have been found. And they are also correct to imply, in their rhetorical question, that this time it is for real. From the perspective of youth, it always has been "for real." In the early 1930s, a young Canadian historian remarked that "most people would agree that it is the cursed spite of this generation to have been born to set right a world which is out of joint." He concluded, however, that "it would be nearer the truth to say that setting right a disjointed world is the task of every generation."[7] During the years examined here, youth-watchers were convinced that Canadian society was seriously menaced by a very real youth problem. Young Canadians were equally convinced that their elders exhibited a very real intent to repress their youthful creativity and spirit, as well as their fun. Just as "the times" then posed their own challenges to young and old, in both similar and very different ways, so they do in our own day. This is not to dismiss genuine public concern about, or even moral outrage over, the complications of coming of age in a complex world, but merely to point out that it has always been a complicated process and a complex world. Anxieties that have a real, material basis, in the past as now, tend to mutate into vast and unreal generalizations. If adolescents did not ordinarily face the prospect of being shot in high school cafeterias during the 1920s, neither do they now. If adolescents today are not likely to be maimed or killed in industrial accidents at the age of fourteen because of the harsh conditions of full-time factory labour, neither were they then. Such tragedies were, and remain, very real, but they have not been commonplace experiences of adolescence.

For some young people, of course, class, race, religion, and numerous other variables, then as now, make adolescence a particularly trying passage, albeit in different ways and in different measure. Some of the issues facing contemporary adolescents, especially those concerning drug abuse, casual sex, peer violence and the weakening of family ties and parental authority, are more real for this generation than for any preceding one. Yet twenty-first-century teenagers are also, on the whole, the best-fed, best-schooled, most legally protected, best-informed, most affluent, and healthiest young Canadians of any time. It is also important to consider what history and destiny held out for the "flaming" and otherwise troublesome youth of the past. These were the generations that stepped up to the threshold of adulthood carrying the weight—individual and collective, personal and historical—of two world wars, the decade-long, profound dislocation known as the Great Depression, and the dawn of the Atomic Age. Despite all this, they endured, reconstructed, thrived, and prospered, making the Canada of our own times internationally recognized for its quality of life. A little history offers some perspective on the youth problem, and perhaps not a little hope.

Notes

Introduction

1 Charles G.D. Roberts, cited in J.T.M. Anderson, *The Education of the New Canadian* (Toronto: J.M. Dent and Sons, 1918), 243. New Brunswick-born Sir Charles G.D. Roberts (1860–1943), known as "the Father of Canadian poetry," served as a commissioned officer for the British Army during the Great War, at the age of 54. J.T.M. Anderson was Inspector of Schools, Yorkton, Saskatchewan.

2 P. Ariès, *Centuries of Childhood: A Social History of Family Life*, trans. R. Baldick (New York: Knopf, 1962), 30; G.S. Hall, "Child Study and Its Relation to Education," *Forum* 29 (1900): 689; see also N. Lesko, "Denaturalizing Adolescence: The Politics of Contemporary Representations," *Youth and Society* 28 (1996): 139–61.

3 R.E. Muus, *Theories of Adolescence*, 5th ed. (New York: Random House, 1988), 268.

4 E.H. Erikson, *Identity and the Life Cycle* (New York: Norton, 1959), 17–18, 94–96; on Erikson's influence as the foremost theorist of human development of the latter part of the twentieth century, see J.E. Côté and A.L. Allahar, *Generation on Hold: Coming of Age in the Late Twentieth Century* (Toronto: Stoddart, 1994), 70–75.

5 Hall, "Child Study and Its Relation to Education," 689.

6 M. Danesi, in *Forever Young: The "Teen-Aging" of Modern Culture* (Toronto: University of Toronto Press, 2003), contends that the term *teenager* was first publicly used in a 1939 journal article, which he does not reference. J. Ayto, *Twentieth Century Words* (London: Oxford University Press, 1999), 181 and 309, locates *teenage* used as an adjective as early as 1921, and finds *teenager* to have emerged in 1941. Yet there are references in the press, American and Canadian, to *teenage* and *teenager* between these dates, as the following chapters will show. The apostrophe, indicating the contraction of *between*, is found in the most common spelling of *teenager* before 1950; it appears to have been dropped by the 1960s.

7 H. Graff, *Conflicting Paths: Growing Up in America* (Cambridge, MA: Harvard University Press, 1995), 301.

8 See the essays in V.F. Calverton and S.D. Schmalhausen, eds., *The New Generation: The Intimate Problems of Modern Parents and Children* (New York: Macaulay, 1930), especially the introduction, by Bertrand Russell, 17–24.

9 Pierre Bourdieu, for example, regards the acceleration of change in the consumer marketplace since World War II as the outcome of generational turnover rather than of class membership; see P. Bourdieu, *Sociology in Question*, trans. R. Nice (London: Sage, 1993), 94–102. For an overview of the sociology of generations, see J. Edmunds and B.S. Turner, introduction to *Generational Consciousness, Narrative, and Politics*, ed. J. Edmunds and B.S. Turner (Lanham, MD: Rowman and Littlefield, 2002), 2–3; also B.S. Turner, "Strategic Generations: Historical Change, Literary Expression, and Generational Politics," in *Generational Consciousness*, 15.

10 Glen Elder's landmark study *Children of the Great Depression: Social Change in Life Experience* (Chicago: University of Chicago Press, 1974) conceptualized this experience in terms of four key elements: location in time and place; mediation of social relations or linked lives; the intersection of age, period, and cohort timing; and development of the individual in terms of human agency. See also G. Elder and S.E. Dragastin, eds., *Adolescence in the Life Cycle: Psychological Change and Social Context* (New York: Halsted Press, 1975).

11 See the fascinating studies compiled by William Strauss and Neil Howe, spanning American generations from 1584 to 2059, in Strauss and Howe, eds., *Generations: The History of America's Future* (New York: William Morrow, 1991); Strauss and Howe argue that "without a sense of trajectory, the future becomes almost random," 7. This is a particularly strong trend among demographers; see D.K. Foot with D. Stoffman, *Boom, Bust and Echo: How to Profit from the Coming Demographic Shift* (Toronto: Macfarlane Walter and Ross, 1996).

12 On American literature concerned with the generations of the 1920s and the 1960s, see J.D. Hazlett, "Generational Theory and Collective Biography," *American Literary History* 4 (1992): 72–96; D. Coupland, *Generation X: Tales for an Accelerated Culture* (New York: St. Martin's Press, 1991).

13 N. Ryder, "The Cohort as a Concept in the Study of Social Change," *American Sociological Review* 30 (1965): 843–61; H. Schuman and J. Scott, "Generations and Collective Memories," *American Sociological Review* 54 (1989): 359–81. Ryder, 845, uses the term *cohort* descriptively to refer to "the aggregate of individuals within some population definition who experienced the same event within the same time interval."

14 J.S. Smith, "The Strange History of the Decade: Modernity, Nostalgia, and the Perils of Periodization," *Journal of Social History* 32 (1998): 263–85.

15 "The Fight for the Future," editorial, *Waterford Star,* September 29, 1927, 7. Waterford is a rural town in southwestern Ontario.

16 Turner, "Strategic Generations," 15.

17 On the use and misuse of the term, see, for example, A. Krieger, "Generational Conflict: The History of an Idea," *Daedalus* 108 (1979): 23–38.

18 Erikson, *Childhood and Society*, 141; Hazlett, "Generational Theory and Collective Biography," 77.

19 S.S. Friedman, "Women's Autobiographical Selves: Theory and Practice," in *The Private Self: Theory and Practice of Women's Autobiographical Writing,* ed. S. Benstock (Chapel Hill: University of North Carolina Press, 1988), 34–35. See also H. Buss, *Mapping Our Selves: Canadian Women's Autobiography in English* (Montreal: McGill-Queen's University Press, 1993), especially 3–29, where she provides an incisive overview of theories of autobiography and self-formation in regard to women.

20 Ryder, "The Cohort as a Concept," 846–47.

21 Krieger, "Generational Conflict," 31–32.

22 Ibid., 24–25. Krieger points out that the Catholic Church at this time was also becoming increasingly keen to establish the "correct age" for receiving the sacraments, especially those of infancy, childhood, and adolescence, such as baptism, first communion, and confirmation.

23 Ibid., 31. See also J. Austin and M.N. Willard, "Introduction: Angels of History, Demons of Culture," in *Generations of Youth: Youth Culture and History in Twentieth-Century America*, ed. J. Austin and M.N. Willard (New York: New York University Press, 1998), 6–8.

24 Ibid., 31.

25 Hazlett, "Generational Theory and Collective Biography," 81. Hazlett discusses the ideas of American writer Randolph Bourne, who believed that the consciousness of each generation was contingent with "the particular portion of history that it possesses in its youth."

26 K. Mannheim, "The Problem of Generations" (1927), in *Essays on the Sociology of Knowledge* (London: Routledge and Kegan Paul, 1972; originally published 1927), 320.

27 Ibid., 281–82, 306–307, 291.

28 Ibid., 283; Mannheim ascribes the term to German art historian Pinder's 1927 work. See also P. Kecskemeti, introduction to Mannheim, *Essays on the Sociology of Knowledge*, 21–22; Mannheim, "The Problem of Generations," 302, 309–10. Turner, "Strategic Generations," 14, contends that "war and its social consequences have been a particularly important lever for the formation of generational consciousness and leadership;" Turner, "Strategic Generations," 11.

29 This is what Mannheim refers to as "the non-contemporaneity of the contemporaneous" in relation to generations: for each generation living at the same time, the "same time" is also a different time; Mannheim, "The Problem of Generations," 288–89; Kecskemeti, introduction, 23.

30 The Renfrew records are available online at the National Library and Archives website, www.archives.ca. Eight young men were eighteen years old, nine were nineteen; E. Anderssen, "Obituaries: Clifford Holliday, Canada's Last Vimy Vet," 1898–2004, *Globe and Mail*, May 8, 2004. Holliday was from a farm family of sixteen in Plus, Manitoba; he signed on with the 43rd Battalion of the Cameron Highlanders in Winnipeg in 1914, as a bugle boy, but spent almost eighteen months in the trenches. He was injured twice; the second injury, in which his jaw was shattered by shrapnel, landed him in England for surgery. A doctor arranged to send him to the Boys' Battalion in Britain for the remainder of the war. Recollections of Burt Woods, in D. Read and R. Hann, eds., *The Great War and Canadian Society: An Oral History* (Toronto: New Hogtown Press, 1978), 101; also Keith Fallis, who joined at eighteen in 1917, 98, and Robert Franklin, who enlisted at eighteen in 1916, 93. See also J. Heath-Rawlings, "Alice Strike, 108, Last Woman WWI Vet," *Globe and Mail*, December 30, 2004. Born Alice Hosgood in Godalming, England, on August 31, 1896, she served her time on a military base near Aldershot, England.

31 National Archives of Canada, Canadian Welfare Council papers, MG 28 I 10, v. 8, file 38, Correspondence of Charlotte Whitton, November 29, 1927, 4.

32 Mrs. Sally Hill grew up in a farm near Alliston, Ontario; in Read and Hann, eds., *The Great War*, 40.

33 A.W. Currie, *Growing Up in Rural Ontario, 1908 to 1926*, unpublished memoirs, 1971, University Archives, Queen's University, Kingston, Ontario, 39.

34 H. MacLennan, "What It Was Like to Be in Your Twenties in the Thirties," *The Great Depression*, ed. V. Hoar (Toronto: Copp, Clark, 1969), 144.

35 J.F.B. Livesay, letter to Dorothy Livesay, June 21, 1927, Dorothy Livesay Collection, MSS 37, Box 37, Folder 7, University of Manitoba Archives. While the family lived in Winnipeg, Livesay was manager of the Western Associated Press; he became general manager of the Canadian Press and they moved to Toronto in the early 1920s.

36 L. Davidow Hershbein, "The Flapper and the Fogey: Representations of Gender and Age in the 1920s," *Journal of Family History* 26 (2001): 113–14. See also R.R. Pierson, "Gender and the Unemployment Insurance Debates in Canada, 1934–1940," *Labour/Le travail* 25 (1990): 77–103.

37 H. Garner, "On the Road through the 'Thirties," *Weekend Magazine*, February 27, 1971, 6. See also "Experiences of a Depression Hobo," *Saskatchewan History* 22 (Spring 1969): 60–63.

38 M. Richler, *The Street* (Toronto: McClelland and Stewart, 1969), 69.

39 B. McNeil, *Voices of a War Remembered: An Oral History of Canadians in World War II* (Toronto: Doubleday, 1991), 2–3.

40 J. Friesen, "Facing German Guns, Soldier Knew He Had to Kill," *Globe and Mail*, June 1, 2004.

41 R. Collins, *You Had to Be There: An Intimate Portrait of the Generation That Survived the Depression, Won the War, and Re-invented Canada* (Toronto: McClelland and Stewart, 1997), 6.

42 Letter to George Antheil, *Toronto Star*, November 10, 1943.

43 *Adventure*, Magee High School Annual (1945), 6.

44 American sociologists Howard Schuman and Jacqueline Scott, in examining cohort memories of world events, found that all their subjects spoke of the Great War, the Depression, and World War II as the formative events of their youth; see Schumann and Scott, "Generations and Collective Memories," 359–60. N. Brown, S. Shevell, and L. Rips, "Public Memories and Their Personal Context," in *Autobiographical Memory*, ed. D.C. Rubin (Cambridge: Cambridge University Press: 1986), 137–58; D.C. Rubin, S. Wetzler, and R. Nebes, "Autobiographical Memory across the Lifespan," in *Autobiographical Memory*, 202–21; see also M. Freeman, *Rewriting the Self: History, Memory, Narrative* (London: Routledge, 1993); Turner, "Strategic Generations," 19.

45 P. Bourdieu, *Outline of a Theory of Practice*, trans. R. Nice (Cambridge: Cambridge University Press, 1977): 95; Bourdieu uses the term *habitus* to explain the historical context of this struggle; see also J.M. Ostrow, "Culture as a Fundamental Dimension of Experience: A Discussion of Pierre Bourdieu's Theory of Human Habitus," *Human Studies* 4 (1981): 289–90; Austin and Willard, "Introduction: Angels of History, Demons of Culture," 14–15.

46 R. Van Krieken, *Norbert Elias* (London: Routledge, 1998), 115; N. Elias, "From *The Germans*," in S. Mennell, *Norbert Elias: An Introduction* (Oxford, UK: Blackwell, 1982), 242–24. Elias was a sociologist who trained under Mannheim; he was particularly interested in the relationship between civilization and culture, a relationship to which he saw the childrearing process as integral. Although Elias was concerned to explain the youth counterculture and rebellion of the 1960s, his views, adapted from Mannheim's discussions of 1920s youth, apply very well to discussion here.

47 Mennell, *Norbert Elias: An Introduction*, 31.

48 Turner, "Strategic Generations," 5–7. See also D. Kertzer, "Generation as a Sociological Problem," *Annual Review of Sociology* 9 (1983): 125–49. An increase in such "self-socialization" is understandable during times of rapid change because this makes the cohort/peer group experiences unique while differentiating them from other cohorts. See D. Riesman, *The Lonely Crowd: A Study of the Changing American Character* (New Haven, CT: Yale University Press, 1950); one of Riesman's themes is the replacement of inner-directed types whose standards are their parents' by other-directed types whose standards are those of their peers.

49 K. Davis, "The Sociology of Parent-Youth Conflict," *American Sociological Review* 5 (1940): 523–35. For a view that counters the notion of increased parent-youth conflict, see the study by Canadian sociologists W.A. Westley and F. Elkin, "The Protective Environment and Adolescent Socialization," *Social Forces* 35 (1957): 243–49.

50 Mrs. Sally Hill, in Read and Hann, eds., *The Great War*, 40.

51 Westley and Elkin, "The Protective Environment and Adolescent Socialization," 243–49. The McGill sociologists examined "Suburban Town," an anglophone suburb of Montreal with a population in 1951 of fewer than 12,000; over two-thirds of family heads had managerial or professional positions and worked in Montreal; twenty adolescents, all fourteen to fifteen years old, and their families were studied intensively.

52 Davidow Hershbein, "The Flapper and the Fogey," 115–17.

53 See M. Danesi, *Forever Young: The "Teen-Aging" of Modern Culture* (Toronto: University of Toronto Press, 2003).

54 Davidow Hershbein, "The Flapper and the Fogey," 115–17. On nostalgia, see Michael Kamman, *The Mystic Chords of Memory: The Transformation of Tradition in*

American Culture (New York: Vintage, 1991), 293–96; Kamman argues that modernism could be countered through systematic recollections of the past; see also J. Lears, *No Place of Grace: Antimodernism and the Transformation of American Culture, 1880–1920* (Chicago: University of Chicago Press, 1981), and for Canada, I. McKay, *The Quest of the Folk: Antimodernism and Cultural Selection in Twentieth-Century Nova Scotia* (Montreal: McGill-Queen's University Press, 1994). See also K. Walden, *Becoming Modern: The Industrial Exhibition and the Shaping of a Late Victorian Culture* (Toronto: University of Toronto Press, 1997).

55 On consumerism and modernity, see L. Cohen, "The Class Experience of Mass Consumption," and J.S. Rubin, "Between Culture and Consumption: The Mediation of the Middle-brow," both in *The Power of Culture: Critical Essays in American History*, ed. R.W. Fox and T.J. Lears (Chicago: University of Chicago Press, 1993): 135–60, 163–91; W. Leach, *Land of Desire: Merchants, Power, and the Rise of a New American Culture* (New York: Vintage, 1993), 4–5; R. Johnston, *Selling Themselves: The Emergence of Canadian Advertising* (Toronto: University of Toronto Press, 2001); J. Lears, *Fables of Abundance: A Cultural History of Advertising in America* (New York: Basic Books, 1994).

56 On these themes, see J. Stanton, "Modernism and Post-modernism: Canada's Century Reconsidered," *The Round Table* 329 (1994): 77–87. On the impact of science, see S. Zeller, *Inventing Canada: Early Victorian Science and the Idea of a Transcontinental Nation* (Toronto: University of Toronto Press, 1987).

57 R. Wohl, "Heart of Darkness: Modernism and Its Historians," *Journal of Modern History* 74 (2002): 573–621. See also the classic by M. Berman, *All That Is Solid Melts into Air: The Experience of Modernity* (New York: Simon and Schuster, 1982); for Canada, see R. Cook and R. Brown, *Canada, 1896–1921: A Nation Transformed* (Toronto: McClelland and Stewart, 1974).

58 See W.R. Everdell, *The First Moderns: Profiles in the Origins of Twentieth-Century Thought* (Chicago: University of Chicago Press, 1997), 9–11. Everdell contends that modernism was born out of the collapse of the world view that gave rise to "modernity"—the failure of the paradigm of continuity that prevailed in nineteenth-century thought; it was in 1913, he concludes, that the modernists "found their audience, their age, and each other," 324. See also the expansive synthesis by P. Watson, *A Terrible Beauty: The People and Ideas That Shaped the Modern Mind* (London: Phoenix Press, 2000), especially chapter 16, 273–99. Allan Levine admirably discusses "the modern" in Canada within a North American context in *The Devil in Babylon: The Fear of Progress and the Birth of Modern Life* (Toronto: McClelland and Stewart, 2005).

59 P. Nicholls, *Modernisms: A Literary Guide* (Berkeley: University of California Press, 1995), 85. Here Nicholls refers specifically to the futurist movement in northern Italy, but his phrase captures the essence of the tensions felt by Canadians at this time.

60 J.T.M. Anderson, *The Education of the New Canadian: A Treatise on Canada's Greatest Problem* (Toronto: Dent, 1918), 129.

61 Wohl, "Heart of Darkness," 576, 614–15.

62 Contemporary commentaries include, for example, T.R. Robinson, "Youth and the Virtues," *Social Welfare* (October 1928): 9; H. Dobson, "Youth: Scapegrace or Scapegoat," *Social Welfare* (July 1929): 228; "Hygiene of Recreation," editorial, *Canadian Practitioner* (June 1924): 309. These anxieties are described more fully in C.R. Comacchio, "Dancing to Perdition: Adolescence and Leisure in Interwar English Canada," *Journal of Canadian Studies* 32, no. 3 (1997): 5–27. On post–World War II developments, see M.L. Adams, *The Trouble with Normal: Postwar Youth and the Making of Heterosexuality* (Toronto: University of Toronto Press, 1997). On similar European developments regarding "modern youth," see K. Alaimo, "Shaping

Adolescence in the Popular Milieu: Social Policy, Reformers, and French Youth, 1870–1920," *Journal of Family History* 17 (1992): 420; W.S. Haine, "The Development of Leisure and the Transformation of Working-Class Adolescence in France," *Journal of Family History* 17 (1992): 451. Among the seminal works on the historical experience of adolescence are: J. Kett, *Rites of Passage: Adolescence in America* (New York: Basic Books, 1977); J. Springhall, *Coming of Age: Adolescence in Britain, 1860–1960* (London: Oxford University Press, 1986); J. Modell, *Into One's Own: From Youth to Adulthood in the United States* (Berkeley: University of California Press, 1988); R. Wegs, *Growing Up Working Class: Youth in Vienna, 1870–1920* (Philadelphia: University of Pennsylvania Press, 1989); D. Linton, *Who Has the Youth Has the Future: The Campaign to Save Young Workers in Imperial Germany* (Cambridge, MA: Harvard University Press, 1990); H. Hendrick, *Images of Youth: Age, Class, and the Male Youth Problem* (London: Oxford University Press, 1990); J. Neubauer, *The Fin-de-Siècle Culture of Adolescence* (New Haven, CT: Yale University Press, 1992); M. Childs, *Labour's Apprentices: Working-Class Lads in Late Victorian and Edwardian England* (Montreal: McGill-Queen's University Press, 1993).

63 I have focused on evidence that specifies this group, wherever possible weeding out the older, or university-located, youth component, primarily as a way of establishing reasonable boundaries on my subject. My reasons for choosing not to look at university-level adolescents are purely practical: given their decidedly elite and minority status during the years under study and the heft of the sources for the non-university set, I felt justified in narrowing my sample to the non-university group. See Paul Axelrod's seminal *Making a Middle Class: Student Life in English Canada during the Thirties* (Montreal: McGill-Queen's University Press, 1991), which has yet to be surpassed, as well as the essays in P. Axelrod and J.G. Reid, eds., *Youth University and Canadian Society: Essays in the Social History of Higher Education* (Montreal: McGill-Queen's University Press, 1989).

64 Graff, *Conflicting Paths*, 302. For Canada, see N. Sutherland, *Growing Up: Childhood in English Canada from the Great War to the Age of Television* (Toronto: University of Toronto Press, 1997), especially chapter 1, "Listening to the Winds of Childhood," 7–12.

Chapter 1

1 There is no historical study specifically about adolescence in Canada, although several touch on the experience: for example, Neil Sutherland's inaugural, and unsurpassed, *Children in English Canadian Society,1880–1920: Framing the Twentieth-Century Consensus* (1976; Waterloo, ON: Wilfrid Laurier University Press, 2000); V. Strong-Boag, *The New Day Recalled: Lives of Girls and Women in English Canada, 1919–1939* (Markham, ON: Penguin, 1988); and, more recently, B. Bradbury, *Working Families: Age, Gender, and Daily Survival in Industrializing Montreal* (Toronto: McClelland and Stewart, 1993). See also K. Dubinsky, *Improper Advances: Rape and Heterosexual Conflict in Ontario, 1880–1929* (Chicago: University of Chicago Press, 1993); J. Taylor, *Fashioning Farmers: Ideology, Agricultural Knowledge and the Manitoba Farm Movement, 1890–1925* (Regina, SK: Canadian Plains Research Centre, 1994), which discusses rural youth in Manitoba; S. Morton, *Ideal Surroundings: Domestic Life in a Working-Class Suburb in the 1920s* (Toronto: University of Toronto Press, 1995), on Halifax working-class families; and C. Strange, *Toronto's Girl Problem: The Perils and Pleasures of the City, 1880–1930* (Toronto: University of Toronto Press, 1995). On the

post–World War II years, see M.L. Adams, *The Trouble with Normal: Postwar Youth and the Making of Heterosexuality* (Toronto: University of Toronto Press, 1997), and D. Owram, *Born at the Right Time: A History of the Baby Boom Generation* (Toronto: University of Toronto Press, 1996).

2 Philippe Ariès, *Centuries of Childhood: A Social History of Family Life,* trans. R. Baldick (New York: Knopf, 1962), 30. See also K. Walden, *Becoming Modern: The Industrial Exhibition and the Shaping of a Late Victorian Culture* (Toronto: University of Toronto Press, 1997).

3 E.H. Erikson, *Identity, Youth, and Crisis* (New York: Norton, 1968), 102.

4 K. Mannheim, "The Problem of Generations" (1927) in *Essays on the Sociology of Knowledge* (1952; London: Routledge and Kegan Paul, 1972), 320.

5 "Hygiene of Recreation," editorial, *Canadian Practitioner* 49 (June 1924): 309.

6 S. Aitken, *Geographies of Young People: The Morally Contested Spaces of Identity* (London: Routledge, 1999), 77.

7 K. Alaimo, "Shaping Adolescence in the Popular Milieu: Social Policy, Reformers, and French Youth, 1870–1920," *Journal of Family History* 17 (1992): 419–21; see also H.P. Chudacoff, *How Old Are You? Age Consciousness in American Culture* (Princeton, NJ: Princeton University Press, 1989), especially chapter 4, 65–91; P. Fass, "Testing the IQ of Children," in *Childhood in America*, ed. P.S. Fass and M.A. Mason (New York: New York University Press, 2000).

8 On the subject of changing views on childhood and the development of child welfare movements, see Sutherland, *Children in English-Canadian Society*; T.R. Richardson, *The Century of the Child: The Mental Hygiene Movement and Social Policy in the United States and Canada* (Albany: State University of New York Press, 1989); C.R. Comacchio, *"Nations Are Built of Babies": Saving Ontario's Mothers and Children, 1900–40* (Montreal: McGill-Queen's University Press, 1993), especially 2, 16–42; K. Arnup, *Education for Motherhood: Advice for Mothers in Twentieth-Century Canada* (Toronto: University of Toronto Press, 1994).

9 G.S. Hall, *Adolescence: Its Psychology and Its Relation to Physiology, Anthropology, Sociology, Sex, Crime, Religion and Education*, vol.1 (New York: D. Appleton, 1904), vii, 614; see also Chudacoff, *How Old Are You?* 66. Hall was a professor of psychology at Johns Hopkins University; in 1888, he became president of newly established Clark University in Worcester, Massachusetts. He is considered one of the founding fathers of experimental psychology, and child psychology in particular, as well as the leading American figure in the child-study movement. See N. Lesko, "Denaturalizing Adolescence: The Politics of Contemporary Representations," *Youth and Society* 28 (1996): 144–47; R.E. Muus, *Theories of Adolescence*, 5th ed. (New York: Random House, 1988), 17–21. On Hall and recapitulation theory, see J. Kett, *Rites of Passage: Adolescence in America, 1790 to the Present* (New York: Basic Books, 1977), 218–19; H. Munro Prescott, *A Doctor of Their Own: The History of Adolescent Medicine* (Cambridge, MA: Harvard University Press, 1998), 6–8; Adams, *The Trouble with Normal*, 43–47. The definitive biography remains D. Ross, *G. Stanley Hall: The Psychologist as Prophet* (Chicago: University of Chicago Press, 1983), 332–33. On early-twentieth-century child pyschology in Canada and the United States, see Richardson, *The Century of the Child*.

10 G.S. Hall, *Youth: Its Education, Regimen and Hygiene* (New York: Appleton, 1907), 135; Chudacoff, *How Old Are You?* 67.

11 See the influential parenting manual by D.A. Thom, *Normal Youth and Its Everyday Problems* (New York: Appleton, 1932), ix; also, A. Goldbloom, "Problems of the Adolescent Child," *Canadian Medical Association Journal* 43 (1940): 336–39; Alaimo, "Shaping Adolescence," 423; Hall, *Adolescence*, 1, xvi–xvii.

12 Theories about adolescence were circulating long before Hall's work: it is clear that he was inspired not only by Darwinian biology but also by the philosophies of

Enlightenment *philosophe* Jean-Jacques Rousseau and the German Romantic school of *Sturm und Drang*; see Kett, *Rites of Passage*, 221; Sutherland, *Children in English-Canadian Society*, 6–13. As Sutherland notes, compulsory education laws brought unprecedented numbers of children together in the classroom, sparking, by the 1880s, a "prolonged and unprecedented public discussion" of their mental and physical condition and, above all, the perfect situation for "investigation" through survey, testing, and all manner of research. See, for example, Thom, *Normal Youth and Its Everyday Problems*, ix.

13 V. Getis, "Experts and Juvenile Delinquency, 1900–35," in *Generations of Youth: Youth Culture and History in Twentieth-Century America*, ed. J. Austin and M.N. Willard (New York: New York University Press, 1998), 30–31.

14 Muus, *Theories of Adolescence*, 270. If, as Rolf Muus contends, "the hypothesis of a universal period of storm and stress is no longer tenable," it is clear that it remains an important characteristic of the life stage for at least some of our present-day experts, as well as for much of the public.

15 As president of Clark University, Hall invited Freud to give a lecture series in 1909 and personally wrote the preface to the American edition of Freud's *A General Introduction to Psychoanalysis* (New York: Liveright, 1920); see Muus, *Theories of Adolescence*, 45.

16 H. Graff, *Conflicting Paths: Growing Up in America* (Cambridge, MA: Harvard University Press, 1995), 302.

17 On Addams's influence, see C.L. James, "Practical Diversions and Educational Amusements: Evangelia Home and the Advent of Canada's Settlement Movement, 1902–09," *Historical Studies in Education* 10, nos. 1–2 (1998): 49–51. On newspaper and magazine circulation, see R. Johnston, *Selling Themselves: The Emergence of Canadian Advertising* (Toronto: University of Toronto Press, 2001); the *Saturday Evening Post* had the highest circulation of any magazine in Canada.

18 The interactionist approach was imported to Canada by the University of Chicago–trained Carl Addington Dawson, who was instrumental in establishing sociology at McGill University. With Warner Gettys, Dawson produced an influential textbook, *An Introduction to Sociology* (New York: Ronald, 1929), in which they catalogued modernization's undermining impact on families (61, 77–79). Ostensibly targeting the relations of industry and community during the economic crisis of the 1930s, McGill's Social Science Research Project discussed family as an integral player in these interactions. See M. Shore, *The Science of Social Redemption: McGill, the Chicago School, and the Origins of Social Research in Canada* (Toronto: University of Toronto Press, 1987), xvi, 118, 227–30.

19 H. Miner, *St. Denis, a French-Canadian Parish* (Chicago: University of Chicago Press, 1939), 233, 268. The parish consisted of 700 people in 120 households. Young women were as likely to leave as were young men. According to Miner, the intense structural changes wrought by World War II had fostered a "growing resistance among unmarried girls to assuming the burden of bearing and rearing a family of ten" while also performing all the necessary household and farm labour: "In the present glow of economic expansion, a girl can assert her preference for an easier life" (263–69). Here Miner speaks of his observations on a return visit in 1949.

20 See C.H. Young, *The Ukrainian Canadians: A Study in Assimilation* (Toronto: Nelson, 1931); C. Dawson, *Group Settlement: Ethnic Communities in Western Canada* (Toronto: Macmillan, 1936). Dawson mentored both Young and Miner.

21 Muus, *Theories of Adolescence*, 137; Boas was a Columbia University scholar.

22 Ibid., 138. Muus contends that "theories of adolescence became the battleground" for testing Boas's ideas.

23 K. Lewin, "From the Field Theory Approach to Adolescence," *American Journal of Sociology* 44 (1939): 868–97.

24 Muus, *Theories of Adolescence*, 269.

25 Ibid., 53.

26 Thom, *Normal Youth and Its Everyday Problems*, 18.

27 Ibid., 19.

28 A. Brown, "Toronto as a Paediatric Centre," *Canadian Medical Monthly* 5 (June 1920): 205. Prescott, *A Doctor of Their Own*, 14, notes that this "cross-training" in medicine and psychology was actively promoted by the Commonwealth Fund during the 1930s.

29 No less an authority than Dr. J. Roswell Gallagher, who is credited with establishing adolescent medicine in the United States, argued that "adolescents are no more enigmatic than any other people." But Gallagher also recognized that "adolescence puts the result of heredity and environment and childhood training to a severe test." See J.R. Gallagher, *Your Son's Adolescence* (Boston: Little, Brown, 1951); also Gallagher, *Medical Care of the Adolescent*, 2nd ed. (New York: Appleton-Century-Crofts, 1966), 12. A 1970 publication intended for use in medical schools still proclaimed adolescence to be distinguished by "a restlessness of body and a discontentment of mind...brought about by biological changes": see W.A. Daniel, *The Adolescent Patient* (St. Louis, MI: Mosby, 1970), 19. The authoritative text by Dr. I.N. Kugelmass, *Adolescent Medicine: Principles and Practice* (Springfield, IL: Charles C. Thomas, 1975), opens with the declaration that "adolescent life is a revolt against the rules of Nature" (3).

30 D.V. Currey and A.G. Nicolle, "Development of a Health Program in the Secondary School," *Canadian Public Health Journal* 31 (April 1940): 176; also, "School Health Supervision in Secondary Schools," editorial, *Canadian Public Health Journal* 31 (April 1940): 199. See the psychiatrists' viewpoint on the "mental, social and moral difficulties" of adolescence in W.T.B. Mitchell, "The Clinical Significance of Some Trends in Adolescence," *Canadian Medical Association Journal* 22 (1930): 182–87. Similar views are found in Thom, *Normal Youth and Its Everyday Problems*, ix; also, A. Goldbloom, "Problems of the Adolescent Child," *Canadian Public Health Journal* 43 (1940): 336–39.

31 Hall, *Adolescence*, 1, xvi–xvii, 438–39; Prescott, *A Doctor of Their Own*, 24–25; Adams, *The Trouble with Normal*, 43–47.

32 Lesko, "Denaturalizing Adolescence," 150; on this model and its context, see also A. James and A. Prout, *Constructing and Reconstructing Childhood: Contemporary Issues in the Sociological Study of Childhood* (London: Falmer, 1990).

33 G.S. Hall, "Child Study and Its Relation to Education," *Forum* 29 (1900): 689; see also Lesko, "Denaturalizing Adolescence," 139.

34 "Hygiene of Recreation," editorial, *Canadian Practitioner* 49, 6 (1924): 309.

35 Mitchell, "The Clinical Significance of Some Trends in Adolescence," 182–87.

36 At Montreal High School, a private boys' academy, the principal observed in 1897 that "exercises in the gymnasium and on the field revealed many bodily defects," bringing about compulsory medical examinations for each boy at the beginning of the school year, "to determine whether...he should have remedial exercises to correct less serious weaknesses. E. Rexford, I. Gammell, and A.R. McBain, "The History of the High School of Montreal," citing *Annual Report*, 1897, McGill University Archives, 117. For girls, as Wendy Mitchinson has demonstrated, "health" entailed protection of the reproductive organs and conservation of the delicate nervous system thought to be closely associated with them during this critical waystation on the path to motherhood; W. Mitchinson, *The Nature of Their Bodies: Women and Their Doctors in Victorian Canada* (Toronto: University of Toronto Press, 1991), especially chapter 3, 81–88. On the U.S. and Great Britain, see J. Roswell, "The Origins, Development and Goals of Adolescent Medicine," *Journal of Adolescent Health Care* 3 (1982): 57–63. On muscular Christianity in Canada, see D. Howell and P. Lindsay,

"Social Gospel and the Young Boy Problem, 1895–1925," in *Sports in Canada: Historical Readings*, ed. M. Mott (Toronto: Copp Clark Pitman, 1989), 220–33; J. Barman, "Sports and the Development of Character," *Sports in Canada*, 234–46. On similar themes, focusing on manliness in the post-Great War years, see B. Kidd, *The Struggle for Canadian Sport* (Toronto: University of Toronto Press, 1996), 44–93. An interesting imperialist theme is pursued in D. Randall, *Kipling's Imperial Boy: Adolescence and Cultural Hybridity* (New York: Palgrave, 2000), 8–9. For Canada, see also M. Moss, *Manliness and Militarism: Educating Young Boys in Ontario for War* (Toronto: Oxford University Press, 2001), especially 21–35.

37 L.A. Banks, *A Manly Boy: A Series of Talks and Tales for Boys* (Toronto: William Briggs, 1900), 2.

38 University of British Columbia Archives, Tuxis papers, Boys Parliaments, A. Max Herity, Belleville, Report of the Minister of the Physical Standard, *Proceedings of the Ontario Boys' Parliament*, 1928, 22. The Tuxis, established in 1918, are discussed in chap. 7, 194–96.

39 Hall, *Adolescence*, 2, 566, 624, also 572, 646; on menstruation, see Hall, *Adolescence*, 1, xiv, 472, 494.

40 Dr. M.R. Melendy, "Becoming a Woman," *Vivilore: The Pathway to Mental and Physical Perfection* (Toronto: J.L. Nichols, 1904), 300. Melendy was a Chicago physician and "lecturer on the diseases of women and children," according to the book's jacket biography.

41 Hall, *Adolescence*, 2, 617.

42 "Is This Fashion?," letter to the editor, *The Globe*, January 23, 1922, 5. For a contemporary view about these fears, see L. Pruette, "The Flapper," in *The New Generation: The Intimate Problems of Modern Parents and Children*, ed. V.F. Calverton and S.D. Schmalhausen (New York: Macaulay, 1930), 572–90. Pruette was a Columbia-trained psychologist and author of a biography of G. Stanley Hall, whose views on women she disputed.

43 E.S. Dummer, foreword, *The Unadjusted Girl, with Cases and Standpoint for Behavior Analysis*, by W.I. Thomas (Boston, MA: Little, Brown, 1923), xi–xvii. J. Sangster, *Regulating Girls and Women: Sexuality, Family, and the Law in Ontario, 1920–1960* (Don Mills, ON: Oxford University Press, 2001), makes much the same point about the correlation of youthful "maladjustment" and delinquency with female sexuality.

44 K. Gordon, "Wherein Should the Education of a Woman Differ from That of a Man?," *School Review* 13 (1905): 790–94.

45 W.F. Roberts, Minister of Public Health, New Brunswick, "The Reconstruction of the Adolescent Period of Our Canadian Girl," *Social Welfare* (January 1920): 100.

46 Roberts, "The Reconstruction of the Adolescent Period of Our Canadian Girl," 100; similar views are expressed in A.F. Hodgkins, "Recreation for Woman and Girls," *Canadian Public Health Journal* 14 (July 1923): 314–17. A 1924 survey of adolescent girls by American psychologist Lorine Pruette reported that 61 per cent would choose a career above all else. Pruette, *Women and Leisure: A Study of Social Waste* (New York: Dutton, 1924); also cited in Pruette, "The Flapper," 583. See also B. Hanawalt, "Historical Descriptions and Prescriptions for Adolescence," *Journal of Family History* 17 (1992): 341–44; G. Elder, "Adolescence in the Life Cycle," in *Adolescence in the Life Cycle*, ed. G. Elder and S.E. Dragastin (New York: Cambridge University Press, 1974), 1–3; J. Brumberg, "Chlorotic Girls, 1870–1920: A Historical Perspective on Female Adolescence," *Child Development* 53 (1982): 1468–77; J. Brumberg, *The Body Project: An Intimate History of American Girls* (New York: Random House, 1997). Strong-Boag, *The New Day Recalled*, 21–22, notes that the percentage of girls fifteen to nineteen in high school surpassed that of boys for each census year from 1921 to 1941. On the influence of medical views about education for girls, see also Mitchinson, *The Nature of Their Bodies*, especially chapter 2, 83–87.

47 See G. Kinsman, *The Regulation of Desire: Sexuality in Canada*, 2nd ed. (Montreal: Black Rose, 1987, 1996).

48 P. Blanchard and C. Manassas, *New Girls for Old* (New York: Macaulay, 1930), cited in Pruette, "The Flapper," 583.

49 See M. Mead, "Adolescence in Primitive and Modern Societies," in *The New Generation*, ed. V.F. Calverton and S.D. Schmalhausen, 180–81.

50 On early-twentieth-century sex education, see M. Bliss, "Pure Books on Avoided Subjects: Pre-Freudian Sexual Ideas in Canada," in *Studies in Canadian Social History*, ed. M. Horn and R. Sabourin, (Toronto: McClelland and Stewart, 1974), 338–51; C. Sethna, "Men, Sex and Education: The Ontario Women's Temperance Union and Children's Sex Education, 1900–20," *Ontario History* 88 (1996): 186–206.

51 J. Kett, *Rites of Passage*, 214–44. Kett notes that adolescents became increasingly dependent as the life stage itself became more regulated in the early twentieth century; see also H. Graff, *Conflicting Paths*, 305.

52 See S. Houston, "The Waifs and Strays of a Victorian City," in *Childhood and Family in Canadian History*, ed. J. Parr (Toronto: McClelland and Stewart, 1982). J. Springhall, *Youth, Popular Culture and Moral Panics: Penny Gaffs to Gangsta-Rap, 1830–1996* (New York: St. Martin's Press, 1998), discusses how the "working-class lad" was seen to be the chief audience for the penny gaff, penny dreadful, gangster film, comic book, and gangsta rap, which span contentious popular culture since the late nineteenth century; see also D. Nasaw, *Going Out: The Rise and Fall of Public Amusements* (Cambridge, MA: Harvard University Press, 1993), for the American version of the story.

53 National Library and Archives, Canadian Welfare Council, vol. 29, file 38, typescript, "Laws Relating to Child Labour in Canada," 25 November 1925.

54 A Juvenile Court Probation Officer, "As the Twig Is Bent: What Are We Doing to Keep Children from the Reformatory?" *Chatelaine*, March 1928, 3–6. See also Judicial and Penitentiary Statistics: Juvenile Delinquency," *Canada Yearbook* 1939, 1067–68. The statistics for 1922–37 showed a definite upward trend overall, for all offences and all ages; however, the sixteen-to-under-twenty-one group showed a much higher crime rate than the juvenile group (seven to sixteen) or the total young persons group (seven to twenty-one). Total convictions of persons seven to under twenty-one rose steadily from 3,079 in 1911 to 6,535 in 1921, to 11,764 in 1931. See also Canadian Welfare Council, *The Juvenile Court in Law* (Ottawa: Canadian Welfare Council, 1952); Canadian Welfare Council, *Your Town against Delinquency* (Ottawa: Canadian Welfare Council, 1948). D.O. Carrigan, *Juvenile Delinquency in Canada: A History* (Concord, ON: Irwin, 1995), 109, provides statistics for convictions in all provinces, 1922–1945. On girls, see J. Sangster, *Girl Trouble: Female Delinquency in English Canada* (Toronto: Between the Lines, 2002), and Sangster, *Regulating Girls and Women*. Note that various steps were taken to distinguish youthful offenders before the all-encompassing 1908 law, including changes to the Criminal Code in 1892; for a summary of legal changes, see P. Dubois and J. Trépanier, "L'adoption de la loi sur les jeunes délinquants de 1908: Étude comparée des quotidiens montrealaise et torontois," *Revue d'histoire de l'Amerique francaise* 52 (1999): 345–81. The 1908 law was spearheaded by William L. Scott, president of Ottawa's Children's Aid Society, in consultation with J.J. Kelso, its Ontario leader, and was modelled on American legislation. Dubois and Trépanier point out that, as the bill was being discussed in Parliament in 1907, convictions in the under-sixteen category constituted only 11.2 per cent of all convictions in Quebec and 12.8 in Ontario. On boys, see also P. Rains and E. Teram, *Normal Bad Boys: Public Policies, Institutions, and the Politics of Client Recruitment* (Montreal: McGill-Queen's University Press, 1992), especially 21–32. For a contemporary example of this ambivalence regarding girls or boys as more prone to delinquency, see D.N. McLachlan, "The Spiritual and Ethical Development of the Child," *Social Welfare* (December 1929): 68.

55 There was a spate of reporting on delinquency in Toronto in 1920. For a small sample from the *Globe and Mail*, see "Records Indicate Crime Increasing among Youths," January 6, 1920, 6, which comments on the police court records showing a rise in criminal charges against sixteen- and seventeen-year-old boys; "School Boards Ask Delegates from All Over," January 7, 1920, 1, which reports on the pledge by board trustees from eight cities without juvenile courts to lobby for them; "Calls School Reform Field," January 14, 1920, 4; "Juvenile Court Is Promised," January 14, 1920, 6; "A Cure for Juvenile Crime," editorial, January 24, 1920, 10; "Judge Discusses Juvenile Problem," April 3, 1920, 10, which reports on a lecture to social service workers at the University of Toronto by juvenile court judge E.S. Mott. Mott also appeared at the monthly meeting of the York Pioneer and Historical Society: "Object of Court to Help Children," April 7, 1920, 11.

56 For 1911, the sixteen-to-under-twenty-one group shows a rate (per 100,000 of the same age cohort in the general population) that was 127 greater than that shown for juveniles and 83 times greater than the general rate for young persons; for 1921, the proportion was 227 per 100,000 greater than the juvenile rate and 155 greater than the general rate; by 1931, it had increased to 359 greater than the former and 236 greater than the latter. See "Juvenile Delinquency," *Canada Yearbook* (1939), 1066–67. The yearbook reports the following total convictions of persons seven to under twenty-one: 1911: 3,079; 1921: 6,535; 1931: 11,764; 1936: 11,845; 1937: 12,727.

57 Public Archives of Nova Scotia, MG 20, no. 176, Minutes of Meetings of the Directors, 1906–8, Minutes of Annual Meeting, 1906. The Boys' Club, which was established in 1902, ran into serious difficulties by 1908: see "Boys' Club Burned Out at Early Hour," *Halifax Evening Mail*, March 7, 1908, 3. The Directors' Meeting Minutes, September 2, 1908, report that it was "resolved that the work of the Boys' Club be closed for the time being."

58 Sessional Papers of the Province of Ontario, Committee on Child Labour, *Annual Report,* 1906–1907, "Employment of Children," 129.

59 "Big Brothers Care for Over 400 Boys," *Globe and Mail*, January 20, 1920, 9.

60 Rains and Teram, *Normal Bad Boys*, 21, Table 1, 22, indicate that the numbers rose from 367 in 1911 to 678 in 1919; D. Chunn, *From Punishment to Doing Good: Family Courts and Socialized Justice in Ontario, 1880–1940* (Toronto: University of Toronto Press, 1993), details the reformist discourses on delinquency, and the resulting framework of family courts that was constructed to address those anxieties about youth criminality; see also Judge H. Gregory MacGill, *The Work of the Juvenile Court* (Vancouver, BC: Moore, 1943).

61 "Old-fashioned" punishment, such as strapping, had its public supporters: see "Old-Fashioned Cure for Boy Offenders," *Globe and Mail*, February 5, 1920, 18; "Illness Saves Youth Spanking," *Globe and Mail*, February 18, 1920, 8; "Three Years for Bandit," *Globe and Mail*, March 25, 1920, 4.

62 J. Modell, *Into One's Own: From Youth to Adulthood in the United States* (Berkeley: University of California Press, 1988), 86; P. Fass, *The Damned and the Beautiful: American Youth in the 1920s* (New York: Oxford University Press, 1977), 262–73, 324–25; B. Bailey, *From Front Porch to Back Seat: Courtship in Twentieth-Century America* (Baltimore, MD: Johns Hopkins University Press, 1988), 78–80.

63 "Big Sisters Doing Wonderful Work," *Globe and Mail*, January 7, 1920, 10; J.M. Wyatt, "Causes of Juvenile Delinquency," *Social Welfare* (July 1920): 10; A.E. Dodds, "What Can Our Cities Do in Their Leisure Hours?" *Social Welfare* (July 1920): 180; K.H. Rogers, *Street Gangs in Toronto: A Study of the Forgotten Boy* (Toronto: Ryerson, 1945), 111–116.

64 Public Archives of New Brunswick, M53 A-B, typescript, Rev. K.F. Drew, "Some Highlights from the History of the Inter-provincial Home for Young Women, 1920,"

80. The Home's board consisted of representatives of the Anglican, Baptist, Methodist, and Presbyterian churches of New Brunswick, Nova Scotia, and Prince Edward Island.

65 "Among Ourselves: Runaways," *Globe and Mail*, September 25, 1924, 16.

66 Ibid.

67 "Girl Returns after Escape from Refuge," *Globe and Mail*, March 4, 1920, 10. The difficulties of "delinquent girls" have been thoroughly examined by Joan Sangster, in *Girl Trouble* and *Regulating Girls and Women*; see also, Sangster, "Incarcerating Bad Girls: The Regulation of Sexuality through the Female Refuges Act in Ontario, 1920–45," *Journal of the History of Sexuality* 7 (1996): 239–75.

68 "15-Year-Old Toronto Girls Run Away to Join Movies," *Globe and Mail*, March 4, 1920, 2.

69 "Seeking for Adventure; Glad to Go Back Home," *Globe and Mail*, January 19, 1920, 5; see also "Runaways," editorial, *Toronto World*, March 2, 1918, 3.

70 Rogers, *Street Gangs in Toronto*, 116.

71 "Big Brothers Care for Over 400 Boys," 9.

72 "Forum: Are Parents What They Used to Be?" *Maclean's* (August 1927): 12, quoting S.J. Dickson, Toronto Chief of Police; also "Parental Delinquency," *Canadian Child Welfare News* (August–December 1924): 38; A. Plumptre, "What Shall We Do with Our Flapper?" *Maclean's* (June 1922): 66; P.J. Bend, "Juvenile Delinquency: Its Causes," *Social Welfare* (March 1919): 126; Judge E. MacLachlan, "The Delinquent Girl," *Social Welfare* (December 1921): 56. In their analysis of Toronto and Montreal daily newspapers (both anglophone and francophone in the latter city), P. Dubois and J. Trépanier, "L'adoption de la loi sur les jeunes délinquants de 1908" found unanimity in both cities and languages on the negligence of parents as the foremost cause of delinquency.

73 "Three Youths Found Guilty of Killing Man," *Globe and Mail*, April 9, 1920, 3. The youths, seventeen to nineteen, who had been "indulging freely in alcoholic liquors," beat a sixty-year-old man to death at a Sault Ste. Marie employment office.

74 "As the Twig Is Bent," 5.

75 Muus, *Theories of Adolescence*, 308; see also Chudacoff, "How Old Are You?," 90–91.

76 "Juvenile Purse-Snatchers," *Globe and Mail*, March 19, 1920, 3.

77 Rogers, *Street Gangs in Toronto*, 111.

78 "Youthful Hoodlums Becoming Nuisance," *Globe and Mail*, March 15, 1920, 13.

79 Kett, *Rites of Passage*, 255–57.

80 "Deplorable Depravity of Young Girls and Boys," editorial, *Globe and Mail*, April 3, 1920, 3.

81 "Many Aliens Hold Licenses in City," editorial, *Toronto World*, January 1, 1918, 4.

82 "As the Twig Is Bent," 5. See also R. Coulter, "Not to Punish but to Reform: Juvenile Delinquency and the Children's Protection Act," in *Social Welfare Policy in Canada*, ed. R.B. Blake and J. Keshen (Toronto: Copp Clark, 1995), 137–52.

83 Young, *Ukrainian Canadians*, 282–83. To explain the low numbers, Young contends that the Ukrainian youth arrested "must have given some other origin—or none at all" to reformatory officials. See also W.B. Hurd, "The Decline in the Canadian Birth Rate," *Canadian Journal of Economics and Political Science* 3 (February 1937): 40–57.

84 F. Sharf, "Beatrice Street and the Pits Gang," in *Growing Up Jewish: Canadians Tell Their Own Stories*, ed. R. Sharp, I. Abella, and E. Goodman (Toronto: McClelland and Stewart, 1997), 45–50. See also C. Levitt and W. Shaffir, *The Riot at Christie Pits* (Toronto: Lester and Orpen Dennys, 1987); for the broader context of Canadian anti-Semitism during the 1930s, see L.R. Betcherman, *The Swastika and the Maple Leaf: Fascist Movements in Canada* (Toronto: Fitzhenry and Whiteside, 1975).

85 Kett, *Rites of Passage*, 256; see also Peter Rush, "The Government of a Generation: The Subject of Juvenile Delinquency," in *Youth Justice: Critical Readings*, ed. E. McLaughlin, J. Muncie, and G. Hughes (London: Sage, 2002): 138–58.

86 Kett, *Rites of Passage*, 257–58.

87 Sharf, "Beatrice Street and the Pits Gang," 94.

88 V. Getis, "Experts and Juvenile Delinquency, 1900–35," 30–31.

89 The terms "folk devil" and "moral panic" are attributed to Stanley Cohen's seminal study, *Folk Devils and Moral Panics: The Creation of the Mods and Rockers* (Oxford: Basil Blackwell, 1990; originally published 1972). See the discussion in Summerfield as well as E. McLaughlin, J. Muncie, and G. Hughes, introduction, in *Youth Justice: Critical Readings*, ed. E. McLaughlin, J. Muncie, and G. Hughes (London: Sage, 2002) 19–21. See also J. Clarke, "The Three Rs—Repression, Rescue and Rehabilitation: Ideologies of Control for Working-Class Youth," in *Youth Justice*, 121–37.

90 R. Pierson, "Gender and the Unemployment Insurance Debates in Canada," *Labour/Le travail* 25 (Spring 1990): 82–84.

91 H. Weir, "Unemployed Youth," in *Canada's Unemployment Problem*, ed. L. Richter (Toronto: Macmillan, 1939), 146. See also J.P. Huzel, "The Incidence of Crime in Vancouver during the Great Depression," *BC Studies* 69–70 (1986): 211–48; B. McCarthy and J. Hagen, "Gender, Delinquency and the Great Depression," *Canadian Review of Sociology and Anthropology* 24 (1987):153–77. D.O. Carrigan, *Crime and Punishment in Canada: A History* (Toronto: McClelland and Stewart, 1991), 219, argues that youth gangs emerged in Canadian cities during the 1930s, but concerns about their proliferation certainly abounded in the previous decade, as this discussion shows.

92 Weir, "Unemployed Youth," 140; H.M. Cassidy, "Relief and Other Social Services for Transients," in *Unemployment in Canada*, ed. L. Richter (Toronto: Macmillan, 1939), 174.

93 Interview with Wilda S., Living History Project, Riverview Health Centre, Winnipeg, Manitoba, 1999, http://www.riverviewhealthcentre.com/.

94 Cassidy, "Relief and Other Social Services for Transients," 176–77, 180.

95 Ibid., 180–81. They were provided with eight hours work per day in return for room and board, clothing and medical service, and an allowance of twenty cents per day. In 1934 and 1935, there were an estimated 19,000 to 25,000 in the camps, more than half of these in the western provinces. See also J. Struthers, *No Fault of Their Own: Unemployment and the Canadian Welfare State, 1914–1941* (Toronto: University of Toronto Press, 1983), 100, 132–35.

96 W.A. Waiser, *"All Hell Can't Stop Us": The On-to-Ottawa Trek and Regina Riot* (Calgary, AB: Fifth House, 2003), 61; "To the Citizens of Vancouver and District, Statement of the Conference Committee on Relief Camp Workers," advertisement, *Vancouver Sun*, May 27, 1935, 18.

97 "The Revolt of Youth," editorial, *National Home Monthly* (June 1934): 3.

98 D.L. Ritchie, "The Plight of Youth," *Social Welfare* (June 1934): 50.

99 G. Arnold, "Flaming Youth," *Maclean's* (July 1934): 13.

100 *Canada Yearbook*, 1936; see also Arthur P. Woollacott, "Junior G-Men of Canada," *Maclean's* (January 1939): 26.

101 "The Revolt of Youth," 3.

102 F.T. Sharpe, "Stopping before Starting," *Child Welfare News* (January 1934): 43–44; "Moral Standards," editorial, *Social Welfare* (September 1936): 94; "Youth Tells," *Maclean's* (December 1933): 25.

103 W. Bowie, "The Character of a Nation," *Social Welfare* (July 1931): 199; "Leisure Time Problems in the Isolated Home," *Child and Family Welfare* (January 1934): 46; W.R. Cook, "Getting Down to Brass Tacks in Community Planning for Leisure Time," *Social Welfare* (March 1938): 10–11.

104 Elsie Freeman, cited in A. Skeoch, *Years of Hope, 1921–1929* (Toronto: Grolier, 1988), 109. Freeman left her family's farm in Acton, Ontario, in 1918 at the age of fifteen.

105 On delinquency fears during World War II, see J. Keshen, *Saints, Sinners and Soldiers: Canada's Second World War* (Vancouver, BC: University of British Columbia Press,

2004), especially chapter 8, "The Children's War: Youth Run Wild"; M. Valverde, "Building Anti-delinquent Communities; Morality, Gender and Generation in the City," in *A Diversity of Women: Ontario, 1945–80*, ed. Joy Parr (Toronto, ON: University of Toronto Press, 1995), 25–31.

106 Public Archives of Ontario, YWCA Toronto, Annual Reports, F794 ACC 9844, box 11, B-1, MU 3527, *Annual Report*, 1941; A.E. Robinson, general secretary, Big Sister Association of Toronto, "Memo on Big Sisters," dated February 7, 1941: 1; G.E. Millard, principal, Havergal College, Toronto, "The Psychiatry of the Older Girl," *The Canadian Guider* 9 (March 1940): 5. The principal of the elite Toronto girls' school Havergal College considered that the problems of girls between the ages of thirteen and seventeen were "perhaps the most complicated" of all possible girl problems, and that there should consequently "be some opportunity for girls of this age to take part in intelligent community service and in social activities with boys."

107 Public Archives of Ontario, YWCA Toronto, Annual Reports, F794 ACC 9844, box 11, B-1, MU 3527, *Annual Report*, 1939, 11; also 1941, 4–5.

108 Public Archives of Ontario, YWCA Toronto, Annual Reports, F794 ACC 9844, box 11, B-1, MU 3527, *Annual Report*, 1943, 9; 1946, 10.

109 Dr. W. Clarke, director, American Social Hygiene Association, "They Are in Danger," *Health* (March 1941): 12–14. Clarke was speaking before the Vancouver Social Hygiene Council on the event of Social Hygiene Day.

110 C. Smith, "Teen Age Tragedy," *Health* (Autumn 1945): 10–14. See also C. Sethna, "Wait Till Your Father Gets Home: Absent Fathers, Working Mother and Delinquent Daughters in Ontario during World War II," in *Family Matters: Papers in Post-Confederation Canadian Family History*, ed. E.A. Montigny and L. Chambers (Toronto: Canadian Scholars' Press, 1998), especially 22–23. Adams, *The Trouble with Normal*, 108, points out that the actual number of teenagers affected by VD was greatly exaggerated, amounting to no more than 10 per cent of the whole. The same was true for the rise in unwed pregnancy, as noted.

111 "The Health of Secondary School Pupils," editorial, *Canadian Public Health Journal* 33 (1942): 464.

112 Major I. Eisenhardt, director, National Physical Fitness Plan, "Physical Fitness in Canada," *Health* (Spring 1945): 9–12. The act was part of the proposed health insurance act, but the need for action in this field persuaded the minister, Ian Mackenzie, to move on it. See also V.S. Blanchard, "School Health Problems," *Canadian Public Health Journal* 36 (September 1945): 217–22. On the Act, see Kidd, *The Struggle for Canadian Sport*, 252–54. Kidd notes that the plan never measured up to its directors' high hopes, had its finances cut repeatedly, and was finally repealed in 1954, bringing down all provincial programs that it had supported, meagre as they were.

113 Hershbein, "The Flapper and the Fogey: Representations of Gender and Age in the 1920s," *Journal of Family History* 26 (January 2001): 112–37.

Chapter 2

1 K. Mannheim, "The Problem of Generations," in Mannheim, *Essays on the Sociology of Knowledge* (London: Routledge and Kegan Paul, 1972; essay originally published 1928), 320.

2 A recent national youth survey, June 2004, indicates that, in a time when youth dependency extends ever longer and generational differences increase proportionately with the intensified pace of change, 85 per cent of young people aged thirteen

to nineteen polled expressed satisfaction with their parents and family lives. See "The Kids Are All Right," editorial, *Globe and Mail*, July 6, 2004, 16.

3 S.T. Wargon, *Children in Canadian Families* (Ottawa: Statistics Canada, 1997), 1. Uniform vital statistics date only from 1926.

4 Within the pre-adult age group comprising those from fourteen to twenty years old, there were comparatively few young immigrants, the average number under the age of twenty accounting for about 2,000 per year between 1921 and 1951. The numbers and proportion of youth dropped somewhat in 1951, when, of 14,009,429 Canadians, 1,058,000 were fifteen to nineteen. See Wargon, *Children in Canadian Families*, 21; Canada, Department of Labour, *Employment of Children and Young Persons* (Ottawa: King's Printer, 1930), 14; L. Marsh, *Employment Research: An Introduction to the McGill Programme of Research in the Social Services* (Toronto: Oxford University Press, 1935), 55–57. See also J.H. Thompson and Allen Seager, *Canada 1922–1939: Decades of Discord* (Toronto: McClelland and Stewart, 1985), 4–5.

5 W.B. Hurd, "The Decline in the Canadian Birth Rate," *Canadian Journal of Economics and Political Science* 3 (1937): 40–57. Hurd notes a decline in the birth rate of 23.3 per cent for women fifteen to forty-four over the previous half-century.

6 J.E. Robbins, *Dependency of Youth*, Census Monograph 9, Dominion Bureau of Statistics (Ottawa: King's Printer, 1937), 22. Robbins was chief of the Education Branch of the Dominion Bureau of Statistics. This in-depth study derived its information from volume 13, Seventh Census of Canada, 1931 and "supplementary data." According to Robbins's calculations, the "average man" in Canada, with average annual earnings amounting to $927, would have to spend his total salary for six years to "repay the expense incurred by society in rearing him for the first 18." See also B. Davies, *Youth Speaks Its Mind* (Toronto: Ryerson, 1948), 65. Davies estimated that "it requires about two years for the average Canadian youth, after leaving school, to become self-supporting."

7 Wargon, *Children in Canadian Families*, 20–21.

8 See the detailed census examination by G. Darroch, "Home and Away: Patterns of Residence, Schooling and Work among Children and Never-Married Young Adults, Canada, 1871 and 1901," *Journal of Family History* 26 (2001): 220–50. Darroch also finds a high proportion of youth leaving home during these years.

9 On fatherhood in the early twentieth century, see R. Griswold, *Fatherhood in America: A History* (New York: Basic Books, 1993); R. LaRossa, *The Modernization of Fatherhood: A Social and Political History* (Chicago: University of Chicago Press, 1997). For Canada, see C. Comacchio, "A Postscript for Father: Defining the New Fatherhood in Interwar Canada," *Canadian Historical Review* 78 (1997): 385–408; R. Rutherford, "Fatherhood and Masculine Domesticity during the Baby Boom," in *Family Matters: Papers in Post-Confederation Canadian Family History*, ed. L. Chambers and E. Montigny (Toronto: Canadian Scholars' Press, 1998): 309–33.

10 A. Brookes, "Family, Youth, and Leaving Home in Late-Nineteenth-Century Rural Nova Scotia: Canning and the Exodus, 1868–1885," in *Childhood and Family in Canadian History*, ed. J. Parr (Toronto: McClelland and Stewart, 1982), 121–24.

11 M. de la Roche, *Ringing the Changes: An Autobiography* (Toronto: Macmillan, 1957), 200. De la Roche was born in 1879.

12 Wargon, *Children in Canadian Families*, 24–25. The statistics demonstrate that the number of never-married adult sons and daughters living in the family home was at just about the same level in 1931 as in 1976.

13 Wargon, *Children in Canadian Families*, 21. Wargon finds that the number of unmarried young adults ages fifteen to twenty-four still living at home, in relation to the total population of the same ages, experienced a decline over the whole period 1941–1976, the largest drop occurring over the twenty years from 1941–1961. During this time, unmarried young adults of that age group living at home represented well

over four-fifths of the unmarried population of that group, a proportion that remained fairly stable at between 0.83 and 0.84 during those three decades.

14 C.M. Bayley, "The Social Structure of the Italian and Ukrainian Immigrant Communities in Montreal, 1935–1937," MA thesis, McGill University, 1939, 264. Bayley lived for fifteen months among the Italians and another seven months among the Ukrainians in Montreal between 1935 and 1937 to do his research under the supervision of Carl Dawson. Although the largest European group in city, the Italians represented barely 3 per cent of the total population; the Ukrainians were the fifth largest group.

15 Robbins, *Dependency of Youth*, 9–10. Wargon, *Children in Canadian Families*, 24, n. 3, in citing Robbins's work, points out that "it is not completely clear . . . whether 'dependency' or 'independence' referred to the financial or wage-earning status of young adult children still living at home, or to both financial and residential independence from parents. Certain tabular data in the monograph seem to imply that independence referred only to the wage-earning capacity of young adult children 15 and over, most of whom probably continued to live at home and to contribute to the maintenance of their families and family households until they married"; see Robbins, 44.

16 Robbins, *Dependency of Youth*, 17, predicted that the average age of school-leaving in 1941 would be about seventeen, rather than 16.25 as in 1931, and that "the younger generation [in 1941] as a whole will probably not be self supporting until the age of 19 or thereabouts."

17 Ibid., 21–22.

18 Ibid., 9–10.

19 A.W. Currie, *Growing up in Rural Ontario, 1908 to 1926*; unpublished memoirs, 1971, University Archives, Queen's University, Kingston, Ontario, 68.

20 Elsie Freeman, cited in A. Skeoch, *Years of Hope, 1921–1929* (Toronto: Grolier, 1988), 9–12.

21 Interview with Betty L., Living History Project, Riverview Health Centre, Winnipeg, Manitoba, http://www.riverviewhealthcentre.com/livinghistory/. The Living History Project was begun by Riverview Health Centre volunteers in 1999, when the United Nations celebrated the International Year of Older Persons.

22 Basil H. Johnston, *Indian School Days* (Toronto: Key Porter, 1988), 174, 176. Johnston, born in 1929 at Cape Croker on Georgian Bay in Ontario, attended the Jesuit-run Garnier Residential School for Indian Boys in Spanish, Ontario.

23 Wargon, *Children in Canadian Families*, 23; Wargon infers that, since approximately 1956, young adults have increasingly chosen to live in non-family households, either alone or with their peers. This trend seems to have reversed since the recessionary 1980s.

24 "On the Spirit of the Strike," *Chatelaine* (May 1928): 16; see also Judge Emily Murphy's indictment of the "companionate marriage," which she interprets as "trial" marriage; E. Murphy, "Companionate Marriage," *Chatelaine* (May 1928): 4.

25 This is discussed in C.R. Comacchio, *The Infinite Bonds of Family: Domesticity in Canada, 1850–1940* (Toronto: University of Toronto Press, 1999),

26 C.W. Topping, "The Equalitarian Family as a Fundamental Invention," *Canadian Journal of Economics and Political Science* 8 (1942): 600. Topping contends that the "paternal" family was still predominant in large rural families, in Quebec, and in immigrant urban families.

27 Ibid., 604.

28 "Democracy in the Home," editorial, *Canadian Unionist* (January 1939): 5. This discussion is reiterated in Canadian Youth Commission, *Youth, Marriage and the Family* (Toronto: Ryerson Press, 1947), 1–7.

29 H. Graff, *Conflicting Paths: Growing Up in America* (Cambridge, MA: Harvard University Press, 1995), 305.

30 Bayley, "The Social Structure of the Italian and Ukrainian Immigrant Communities in Montreal, 1935–37," 282, Case 7, Miss E. This young woman, twenty-three years old, had been born in Naples and moved to Canada at the age of eight.

31 C.H. Young, *The Ukrainian Canadians: A Study in Assimilation* (Toronto: Nelson, 1931), 155. This book is based on eight hundred interviews over eighteen months that McGill sociologist Young spent visiting Ukrainian communities across Canada, the majority in the Prairies. It was edited by Helen R.Y. Reid, chair of the Immigration Division, Canadian National Committee for Mental Hygiene. Young found that the patriarchal family "in which the power of the husband and father . . . was very great" persisted, but that the younger generation was less inclined to take up this family form.

32 Ibid., 158.

33 Ibid., 158–60.

34 C. Dawson, *Group Settlement: Ethnic Communities in Western Canada* (Toronto: Macmillan, 1936), 159–60.

35 Ibid., 161.

36 Young, *The Ukrainian Canadians*, 105, 112–13. See also H. Atkinson, "Boys in Trouble," *Child and Family Welfare* 7 (March 1932): 2; also the contemporary sociological survey in Ross, "Juvenile Delinquency in Montreal," 1932, 34–35. On intergenerational conflict in the Ukrainian community in the west, see F. Swyripa, *Wedded to the Cause: Ukrainian-Canadian Women and Ethnic Identity, 1891–1991* (Toronto: University of Toronto Press, 1993), 90–95.

37 Dawson, *Group Settlement*, 160; see also N. Ryder, "The Cohort as a Concept in the Study of Social Change," *American Sociological Review* 30 (1965): 850.

38 Swyripa, *Wedded to the Cause*, 90–95.

39 Bayley, "The Social Structure of the Italian and Ukrainian Immigrant Communities," Case 7, Miss E., 278.

40 Mrs. Anna Smokorowsky, in D. Read and R. Hann, eds., *The Great War and Canadian Society: An Oral History* (Toronto: New Hogtown Press, 1978), 82–83. Smokorowsky was born in Venlaw, Manitoba, in 1902, three years after her parents came to Canada from Ukraine.

41 Bayley, "The Social Structure of the Italian and Ukrainian Immigrant Communities," 35.

42 Ibid., 101.

43 Dawson, *Group Settlement*, 162. These observations are from Dawson's field notes.

44 Bayley, "The Social Structure of the Italian and Ukrainian Immigrant Communities," 70–73, 80. Over 60 per cent of the Italian population of Montreal at that time had been born in the city.

45 Ibid., 71, 78.

46 Ibid., 278, 71.

47 Ibid., 87.

48 H.G. MacGill, "The Oriental Delinquent in the Vancouver Juvenile Court," *Sociology and Social Research* 22 (1938): 428, 438.

49 E.A. Guest, "The Home, a Boy's One Safe Harbour," *Canadian Mentor* 11, 3 (1929): 1–2. The *Canadian Mentor* was the official organ of the Tuxis and Trail Rangers movement; see chap. 7.

50 W.G. Hammond, "The Teacher Father," letter to the editor, *Globe and Mail* (June 12, 1945), 8. Hammond identified himself as head of the English Department, Lawrence Park Collegiate, Toronto.

51 University of British Columbia Archives, Journals of the Tuxis, 9th Annual Boys Parliament, Calgary, Alberta, 1928, 5; see also 10th Annual Boys Parliament, Victoria, BC, 1929, "Report of the Committee on Home Affairs," 24; also, pamphlet promoting Father and Son Week, 3–10 February 1929; see chap. 7.

52 "Your Boy Is Growing Up!" advertisement, Manufacturers Life Insurance Company, Toronto, in Chatelaine, May 1928.

53 H. Boyle, Homebrew and Patches (Toronto: Clarke. Irwin, 1963), 54, 64. A long-time CBC broadcaster and writer, Boyle grew up on a farm near Cargill, Ontario.

54 "Letters from a Schoolmaster," Maclean's (February 1938): 17; (March 1938): 22; and (March 1938): 40.

55 "Letters from a Schoolmaster," Maclean's (May 1938): 71.

56 Interview, Mrs. Jim Lawson, 1967, in D. Livesay, Right Hand, Left Hand (Erin, ON: Porcepic, 1977), 46.

57 Ibid., 45–46.

58 D. Livesay, Journey with My Selves: A Memoir (Vancouver: Douglas and McIntyre, 1991), 15. Livesay (1909–1996) was born in Winnipeg; her parents were Florence Randal Livesay, a journalist and poet, and J.F.B. Livesay, general manager of the Canadian Press. Beginning with her first publication, Green Pitcher, in 1928, Livesay wrote short fiction, journalism, political commentary, and the poetry for which she is best known. She was a leftist political activist and a social worker during the Depression. See P. Stevens, Dorothy Livesay: Patterns in a Poetic Life (Toronto: ECW Press, 1992).

59 University of Manitoba Archives, Dorothy Livesay Papers, MSS 37, Box 2, Folder 1, Diary entry, October 11, 1923; also December 17, 1927. Livesay was fourteen in the former, eighteen in the latter.

60 Library and Archives Canada, MG 28 I 10, vol. 40, File 173C, Council on Child and Family Welfare, Postnatal Letters, no. 2 and no. 3. Along with Prenatal Letters, this was a published series sent out to mothers across Canada.

61 "Letters from a Schoolmaster," Macleans (April 1938): 43.

62 H. Russell Ross, "Juvenile Delinquency in Montreal," MA thesis, McGill University, 1932, 79.

63 Library and Archives Canada, Mg 28, I 10, vol. 3, file 599, 1942–44, Canadian Youth Commission papers, typescript, interview with "Hugh," Halifax, Nova Scotia, August 1944, 3. These intensive interviews were conducted by the CYC as part of a national survey of citizenship and youth services; many were published, on a number of subject areas.

64 I. LePage, "Group Organization and the Development of the Adolescent Girl," MA thesis, McGill University, 1932, 27.

65 M. Peate, Girl in a Sloppy Joe Sweater: Life on the Canadian Home Front during World War II (Montreal: Optimum, 1988), 114.

66 Library and Archives Canada, Mg 28, I 10, vol. 3, file 599, 1942–44, Canadian Youth Commission papers, typescript, interview with "Vi," Toronto, August 1944, 2.

67 Library and Archives Canada, Canadian Youth Commission papers, typescript, interview with "Mrs A.," Toronto, August 1944, 3; interview with "Anne," rural Ontario, August 1944, 4.

68 Library and Archives Canada, Canadian Youth Commission papers, typescript, interview with "A.K.," Antigonish, Nova Scotia, August 1944, 5.

69 E. Jaques, Uphill All the Way: An Autobiography (Saskatoon: Western Producer Prairie Books, 1977), 111.

70 C.D. Taylor, The Surprise of My Life: An Autobiography (Waterloo, ON: Wilfrid Laurier University Press, 1998), 43–44. Claire Wodlinger Drainie Taylor grew up in a middle-class Jewish Canadian family in Regina, Saskatchewan; she would go on to a career as a radio and television actress and scriptwriter.

71 Interview with Wilda S., Living History Project, Riverview Health Centre, www.riverview healthcentre.com. Wilda lived in a family of twelve, including five brothers and four sisters, on the north side; her father was a tinsmith.

72 University of Toronto Archives, J.D. Ketchum papers, File 3A, Box 37. Ketchum was on the university's psychology faculty; the writer is identified as "girl 25."

73 George Antheil, "A Word to Women," *Toronto Star*, April 2, 1941, 24.

74 Ibid., *Toronto Star*, May 28, 1941, 26.

75 "No Discrimination in 'Teen-Age Clubs: Social and Racial Differences Absent in Youth Recreation Centres," *Simcoe Reformer*, June 28, 1945, 2. Simcoe is a rural town in southwestern Ontario. The speaker, Miss Donalda MacRae, was identified as "Secretary for the younger membership of the National Council, YWCA."

76 Interview with Wilda S., Living History Project, Riverview Health Centre, www.riverview healthcentre.com.

77 Currie, *Growing Up in Rural Ontario*, 93.

78 N. Enstad, *Ladies of Labor, Girls of Adventure: Working Women, Popular Culture and Labor Politics at the Turn of the Twentieth Century* (New York: Columbia University Press, 1999): 2–3.

79 Ibid., 9–10. Enstad discusses the ability of fashion to bridge ethnic boundaries among young women of immigrant families, helping them to "signal . . . their Americanism." See also Bayley, "The Social Structure of the Italian and Ukrainian Immigrant Communities," 90.

80 "Ontario's Sunny Riviera," *Waterford Star*, September 4, 1930, 6.

81 L. Davidow Hershbein, "The Flapper and the Fogey: Representations of Gender and Age in the 1920s," *Journal of Family History* 26 (January 2001): 113–14.

82 E. Welles Page, "A Flapper's Appeal to Parents," *Outlook Magazine*, December 6, 1922, 607.

83 *Understanding Your Teenager* (Toronto: Metropolitan Life Insurance Company, 1953), 1, 18–20.

84 Ibid., 20.

85 Westley and Elkin, "The Protective Environment," 245.

86 Ibid., 246–47.

87 Ibid., 245–46. The authors comment on this study in footnote 4; I have not been able to track it. See also their earlier study, W.A. Westley and F. Elkin, "The Myth of Adolescent Culture," *American Sociological Review* 20 (1955): 680–84.

Chapter 3

1 Reminiscences of Jake Foran, in D. Read and R. Hann, eds., *The Great War and Canadian Society: An Oral History* (Toronto: New Hogtown Press, 1978), 211.

2 G. Pringle, "Is the Flapper a Menace?" *Maclean's* (June 1922): 19. Dr. Thom also discusses "the accepted petting convention of modern adolescence," in D.A. Thom, *Normal Youth and Its Everyday Problems* (New York: Appleton, 1932), 69–70.

3 University of Manitoba Archives, Lillian Beatrice Allen papers, MSS 45, Box 14, file 1, typescript, undated, "Growing Up," 21. Allen was born in Winnipeg, November 9, 1904. She was the only daughter of Frank Allen, the first physics professor at the University of Manitoba. She earned a master's degree in home economics at the University of Syracuse in 1947 and lectured at Manitoba's Faculty of Agriculture and Home Economics.

4 C.M. Bayley, "The Social Structure of the Italian and Ukrainian Immigrant Communities in Montreal," MA thesis, McGill University, 1937, 87.

5 M. Peate, *Girl in a Sloppy Joe Sweater: Life on the Canadian Home Front during World War II* (Montreal: Optimum, 1988), 108.

6 Letter, "Dorothy Dix Says," *Montreal Gazette*, December 14, 1944, 18.

7 I. LePage, "Group Organization and the Development of the Adolescent Girl," MA thesis, McGill University, 1932, 23.

8 University of Toronto Archives, J.D. Ketchum papers, Box 32, B740072, File 155, Life History no. 3, 22.

9 University of Manitoba Archives, Lillian Beatrice Allen papers. MSS 45, Box 14, file 1, typescript, [late 1970s], "My Life with Sex," 4.

10 G. Antheil, "A Word to Women," *Toronto Star*, June 18, 1941, 26.

11 D. Baillargeon, "Beyond Romance: Courtship and Marriage in Montreal between the Wars," in *Rethinking Canada: The Promise of Women's History*, 4th ed., ed. V. Strong-Boag, M. Gleason, and A. Perry (Toronto: Oxford University Press, 2002) 203–19. See also A. Gagnon, "The Courtship of Franco-Albertan Women, 1890–1930)," in *Family Matters: Papers in Post-Confederation Canadian Family History*, ed. L. Chambers and E. Montigny (Toronto: Canadian Scholars' Press, 1998), 177–98. On the United States, see E.K. Rothman, *Hands and Hearts: A History of Courtship in America* (New York: Basic Books, 1984); B. Bailey, *From Front Porch to Back Seat: Courtship in Twentieth-Century America* (Baltimore, MD: Johns Hopkins University Press, 1988), 78–80.

12 W. Waller, "The Rating and Dating Complex," *American Sociological Review* 2 (1937): 727–28, discusses customs of courtship among adolescents, based on a survey of college students. On commercialized leisure, see D. Nasaw, *Going Out: The Rise and Fall of Public Amusements* (Cambridge, MA: Harvard University Press, 1999), 1–9.

13 T. Newcombe, "Recent Changes in Attitudes toward Sex and Marriage," *American Sociological Review* 2 (1937): 659–67.

14 G. Antheil, "A Word to Women," *Toronto Star*, February 7, 1945, 20.

15 W.A. Buck, "Measurement of Changes in Attitudes and Interests of University Students over a Ten-Year Period," *Journal of Abnormal and Social Psychology* 31 (1936): 2–19; Buck compared his surveys of college students for 1923 and 1933 and found that boys "grew more tolerant" as they approached college age while girls did not become tolerant until that age, suggesting to him that gender-differentiated socialization made girls "closer to convention" than boys. See also H. Hart, "Changing Attitudes and Interests," *Fortune Magazine* (January 1937): 22–27. The magazine conducted a quarterly survey on "Recent Social Trends."

16 Newcombe, "Recent Changes in Attitudes," 662. Newcombe cites R.S. Lynd and H.M. Lynd, *Middletown: A Study in Contemporary American Culture* (New York: Harcourt, Brace, 1929) and *Middletown in Transition: A Study in Cultural Conflicts* (New York: Harcourt, Brace, 1937), 664–65.

17 Waller, "The Rating and Dating Complex," 728–79.

18 K. Lukasiewicz, "The Polish Community in the Crows Nest Pass," *Alberta History* 36 (Autumn 1988): 1–9. The first Polish emigrants arrived in Crowsnest Pass, one of the largest coalfields in Canada, in 1903.

19 On Ukrainian child brides, see F. Swyripa, *Wedded to the Cause: Ukrainian-Canadian Women and Ethnic Identity, 1891–1991* (Toronto: University of Toronto Press, 1993), 90–95.

20 "Perjury Case Arises from Child Marriage," *The Globe*, July 7, 1920, 3; see also "Girl's Mother Has Bridegroom Arrested," *The Globe*, July 27, 1920, 3. In the latter case, the young woman "misrepresented her age" as eighteen when she was only fifteen. The twenty-year-old groom had boarded at the girl's home for a year and declared that he would "put up a fight for her."

21 "Early Marriages," editorial, *Grain Growers Guide*, June 17, 1925, 19.

22 E. Jaques, *Uphill All the Way: An Autobiography* (Saskatoon, SK: Western Producer Prairie Books, 1977), 119–20.

23 Reminiscences of Alex Boulton, in Read and Hann, eds., *The Great War and Canadian Society*, 44. Boulton grew up in the rural hamlet of South Fredericksburg, Ontario;

in this oral testimony, he recalls "the old-fashioned courtship approach" of his adolescent years during the war.

24 Jaques, *Uphill All the Way*, 120.

25 B. Johnston, *Indian School Days* (Toronto: Key Porter, 1988), 185. Born on the Cape
Croker Ojibway Reserve in Ontario in 1929, Johnston is a renowned author and eth-
nologist.

26 A. Anderson, *Remembering the Farm: Memories of Farming, Ranching and Rural Life in
Canada, Past and Present* (Toronto: Macmillan, 1979), 120.

27 Bayley, "The Social Structure of the Italian and Ukrainian Immigrant Communities,"
281.

28 Ibid., 67; Bayley noted the trend of the Canadian-born daughters of both groups to
marry Canadian-born men of their communities rather than those who were "foreign-born." Among Italians in 1935, 14.8 per cent of those married in Mont Carmel
and Notre Dame parishes wed out of their own ethnic group, while the Ukrainians
had "scarcely commenced to intermarry."

29 Ibid., 80, 283. Mr. A. was twenty-four years old, born in Montreal, and had a sixth-
grade education; he worked as a mechanic for nine dollars per week, but "tips and
side graft bring it up to between $25 and $40 per week."

30 University of Manitoba Archives, Lillian Beatrice Allen papers. MSS 45, Box 14, file
1, "Growing Up," 26.

31 Peate, *Girl in a Sloppy Joe Sweater*, 136. Peate notes that "the situation spawned a
social phenomenon called the 'hen party.'"

32 D. Dix, "Dorothy Dix Says," *Montreal Gazette*, December 14, 1944, 18.

33 "No Men in Their Lives," *Toronto Star*, April 27, 1946: 22. Described as "brighter than
the average of topical verse in school magazines," the poem by Mona Van Ark, "A
Class of 32," was originally printed in *Norvoc*, the annual publication of Toronto's
Northern Vocational High School.

34 Miss Rosalind, "Advice to Girls," *Waterford Star*, February 10, 1921, 5. The *Star* was
a weekly newspaper; Miss Rosalind gave a Hamilton address for advice-seekers.

35 University of Manitoba Archives, Lillian Beatrice Allen papers, MSS 45, Box 14, file 3,
typescript, [probably late 1970s], "My Life with Sex," 4. See also Allen, Box 1, Folder
2, Diary 1921–22, 11. Allen, who never married, was quite candid about sexuality.

36 Jaques married Jimmy in 1921, after several years of living and working on her own
in Calgary and Vancouver; Jaques, *Uphill All the Way*, 120–21.

37 K.R. Strange, *With the West in Her Eyes* (Toronto: George J. McLeod, 1937), 252–54.
British-born Strange and her husband homesteaded in Fenn, Alberta; she was a regular contributor to the *Grain Growers Guide*. This book details her life there during
the 1920s; they left the town in 1930.

38 See Gagnon, "The Courtship of Franco-Albertan Women, 1890–1930," 177–98.

39 H. Miner, *St. Denis, a French-Canadian Parish* (Chicago: University of Chicago Press,
1939), 209–11.

40 Baillargeon, "Beyond Romance," 206–208.

41 C.D. Taylor, *The Surprise of My Life: An Autobiography* (Waterloo, ON: Wilfrid Laurier
University Press, 1998), 46.

42 University of Toronto Archives, J.D. Ketchum papers, Box 32, B740072, File 155, Life
History no. 3, 27–28. The anonymous writer was born in 1909.

43 Anderson, *Remembering the Farm*, 117.

44 Mrs. Sally Hill, in Read and Hann, eds., *The Great War and Canadian Society*, 44.

45 University of Toronto Archives, J.D. Ketchum papers, Box 32, B740072, File 155, Life
History no. 3, 21. She started high school in 1921.

46 Johnston, *Indian School Days*, 230.

47 I. Knockwood, *Out of the Depths: The Experiences of Mi'kmaw Children at the Indian
Residential School at Shubenacadie, Nova Scotia* (Lockport, NS: Roseway, 1992), 52–53.

48 University of Toronto Archives, J.D. Ketchum papers, Box 32, B740072, File 155, Life History no. 3, 57.

49 Taylor, *The Surprise of My Life*, 64. Taylor eloped with an "older" man (in his thirties) at the age of sixteen, the first of her three marriages.

50 University of Manitoba Archives, Lillian Beatrice Allen papers, MSS 45, Box 14, file 1, "Growing Up," 21.

51 R. Collins, *You Had to Be There: An Intimate Portrait of the Generation That Survived the Depression, Won the War, and Re-invented Canada* (Toronto: McClelland and Stewart, 1997), 46–47. This is the story of Gladys Graham Byrnes, of Creemore, Ontario, who came of age during the 1930s; "clueless" when she started menstruating, her mother told her to ask her sister, who was four years older, about sex.

52 Reminiscences of Mrs. Helen Gloucester, in Read and Hann, eds., *The Great War and Canadian Society*, 62; also those of Larry Nelson, from Toronto, in Collins, *You Had to Be There*, 59, and Patricia Ritz Anders, who married at the age of nineteen during the late 1930s and recalls "knowing nothing about sex," also in Collins, 60.

53 Collins, *You Had to Be There*, 44.

54 H. Garner, "On the Road through the Thirties," *Weekend Magazine*, February 27, 1971, 7.

55 "Love in Hidden Places," in *Ten Lost Years, 1929–1939: Memories of Canadians Who Survived the Depression*, ed. B. Broadfoot (Don Mills, ON: General, 1973), 241.

56 H. MacLennan, "What It Was Like to Be in Your Twenties in the Thirties," in *The Great Depression: Essays and Memoirs from Canada and the United States*, ed. V. Hoar (Toronto: Copp, Clark, 1969), 144.

57 See A. Levèsque, *Le Norme et les déviantes: Des femmes au Québéc pendant l'entre-deux-guerres* (Montreal: Rémue-Ménage, 1989), translated by Y. Klein, *Making and Breaking the Rules: Women in Quebec, 1919–1939* (Toronto: McClelland and Stewart, 1994); M.A. Cliche, "Morale chrétienne et double standard sexuel: Les filles-meres à l'hôpital de la Miséricorde à Québec, 1874–1972," *Histoire sociale/Social History* 47 (1991): 85–125. See also J. Sangster, *Regulating Girls and Women: Sexuality, Family, and the Law in Ontario, 1920–1960* (Don Mills, ON: Oxford University Press, 2001).

58 Peate, *Girl in a Sloppy Joe Sweater*, 157–58; she is recalling the situation of her friend Cath.

59 Boulton, in Read and Hann, eds., *The Great War and Canadian Society*, 44.

60 R.D. Sharma, "Pre-marital and Ex-nuptial Fertility in Canada, 1921–72," *Canadian Studies in Population* 9 (1982): 1–15. Sharma notes that there was an upward trend in illegitimacy from 1921 to 1970, excluding Newfoundland, Quebec, and the Northwest Territories; the trend would reverse itself after 1970, 2–3.

61 Canadian Youth Commission, *Youth, Marriage and the Family* (Toronto: Ryerson Press, 1947), 15.

62 H. Weir, "Unemployed Youth," in *Canada's Unemployment Problem*, ed. L. Richter (Toronto: Macmillan, 1939), 141, 146.

63 Ibid., 141–42. The marriage rate in 1926 was 66,658; it peaked at 77,288 in 1929, dropped back to 66,591, and bottomed out at 62,531 the following year, when it began a gradual rise. By 1935, it was 76,893, just short of the 1929 total. See W.B. Hurd, "The Decline in the Canadian Birth Rate," *Canadian Journal of Economics and Political Science* 3, 1 (1937): 40–57; Hurd, "Some Implications of Prospective Population Changes in Canada," *Canadian Journal of Economics and Political Science* 5, 4 (1939): 492–503. See also Ontario Young Men's Council, YMCA, *Survey: A Youth's Eye View of Some Problems Connected with Getting Married* (1934), 10.

64 Weir, "Unemployed Youth," 142–43. The figures are as follows: 1926: 6,121; 1927: 6,715; 1928: 7,280; 1929: 7,516; 1930: 8,059; 1931: 8,365; 1932: 8,460; 1933: 8,426; 1934: 8,070; 1935: 8,344; 1936: 8,633. The figures for each individual province show an increase in each case over the ten-year period, varying from 5.8 per cent for the

province of Manitoba to 94 per cent for British Columbia. The distribution of illegitimate births by age did not change to any considerable extent between 1931 and 1951; during those twenty years, it actually declined for the group under age twenty. See Canadian Marketing Analysis, *The Liberty Study on Young Canada* (Toronto: Canadian Marketing Analysis, Ltd., 1955), chart 13, 17. The percentage of mothers under twenty in 1931 was 38.8; for 1941, 29.9; for 1951, 33.

65 Sharma, "Pre-marital and Ex-nuptial Fertility in Canada, 3. Sharma contends that, although the illegitimacy ratio is frequently used as measure of the level of illegitimacy, it is not as good a a measure as age-specific illegitimacy fertility rates. The age-specific illegitimacy fertility rates are not influenced by the age structure of the mothers because illegitimate births are related to the group of unmarried women to which the mother belongs. He notes that "illegitimate" births are more likely to be under-registered; he does not attempt to explain the blip during the Depression years. See Table 3.3: Percentage Change in Illegitimate Birth Rate, 15 to 49 years: 1921–31: +35.3; 1931–41: +3.9; 1941–51: +60.2; 1951–56: +18.7.

66 D. Livesay, *Right Hand, Left Hand* (Erin, ON: Press Porcepic, 1977), 123.

67 A. Woywitka, "Out of the Roaring 20s into the Hungry 30s," *Alberta History* (Summer 1999): 17.

68 G. Bates, "The Venereal Disease Problem," *Canadian Public Health Journal* 13 (April 1922): 265–69; Bates, who headed the Social Hygiene Council of Canada (founded in 1921) presented this paper to the Hamilton Social Hygiene Council. Similar views are expressed in Mrs. L.A. Hamilton, "Educational Opportunities," *Canadian Public Health Journal* 12 (February 1921): 59–64; W.H. Roberts, "The Venereal Problem in Large Towns and Small Cities," *Canadian Public Health Journal* 11 (September 1920): 63–65. On VD scares during World War I, see J. Cassel, *The Secret Plague: Venereal Disease in Canada, 1838–1939* (Toronto: University of Toronto Press, 1987), 24–45.

69 Public Archives of Ontario, RG 10-30-A.1-4.08, Department of Health, Historical Pamphlets and Bulletins, file 4.1, Arthur Beall, 1. Sethna discusses Beall's work thoroughly in "Men, Sex and Education," 191–97.

70 P. Sandiford, "The School Programme and Sex Education," *Canadian Public Health Journal* 13 (March 1922): 60–61.

71 D.A. Thom, *Normal Youth and Its Everyday Problems* (New York: Appleton, 1932), 42, 68–79.

72 E. Guest, "Problems of Girlhood and Motherhood," *Canadian Public Health Journal* 13 (May 1922):193–95. Oral testimony from the time suggests that there may have been some truth to this medical worry; see the memories of Helen Gloucester, who was hospitalized at Toronto General Hospital to deliver her first child during the war, and whose doctor discovered that she "didn't know which way the baby was coming," in Read and Hann, eds., *The Great War and Canadian Society*, 62; see also V. Strong-Boag, *The New Day Recalled: Lives of Girls and Women in English Canada, 1919–1939* (Markham, ON: Penguin, 1988), 15, 86–89; and the recollections of Montreal housewives about the interwar years in D. Baillargeon, *Making Do: Home and Family in Montreal during the Great Depression* (Waterloo, ON: Wilfrid Laurier University Press, 1998).

73 E.S. Dummer, foreword to *The Unadjusted Girl, with Cases and Standpoint for Behavior Analysis*, by W.I. Thomas (Boston: Little, Brown, 1923), xi–xvii. Thomas's sample consisted largely of girls who were either unwed mothers or prostitutes.

74 Thomas, *The Unadjusted Girl*, 109.

75 G. Pringle, "Is the Flapper a Menace?" 19; M.J. Exner, *The Question of Petting* (New York: American Social Hygiene Association, 1926), 32–35; F.E. Williams, *Adolescence: Studies in Mental Hygiene* (New York: Appleton-Century, 1932), 54; Thom, *Normal Youth and Its Everyday Problems*, 69–70. See also some of the material published during the interwar years by various social hygiene organizations, e.g., United States,

Public Health Service, *The Wonderful Story of Life: A Mother Talks with Her Daughter Regarding Life and Reproduction* (Washington, DC: Government Printing Office, 1921); O. Davies, *The Story of Life: As Told to His Sons and as Told to Her Daughters* (Naperville, IL: J.L. Nichols, 1922); H.W. Brown, *Sex Education in the Home* (New York: American Social Hygiene Association, 1933); J. Robertson, *What Every Lad Should Know about Sex* (London: Peoples League of Health, 1935); G.L.M. McElligott, *Ourselves: A Few Facts for Young Men* (Birmingham, UK: British Social Hygiene Council, 1935); V.H. Parker, *Social Hygiene and the Child* (New York: American Social Hygiene Association, 1939). These and many others are in the Public Health Nursing Division Records, Public Archives of Ontario, RG10-30-A-1, 7.02–7.03.

76 Thom, *Normal Youth*, 60–63; J.R. Gallagher, *Your Son's Adolescence* (Boston: Little, Brown, 1951), 104. Gallagher's view was more tolerant in regard to adolescent experimentation, but he still considered homosexuality aberrant.

77 Davis, *Factors in the Sex Life of Twenty-Two Thousand Women* (New York: Harper and Row, 1929); cited also in L. Pruette, "The Flapper," in *The New Generation: The Intimate Problems of Modern Parents and Children*, ed. V.F. Calverton and S.D. Schnalhausen (New York: Macaulay, 1930), 585. Of the 1,000 married women who constituted the remainder of the study group, 71 admitted to intercourse before marriage; of the 1,200 unmarried college girls, the number was 136. Davis (1860–1935) received a PhD in economics in 1900 from the University of Chicago. She became Commissioner of Corrections for New York City in 1914; as general secretary of the Board of Directors of the Bureau of Social Hygiene, she directed research into the narcotics trade and addiction, the "white slave trade," juvenile delinquency, and other aspects of public health and social hygiene. She died in 1935. See L.D. Gordon, "Katherine Bement Davis," in *Biographical Dictionary of Social Welfare in America*, ed. W.I. Trattner (New York: Greenwood, 1986), 207–10.

78 University of Toronto Archives, J.D. Ketchum papers, Box 32, B740072, File B89, Life History no. 8, 86. The writer was born in 1909 to a "well-to-do family."

79 Ibid.

80 University of Manitoba Archives, Lillian Beatrice Allen papers, MSS 45, Box 14, folder 3, "My Life with Sex," 5–7.

81 University of Toronto Archives, J.D. Ketchum papers, Box 32, B740072, File 82, Life History no. 9, 25. The writer was born in Toronto in 1914; her father was "in business."

82 University of Toronto Archives, J.D. Ketchum papers, Box 32, B740072, File 3A, Life History no. 40, 7. Ketchum notes in brackets that "the writer is a homosexual, emotionally unstable, cannot adjust to marriage." The writer was twenty-two years old at the time of her writing, in 1934.

83 Davis, "The Sociology of Parent-Youth Conflict," *American Sociological Review* (1940): 333–34.

84 Bates, "The Venereal Disease Problem," 269.

85 Already by 1911, the Vancouver Medical Association was recommending the teaching of "sex hygiene" to high school pupils, though Vancouver doctors soon concluded that it was impossible to deal adequately with this subject in a series of lectures delivered by a physician at the close of a high school course; see T.G. Hunter and C.H. Gundry, "School Health Practices: Ritualistic or Purposeful?" *Canadian Journal of Public Health* 46 (January 1955): 9–14.

86 Roberts, "The Venereal Problem in Large Towns and Small Cities," 65.

87 Public Archives of Ontario, RG 10-30-A.1-4.08, Department of Health, Historical Pamphlets and Bulletins, file 4.1, A. Beall, 3.

88 Public Archives of Ontario, RG 10-30-A.1-4.08, Department of Health, Historical Pamphlets and Bulletins, file 4.1, A. Beall. One social hygiene activist estimated that 78 per cent of both boys and girls had not been taught the facts of sex by parents,

and suggested the adoption of an American approach to high school biology courses, where discussions of the reproductive process were allegedly "very frank, even in
mixed classes"; see Hamilton, "Educational Opportunities," 64.

89 Thom, *Normal Youth*, 21.

90 Sandiford, "The School Programme and Sex Education," 59–63; Thom, *Normal Youth*, 44; 46.

91 "Powerful Drama Draws Record Audience," *The Globe*, January 6, 1932, 11. Dr. Gordon Bates, general secretary of the Social Hygiene Council, and Dr. Robb, provincial minister of public health, both spoke at the film's opening.

92 Dorothy Dix's Letter Box, *Guelph Daily Mercury*, May 12, 1938, 11. Elizabeth Meriwether Gilmer (1861–1951), writing under the pen name "Dorothy Dix," was America's highest-paid and best-known female journalist. Her papers are held at Austin Peay University, Tennessee; http://library.apsu.edu/dix/dix.htm.

93 "Man Dares Invade Realm of Women," *Toronto Star*, December 11, 1937, 1. The col- umn was announced as being "as modern as the young people of today," while demonstrating "a wholesome thread of practical common sense." Antheil would begin dedicating the Wednesday column specifically to teenagers in June 1940. The column appears to have been dropped in March 1945 without announcement. See also "Antheil's 'Bad Boy of Music' Recalls Europe in Mad 1920s," a review of his autobiography, *Toronto Star*, December 22, 1945, 4. Born in New Jersey to parents of Polish-Prussian origins, Antheil was an avant-garde American composer and pianist, known for his *Ballet Mecanique*. The *Star* called him "one of the six most important composers of the continent."

94 Antheil, "A Man Talks to Women," *Toronto Star*, July 24, 1940, 22.

95 Ibid.

96 Ibid.

97 Ibid., October 1, 1940, 24.

98 "Let Mary Starr Solve Problems," *Toronto Star*, May 12, 1945, 19. The new column would start May 14, 1945, and run until November 1967.

99 Mary Starr, "If You Take My Advice," *Toronto Star*, April 27, 1946, 5. The letter from "Blue Eyes" (4 May 1946) is "debunking" (the writer's term) her advice on necking.

100 Ibid., March 25, 1946, 6.

101 L.A Kirkendall and R.F. Osborne, *Dating Days* (Chicago: Science Research Associates, 1949), 8. This was a pamphlet designed to be circulated through high school health classes.

102 Ibid., 25, 29, 16.

103 Girl Guides of Canada, *A Checklist on Looks, "Poise-onality," Social Habits, Health, and "A Serious Note" on Tolerance* (Ottawa: Girl Guides of Canada, 1950). This pamphlet stressed good family relations, the importance of belonging to a church, and racial tolerance, while providing "tips" for attracting boys and dating behaviour.

104 Antheil, "A Man Talks to Women," *Toronto Star*, October 1, 1940, 24.

105 Canadian Youth Commission,*Youth, Marriage and the Family*, 56–57, 103.

106 Ibid., 163, 172–73.

107 Ibid., 178.

108 E.M. Duvall, *Facts of Life and Love for Teenagers* (Toronto: Popular Library, 1950). The book was printed "by arrangement with the National Board of YMCAs." The author is identified as having a PhD and working as "consultant to the National Council on Family Relations" of the United States.

109 Ibid., 38–39, 56–57, 60–61.

110 C.R. Adams, "Teen-Age Special: Romance Isn't Easy," *Chatelaine* (September 1948): 4–5. The article includes a twenty-four-question quiz, "How Good Are You at Romance?" Adams is identified as a marriage counsellor from Pennsylvania State University.

111 L. Dempsey, "Ten Strings to Your Beau," *Chatelaine* (July 1947): 56.
112 University of Alberta Library, Alberta Folklore and Local History Collection, *En Avant*, 1945 yearbook, Alexandra High School, Medicine Hat, Alberta, 3.
113 University of Alberta Library, Alberta Folklore and Local History Collection, Stan Stadnyk, "Ode to a Girlfriend (Composed While Working in a Cow Barn)," *Wings*, 1944–45 yearbook, Sangudo High School, Sangudo, Alberta, 18.
114 Antheil, "A Man Talks to Women," *Toronto Star*, August 21, 1940, 22.
115 W.A. Westley and F. Elkin, "The Protective Environment and Adolescent Socialization," *Social Forces* 35 (1957): 248–49.
116 Gagnon, "The Courtship of Franco-Albertan Women," 179–80.

Chapter 4

1 Ontario, Department of Education, *Report of the Inspectors of High Schools* (Toronto: King's Printer, 1919), 32–33; Ontario, Department of Education, *Report of the Inspectors of High Schools* (Toronto: King's Printer, 1922), 45–46; R. Ueda, *Avenues to Adulthood: The Origins of the High School and Social Mobility in an American Suburb* (Cambridge: Cambridge University Press, 1987), 141.
2 "Educational Committee Report," *Industrial Canada* (June 1920): 76.
3 "Criticism of Nova Scotia System," editorial *Halifax Herald*, June 22, 1912, 3; F.H. Sexton, "The Value of Technical Education," *Industrial Canada* (January 1927): 129.
4 On "the second great transformation" in American schools, see C. Goldink and L.F. Katz, "Human Capital and Social Capital: The Rise of Secondary Schooling in America, 1910 to 1940," *Journal of Interdisciplinary History* 29 (1999): 685–86.
5 R. Stamp, "Canadian High Schools in the 1920s and 1930s: The Social Challenge to the Academic Tradition," Canadian Historical Association, *Historical Papers* (1978): 77–78.
6 See D. Marshall, *The Social Origins of the Welfare State: Quebec Families, Compulsory Education, and Family Allowances*, trans. N. Danby (Waterloo, ON: Wilfrid Laurier University Press, forthcoming), 1. This was a Liberal measure spearheaded by Premier Adelard Godbout.
7 In New Brunswick, attendance of children under fourteen for the full school term was required in Fredericton, Saint John, Newcastle, Chatham, Marysville, Edmundston, and Campbellton. The law did not impose any limit on the absence from school of children in Saskatchewan if their own or others' needs required them to work for wages. See "Legal Minimum Age for the Employment of Children in Canada," *The Labour Gazette* (April 1939): 398–99.
8 Ontario, Department of Education, *Report of the Inspectors of High Schools* (Toronto: King's Printer, 1922), 34. Stamp, "Canadian High Schools in the 1920s and 1930s," 78–79.
9 Stamp, "Canadian High Schools in the 1920s and 1930s," 78. See also University of New Brunswick Archives, RS 118, file 14, brochure addressed to "Graduates at Yuletide," 21 December 1931, signed by Principal Fletcher Peacock; Ontario, Department of Education, *Report of the Inspectors of High Schools* (1922), 45–46. In the view of the three high school inspectors, the growing numbers were not merely the outcome of legislation: they saw the "greatest cause" as a new public appreciation of the importance of education, as well as "a general desire among parents to have their children share in its benefits."

10 Of all Quebec residents in the fourteen to twenty age group, only 27 per cent were at school in 1931, by comparison to 37 per cent of the total juvenile population of the country. See L. Marsh, *Canadians In and Out of Work: A Survey of Economic Classes and Their Relation to the Labour Market* (Toronto: Oxford University Press, 1940), 162–63.

11 Ibid., 162–63; P. Axelrod, *The Promise of Schooling: Education in Canada, 1800–1914* (Toronto: University of Toronto Press, 1997), 68. See also J. Modell and J.T. Alexander, "High School in Transition: Community, School, and Peer Group in Abilene, Kansas, 1939," *History of Education Quarterly* 37, 1 (1997): 1–2. P. Axelrod, *Making a Middle Class: Student Life in English Canada during the Thirties* (Montreal: McGill-Queen's University Press, 1995), discusses the class, gender, and ethnic basis of the university population during the 1930s.

12 Ontario, Department of Education, *Annual Report* (Toronto: King's Printer, 1923), ix; Stamp, "Canadian High Schools in the 1920s and 1930s," 107.

13 Ontario, Department of Education, *Report of the Minister of Education* (Toronto: King's Printer, 1919), 15; W.F. Dyde, *Public Secondary Education in Canada* (New York: Columbia University, 1929), 41; J.M. McCutcheon, *Public Education in Ontario* (Toronto: Best, 1941), 171; F. Johnson, *A Brief History of Canadian Education* (Toronto: McGraw-Hill, 1968), 142–43; see also Stamp, "Canadian High Schools in the 1920s and 1930s," 77–80; N. Sutherland, *Children in English-Canadian Society: Framing the Twentieth-Century Consensus* (1976; Waterloo, ON: Wilfrid Laurier University Press, 2000).

14 Public Archives of Ontario Pamphlet Collection, "Laying the Cornerstone of New Jarvis Street Collegiate," programs, September 29, 1922, 1–2. The collegiate opened as Toronto Grammar School in 1807; it became Toronto High School in 1871.

15 Public Archives of Ontario Pamphlet Collection, "Riverdale Collegiate Institute: Golden Anniversary, 1907–57," pamphlet, 1957. There were 179 students in 1908, 448 in 1918, and 962 by 1923; the peak was reached in 1933, when the school had 1,194 students.

16 Public Archives of New Brunswick, PS 116, Department of Education, Annual Reports, Fredericton High School, Fredericton, NB, 1932. A similar expansion was taking place at Barrie Collegiate, in Barrie, Ontario, between 1918 and 20; see Public Archives of Ontario Pamphlet Collection, A.R. Girdwood, principal, foreword to *History of the Barrie Collegiate Institute, 1843–1943*, 1943.

17 B. Davies, *Youth Speaks Its Mind* (Toronto: Ryerson, 1948), 89.

18 Ontario, Department of Education, *Annual Report* (Toronto: King's Printer, 1920), 56; the report notes that the yearly expansion of high schools is the "outstanding feature of the system," an assessment that is repeated in every report through the decade. In 1929 there were 63 collegiate institutes and 142 high schools in the province; of the collegiates, only 7 of 63 had retained their original buildings, and of the high schools, more than half were in new buildings or expanded and modernized structures; see Ontario, Department of Education, *Annual Report* (Toronto: King's Printer, 1929), 38. The minister reported in 1923 that attendance had reached a "point never reached before" during the 1922 school year: enrolment was 60,395, an increase of 41.9 per cent during the two years under the Adolescent Attendance Act; see Ontario, Department of Education, *Report of the Minister of Education* (Toronto: King's Printer, 1923), iii.

19 Sutherland, *Children in English-Canadian Society*, 164. The Ontario population grew by 17 per cent in the 1920s, but secondary school population quadrupled during that decade; R. Stamp, "Canadian High Schools in the 1920s and 1930s," 80. On working-class attendance, see C. Heron, "The High School and the Household Economy in Working-Class Hamilton, 1890–1940," *Historical Studies in Education* 7 (1995): 242, 246; see also the oral histories in J. Synge, "The Transition from School to Work:

Growing Up Working Class in Early Twentieth Century Hamilton, Ontario," in *Childhood and Adolescence in Canada,* ed. K. Ishwaran (Toronto: McGraw-Hill Ryerson, 1979), 249–69. On London, see I.F. Goodson and I.R. Dowbiggin, "Vocational Education and School Reform: The Case of the London Technical School, 1900–1930," *History of Education Review* 20, 1 (1991): 55.

20 C. Campbell, "Family Strategy, Secondary Schooling and Making Adolescents: The Indian Summer of the Old Middle Class, 1945–60," *History of Education Review* 22, 2 (1993): 19, 38.

21 P. Fass, "Creating New Identities: Youth and Ethnicity in New York City High Schools in the 1930s and 1940s," in *Generations of Youth: Youth Culture and History in Twentieth-Century America,* ed. J. Austin and M.N. Willard (New York: New York University Press, 1998), 95–96.

22 J.T.M. Anderson, *The Education of the New Canadian: A Treatise on Canada's Greatest Educational Problem* (Toronto: Dent, 1918), 9. Sociologist Charles Young also observed the emerging "Canadian" perception that made the public school "the most important means of assimilating the foreign-born or their children"; see C.H. Young, *The Ukrainian Canadians: A Study in Assimilation* (Toronto: Thomas Nelson, 1931), 178.

23 Ibid., 201. Young is quoting J.S. Woodsworth.

24 Ibid., 183–84.

25 C. Dawson, *Group Settlement: Ethnic Communities in Western Canada* (Toronto: Macmillan, 1936), 156. The total Mennonite church membership was, by Dawson's estimation, about five thousand. The Mennonite Collegiate Institute opened in Gretna in 1891.

26 Young, *The Ukrainian Canadians,* 195.

27 Ibid., 201.

28 Marsh, *Canadians In and Out of Work,* 227–78.

29 Ibid., 203–4.

30 S.S. Dhai, "Discovering the New World," *Queen's Quarterly* 76 (1969): 200.

31 Reminiscences of Mrs. Anna Smokorowsky, in *The Great War and Canadian Society: An Oral History,* ed. D. Read and R. Hann (Toronto: New Hogtown Press, 1978), 82–83.

32 M.Y. Hubbert, *Since the Day I Was Born* (Thornbury, ON: Conestoga Press, 1991), 218.

33 B.H. Johnston, *Indian School Days* (Toronto: Key Porter, 1988), 185.

34 I. Knockwood, *Out of the Depths: The Experiences of Mi'kmaw Children at the Indian Residential School at Shubenacadie, Nova Scotia* (Lockport, NS: Roseway, 1992), 125.

35 H. Liss, "Editor's Message," *Wings,* 1944 yearbook of Sangudo High School, Sangudo, Alberta, 3. This is the yearbook's first issue.

36 *Wings,* 1944, 3.

37 "Education," editorial, *The Dawn of Tomorrow,* July 21, 1923, 2. The newspaper served the black community and was published in London, Ontario.

38 W.P. Oliver, "The Negro in Nova Scotia," *Journal of Education* (1949): 20. The journal was an in-house production of the Halifax Department of Education. See also R. Winks, "A History of Negro School Segregation in Nova Scotia and Ontario," *Canadian Historical Review* (June 1969): 168–69. On conditions in black communities in Canada in the immediate post–World War II years, see E. Staebler, "Would You Change the Lives of These People?" *Maclean's* (May 1956): 30.

39 University of British Columbia Archives, Grace McInnis papers, Box 4, file 4–8, Canadian Youth Congress, Report on Education, in Reports of the Ontario-Quebec Regional Youth Conference, Toronto, April 11–12, 1941, 8. McInnis, who was J.S. Woodsworth's daughter, was involved in the Canadian Youth Congress as a young woman. See also "Our Young Men Pass On," editorial, *The Dawn of Tomorrow,* August 4, 1923, 3.

40 M. Yuasa, "We Must Lose to Win," *The BC Teacher* 19 (February 1940): 305; cited in M. Ashworth, *The Forces Which Shaped Them: A History of the Education of Minority Group Children in British Columbia* (Vancouver, BC: New Star Books, 1979): 105.

41 C.H. Young and H.Y. Reid, *The Japanese Canadians* (Toronto: University of Toronto Press, 1938), 81.

42 In Manitoba, for example, nearly 30 percent of unskilled manual labourers had less than five years of elementary schooling, rendering a close association of "the lowest paid and least pleasant work" with the lowest educational achievement. Marsh, *Canadians In and Out of Work*, 227–28, 234, 243.

43 Ibid., 248.

44 Public Archives of Nova Scotia, Alexander Mowat papers, MG 2408, file 2, F.C. Purdy, supervisor of schools, "School Survey of Mahone School," November 1948. An unstated number of pupils and seven "citizens" of the town (Mahone Bay) were interviewed about the school and its curriculum. The students ranged from grades 8 through 11. Most of the interviewees were identified as "working class," mostly in boat- and shipbuilding occupations.

45 "The Education of the Poor Man's Child," *Globe*, January 7, 1920, 5. From the 1870s, there were two types of secondary schools in Ontario: the high schools and the collegiates. Initially, the collegiates had a curriculum more on the classical model and were mainly for young men, but the distinction between the two types of schools would disappear in the twentieth century. See R.D. Gidney and W. Millar, *Inventing Secondary Education: The Rise of the High School in Nineteenth-Century Ontario* (Kingston: McGill-Queen's University Press, 1990).

46 National Library and Archives Canada, Canadian Welfare Council, vol. 8, file 38, "Canadian and International Child Labour Conventions" (March 1924): 1–5.

47 "Montreal Children Must Get Certificates to Work," *Globe*, March 18, 1920, 18.

48 "Children Throng Office for Work Certificates," *Globe*, March 23, 1920, 11.

49 Public Archives of New Brunswick, Ministry of Education, C.H. Blakeney, 1940–45, author not stated, undated typescript, "Some Present Policies and Future Plans of the New Brunswick Department of Education," 6.

50 University of British Columbia Archives, Tuxis Boys papers, Proceedings of the 7th Manitoba Boys Parliament, 1928, "The Christian's Attitude to Preparation for and Motives in the Choice of His Life Work: Summary of General Discussion," 10.

51 Public Archives of Nova Scotia, Ministry of Education, MG 17, Series A, Correspondence, June 18, 1930, 2.

52 Hubbert, *Since the Day I Was Born*, 228–29.

53 Knockwood, *Out of the Depths*, 116–17.

54 Letter signed "Tick," "Circle of Young Canada" column, *Globe*, January 5, 1918, 14. "Tick" is responding to a previously published letter from "Harbour Lassie," describing "lively pranks" at her school, which he believes is the high school that he used to attend.

55 See, for example, the debate on technical education that took place in the House of Commons, especially the comments of Rodolphe Lemieux, Rouville, *House of Commons Debates*, March 27, 1916, 2270–73. The *Report of the Royal Commission on Industrial Training and Technical Education* (Ottawa: King's Printer, 1911) is replete with discussion of vocational training in secondary schools and night classes to substitute for apprenticeship. See, for example, "Industrial Training and Technical Education in Relation to Apprentices, Foremen and Leaders," 273; "Apprenticeship in New Brunswick," 1820; Statement of the Canadian Manufacturers Association, Toronto, 2087; Report of the Educational Commission of Toronto, 2115; Report of the Building Trades of Kingston, Ontario, 2143; Report of the Maritime Commission on Technical Education, 2239. See also *Statutes of Ontario*, Apprenticeship Act, c. 25, 1928; the Act provided an inspector to regulate contracts and working conditions on behalf of

apprentices. Also National Library and Archives, Canadian Welfare Council, J. Pigott, "Youth Training," unpublished paper presented at CWC Convention, Winnipeg, 1939.

56 I.F. Goodson and C.J. Anstead, eds., *Through the Schoolhouse Door: Working Papers* (Toronto: Garamond, 1993), 128–29.

57 Public Archives of New Brunswick, RG 118 C2, Ministry of Education Reports, St. John Vocational School, Report of the Department of Practical Arts for Girls, 1928, 5.

58 "An Act Respecting Education for Industrial Purposes," *Statutes of the Province of Ontario*, 1911. The federal government would follow suit in 1919 with its Technical Education Act; see Ontario, Department of Education, "Report of the Division of Industrial and Technical Education," *Annual Reports* (1919): 13; Technical Education Act, *Statutes of the Dominion of Canada*, 1919, chapter 73: 9–10.

59 Stamp, "Canadian High Schools in the 1920s and 1930s," 90.

60 Special industrial schools in both theory and practice in a number of trades were established in Haileybury, Sudbury, Toronto, and technical high schools or departments were also set up at Haileybury, Hamilton, Sault Ste. Marie, Sudbury, and Toronto. Night classes for those employed during the day were held at Berlin (Kitchener), Brockville, Collingwood, Galt, Guelph, Hamilton, London, Stratford, St. Thomas, and Toronto; Technical Education Act, *Statutes of the Dominion of Canada*, 1919, chapter 73: 9–10. See also Sutherland, *Children in English-Canadian Society*, especially 12 and 13; and R. Stamp, "Those Yankee Frills: The New Education in Ontario," in *History of Ontario: Selected Readings*, ed. M. Piva (Toronto: McClelland and Stewart, 1985).

61 K. Alaimo, "Shaping Adolescence in the Popular Milieu: Social Policy, Reformers, and French Youth, 1870–1920," *Journal of Family History* 17 (1992): 420–21.

62 Public Archives of Nova Scotia, Alexander Mowat papers, MG 2408, file 2, A. Mowat, handwritten survey notes, "Outside School Hours." Mowat was a professor of education at Dalhousie University, Halifax. This is an account of answers to fifteen questions that he posed to young people about how they spent their leisure time. The participants are identified as sixty girls and forty boys in an unnamed Halifax school, ages eleven to fourteen, who are "representative of a fairly homogenous social class," live in families averaging 2.91 children, and whose fathers belong to "what may be described as the better working class."

63 Goodson and Dowbiggin, "Vocational Education and School Reform," 55. On vocational education, see also N.S. Jackson and J.S. Gaskell, "White Collar Vocationalism: The Rise of Commercial Education in Ontario and British Columbia, 1870–1920," in *Gender and Education in Ontario: An Historical Reader*, ed. R. Heap and A. Prentice (Toronto: Canadian Scholars' Press, 1991), 165–94; T.A. Dunn, "Teaching the Meaning of Work: Vocational Education in British Columbia, 1900–29," in *Shaping the Schools of the Canadian West*, ed. D.C. Jones, N.M. Sheehan, and R.M. Stamp (Calgary, AB: Detselig, 1979), 237–53.

64 A new building with up-to-date equipment was built in 1918; see Goodson and Anstead, *Through the Schoolhouse Door*, 123–25.

65 University of New Brunswick Archives, RS 118, file 9, memo, undated. According to this record, the 1929 day enrolment was 552; night classes had 911 students. The Act for the Promotion of Vocational Education in Canada was suspended indefinitely in 1931 due to Depression constraints.

66 Stamp, "Canadian High Schools in the 1920s and 1930s," 86. In 1932, Ontario high schools showed a 10.6 per cent enrolment gain over the previous year, a rate of increase sustained through the Depression.

67 Marsh, *Canadians In and Out of Work*, 248.

68 E.C. Webster, *Guidance for the High School Student*, McGill University Social Research Series, no. 8 (Montreal: 1939), 128. In a sample of high schools in Montreal studied over several years, one in ten students, on average, graduated from high school.

69 Canadian Youth Congress, *Report on Education* (Toronto: CYC, April 1941), 4.

70 Ford Motor Company, "War Comes to a Classroom," *Saturday Night* (October 1942): 9. This is a full-page advertisement showing a young man with goggles working on a lathe, with other boys at their books, and the (male) teacher writing on a blackboard.

71 "Central Tech Fair," *Toronto Star*, March 5, 1941, 16. A special aspect of the annual industrial fair that year was the showing of "war work, and the preparation of goods and weapons of war."

72 R.B. Matthews, "The Air Force Needs 50,000 Model Planes...40,000 Schoolboys Will See It Gets Them!" *Saturday Night* (December 1942): 4–6. See also B. Coffey, "Canada's Children Look Forward to the Future in the Skies," *Saturday Night* (February 1944): 19.

73 Marsh, *Canadians In and Out of Work*, 239–40. Marsh found that, among those twenty and older, the rural/urban differentials were much lower, reflecting the overall low attendance at postsecondary institutions; see also Johnson, *A Brief History of Canadian Education*, 142–43; McCutcheon, *Public Education in Ontario*, 171.

74 Public Archives of New Brunswick, MC 1771, MS 1B1, December 12, 1989, reminiscences of Red Atkinson, 1. Atkinson grew up in Jolicure, Westmorland County, attended high school in Sackville, and graduated from Normal School in Fredericton in 1931.

75 Written reminiscences, Lorna (Hood) McCutcheon, National Adult Literacy Database, Learning for Life project, http://www.nald.ca/. McCutcheon was born in Magaguadavic, New Brunswick, the second child in a family of five. She and her sister Frances attended Fredericton High School, staying at a boarding house across the street. This project of "life stories" was undertaken by the Fredericton Regional Family Resource Centre.

76 Interview with Hazel Huckvale, Williams Lake, British Columbia, October 24, 1998, Prince George Oral History Page, http://www2.pgohg.org:8080.

77 Strange, *With the West in Her Eyes* (Toronto: George J. McLeod, 1937), 35.

78 Public Archives of New Brunswick, RS 116, Department of Education, A1a–A1r, Box no. 2, Correspondence, A.P. Paterson, Minister of Education. See the letter from Herbert Edward, Loggieville, NB, to Paterson, September 20, 1938, 4. The province's Women's Institutes were also wholly behind rural high schools, actively petitioning the provincial government and even attempting to take on the project in certain communities; see letter to Paterson from Tabusintac, NB, August 15, 1938; also from Port Elgin, NB, August 27, 1938.

79 Public Archives of New Brunswick, RS 116, Department of Education, Minister of Education C.H. Blakeney, 1940–45, undated typescript, "Some Present Policies and Future Plans of the New Brunswick Department of Education," 8.

80 Reminiscences of Irene Rigler, Prince George Oral History Page, http://www2.pgohg.org:8080. The site, run by the Prince George Oral History Group, is the winner of the first-ever BC History Website Prize. Rigler was born in Winnipeg and moved with her parents to Sylvan Glade, near Prince George, in 1929. She finished primary school in 1935. In some cases an entire family moved so that a promising adolescent could continue. See also C. McKenzie, "Growing Up in Alberta," *Alberta History* 37, 3 (1989): 14–23. McKenzie was born in Ontario in 1897 and moved to the Okotoks–High River area of Alberta with his homesteading parents. The family moved from High River, Alberta, to Calgary so that he could do grade 12 and achieve senior matriculation at the city's Central Collegiate Institute. He graduated with the highest marks in the class and went on to become a teacher before enlisting in 1918 and studying medicine after his stint in the armed forces.

81 Public Archives of Nova Scotia, Alexander Mowat papers, MG 2408, file 2, article offprint, "Planning Tomorrow's Rural High Schools," published in *Municipal Affairs:*

Monthly Bulletin of the Nova Scotia Municipal Bureau 11, 3 (1946): 6; See also, Mowat, "The Rural High School Serving Its Community," *Journal of Education* (June 1950): 172.

82 Public Archives of Ontario, RG16-280-4, Extension Branch, Department of Agriculture, Box 1, "History of the Extension Branch, 1907–57," typescript (March 1959), 1. See also J.H. Putman, inspector of Schools, Ottawa, "Ontario's Biggest Problem: The Rural School," *Globe*, January 2, 1920, 6, January 6, 1920, 6.

83 Mowat, "The Rural High School Serving Its Community," 174.

84 Ontario, Department of Education, *Annual Report of the Inspectors of High Schools* (1920), 49; ibid. (1922: 45–46. The latter also notes the increase in juvenile delinquency since the war, and comments on the "great need for moral training."

85 G.S. Hall, *Adolescence: Its Psychology and Its Relation to Physiology, Anthropology, Sociology, Sex, Crime, Religion and Education*, vol. 1 (New York: Appleton, 1904), xvi–xvii.

86 T.W. Gutowski, "Student Initiative and the Origins of the High School Extracurriculum: Chicago, 1880–1915," *History of Education Quarterly* 28 (1988): 49–72.

87 *Statutes of the Dominion of Canada*, 9–10 George V, c. 73, 7 (1919).

88 Ontario, Department of Education, *Report of the Inspectors of High Schools* (Toronto: King's Printer, 1920), 49–50.

89 *Constitution of the Strathcona Trust: For the Encouragement of Physical Training and Military Drill in Public Schools* (Ottawa: Government Printing Bureau, 1910), 5.

90 In Galt, Waterloo County, Ontario, a cadet corps was formed immediately on the announcement of war in August 1914; in December of the following year, the Berlin-Waterloo school board authorized a cadet corps at its collegiate institute with an initial membership of fifty-five boys; see *Berlin News Record*, August 27, 1914, 1; *Berlin Daily Telegraph*, December 18, 1915, 1. See also R. Stamp, "Canadian High Schools in the 1920s and 1930s," 93–94; M. Moss, *Manliness and Militarism: Educating Young Boys in Ontario for War* (Toronto: Oxford University Press, 2001), 15–16, 34–35.

91 Ontario, Department of Education, *Annual Report* (Toronto: King's Printer, 1915), 34.

92 Stamp, "Canadian High Schools in the 1920s and 1930s," 106.

93 Public Archives of Ontario, pamphlet no. 22, *History of the Barrie Collegiate Institute, 1843–1943*, 1943, 60–62. The Barrie cadet corps was organized in 1899; it grew throughout the interwar years, peaking in 1940 with two hundred members; girls' marching and drills began in that year.

94 "Citizens Join in Discussing Cadet Problem," *Edmonton Journal*, March 18, 1927, 4.

95 "Riverdale Collegiate Institute, Golden Anniversary, 1907–57," 42.

96 "Drill vs. Culture," editorial, *Guelph Mercury*, April 12. 1939, 3. This was regarding a motion before the Toronto Board of Education to revive cadet training in the high schools.

97 See the Department of National Defence website, www.dnd.ca, for information on the development of cadet programs in Canada.

98 Editorial, *The Grumbler* (1931), 18. Yearbook of the Kitchener Collegiate Institute, *The Grumbler* began publication in 1907 as "a few mimeographed sheets" produced biweekly by the Literary Society. By 1931 it had become a hybrid newspaper/annual, published three times a year, with as many as three hundred students involved; see "Principal's Message," *The Grumbler* (1938), 5. By 1938 there was also discussion of making it a monthly venture: "Shall We Change *The Grumbler*?" (1938), 4.

99 *FWCI Oracle* (1930–31). This was the yearbook of the Fort William Collegiate and Technical Institute, Fort William (now Thunder Bay), Ontario.

100 M.W Beckleman, "The Group Worker in the Modern Scene," *Canadian Welfare Summary* (July 1938): 64.

101 Ueda, *Avenues to Adulthood*, 150.

102 "Principal's Message," *The Grumbler* (1937), 2.

103 Ontario, Department of Education, *Report of the Inspectors of High Schools* (1919), 39. The report notes similar events taking place at other Ontario schools.

104 *En Avant* (1945), 4. This was the yearbook of Alexandra High School, Medicine Hat, Alberta.

105 Ontario, Department of Education, *Report of the Minister of Education* (Toronto: King's Printer, 1929), 14.

106 *Acta Nostra* (1926), 90. This was the first edition of the yearbook of Guelph Collegiate and Vocational Institute. In 1879, the Guelph Grammar School became the Guelph High School, then the Collegiate Institute in 1886, when a gymnasium was added. A new school building was erected in 1923, with technical education facilities. By the 1920s, it was the largest high school in Wellington District and served a combined rural/urban population of about ten thousand; see G. Shutt, *The High Schools of Guelph* (Toronto: University of Toronto Press, 1961).

107 J.F. Ross, "Principal's Message," *Acta Nostra* (1926), 11.

108 C.E. Phillips, *The Development of Education in Canada* (Toronto: Gage, 1957), 534–40.

109 *The Collegiate Oracle* 1 (December 1922). This was the newspaper of the Fort William Collegiate and Technical Institute; renamed the *Oracle*, it would become the school's annual.

110 "The Advantages of Student Government," *The Grumbler* (1924), 5. KCI was evidently one of the first Ontario high schools to establish a student council, with an elected executive and representatives for each year under a teacher "advisory committee." This was accomplished in 1922; the editorial cited argues that "in the future it will be a recognized organization" throughout Canada. Phillips, *The Development of Education in Canada*, 534, describes student government as "accepted practice" in secondary schools across Canada by the 1930s.

111 D.G. Bell, "Teaching Young Canada to Play," *Maclean's* (July 1926): 9.

112 Editorial, *Canadian Child Welfare News* (May 1927): 31; E. Thomas, "The Church of God and the Homes of His People," *Social Welfare* (November 1920): 48; Ontario, *Report of the Minister of Education* (1929), 14. On funding, see, for example, Ontario High Schools Act, *Revised Statutes of Ontario*, c. 360, 1937.

113 Quoted in H. Gurney, *Girls' Sports: A Century of Progress in Ontario High Schools* (Don Mills, ON: OFSAA, 1979), 24.

114 *Oak Bay Annual* (1939), 2. This was the yearbook of Oak Bay High School in Victoria, BC.

115 Johnston, *Indian School Days*, 192.

116 N. Sutherland, "School Days, School Days, Good Old Golden ... ¿": A Childhood in British Columbia in the 1930s and 1940s," *Historical Studies in Education* 16 (2004): 339–52.

117 "Athletics," *The Grumbler* (1937), 85. KCI was proclaimed "second to none" for its enthusiasm, in terms of both participation and audience support for its teams.

118 *Acta Nostra* (1926), 31–32; also 1929, 15. For similar reports, see "Girls Show Good Work on Field Day," *The Collegiate Oracle* (December 1922), 8 and "Fort William Scores Huge Success on Field Day," ibid., 10.

119 Guelph Public Library Archives, Guelph, Ontario, Shutt Family Papers, Item 7-1, letter to G. Shutt, undated (1960s), signed "A Happy Reader," from a former GCVI student who attended during the 1920s; on sports, see also Axelrod, *The Promise of Schooling*, 116.

120 The earliest record is the Girls' Athletic Club at Jarvis Collegiate in 1897. Jarvis was also the first to affiliate with the YWCA in 1924, naming its new club ROAD to reflect the new emphasis on reading, outdoors, athletics and dramatics; Oakwood Collegiate maintained the two as separate clubs. See Gurney, *Girls' Sports*, 24–26.

121 A.H.D. Ross, *A Short History of the Arnprior High School* (Ottawa: Popham, 1922), 53.

122 "The School Spirit," *Acta Nostra* (1926), 91.

123 *Vox Scholae* (1930), 3. This was the yearbook of Fergus High School, Fergus, Ontario.

124 *En Avant* (1945), 3.

125 *The Grumbler* (1928), 21.

126 *The Grumbler* (1931), 8.

127 Sutherland, "School Days, School Days, Good Old Golden...?" 352.

128 Peate, *Girl in a Sloppy Joe Sweater*, 47–48.

129 *Acta Nostra* (1927), 47–48. Guelph Public Library Archives, Shutt Family Collection, Item 7-1; letter to G. Shutt, unsigned, undated (references to 1920s), 2.

130 *Acta Nostra* (1933): 3. The yearbook ceased publication with this issue, as advertising revenues from local businesses dwindled; it resumed publication only in 1942. Similarly, see *The Grumbler* (1938): 77.

131 Dorothy Williams, "Social Chit-Chat," *En Avant* (1945): 17.

132 *The Souvenir* (1945–46): 30. This was the yearbook of the John Oliver High School, Vancouver, BC.

133 Johnston, *Indian School Days*, 228–29.

134 *Wings* (1944–45): 12. This was the yearbook of Sangudo High School, Sangudo, Alberta.

135 "Avoid Extremes," editorial, *Toronto Star*, January 13, 1921, 4.

136 Public Archives of Ontario, RG 18-88, Box 1, B-72, Royal Commission: Ottawa Collegiate Institute Inquiry, January 6, 1927, file 2, Evidence, 11–15.

137 Ibid., 22, 29.

138 Ibid., 72.

139 J. Struthers, *No Fault of Their Own: Unemployment and the Canadian Welfare State, 1914–1941* (Toronto: University of Toronto Press, 1983), 100, 132–35; R. Pierson, "Gender and the Unemployment Insurance Debates in Canada," *Labour/Le travail* 25 (Spring 1990): 82–84.

140 Ontario, Department of Education, *Report of the High School Inspectors* (Toronto: King's Printer, 1932) 15; also Ontario, Department of Education, *Report of the Minister of Education* (Toronto: King's Printer, 1934), 3; ibid. (1939), viii. By 1939, there were 198 high schools in Ontario, including 58 collegiate institutes; there were also 217 continuation schools. Enrolment in the former was 53,400, with 9,654 in the latter.

141 See the letters to R.B. Bennett in M. Bliss and L. Grayson, eds., *The Wretched of Canada: Letters to R.B. Bennett, 1930–1935* (Toronto: University of Toronto Press 1971); see also B. Broadfoot, *Ten Lost Years, 1929–1939: Memories of Canadians Who Survived the Depression* (Toronto: Doubleday, 1977); W. Johnson, "Keeping Children in School: The Response of the Montreal Catholic School Commission to the Depression of the 1930s," Canadian Historical Association, *Historical Papers* (1985): 197.

142 Ontario, Department of Education, *Report on Vocational Guidance* (Toronto: King's Printer, 1931), 4.

143 Ontario, Department of Education, *Report of the High School Inspectors* (1932), 17; (1934), 3.

144 Editorial, *Acta Nostra* (1933): 11; Gurney, *Girls' Sports*, notes that sports competitions and such groups as the Hi-Y seem to have "faded" by the mid-1930s.

145 R.A. Morton, "Principal's Message," *Wings* (1944–45): 4. The principal makes much of the fact that this is the "invasion year" of 1944.

146 Peate, *Girl in a Sloppy Joe Sweater*, 96.

147 *Adventure* (1944): 46, 54. This was the yearbook of Magee High School, Vancouver, BC.

148 J. Porter, *The Vertical Mosaic: An Analysis of Social Class and Power in Canada* (Toronto: University of Toronto Press, 1965), 169, 146. In addition to class, size of family, and

regional educational and economic disparities, religion is also a factor in the amount of schooling received. Porter argues that due to the classical college tradition in Quebec, Catholic boys left school much earlier than did their Protestant peers. He cites a 1956 study by Quebec sociologist Arthur Tremblay that found that, even as early as twelve years of age, there was a greater proportion of Protestant than Catholic boys in school in the province, with the differences between Catholics and Protestants increasing as they got older: at sixteen, one-quarter of Catholic boys were still in school, compared to one-half of Protestant boys.

149 Canada, Department of Citizenship and Immigration, *Report of Indian Affairs Branch for the Fiscal Year Ended 31 March 1950* (Ottawa: Queen's Printer, 1950), 55.

150 H. Garner, *Cabbagetown* (Toronto: Ryerson Press, 1968). This is a semi-autobiographical set in Toronto's notorious working-class district. According to the author who grew up there, Cabbagetown was "a sociological phenomenon, the largest Anglo-Saxon slum in North America" (author's preface, i).

151 "Marigold," Circle of Young Canada, *Toronto Star*, March 10, 1923, 16; D. Livesay, *Right Hand, Left Hand* (Erin, ON: Press Porcepic, 1977), 20.

152 W.A. Westley and F. Elkin, "The Protective Environment and Adolescent Socialization," *Social Forces* 35 (1957): 248. The authors found the average allowance among comparable wage groups in a working-class section of Montreal to be two dollars weekly.

153 On "secret societies," see W. Graebner, "Outlawing Teenage Populism: The Campaign against Secret Societies in the American High School, 1900–1960," *Journal of American History* 74 (1987): 412–15; Ueda, *Avenues to Adulthood*, 119–20.

154 Public Archives of New Brunswick, Ministry of Education, MC 1771, MS 1B1, December 15, 1908, interview with Murray Sargeant, 11. Sargent graduated from St. John High School in 1924, and taught there during the later 1920s and the 1930s.

155 *The Challenger* (June 1940): 4. This was the newspaper of St. John Vocational School.

156 P. Bourdieu, *Reproduction in Education, Society and Culture*, 2nd ed., trans. R. Nice (London: Sage, 1990), ix–xi, 102, 158. Similar themes are explored for Australia by C. Campbell, "Family Strategy, Secondary Schooling and Making Adolescents: The Indian Summer of the Old Middle Class, 1945–60," *History of Education Review* 22, 2 (1993): 19, 38. For the United States, see C. Goldink and L.F. Katz, "Human Capital and Social Capital: The Rise of Secondary Schooling in America, 1910–40," *Journal of Interdisciplinary History* 29 (1999): 685–86.

157 S. Crawford, "Magee 1945, a Class Portrait: Memoir of a Homecoming," *Vancouver Sun*, September 18, 1999, D5.

158 Modell and Alexander, "High School in Transition," 23.

Chapter 5

1 On the socio-cultural aspects of "efficiency" and scientific management, see C.R. Comacchio, "Mechanomorphosis: Scientific Management and the Efficient Body in Industrial Canada," *Labour/Le travail* 41 (1998): 35–67.

2 See the memories collected by Neil Sutherland, which show without any doubt how many children and young people "earned their keep," well into the twentieth century through part-time, often "invisible" labour; N. Sutherland *Growing Up: Childhood in English Canada from the Great War to the Age of Television* (Toronto: University of Toronto, 1997); also N. Sutherland, "'I Can't Recall When I Didn't Help': The Working Lives of Pioneering Children in Twentieth-Century British

Columbia," *Histoire sociale/Social History* 24 (1991): 263–88; N. Sutherland, "'We Always Had Things to Do': The Paid and Unpaid Work of Anglophone Children between the 1920s and the 1960s," *Labour/Le travail* 25 (1990): 105–41.

3 Department of Labour, *The Employment of Children and Young Persons in Canada* (Ottawa: King's Printer, 1930), 75. Certainly the brief discussion of such part-time work for "schoolchildren" in this study is very negative, commenting on its interference with health, education, and, of course, morality.

4 S.C. Hollander and R. Germain, *Was There a Pepsi Generation before Pepsi Discovered It? Youth-Based Segmentation in Marketing* (Lincolnwood, IL: NTC Business Books, 1992), especially chapter 2, "A History of Marketing to Youth: 1880–1940," 11–26.

5 S. Houston, "The 'Waifs and Strays' of a Late Victorian City: Juvenile Delinquency in Toronto," *Childhood and Family in Canadian History*, ed. J. Parr (Toronto: McClelland and Stewart, 1982), 129–42; see also R. Coulter, "The Working Young of Edmonton, 1921–1931," in ibid. 143–59.

6 *The Employment of Children and Young Persons*, 39. The Factory Act of New Brunswick did not prohibit the employment of children; agricultural Prince Edward Island had no factory law.

7 "Child Labour," *The Canadian Unionist* (April 1931): 272–73. See also L. Marsh, "Reports of the National Employment Commission," *Canadian Journal of Economics and Political Science* 5 (1939): 80–86.

8 Canada, Department of Labour, *The Employment of Children and Young Persons*, 31; also "Employment of Children and Young People," *The Labour Gazette* (February 1937): 170. *The Labour Gazette* was the official organ of the federal labour department.

9 "Child Labour," 272–73.

10 L. Marsh, *Employment Research: An Introduction to the McGill Programme of Research in the Social Sciences* (Toronto: Oxford University Press, 1935), 55–57.

11 "New Bulletin Issued by the Department of Labour," *The Labour Gazette* (January 1931): 29–30.

12 Although the employment crisis of the Depression helped to reduce the total number of employed children, those as young as twelve years of age could still be found in mines, and those as young as fourteen years were still being employed in factories as World War II commenced; "Child Labour," 170. On young miners, see R. McIntosh, *Boys in the Pits: Child Labour in Coal Mines* (Montreal: McGill-Queen's University Press, 2000).

13 Library and Archives Canada, Canadian Welfare Council, 29, file 38, Memorandum Re: Night Employment of Children in Ontario, March 9, 1925, Provincial Secretary L. Goldie to C. Whitton, Executive Director; see also "Wants 15 Years as Minimum Age for Employment," *Montreal Gazette*, September 28, 1925, 16. N. Sutherland, *Children in English-Canadian Society: Framing the Twentieth–Century Consensus* (1976; Waterloo, ON: Wilfrid Laurier University Press, 2000), 165, notes that, in 1891, 13.8 per cent of children between the ages of ten and fourteen were "officially" employed in industry; by 1921, the percentage was 3.2. The drop was even more precipitous in agriculture (at least by official count), from 11.4 to 1.9 per cent.

14 I. MacMillan, "Strikes, Bogeys, Spares and Misses: Pin-boy and Caddy Strikes in the 1930s," *Labour/Le travail* 44 (Fall 1999): 149–90.

15 "Legal Minimum Age for Employment of Children in Canada," *The Labour Gazette* (April 1939): 398–99.

16 "Need for Regulation of Children in Street Trades," *The Labour Gazette* (February 1933): 113.

17 *The Employment of Children and Young Persons*, 131, 134.

18 "Crime Wave Affects Errand Boys of City," *The Globe*, February 13, 1920, 8.

19 "Industrial Employment of Children in Canada," *The Labour Gazette* (January 1930): 6; "Child Welfare," *The Labour Gazette* (March 1930): 290; "Age of Children in Non-

Industrial Occupations," *The Labour Gazette* (December 1930): 1419; "Employment of Children and Young People in Canada," *The Labour Gazette* (January 1931): 29; "Age of Admission of Children to Employment in Non-Industrial Occupations," *The Labour Gazette* (July 1931): 801–802; "Children in Non-Industrial Occupations," *The Labour Gazette* (October 1931): 1104–105; "Draft Convention Concerning the Age for Admission of Children to Non-Industrial Employment," *The Labour Gazette* (May 1932): 563–67; "Child Labour Problems during the Present Emergency," *The Labour Gazette* (February 1933): 113; "Committee to Investigate Youth Problems in Toronto," *The Labour Gazette* (February 1935): 98; "Legal Minimum Age for Employment of Children in Canada," *The Labour Gazette* (April 1939): 398–99.

20   See J. Synge, "The Transition from School to Work: Growing Up Working Class in Early Twentieth Century Hamilton, Ontario," in *Childhood and Adolescence in Canada*, ed. K. Ishwaran (Toronto: McGraw-Hill Ryerson, 1979), 249–69.

21   "Girl's Hair Catches in Factory Shafting," *Globe*, February 7, 1920, 14.

22   H. Michell, "A Study of the Efficiency of Canadian Labour," *Industrial Canada* (June 1928): 183; O.A. Cannon, "Health Opportunities in Industry," *Canadian Public Health Journal* 21, no. 1 (1930): 2–3. See also R.M. Hutton, committee secretary, "Industrial Hygiene in Canadian Factories," *Industrial Canada* (June 1920): 80–83; Dominion of Canada, Honorary Advisory Council for Scientific and Industrial Research, *Survey of General Conditions of Industrial Hygiene in Toronto* (Ottawa: Privy Council of Canada, 1921), 3; "Industrial Fatigue," editorial, *Canadian Medical Association Journal* 15 (1925): 737; A. Mitchell, "The Scope of Medical Services in Industry," *Canadian Public Health Journal* 30, 11 (1939): 521; F.S. Parney, "Division of Industrial Hygiene," *Canadian Public Health Journal* 23, 4 (1939): 149.

23   *The Employment of Children and Young Persons*, 79–84.

24   Ibid., 31.

25   "New Bulletin," *The Labour Gazette* (January 1931): 29–30; Canada, Department of Labour, *The Employment of Children and Young Persons*, 81–92.

26   *The Employment of Children and Young Persons*, 39. The committee was headed by Lord Atholstan.

27   Dr. A.B. Chandler, "The Relation of Child Labour to Child Health," *Canadian Journal of Public Health* 12, 7 (1921): 397.

28   J. Martin, "The Married Woman in Industry," *Canadian Public Health Journal* 43, no. 3 (1919): 380; J. Martin, "The Four Ages of Woman: How Far Is Industrial Subjugation of the Sex Involved in Certain Phases of Feminism," *Canadian Public Health Journal* 43, 4 (1919): 186–88; see also Mrs. R. Asals, representing the Women's Labour League of the Grades and Labour Council, Regina, Testimony to the Royal Commission on Industrial Unrest (1919), and the excerpt from *The Report of the Social Survey Commission*, Toronto (1915), 114–19, both in I. Abella and D. Millar eds., *The Canadian Worker in the Twentieth Century* (Toronto: Oxford University Press, 1978). C. Strange, *Toronto's Girl Problem: The Perils and Pleasures of the City, 1880–1930* (Toronto: University of Toronto Press, 1995), discusses the commission's findings in some detail.

29   C.M. Bayley, "The Social Structure of the Italian and Ukrainian Immigrant Communities in Montreal, 1935–37," MA thesis, McGill University, 1939, 278.

30   "Still More Profits for Canadian Boys and Girls," advertisement, *Chatelaine*, March 1928. This ad is repeated several times, with slightly different wording, in each monthly issue.

31   A.W. Currie, *Growing Up in Rural Ontario, 1908 to 1926*, unpublished memoirs, 1971, University Archives, Queen's University, Kingston, Ontario, 89.

32   T. Arruda, "You Would Have Had Your Pick: Youth, Gender and Jobs in Williams Lake, BC, 1945–75," in *Beyond the City Limits: Rural History in British Columbia*, ed. R. Sandwell (Vancouver: University of British Columbia Press, 1999), 225.

33 W.A. Westley and F. Elkin, "The Protective Environment and Adolescent Socialization," *Social Forces* 35 (1957): 248.

34 Marsh, *Canadians In and Out of Work: A Survey of Economic Classes and Their Relation to the Labour Market* (Toronto: Oxford University Press, 1940), 262–63.

35 Ibid., 264.

36 Ibid., 275, 203, 210, 207–208.

37 Canada, Department of Labour, *The Employment of Children and Young Persons*, 41. The Quebec labour department report for 1928–29 showed a decline in the number of female apprentices in the textile industry, particularly in the factories outside the island of Montreal. The decline occurred among the lowest-paid workers and was thought to be due to the instigation of the minimum-wage order for female employees in September 1928.

38 Marsh, *Canadians In and Out of Work*, 162–63.

39 Ibid., 44.

40 Ibid.

41 Marsh, *Employment Research*, 55–57; he set it at approximately 25 per cent.

42 Marsh, *Canadians In and Out of Work*, 265.

43 Ibid., 218–19.

44 Ibid., 219. Marsh gives the following figures for farm workers as a percentage of all the gainfully employed up to the age of twenty-one: under fourteen: 85.6; fourteen: 79.1; fifteen: 73.3; sixteen: 61.3; seventeen: 53; eighteen: 47.4; nineteen: 41.6; twenty: 35.8; twenty-one: 30.4; total, up to twenty-one: 46.5. There were 683,000 farmers in Canada enumerated in the 1931 census.

45 Marsh, *Employment Research*, 67–71.

46 "Child Labour," *The Labour Gazette* (January 1931): 29–30. The *Gazette* found over fourteen thousand children under sixteen years of age employed in factories in Canada in 1921, the largest number working in cotton, clothing, lumber, metal, and printing and bookbinding establishments. Juveniles of sixteen and seventeen were employed in similar places and in factories producing boots and shoes, biscuits and confectionery, tobacco, and rubber goods.

47 Marsh, *Canadians In and Out of Work*, 219–20.

48 On Quebec, see D. Marshall, *The Social Origins of the Welfare State: Quebec Families, Compulsory Education, and Family Allowances*, trans. Nicola Danby (Waterloo, ON: Wilfrid Laurier University Press, forthcoming), especially chapters 4 and 5, where she details both the decline of the labour of children and very young adolescents (under fourteen), as well as the persistent economic needs of families to send older adolescents to work.

49 Canada, Department of Labour, *The Employment of Children and Young Persons*, 129. This was the Ontario government's Committee on Child Labour of 1906–7.

50 Marsh, *Canadians In and Out of Work*, 46, 47–48.

51 Marsh, *Employment Research*, 77–78.

52 Elsie Freeman, cited in A. Skeoch, *Years of Hope, 1921–1929* (Toronto: Grolier, 1988), 9.

53 Reminiscences of Shirley T., Living History Project, Riverview Health Centre, Winnipeg, Manitoba, http://www.riverviewhealthcentre.com/livinghistory/.

54 Canada, Department of Labour, *The Employment of Children and Young Persons*, 41.

55 The most important book on this subject remains J. Parr, *Labouring Children: British Immigrant Apprentices to Canada, 1869–1924*, 2nd ed. (Toronto: University of Toronto Press, 1994).

56 Library and Archives Canada, MG 28 I 10, Canadian Welfare Council, vol. 6, file 33, 1928, Charlotte Whitton, Letter to Miss Gladys Pott, Society for Overseas Settlement of British Juveniles, August 16, 1928, 2. Whitton was the Council's executive secretary.

57 "British Youngsters Arrive on Prairies," *Globe*, March 13, 1923, 13.

58 Whitton, Letter to Miss Gladys Pott, 2. Whitton, who was strongly opposed to juvenile emigration, described "a most terrible case of criminal assult on the little daughter of a Canadian employer by a British boy placed there by one of the British societies." The girl was four years old, while the boy "had an extremely bad sex history himself, and on the part of his family, and undoubtedly was a sex moron." She also speaks of the "suicides of recent years."

59 "Urge a Readjustment—Children's Aid Staff," *Toronto Star*, February 28, 1924, 22; also "Seek to Guard Young Who Come to Ontario," *Toronto Star*, May 8, 1924, 1.

60 "Lonely 'Home' Boy, Licked by Farmer, Hanged Himself," *Globe*, January 23, 1924, 1; "London Wants Probe into Tragic Deaths of Immigrant Boys," *Globe*, January 31, 1924, 1; "Two Months in Prison for Bulpitt's Employer," *Globe*, February 1, 1924, 1; "Farmer Sent to Jail for Assaulting Boy Who Hanged Himself," *Globe*, February 2, 1924, 9.

61 "Funeral of Home Boy Moves Many to Tears," *Globe*, January 28, 1924, 1; "Farmer Exonerated at Omemee Inquiry into Boy's Suicide," *Globe*, February 3, 1924, 1.

62 Library and Archives Canada, MG 28 I 10, Canadian Welfare Council, vol. 6, file 33, 1928, Minutes of the Conference on Juvenile Emigration, called by the Department of Immigration and Colonization at the Request of the Council on Child Welfare, Ottawa, October 23, 1928; also "Immigration and Colonization in Canada, 1920–1931," *The Labour Gazette* (March 1932): 295–97.

63 Canadian Welfare Council, vol. 6, file 33, 1928, Letter of Charlotte Whitton to F.C. Blair, minister, Department of Immigration, February 22, 1928, 2.

64 "Immigration and Colonization in Canada," 295–97.

65 This was especially the case in Manitoba, although Alberta and Saskatchewan were not far behind; see W. Hurd's reading of the 1931 census, "The Decline in the Canadian Birth Rate," *Canadian Journal of Economics and Political Science* 3, no. 1 (1937): 40–57.

66 C.H. Young, *The Ukrainian Canadians: A Study in Assimilation* (Toronto: Nelson, 1931): 123–25.

67 P.S. Li, "Chinese Immigrants on the Canadian Prairie, 1910–47," *Canadian Review of Sociology and Anthropology* 19 (1982): 528. Li examines the job histories of a group of first-generation Chinese immigrants between 1923 and 1947; of the fifty-five interviewed, thirty-one arrived in Canada between 1910 and 1923 (prior to the Exclusion Act), while the remainder came after World War II.

68 Ibid., 531.

69 J. Modell, *Into One's Own: From Youth to Adulthood in the United States* (Berkeley: University of California Press, 1988), 86; P. Fass, *The Damned and the Beautiful: American Youth in the 1920s* (New York: Oxford University Press, 1977), 262–73, 324–25; B. Bailey, *From Front Porch to Back Seat: Courtship in Twentieth-Century America* (Baltimore, MD: Johns Hopkins University Press, 1988), 78–80. See also D. Fowler, *The First Teenagers: The Lifestyle of Young Wage-Earners in Interwar Britain* (London: Woburn Press, 1995), 42–72.

70 Martin, "The Four Ages of Woman," 186–88.

71 "Girls' Problem Needs Solution," *Globe*, July 30, 1921, 12. K. Dubinsky, *Improper Advances: Rape and Heterosexual Conflict in Ontario, 1880–1929* (Chicago: University of Chicago Press, 1993), effectively dispelled this "rural myth" in regard to sexual danger.

72 Marsh, *Canadians In and Out of Work*, 215. According to the 1931 census figures, about 30 per cent of sixteen-year-old girls were "at home"; ibid., 216.

73 Ibid., 215–17. Marsh notes that 35–40 per cent married in their early twenties; those who kept working are 3.5 per cent of the total gainfully employed in this age group, excluding the widowed or divorced.

74 Reminiscences of Jim and Louise Van Somer, Prince George, BC, Prince George Oral History Page, http://www2.pgohg.org:8080.

75 Marsh, *Canadians In and Out of Work*, 167.

76 Ibid., 199, 202.

77 Ibid., 166, As Marsh explains the findings, "the count for all wage earners without regard to age will obviously show greater inequality than one confined to adults. Juvenile workers earn smaller wages...a good many youths also are not regularly employed or are engaged only in some part-time type of job. That more than 30 per cent of all male wage earners should earn less than 500 a year is in this sense not so bad as it sounds. The focus can best be corrected by confining the measurement to the married men with normal families, 'normal' being used here as elsewhere in this book to mean those families in which both parents are alive and living together in the home."

78 Ibid., 170.

79 Ibid., 195. A higher proportion of wives (15.5 per cent) find work in this than in any other category of workers.

80 Ibid., 195, 196–97. Marsh contends that, for the greater proportion of unskilled workers, both breadwinners' and family resources were inadequate. This is the largest occupational class, with nearly 300,000 families, or 40 per cent of ordinary wage-earner families, in 1931.

81 Ibid., 191–92. By Marsh's estimation, "not more than 55 per cent" of Montreal families could subsist on the earnings of the male breadwinner alone, even leaving "some allowance" for his own understanding that young wage-earners did not contribute their entire pay packet, for the most part, to the family.

82 Ibid., 171.

83 Ibid., 171.

84 Ibid., 182.

85 Ibid., 189–90. The income discrepancy was lower in semi-skilled and unskilled occupations where young men and women did substantially similar work.

86 H. Weir, "Unemployed Youth," in *Canada's Unemployment Problem*, ed. L. Richter (Toronto: Macmillan, 1939), 129–30.

87 University of British Columbia Archives, J.W. Robertson papers, Box 6, Royal Commission on Industrial Training and Technical Education, Correspondence 1910–16, Folder S-5, unsigned memo, "Some Notes for the Use of Hon. W.L. Mackenzie King," 1.

88 Canada, Department of Labour, *The Employment of Children and Young Persons*, 60.

89 Ibid., 60. See also British Columbia, Department of Labour, *Annual Report* (Victoria, BC: King's Printer, 1928), 95–96.

90 Canada, Department of Labour, *The Employment of Children and Young Persons*, 63.

91 "The Technical School," editorial, *Toronto News*, May 26, 1913, 3.

92 "Apprenticeship in Ontario," *The Labour Gazette* (November 1930): 1283.

93 Ibid. Its purview initially took in the building trades, masonry, carpentry, painting, decorating, and plastering, and was later extended to plumbing, steamfitting, sheet metal, and electrical wiring and installation.

94 "Hamilton Technical School," *The Labour Gazette* (February 1933): 173–74. Special day classes for first- and second-year apprentices in the nine designated building trades, from all over the province, were held for eight weeks, beginning January 9, 1933. The total enrolment was ninety-eight, with the largest number—twenty-five—in plumbing.

95 "Apprenticeship in Ontario," *The Labour Gazette* (November 1930): 1283.

96 "Annual Report of Ontario Department of Labour," *The Labour Gazette* (May 1933): 505–508.

97 "Hamilton Technical School," 173–74.

98 "Apprenticeship in Vancouver," *The Labour Gazette* (September 1931): 997–98.

99 "Annual Report of the Ontario Apprenticeship Board for the Year Ending October 31, 1933," *The Labour Gazette* (January 1934): 36–37.

100 "Annual Report of the Ontario Apprenticeship Board for the Year Ending March 31, 1935," *The Labour Gazette* (June 1936): 488. The 319 apprentices were distributed as follows: bricklaying: 38; masonry: 3; carpentry: 24; painting and decorating: 10; plastering: 11; plumbing: 116; steamfitting: 34; sheet metal work: 31; and electrical work: 52.

101 Davies, *Youth Speaks Its Mind*, 85.

102 Ibid.

103 Marsh, *Canadians In and Out of Work*, 281.

104 Ibid., 282. Four thousand were over sixty-five; the total was 202,000.

105 Ibid., 285. 27,942 and 33,500 unemployed youth of both sexes in the Prairies in 1931 and 1936, respectively, representing an increase of 18.7 per cent over those five years.

106 Ibid., 296. The estimates of the chief Dominion statistician for young men fifteen to twenty-four who were unemployed in 1936 suggested that the combination of those who lost jobs and those who were never gainfully employed was "over 16 per cent," or approximately 155,000. This accounted for one and one half times the supply of new workers coming of age annually. The average length of idleness for urban boys was about two years; about 70 per cent of farm workers (the majority were farm family members) were not receiving wages. See also J.E. Robbins, *Dependency of Youth*, Census Monograph no. 9, Dominion Bureau of Statistics (Ottawa: King's Printer, 1937), 10, 24–26.

107 Weir, "Unemployed Youth," 126.

108 Ibid., 121; of 928 boys who left public schools in Toronto in 1936, 642 were employed, 194 unemployed, and the status of the remainder was unknown. Among girls, 1,037 left the public schools; of these, 469 were employed, 422 unemployed, and the status of the remainder was unknown.

109 Ibid., 119. The reports resulted from a symposium held at the Institute of Public Affairs at Dalhousie University in 1937. A survey of North Sydney, Nova Scotia, showed that 298 young men aged sixteen to twenty-five were out of work and school in January 1937. Only fifty-three of these belonged to families on relief; more than 80 per cent of the unemployed young men of that town were not collecting relief. More than 25 per cent of these had failed to reach grade 6.

110 D. Livesay, *Right Hand, Left Hand* (Erin, ON: Press Porcepic, 1977), 112–13. The reserve was a mile across the water from Lachine, Quebec.

111 Reminiscences of George Watson, Prince William, New Brunswick, Learning for Life, National Adult Literacy Division, http://www.nald.ca/CLR/harvey/. Watson was born in 1914 in Ayrshire, Scotland; he set sail with his family in 1928 to settle in Dumfries, New Brunswick, "a place where you had a hard time to make a living," 1.

112 J. Synge, "Hamilton's Working Women," *Atlantis* 8, 2 (1988): 130.

113 Davies, *Youth Speaks Its Mind*, 64.

114 MacMillan, "Strikes, Bogeys, Spares and Misses," 149–50.

115 Weir, "Unemployed Youth," 132–33.

116 Ibid., 135.

117 Ibid., 139.

118 Public Archives of New Brunswick, Department of Education, RS 116, file A1b, Vocational Education/Youth Training, 1938–39, letter of Fletcher Peacock, director, Educational Services, to A. Paterson, minister of Education, dated February 3, 1938; Peacock remarks on "a deluge of applications for the boys' courses." Under the provisions of the King government's Unemployment and Agricultural Assistance Act, 1938, New Brunswick received $75,000 toward the cost of any specific project for youth training, on a dollar for dollar basis; see also *Statutes of Canada*, Bill 9Y, 3

George VI, May 1939, An Act to Provide for the Training of Young People to Fit Them for Gainful Employment.

119 "Labour Legislation Enacted by the Parliament of Canada in 1939," *The Labour Gazette* (July 1939): 667–70. In 1939, the program was enlarged to take in all unemployed young Canadians aged sixteen to thirty under a special Youth Training Act administered by the federal department of labour, which provided for the appointment of a supervisor of youth training and appropriated $4.5 million for a period of three years, to be paid out to the provinces.

120 Letter of Fletcher Peacock, director, Educational Services, to A. Paterson, minister of Education, dated February 3, 1938, 2.

121 Public Archives of New Brunswick, Department of Education, RS 116, Department of Education, file A3J2-3b8, Box 4, letter of Fletcher Peacock, director, Educational Services, to C.H. Blakeney, minister of Education, dated July 17, 1940. The Dominion-Provincial Training Programme, conducted under the auspices of the federal Department of Labour, will be discussed further in the chapter.

122 "Dominion-Provincial Youth Training in 1937," *The Labour Gazette* (June 1938): 616–17.

123 Canadian Youth Commission, *Youth and Jobs in Canada* (Toronto: Ryerson Press, 1945): 54. See also Davies, *Youth Speaks Its Mind*, 62–63.

124 Davies, *Youth Speaks Its Mind*, 65.

125 Ibid., 83.

126 Ibid., 85.

127 Marsh, *Canadians In and Out of Work*, 222–23.

128 Ibid., 224.

129 Ibid., 225.

130 Ibid., 224.

131 Canadian Youth Commission, *Youth and Jobs*, 84.

132 Marsh, *Canadians In and Out of Work*, 226; 42 per cent of those who had finished school stated financial reasons for not continuing; familial poverty was legal grounds for non-attendance after the age of fourteen in all Canadian provinces.

133 "Where Will Our Child Labour Problem Lead Us?" *Saturday Night* (January 1943): 2.

134 Editorial, *Toronto Star*, May 9, 1946, 7.

135 Canadian Youth Commission, *Youth, Marriage and the Family* (Toronto: Ryerson Press, 1947), 54, interview with anonymous young man.

136 "Where Will Our Child Labour Problem Lead Us?" 2.

137 M. Peate, *Girl in a Sloppy Joe Sweater: Life on the Canadian Home Front during World War II* (Montreal: Optimum, 1984), 128.

138 M.E. Jukes, "Who Is Rita?" *Saturday Night* (March 1943): 29.

139 Peate, *Girl in a Sloppy Joe Sweater*, 129.

140 Editorial, *Toronto Star*, May 9, 1946, 7.

141 L. Dempsey, "Teen-Age Special: First Job!" *Chatelaine* (December 1945): 12.

142 Ibid., 39.

143 Ibid., 72.

144 Sutherland, *Children in English-Canadian Society*, 165. B. Bradbury, *Working Families: Age, Gender, and Daily Survival in Industrializing Montreal* (Toronto: McClelland and Stewart, 1993), is the only monograph treatment of the family economy in Canada; S. Morton, *Ideal Surroundings: Domestic Life in a Working Class Suburb in the 1920s*, 97–98. Morton notes that, in 1931, only 25 per cent of children over fifteen in Halifax were in school, and only 12 per cent of children in single-parent households. See also N. Sutherland, "We Always Had Work to Do"; J. Taylor, *Fashioning Farmers*, also details the contributions of farm youth in Manitoba.

Chapter 6

1 "Guelph Pastor Scores Dancing," *Guelph Daily Mercury*, October 3, 1921, 3. The controversy seems to have raged awhile in the pages of the paper: see also editorial, October 4, 1921, 3; "Chamber of Commerce...Endorses Action of City Council on Charges of Social Misconduct," October 7, 1921, 5. The minister eventually retracted his statements, saying that he had heard the story about drunkenness and immorality from the mayor and that it was perhaps a "malicious misrepresentation," October 10, 1921, 21. The story ends with a formal letter to the editor by the Rev. T.J. Hind retracting his statement, October 11, 1921, 4.

2 W.S. Haine, "The Development of Leisure and the Transformation of Working-Class Adolescence," *Journal of Family History* 17 (1992): 451; K. Peiss, *Cheap Amusements: Working Women and Leisure in Turn-of-the-Century New York* (Philadelphia, PA: Temple University Press, 1986); and for Canada, C. Strange, *Toronto's Girl Problem: The Perils and Pleasures of the City, 1880–1930* (Toronto: University of Toronto Press, 1995), all discuss the relationship between urban amusements and young women early in this century. For thorough studies of the historical relationship between anxieties about youth and leisure, see J. Springhall, *Youth, Popular Culture and Moral Panics: Penny Gaffs to Gangsta-Rap, 1830–1996* (New York: St. Martin's Press, 1998); D. Nasaw, *Going Out: The Rise and Fall of Public Amusements* (Cambridge, MA: Harvard University Press, 1993).

3 For contemporary views, see T.R. Robinson, "Youth and the Virtues," *Social Welfare* (October 1928): 9; H. Dobson, "Youth: Scapegrace or Scapegoat," *Social Welfare* (July 1929): 228. See also K. Alaimo, "Shaping Adolescence in the Popular Milieu: Social Policy, Reformers, and French Youth, 1870–1920," *Journal of Family History* 17 (1992): 420; Haine, "The Development of Leisure and the Transformation of Working-Class Adolescence," 451, and Peiss, *Cheap Amusements*. On advertising, see W. Leach, *Land of Desire: Merchants, Power and the Rise of a New American Culture* (New York: Vintage Books, 1993), 4–5. The idea of the new youth market is most thoroughly explored in D. Fowler, *The First Teenagers: The Lifestyle of Young Wage-Earners in Interwar Britain* (London: Woburn Press, 1995), especially 93–115.

4 N. Enstad, *Ladies of Labor, Girls of Adventure: Working Women, Popular Culture and Labor Politics at the Turn of the Twentieth Century* (New York: Columbia University Press, 1999): 2–3, 6. Enstad observes that early-twentieth-century consumer culture "offered working women utopian promises and contained painful limitations"; interestingly, neither she nor Peiss makes much of the youth of the women who are their subjects.

5 Haine, "The Development of Leisure," 254; on nineteenth-century shop-floor culture in Canada, there is the unsurpassed work by B.D. Palmer, especially *A Culture in Conflict: Skilled Workers and Industrial Capitalism in Hamilton, Ontario, 1860–1914* (Montreal: McGill-Queen's University Press, 1979). On the breakdown of apprenticeship, see G. Kealey, ed., *Canada Investigates Industrialism: The Royal Commission on the Relations of Labor and Capital, 1889* (Toronto: University of Toronto Press, 1973), 16, as well as the previous chapter. On urban amusements, see Strange, *The Girl Problem*, especially chapter 5, 116–43.

6 C.H. Young, *The Ukrainian Canadians: A Study in Assimilation* (Toronto: Nelson, 1931), 71.

7 D.G. Wetherell and I. Kmet, *Useful Pleasures: The Shaping of Leisure in Alberta, 1896–1945* (Regina, SK: Canadian Plains Research, 1990), 7–9.

8 B. Barnabas, "Progress in Boy Guidance," *Social Welfare* (November 1925): 37; "Earning and Spending Health," editorial, *Social Welfare* (April 1931): 135; M.W. Beckelman, "The Group Worker in the Modern Scene," *Canadian Welfare Summary* (July 1938): 61. Other contemporary Canadian discussions include University of British Columbia Archives, Tuxis papers, Boys' Parliaments, "The Christian's Attitude to His Leisure Time: General Discussion," 6th Annual Saskatchewan Tuxis Boys Parliament, 26–31 December 1928; J.J. Holmes, "Social Consequences of the Long Working Day," *The Canadian Unionist* (February 1930): 115; N. Spencer, "The Six-Hour Day," *The Canadian Unionist* (May 1931): 295; "The Use of Leisure," editorial, *The Canadian Unionist* (March 1938): 261. In fact, the nine-hour work day was commonplace, as was the five-and-a-half- to six-day workweek, and no new statutory holidays were created in Canada between 1896 and 1945; see Wetherell and Kmet, *Useful Pleasures,* 39; Peiss, *Cheap Amusements,* 43–44. The best discussion of the work/leisure debate in the early twentieth century is G. Cross, *Time and Money: The Making of Consumer Culture* (New York: Routledge, 1993). See also M. Brake, *Comparative Youth Culture* (London: Routledge and Kegan Paul, 1985), 147–48; J. Clark and T. Jefferson, "Working Class Youth Cultures," in G. Mungham and G. Pearson, eds., *Working Class Youth Culture* (London: Routledge and Kegan Paul, 1976), 144, 152–53.

9 H. Baker, "Leisure," *Social Welfare* (June 1933): 211, 214; "Caradog," "The Citizen of Tomorrow," *Social Welfare* (February 1931): 94.

10 J. Springhall, "Censoring Hollywood: Youth, Moral Panic and Crime/Gangster Movies of the 1930s," *Journal of Popular Culture* 32, 3 (1998): 136.

11 Ibid., 135.

12 B. Hanawalt, "Historical Descriptions and Prescriptions for Adolescence," *Journal of Family History* 17, 4 (1992): 344; Peiss, *Cheap Amusements,* 4–6. See also "Immodesty of Fashion," editorial, *Canadian Practitioner* 9 (September 1920): 333. On consumerism, see C. Wright, "Feminine Trifles of Vast Importance," in *Gender Conflicts: New Essays in Women's History*, ed. F. Iacovetta and M. Valverde (Toronto: University of Toronto Press, 1992); also D. Nasaw, "Children and Commercial Culture," in *Small Worlds: Children and Adolescents in America, 1850–1950*, ed. P. Petrik and E. West (Kansas City: University Press of Kansas, 1993).

13 On this subject, see the analysis by M. Danesi, *Forever Young: The "Teen-Aging" of Modern Culture* (Toronto: University of Toronto Press, 2003).

14 J. Austin and M.N. Willard, "Introduction: Angels of History, Demons of Culture," in *Generations of Youth: Youth Culture and History in Twentieth Century America*, ed. J. Austin and M.N. Willard (New York: New York University Press, 1998), 30–31.

15 Editorial Brevities, *Guelph Daily Mercury*, January 28, 1921, 3.

16 C.M. Bayley, "The Social Structure of the Italian and Ukrainian Immigrant Communities in Montreal," MA thesis, McGill University, 1937, 284. This case concerned a twenty-four-year-old mechanic, sixth-grade education, born in Montreal.

17 See Nasaw, *Going Out*.

18 *Statutes of Ontario*, c. 71, 1927; also Manitoba, 14 Geo V, 1924 Regulation of Billiard and Pool Rooms; British Columbia, 2 Geo V, c. 28, 1912, Pool Rooms Act.

19 Hon. L.A. David, provincial secretary, Quebec, "Opening Address," *Social Welfare* (December 1921): 423.

20 G. Dickie, "The Menace of Delinquency," *Social Welfare* (April 1921): 185; "Children at the Movies," *Child Welfare News* (February 1930): 266. On film in Canada, see T. Magder, *Canada's Hollywood: The Canadian State and Feature Films* (Toronto: University of Toronto Press, 1993).

21 S.C. Hollander and R. Germain, *Was There a Pepsi Generation before Pepsi Discovered It? Youth-Based Segmentation in Marketing* (Lincolnwood, IL: NTC Business Books, 1992), 66.

22 Public Archives of Nova Scotia, Alexander Mowat papers, MG 2408, file 2, A. Mowat, handwritten survey notes, "Outside School Hours," 3–4. A second survey in February 1940, MG 2403, file no. 6, typescript, "What Influences Educate the Child Other Than the School?" looked at forty-two children aged twelve to fifteen; thirty-two boys, ten girls, at Le Marchant Street School, Halifax, where the majority (twenty-eight) had fathers in business. Of these forty-two, fifteen worked after school; twenty belonged to scouts (only three of these girls), while eleven—ten boys and one girl—belonged to no club.

23 W.M. Bellsmith, "What of the Movie Censor," *Social Welfare* (April 1931): 143. In 1930, there were 910 theatres in Canada, with receipts posting an unprecedented $38,479,500; in 1934, for Canada as a whole, attendance reached a total of 107,718,000, with Ontario accounting for almost half that (45,747,000) and Quebec, one-quarter (24,466,000); see Canada, Dominion Bureau of Statistics, *Census of Merchandising and Service Establishments: Motion Picture Statistics* (Ottawa: Dominion Bureau of Statistics, 1934).

24 Fowler, *The First Teenagers*, 99, 105. Fowler contends that "cinema-going was indisputably the most popular form of commercial recreation" among young people in Britain during the interwar years, with dance halls a close second. On the emergence of "dating" in the 1920s, see J. Modell, *Into One's Own: From Youth to Adulthood in the United States* (Berkeley: University of California Press, 1988), 85–97.

25 M. Peate, *Girl in a Sloppy Joe Sweater: Life on the Canadian Home Front during World War II* (Montreal: Optimum, 1988), 71.

26 Library and Archives Canada, Canadian Welfare Council files, vol. 8, file 41, *Montreal Gazette* clipping, "New Theatre Law Draft Commenced," (17 March 1919), that indicated a fifty-dollar fine or one month's imprisonment to theatre owners for a first offence. See also "76 Perish in Montreal Motion Theatre Fire," *Globe*, January 10, 1927, 1. This was the front-page headline story. The casualties had climbed to seventy-eight by the end; the *Globe* described the fire as a "minor outbreak," attributing the disaster to the stampede down the narrow steps when those at the front stumbled "five steps from safety." This was the "greatest tragedy of its kind" to that point in "all the history of the nation." See also "Thorough Probe Demanded into Cause of Disaster," *Globe*, January 10, 1927, 1; editorial, *Montreal Gazette*, January 10, 1927, 1, calling for a government inquiry in view of the "appalling death list out of all proportion to the damage done to the building"; "Theatre Inspection Ordered in Toronto," *Globe*, January 10, 1927, 1; also "Stern Voice of Opinion Demands All Facts of Montreal Tragedy," *Globe*, January 11, 1927, 2. On legislation, see, for example, *Statutes of Nova Scotia*, 10–11 George V, c. 44, 1920, An Act to Amend Chapter 9, Acts of 1915, Respecting Theatres and Cinematographs; *Statutes of Manitoba*, 11 Geo. V, c. 46, 1921, An Act to Amend the Public Amusements Act (1916); *Statutes of Saskatchewan*, 11 Geo. V, c. 81, 1920, Act to Amend Theatre and Cinematographs Act; *Statutes of British Columbia*, 14 Geo. V, c. 45, 1924, Act to Amend Moving Pictures Act (1914). For Ontario, see *Statutes of Ontario*, 9 Geo V, c. 66, 1919, Act to Amend the Theatre and Cinematographs Act (1917).

27 The age was raised to sixteen in 1930, and attendance was also permitted between 9 a.m. and 6 p.m. on legal and public holidays; "Amendments to the Theatre and Cinematographs Act," *Child and Family Welfare* (November 1930): 30.

28 *Statutes of Manitoba*, 6 Geo. V, c. 109, 1916, Public Amusements Act; *Statutes of British Columbia*, 4 Geo. V, c. 75, 1914, Moving Pictures Act; *Statutes of Nova Scotia*, 5 Geo. V, c. 44, Act Respecting Theatres and Cinematographs; Ontario, 1 Geo. V, 1911, Theatre and Cinematographs Act. There were about forty members altogether on the eight provincial boards, and "their inevitable variety of insight and opinion" suggested that one national board could protect the public morals more effectively. See N. North, "What Can the Movies Teach Us?" *Maclean's* (January 1922): 15; also,

"Deceiving the Censor," *Maclean's* (December 1919): 56–59; R.L. Briscoe, "What the Censor Saves Us From," *Maclean's* (November 1929): 28–29.

29 *Statutes of Manitoba*, 11 Geo. V, c. 46, 1921, An Act to Amend the Public Amusements Act; for similar wording, see *Statutes of Saskatchewan*, 21 Geo. V, c. 70, 1931, Act Respecting Theatres and Cinematographs. On censorship in Manitoba, see J. Skinner, "Clean and Decent Movies: Selected Cases and Responses of the Manitoba Film Censor Board, 1930–50," *Manitoba History* 14 (Autumn 1987). On the U.S., especially during the 1930s, see Springhall, "Censoring Hollywood: Youth, Moral Panic and Crime/Gangster Movies of the 1930s," 136–37. After a series of sex scandals rocked the American film industry in 1922, a group of Hollywood directors hired a midwestern Presbyterian elder and influential Republican, William Harrison (Will) Hays, former postmaster general in President Warren Harding's cabinet, as their front man to clean up the image of the movies. The industry's self-monitoring Motion Picture Producers and Distributors of America Inc. (MPPDA), or Hays Office, tried a variety of ways to regulate films before adopting a formal code. Written in 1930 by two midwestern Catholics—a Jesuit professor of drama in St. Louis and a lay publisher of trade magazines—the new Motion Picture Production Code stipulated, partly in reaction to the increasing popularity of gangster films, that movies stress proper behaviour, respect for government, and "Christian values." The Hays Code, made mandatory in 1934, began with an attack on what was seen as a general tone of lawlessness and on depicting specific criminal methods in recent gangster pictures. Criminal acts were "never [to] be presented in such a way as to throw sympathy with the crime as against law and justice or to inspire others with a desire for imitation." This was followed by eight double-column pages of detailed examples.

30 Public Archives of Ontario, RG 56 B-5, 1932–3, Box 2, Ontario Board of Censors, Elimination Sheets, June 1932.

31 "Experiment in Approved Motion Pictures," editorial, *Social Welfare* (April 1927): 395; Library and Archives Canada, Canadian Welfare Council, Proceedings and Reports of Annual Meetings, Report of the Executive Director, November 1–March 31, 1931, 9.

32 Briscoe, "What the Censor Saves Us From," 28; Magder, *Canada's Hollywood*, details the futile attempts made by Canadians to hold off American domination; see also Nasaw, "Children and Commercial Culture," 19–25.

33 T. Ramsay, *A Million and One Nights: A History of the Modern Motion Picture*, vol. 1 (New York: Simon and Schuster, 1926), xi; see also T. Doherty, *Teenagers and Teenpics: The Juvenilization of American Movies in the 1950s* (Winchester, MA: Unwin Hyman, 1988), for the later period.

34 B.B. Hampton, *History of the American Film Industry from Its Beginnings to 1931* (New York: Dover, 1970; originally published in 1931), 221–22.

35 T. Lussier, "How Hollywood Saw the Reckless Youth of the 1920's," (1999) www.silentsaregolden.com; L. Jacobs, *The Rise of the American Film: A Critical History, 1921–47* (New York: Teachers College Press of Columbia University, 1939, 1948, 1967), 405–406.

36 *Flaming Youth* was produced by First National in 1923 and starred Colleen Moore and Elliott Dexter; it was directed by John Francis Dillon, who also made *The Perfect Flapper* with Moore; see Hampton, *History of the American Film Industry*, Plate 78A; Jacob, *The Rise of the American Film*, 405. The film was based on Walter Fabian's 1923 novel of the same title. See the advertisement for its first showing in Canada (in Toronto), *Toronto Star*, February 16, 1924, 9, and "Reviews," February 19, 1924, 26.

37 Hampton, *History of the American Film Industry*, 296–99, 300–302. See also R. Sklar, *Movie-Made America: A Cultural History of American Movies* (New York: Vintage Books, 1994), 67–157.

38 T. Lussier, "How Hollywood Saw the Reckless Youth of the 1920s," recommends "three excellent Jazz Age films from the 1920's": *The Mad Whirl* (1924) with May

McAvoy and Jack Mulhall; *The Plastic Age* (1925) with Clara Bow and Donald Keith; and *Walking Back* (1928) with Richard Walling and Sue Carol.

39 Jacob, *The Rise of the American Film*, 405. Another of the popular youth films of the time, *Walking Back*, successfully repeated this formula. Its young protagonist, "Smoke" Thatcher (Richard Walling), is failing school and is consequently forbidden by his father to leave the house for a party with his "jazz baby" girlfriend Patsy (Sue Carol). Enraged and defiant, he "borrows" a neighbour's car to attend, and much drinking and carousing ensues. In a modern, manly contest with a drunken rival for Patsy's affections, Smoke wins a demolition derby but destroys the stolen car. He vows henceforth to obey his parents and to work to replace the car, and all ends happily, as he has learned his rightful lesson about the costs of adolescent rebellion.

40 Ibid., 395.

41 Ibid., xiv; R. M. Goldstein and E. Zornow, *The Screen Image of Youth: Movies about Children and Adolescents* (New York: Scarecrow Press, 1980): 341.

42 Jacob, *The Rise of the American Film*, 506–507, 509.

43 J. Springhall, *Youth, Popular Culture and Moral Panics*, 136–40. See also J. McCarty, *Hollywood Gangland: The Movies' Love Affair with the Mob* (New York: St. Martin's Press, 1993).

44 Springhall, *Youth, Popular Culture and Moral Panics*, 296.

45 A.R Jarvis, "The Payne Fund Reports: A Discussion of Their Content, Public Reaction, and Effect on the Motion Picture Industry, 1930–1940," *Journal of Popular Culture* 19, 3 (1991): 127–40; also G.S. Jowett, Ian C. Jarvie, and K.H. Fuller, *Children and the Movies: Media Influence and the Payne Fund Controversy* (Cambridge: Cambridge University Press, 1996): 6, 9–10. Due to public anxiety about the effects of cinema on young minds, the Motion Picture Research Council, in 1928, commissioned a series of studies from the Cleveland-based philanthropic Payne Study and Experiment Fund. The Payne Fund Studies were published from 1933–34 in eight volumes of scholarly reports. On the whole, the authors argued that movies only indirectly inspired criminal activities in youth. See also Springhall, *Youth, Popular Culture and Moral Panics*, 140.

46 Springhall, *Youth, Popular Culture and Moral Panics*, 141. The first popularizaton of the Payne Studies was Forman, *Our Movie-Made Children*, which exaggerated the negative findings of the eight volumes and became a bestseller.

47 Springhall, *Youth, Popular Culture and Moral Panics*, 154. Outside of this series but with similar theme, plot, and resolution, MGM's *Boy's Town* (1938) featured Spencer Tracey as an Irish priest, Father Edward Flanagan, made famous for establishing a rehabilitation centre for juvenile delinquents in Omaha. Mickey Rooney is his toughest customer, torn between loyalty to Boy's Town and to his old life as represented by a gangster older brother.

48 Goldstein and Zornow, *The Screen Image of Youth*, xvii, describe Mickey Rooney and the Andy Hardy series, which made him a national celebrity in his role as the four-teen-year-old son of Judge Hardy, starring in "sugarcoated digestibles for wartime audiences."

49 Ibid., xviii. *The Bachelor and the Bobby-Soxer* (RKO, 1947), directed by Irving Reis and Sidney Sheldon, starring Cary Grant, Myrna Loy, Shirley Temple, and Rudy Vallee.

50 J. Strothard, "The Most Urgent Reform Needed," *Social Welfare* (May 1920): 283.

51 G. Studlar, *This Mad Masquerade: Stardom and Masculinity in the Jazz Age* (New York: Columbia University Press, 1996), 150–98, ably deconstructs the 1920s "dance madness." He points out, 165, that the tango was implicated in Valentino's *The Four Horsemen of the Apocalypse*, in an intertitle that proclaims that, on the eve of the apocalypse itself, "The world was dancing...Paris had succumbed to the mad rhythm of the Argentine tango."

52 Dr. R.A. Adams, *The Social Dance* (Kansas City, KS: R.A. Adams, 1921), 3. According to his own promotion, he also authored *Exalted Manhood, Fighting the Ragtime Devil, Syphilis: The Black Plague,* and *The Negro Girl.* He argued that "habitual dancers" among young women were known to have a life expectancy of twenty-five years, with a host of health troubles along that shortened path. Male dancers, clearly not as seriously affected, could nonetheless expect to die horribly by the age of thirty-seven.

53 "Dancing and the Churches," letter to the editor, signed "Missouri," Whitby, ON, *Toronto Star,* September 1, 1921, 4; see the editor's response in "Is Dancing So Awful?" September 1, 1921, 4. The editorial response, published the same day, declared that "sex appeal" is "universally and forever in play in human affairs and there is nothing evil about it." Moreover, "the sweeping denunciation of all dances and all dancers, and the ascribing of evil thoughts to all, is without warrant and arouses the ire of many good people."

54 "Dancing Craze Is on Increase," *Guelph Daily Mercury,* February 1, 1922, 5.

55 M. Miller, *Such Melodious Racket: The Lost History of Jazz in Canada, 1914 to 1949* (Toronto: Mercury Press, 1997), especially 44–65. Miller notes that Jelly Roll Morton, the self-proclaimed inventor of jazz, worked in Vancouver cabarets as early as 1919. Some African American jazz musicians settled in Montreal's St. Henri community, where the city's black population was located, and this would become a thriving jazz scene in the early 1920s.

56 Hollander and Germain, *Was There a Pepsi Generation before Pepsi Discovered It?* 70.

57 Miller, *Such Melodious Racket,* 58–59; see also "Winnipeg Jazz Babies Concert for Soldiers," *Manitoba Free Press,* June 13, 1919, 8.

58 M. Reynolds, "Toot Sweet: When Jazz Ruled Montreal," *The Beaver* (June/July 2001): 26–32. Miller, *Such Melodious Racket,* 45–46, believes it was "officially" introduced to the Montreal nightclub scene on New Year's Eve 1916, where "a special orchestra with saxophone" was advertised for the Auditorium Studios, a dance "academy" at the corner of Bleury and Ontario streets in downtown Montreal; the first dance-band recordings in that city were made in 1920.

59 See A. Lévesque *La Norme et les déviantes: Des femmes au Québec pendant l'entre-deux-guerres* (1991), trans. Y. Klein as *Making and Breaking the Rules* (Toronto: McClelland and Stewart, 1994), for discussion of the Quebec scene during the interwar years, especially as regards young women.

60 Cited in Miller, *Melodious Racket,* 64; R. Jamieson, "Music: In the House, the Studio and the Concert Hall," *Vancouver Sun,* September 28, 1919, 38; "Music," letter to the editor, 31.

61 Peiss, *Cheap Amusements,* 88–90.

62 Strothard, "The Most Urgent Reform," 285; "Home Authority Is Lax," editorial, *Guelph Daily Mercury,* March 21, 1921, 6.

63 Enstad, *Ladies of Labor,* 9–10.

64 Strothard, "The Most Urgent Reform," 285.

65 "National Conference on Child Welfare," *Social Welfare* (November 1922): 31. See, for example, *Statutes of Nova Scotia,* 17–18 Geo. V, c. 42, 1927, Act to Amend Theatres, Cinematographs and Amusements Act; *Statutes of Ontario,* 9 Geo. V, c. 66, 1919, Act to Amend Theatre and Cinematographs Act, expanded in 12–13 Geo. V, c. 72, 1922, Municipal Institutions Act; expanded again in 21 Geo. V, c. 50, 1931, Municipal Institutions Act.

66 Library and Archives Canada, CWC, vol. 28, file 143, City of Ottawa Survey: Recreation, Memorandum to Captain Bowie, Recreation Division Advisory Committee, 1929, 4.

67 "Mary Marston's Own Column," *Guelph Daily Mercury,* January 28, 1921, 8.

68 Reminiscences of Wilda S., Living History Project, Riverview Health Centre, Winnipeg, MB, http://www.riverviewhealthcentre.com/livinghistory/wilda.html.

69 Ibid.

70 Ibid.

71 Miller, *Such Melodious Racket*, 108–10. The most popular dance bands in Canada were of American origin; only one Canadian band, Guy Lombardo and His Royal Canadians, based in the US after 1924, achieved international success. Mart Kenney and His Western Gentlemen, Canada's leading dance band in the 1930s and 1940s, was formed in 1931 for an engagement at Vancouver's Alexandra Ballroom by Toronto-born saxophonist Mart (Herbert Martin) Kenney. The band made its radio debut on CJOR (Vancouver) in 1934, playing from the Alexandra Ballroom in that city. That was the year of their signature hit, "The West, a Nest, and You, Dear." The Gentlemen also had a regular show on the CBC program *Rocky Mountain Melody Time*. The band began touring eastern Canada in summer 1937, and also made the first of many appearances at Toronto's Royal York Hotel. Until 1940, Mart Kenney and His Western Gentlemen were in residence in the top ballroom on the West Coast—the Panorama Roof of Hotel Vancouver. After 1949, Mart Kenney's Ranch, a dance hall near Woodbridge, Ontario, just north of Toronto, was the location for their CBC broadcasts. See Vicky Gabereau and David Wisdom, "Canadian Popular Music since 1900," http://collections.ic.gc.ca/heirloom_series/volume1/chapter9/312-315.htm.

72 R. Collins, *You Had to Be There: An Intimate Portrait of the Generation That Survived the Depression, Won the War, and Re-invented Canada* (Toronto: McClelland and Stewart, 1997), 61.

73 Peate, *Girl in a Sloppy Joe Sweater*, 166.

74 "Hear 'Voice' Coming, 13,000 Hepcats Riot," *Toronto Star*, May 15, 1945, 4. The alleged riot took place in Philadelphia.

75 Peate, *Girl in a Sloppy Joe Sweater*, 69.

76 Ibid., 85.

77 Reminiscences of George McKnight, www.teentown.ca.

78 The more assertive sound of bebop, developed in New York during the early 1940s, also found devotion among Canadian youth by the late 1940s, as represented in recordings by Moe Koffman and Oscar Peterson. See M. Miller, "Jazz," *Canadian Encyclopedia of Music*, www.canadianencyclopedia.ca.

79 Hollander and Germain, *Was There a Pepsi Generation before Pepsi Discovered It?* xiii.

80 Ibid., 39. The authors' content analysis of popular magazines of the 1920s shows that sexiness and youthfulness were the predominant advertising appeals.

81 Ibid., 15–17.

82 Ibid., 38–41. Fowler, *The First Teenagers*, 338–41, finds the same spending patterns in regard to clothes for British adolescents of the interwar years.

83 Hollander and Germain, *Was There a Pepsi Generation before Pepsi Discovered It?* 21.

84 Ibid., 225. As discussed in chapter 5, the beauty industry became a growth area of the service trades during the interwar years. See L. Banner, *American Beauty* (New York: Knopf, 1983); K. Peiss, *Hope in a Jar: The Making of America's Beauty Culture* (New York: Metropolitan Books, 1998).

85 Hollander and Germain, *Was There a Pepsi Generation before Pepsi Discovered It?* 52, 62–64; the authors point out that, by the late 1920s, advertisers were concerned to differentiate clothing lines and their advertising by age groups within age groups, for example, eight- to fifteen-year-olds and fifteen- to eighteen-year-olds, because of their perceived "marked differences" in taste and style as well as lifestyle. See also Fass, *The Damned and the Beautiful*, 280–86.

86 "Youth Must Be Served," advertisement for Northway's Department Store, *Toronto Star*, March 6, 1945, 7. The store, John Northway and Son Ltd., was part of an Ontario chain; the Toronto location, at 240 Yonge Street, opened in 1928. As the ad proclaimed, Northway's offered "an entire floor to themselves for tiny tots to teenagers; Teenage Shop on 2nd floor."

87 Back page advertisement, *The Collegiate Oracle* (December 1922). The *Oracle* was the newspaper of the Fort William Collegiate and Vocational Institute.

88 See Studlar, *This Mad Masquerade*, especially chapter 3, 150–98. Studlar notes that the 1920 publication by American eugenicist Knight Dunlap, *Personal Beauty and Racial Betterment* (St. Louis, MI: C.V. Mosby, 1920), 87–89, urges women to judge beauty according to a standard of "highest" value, which also meant of the "white race" (163).

89 Hampton, *History of the American Film Industry*, 223, observes that "Cecil B. DeMille made it possible for every girl with the price of a theatre ticket to feast her eyes on fashion shows." See also Jacobs, *The Rise of the American Film*, 282, and Enstad's imaginative discussion of film, fashion, and working women's culture in *Ladies of Labor*, especially 48–58, 163–200.

90 Hollander and Germain, 38–39. The "Betty Betz" ad ran in ninety-six American newspapers, with total newspaper circulation approaching thirty million.

91 B. Haiken, "Plastic Surgery and American Beauty in 1921," *Bulletin of the History of Medicine* 68 (1994): 429–53.

92 The Pickford cap campaign is discussed in Jacob, *The Rise of the American Film*, 282; R. Johnston, *Selling Themselves: The Emergence of Canadian Advertising* (Toronto: University of Toronto Press, 2001), 229. Russell also notes, 247, that *Maclean's* conducted a survey of 1,694 subscribers in 1928, "Detailed Analysis of Distribution," discovering that each issue was read on average by four different people—half women, half men—making it very much a "family" magazine. By that time, with two issues per month, the magazine had a circulation of sixty-five thousand per issue. The most popular American magazine was *The Saturday Evening Post*.

93 Johnston, *Selling Themselves*, 228–29. The highest circulating periodicals in Canada were the *Montreal Star* and its weekend edition, the *Family Herald and Weekly Star*; both had circulations over 100,000 and dominated the national field in advertising. A discussion of the hot topic of youth and American magazines is found in L. Davidow Hershbein, "The Flapper and the Fogey: Representations of Gender and Age in the 1920s," *Journal of Family History* 26 (2001): 112–37. On Canadian magazines, see F. Sutherland, *The Monthly Epic: A History of Canadian Magazines, 1789–1989* (Toronto: Fitzhenry and Whiteside, 1989); also M. Vipond, *The Mass Media in Canada* (Toronto: Lorimer, 2000; first published 1989). Fowler, *The First Teenagers*, 105–106, notes the increasing catering to young people by British magazines during the interwar years.

94 Peate, *Girl in a Sloppy Joe Sweater*, 67.

95 Editorial, *Toronto Star*, June 15, 1945, 6.

96 "Zoot Suit's Day Wanes, in Opinion of Tailors," *Globe*, June 12, 1943, 5.

97 Ibid., 5.

98 Ibid.

99 Peate, *Girl in a Sloppy Joe Sweater*, 122.

100 "Zoots in Uniform," *Globe*, June 19, 1943, 3. John R. MacNicol, Progressive Conservative, Toronto-Davenport, mentioned in the House of Commons a "new life-saving suit" for the navy and another member interjected "a zoot suit," to which Navy Minister Macdonald responded, "The Navy is VERY much against the zoot variety."

101 M. Mazon, *The Zoot-Suit Riots: The Psychology of Symbolic Annihilation* (Austin: University of Texas Press, 1984), 6–8, contends that most zoot-suiters in the United States were more likely rejecting adult ways than government policy; they were more a social than a political grouping. R.D.G. Kelley, "The Riddle of the Zoot: Malcolm Little and Black Cultural Politics during World War II," in *Generations of Youth: Youth Culture and History in Twentieth Century America*, ed. J. Austin and M.N. Willard, sees the zoot suit's adoption by young male African Americans as a "signi-

fier of a culture of opposition" (137). For the Montreal situation, see S.M. Durflinger, "The Montreal and Verdun Zoot-Suit Disturbances of June 1944: Language Conflict, a Problem of Civil-Military Relations or Youthful Over-Exuberance?" in *L'Impact de la deuxième guerre mondiale sur les sociétés canadienne et québécoise*, ed. S. Bernier (Montreal/Ottawa: Université du Québec à Montréal et la Direction Histoire et Patrimoine de la Défense Nationale, 1998). Montreal's zoot-suit disturbances are also mentioned in W. Weintraub, *City Unique: Montreal Days and Nights in the 1940s and '50s* (Toronto: McClelland and Stewart, 1996), 50–52. See also J. Keshen, *Saints, Sinners, and Soldiers: Canada's Second World War* (Vancouver: University of British Columbia Press, 2004), 207–208.

102 Editorial, *Globe*, June 19, 1943, 5.

103 Ibid.

104 "Zoot Suiters Push Kids off Swings," *Globe*, July 4, 1944, 5. "Rough older boys" were "monopolizing swings and other play facilities" at Victoria Park in Kitchener.

105 Letter to the editor, from Brantford, Ontario, *Globe*, July 3, 1943, 4.

106 "Zoot Suit Wearers of Montreal Start Riot in St. Lambert Suburb," *Globe*, May 30, 1944, 3. The newspaper reported one arrested, five injured.

107 Durflinger, "The Montreal and Verdun Zoot-Suit Disturbances," 224.

108 This was reported in the *Verdun Messenger*, cited in Durflinger, "The Montreal and Verdun Zoot-Suit Disturbances," 225.

109 Ibid. On Sunday, June 4, Oland, attempting to defuse the volatile situation, cancelled all leave for Montreal-based sailors as well as for those serving aboard ships in harbour. A 9 p.m. naval curfew was imposed in Montreal, and the Verdun Dance Pavilion was placed out of bounds to naval personnel. A board of inquiry was announced, to commence on June 5, to examine the navy's role.

110 Ibid. The board of inquiry found the zooters were from varied ethnic backgrounds while the sailors were mainly anglophone. Five out of eight witnesses described the zooters as being of Italian background, two believed they were francophone, several described some as "Jewish" or "Syrian," and most agreed that they were predominantly English-speaking.

111 "Teen-agers 'Big Business'" *Toronto Star*, June 15, 1946, 12. The writer is quoting H.J. Fram, president of the Dress Manufacturers Guild of Toronto.

112 Ibid. Teenagers evidently bought 60 per cent of dress goods.

113 E. Kelly, "Teen-Age Special: The West, Young Country, Young Fashions," *Chatelaine* (September 1946): 8–9. All clothes modelled in this spread were "courtesy of the Hudson's Bay Company."

114 Austin and Nevin Willard, "Introduction: Angels of History, Demons of Culture," 30–31.

115 M. Brake, *Comparative Youth Culture*, 148. During the 1930s, sociologist Norbert Elias noted that many "taboos" had been relaxed since the Great War. Elias wondered whether, far from representing the moral "decline" or social degeneration feared by so many, some "specific relaxations," such as in modern dancing practices, were enabled by the widespread adoption of certain middle-class standards of self-restraint—in short, because of the common attainment, through socialization, of a certain level of "habitual, technically and institutionally consolidated self-control." Having internalized the specified moral standards, more people of every class and "racial" background, and in an increasingly cross-generational fashion, were consequently able "to restrain...urges and behaviour in correspondence with the more advanced feelings for what is offensive." Any "relaxation," consequently, had taken place "within the framework of an already established standard." See N. Elias, *The Civilizing Process, vol. 1: The History of Manners*, trans. E. Jephcott (Oxford: Blackwell, 1978), 116, 186. The second volume of this work, originally written in 1939, is *The Civilizing Process, vol. 2: State Formation and Civilization*, trans. E. Jephcott (Oxford:

Basil Blackwell, 1982). See also S. Mennell, *Norbert Elias: An Introduction* (Oxford: Blackwell, 1982), 46, 59–60.

Chapter 7

1 D.N. McLachlan, "The Spiritual and Ethical Development of the Child," *Social Welfare* (December 1929): 68; "A World of Change," editorial, *National Home Monthly* (December 1934): 3.
2 "A World of Change," 3.
3 Insistence on utility in recreation was not new; the repercussions of leisure in industrial-urban societies had been a cause for reformist concern in Britain and the United States since the mid-Victorian years; see the classic study by P. Bailey, *Leisure and Class in Victorian England: Rational Recreation and the Contest for Control, 1830–1885* (Toronto: University of Toronto Press, 1978). On Canada, see D.G. Wetherell and I. Kmet, *Useful Pleasures: The Shaping of Leisure in Alberta, 1896–1945* (Regina, SK: Canadian Plains Research, 1990).
4 "Leisure Hours," *Social Welfare* (July 1923): 206.
5 K. Alaimo, "Shaping Adolescence in the Popular Milieu: Social Policy, Reformers, and French Youth, 1870–1920," *Journal of Family History* 17 (1992): 421–23.
6 C. Whitton, "Ontario's Immediate Problem in Child Welfare," *Social Welfare* (June 1924): 1.
7 "Present Day Problems in Social Life," *Social Welfare* (June–July 1926): 192. While lamenting the lack of "adequate provision for leadership" in community recreation, the council nonetheless applauded its finding of thirty-six community centres in a national survey of 1923, "serving 1,500,000 people, of whom 300,000 were children"; Library and Archives Canada, Canadian Welfare Council papers, MG 28 110, Canadian Council on Child and Family Welfare, Report of the Executive Director, November 1, 1922–March 31, 1923, 10; also special issue on Recreation, *Child and Family Welfare* (July 1931): 329. On "community" concepts, see R. Williams, *Culture and Society, 1780–1950* (London: Chatto and Windus, 1967; originally published 1958), 328. On the post–World War II years, see S. Tillotson, *The Public at Play: Gender and the Politics of Recreation in Post-war Ontario* (Toronto: University of Toronto Press, 2000).
8 Rev. G.A. Woodside, "The Ideal for the Child," *Social Welfare* (May 1919): 191–92.
9 "Flappers Interpret Religion?" *Maclean's* (July 1923): 131; this is a summary of an address by Rev. W.E. Gardiner, secretary, Department of Religious Education, Episcopal Church, originally published in the *New York Times*; see also D. Marshall, *Secularizing the Faith: Canadian Protestant Clergy and the Crisis of Belief, 1850–1940* (Toronto: University of Toronto Press, 1992).
10 C.L. Roman, "Sacrifice and Burnt Incense," *Social Welfare* (August 1924): 224.
11 Ibid., 203; also V.K. Brown, "Street Play," *Social Welfare* (July 1931): 201; "The Boys' Club," *Social Welfare* (July 1931): 204.
12 On Canadian imperialist thought, the classic work remains C. Berger, *The Sense of Power: Studies in the Ideas of Canadian Imperialism, 1867–1914* (Toronto: University of Toronto Press, 1970). See also Mark Moss, *Manliness and Militarism: Educating Young Boys in Ontario for War* (Toronto: Oxford University Press, 2001), especially 21–35; and on Christianity and nationalist-imperialist thought, N. Christie and M. Gauvreau, *A Full-Orbed Christianity: The Protestant Churches and Social Welfare in Canada, 1900–1940* (Montreal: McGill-Queen's University Press, 1996). See also J.

Springhall, *Youth, Empire and Society: British Youth Movements, 1883–1940* (London: Croom Helm, 1977). On the Boy Scouts, see M. Rosenthal, *The Character Factory: Baden-Powell and the Origins of the Boy Scout Movement* (London: Collins, 1986); D. Macleod, *Building Character in the American Boy: The Boy Scouts, YMCA, and Their Forerunners, 1870–1920* (Madison: University of Wisconsin Press, 1983).

13 Rosenthal, *The Character Factory*, 108–15. The structure of Scouting, in addition to its militarism, was based on Canadian naturalist/writer Ernest Thompson Seton's Woodcraft boys' organization, which predated the Scouts and borrowed strongly from Native folklore and iconography. The popularity of the Scouts soon saw the demise of Seton's group; see J. Gillis, *Youth and History: Tradition and Change in European Age Relations, 1770–Present* (New York: Academic Press, 1974), 142–48.

14 R. Baden-Powell, *Scouting for Boys* (London: Horace Cox, 1908), 25.

15 A. Baden-Powell, *The Handbook for Girl Guides, or How Girls Can Help Build the Empire* (London: Thomas Nelson, 1912) vii, 24.

16 Agnes Baden-Powell's leadership position was taken over in 1915 by her brother's wife, Olave. By 1917, the Guides were incorporated under an act of Parliament, which recorded that the purpose of guiding was "to promote and carry out in Canada ... the instruction of girls in the principles of discipline, loyalty and good citizenship." An annual grant of $3,000 was awarded by federal government in 1919; it was raised to $10,000 in 1921; see An Act to Incorporate the Canadian Council of the Girl Guides Association, Toronto, National Girl Guide Headquarters, July 25, 1917, 157; Minute Book of the Dominion Council, 1910–21, April 8, 1921, 3; Rosenthal, *The Character Factory*, 148–52. An extensive description of the Scouts' history and program can be found in J.W. Robertson, "The Boy Scout Movement," *Canadian Boy* (October 1920): 11–16. Robertson was the Scout's chief commissioner from 1919 until his death in 1930, agricultural professor at the Ontario Agricultural College at Guelph, and joint chief commissioner of the Royal Commission on Industrial Training and Technical Education, discussed in chapter 4; see "Our Late Chief Commissioner," *The Scout Leader* (April 1930): 1.

17 Canada, Department of Mines and Resources, *Report of Indian Affairs Branch for the Fiscal Year Ended March 31, 1942* (Ottawa: King's Printer, 1943), 136. The report indicated that youth organizations, predominantly Boy Scouts and Girl Guides, were operating at the following Indian Day Schools: Birch Island, Manitoulin Island Agency, Ontario; Tobique, Maliseet, New Brunswick; Skidegate and Massett, Queen Charlotte Agency, and Port Simpson, Skeena Agency, British Columbia; and Grouard and Morley residential schools, Alberta.

18 "Captain H.A. Pearson," *Toronto World*, January 7, 1918, 5. The captain was addressing the YMCA membership in Toronto.

19 University of British Columbia Archives, Tuxis papers, Boys' Parliament Collection, Typescript, "21 Years of Teenage Work"; also *The Boy's Own Book* (Toronto: National Boys' Work Board of the Religious Education Council of Canada, 1929): 9–13. The latter was the official manual of the Tuxis and Trail Rangers groups.

20 For example, UBC Archives, Boys' Parliament Collection, Ninth Annual Older Boys' Parliament of Alberta, Resolution no. 12, 1928, 10; no. 10, 1929, 10; no. 35, 1929; Sixth Annual Saskatchewan Boys' Parliament, Regina, December 26–31, 1928, Resolution no. 10, 12; Seventh Annual Manitoba Boys' Parliament, Winnipeg, December 26–30, 1928, "The Christian's Attitude to the Use of Alcohol: Summary of General Discussion," 7–9; also Resolution no. 8, 8; "The Christian Attitude to His Leisure Time: Summary of General Discussion," 11; *The Boy's Own Book*, 32–33.

21 First Annual Older Boys' Parliament of Ontario, 1928, 35.

22 There is as yet no comprehensive published study of the Canadian Boy Scouts and Girl Guides; see L.M. McKee, "Voluntary Youth Organizations in Toronto, 1880–1930," dissertation, York University, 1982, 62–66, 266–68. See also "The New

Profession: Boy Leadership," *Social Welfare* (November 1923): 37; "Building Boyhood," editorial, *Social Welfare* (July 1923): 195; J.H. Hodgins, "Fitting Our Sons for Tomorrow," *Maclean's* (July 1924): 82–83. The University of Toronto instigated one such course for social workers; see University of Toronto Archives, Department of Social Service, B84–1089, Special Course in Work with Boys, n.d.

23 Library and Archives Canada, Canadian Welfare Council papers, Winnipeg Survey, Autumn–Winter 1933–34, 9–11.

24 UBC Archives, Boys' Parliaments, "Journals of the Tuxis Parliament of Alberta," Calgary, December 27–31, 1928, 5; Sixth Annual Saskatchewan Boys' Parliament, Regina, December 26–31 1928, 12.

25 Guelph Public Library Archives, Guelph, Ontario, YMCA papers, General Secretary's Report, July–August 1937, 3.

26 Guelph Public Library Archives, Guelph YMCA papers, Minutes of Third Regular Meeting, Board of Directors, November 11, 1913, 2; General Secretary's Report, February 1937, 1; YWCA papers, General Secretary's Report, Summer 1925. There are frequent mentions in both sets of Y papers throughout the interwar period of these recruiting drives, with optimistic statistics as to increased membership among working-class youth. See also Mrs. N.W. Rowell, President, Dominion Council, YWCA, "The Young Women's Christian Association," *Social Welfare* (October 1922) 20–22.

27 *Acta Nostra*, 1927, 50; 1930, 45. This was the yearbook of the Guelph Collegiate and Vocational Institute.

28 Ibid., 1931, 87.

29 E. Pearce, "The Girl and the Group," *Social Welfare* (July 1929): 230; K. MacPherson, "The Delinquent Girl and the Rescue Homes," *Social Welfare* (April 1921): 152; I. Dingman, "Your Teenage Daughter," *Chatelaine* (October 1934): 19.

30 A. Baden-Powell, *Handbook for Girl Guides*, 24.

31 Public Archives of Nova Scotia, MG 898, Girl Guides of Canada, Nova Scotia Council, Canadian Council of the Girl Guides Association, *Annual Reports*, 1–34, starting April 1932.

32 "Resume of Cooperative Girls Work in Canada, *Canadian Child Welfare News* (January–March 1925): 52. On the CGIT, see M. Prang, "The Girl God Would Have Me Be: The Canadian Girls in Training, 1915–39," *Canadian Historical Review* 66 (1985): 154–84; "Girls in Teens Get Attention in Fine Society," *Globe*, June 12, 1921, 18. The latter notes that there were 139 groups registered across the nation, by contrast to only a dozen a year earlier.

33 Public Archives of Nova Scotia, MG 20, MSS Societies, Nova Scotia Girls' Work Boards, CGIT, Phylis Blakely, typescript, undated, "History of the CGIT," 2–5. The first conference was held at Kingston, Ontario, in 1917. In 1919, the group inaugurated ten-day open-air camps to provide "healthful enjoyment" alongside religious training; nearly five hundred CGIT girls went to camp for the first time.

34 Ibid., 4. By 1921, each of the Atlantic provinces had its own Girls' Work Board to plan and coordinate girls clubs and activities.

35 M.Y. Hubbert, *Since the Day I Was Born* (Thornbury, ON: Conestoga Press, 1991), 226. Hubbert was born in Toronto, in a working-class family, in 1924.

36 Library and Archives Canada, Canadian Welfare Council papers, "York Township Survey, Autumn–Winter 1933–34," 10.

37 Bowie, "The Value of Supervised Recreation," 442.

38 L.F. Ward, "The Opportunity of the Pastor in Family Guidance," *Social Welfare* (December 1933): 12.

39 UBC Archives, Boys' Parliaments Collection, British Columbia, Tuxis second Older Boys Parliament, Victoria, December 29–31, 1924, 9–10.

40 "The Fight for the Future," editorial, *Waterford Star*, September 29, 1927, 7; also "Stay with the Farm, Urges Honourable J.S. Martin," *Waterford Star*, November 24, 1927, 6.

41 Public Archives of Ontario, RG 16-280-4, Extension Branch, Department of Agriculture, Box 1, typescript, unsigned, "History of the Extension Branch, 1907–57," March 1959, 1. See also Memorandum, Dr. C.C. James, Deputy Minister of Agriculture, to Nelson Monteith, Minister of Agriculture, 1906, 13. Jeffery Taylor, *Fashioning Farmers: Ideology, Agricultural Knowledge and the Manitoba Farm Movement, 1890–1925* (Regina, SK: Canadian Plains Research Centre, 1994), discusses how these clubs were intended to "educate" farm youth to both modern methods in agriculture and to the advantages of staying on the farm once they came of age.

42 Ontario, Agricultural Enquiry Committee, *Report of the Agricultural Enquiry Committee* (Toronto: King's Printer, 1925), 45. The name was officially changed to 4H Club in 1952. By 1930, the newly organized Canadian Council on Boys and Girls Clubs had given considerable impetus to the movement.

43 Miss K.F. Mackintosh, "Where Girls Have Good Times," *Waterford Star*, February 8, 1923, 5. Miss Mackintosh is identified as a "country home demonstrator" employed by the provincial ministry of agriculture.

44 "What the Girls Are Doing," *Waterford Star*, April 2, 1921, 6. This is a report on the Blackwell Junior Women's Institute of Lambden County; similar reports of proceedings in Leeds and Huron counties are included.

45 Public Archives of Ontario, RG 16-280-4, Department of Agriculture, Agricultural Representatives Office, Minutes of Junior Farmers Groups, Bolton minutes, December 1930, 2.

46 "The New Canada Movement," editorial, *Waterford Star*, February 8, 1934, 3. See also T. Crowley, "The New Canada Movement: Agrarian Youth Protest in the 1930s," *Ontario History* 80 (September 1988): 311.

47 Public Archives of Nova Scotia, Alexander Mowat papers, MG 2408, file 2, A. Mowat, handwritten survey notes, "Outside School Hours," 3–4. A second survey was conducted in February 1940, MG 2403, file no. 6, typescript, "What Influences Educate the Child Other Than the School?" 8–15. As noted in chapter 6, only one-quarter of the forty-two participants (eleven in total) did not belong to after-school clubs or organizations.

48 Library and Archives Canada, Canadian Welfare Council papers, Child Welfare in Manitoba, typescript, "Community Clubs for Boys and Community Clubs for Girls," Winnipeg, April 12, 1933, 4–7.

49 Public Archives of Nova Scotia, MG 898, Girl Guides of Canada, Nova Scotia Council, Canadian Council of the Girl Guides Association, *Annual Reports*, 1–34, April 1932–1937. By 1933 there were 1,015 Guide companies, with 24,537 girls enrolled, and 95 Ranger companies (older Guides, over sixteen), with 1,699 girls. The 1937 annual report showed 50,784 members.

50 Ibid., *Annual Report for the Year Ending April 1933*, 6.

51 F. Fidler, "'Rising Sun' Square of Vancouver Is Example of What Japanese Boys Can Do with Tuxis Program," *The Canadian Mentor* 11, 3 (1929): 3.

52 S. Scheidleiger, "A Comparative Study of the Boy Scout Movement in Different National and Social Groups," *American Sociological Review* 13 (1948): 739.

53 Ibid., 739.

54 C.H. Young, *The Ukrainian Canadians: A Study in Assimilation* (Toronto: Thomas Nelson, 1931), 146. There were eighty-eight branches, including forty branches of the youth section and fifty-two of the women's section.

55 C. Dawson, *Group Settlement: Ethnic Communities in Western Canada* (Toronto: Macmillan, 1936), 82. Dawson cites a "letter written by an educated Doukhobor" to the effect that several attempts were made, mostly by university students and graduates, to give the movement a "wider appeal."

56 Dawson, *Group Settlement*, 163–64.

57 Ibid., 164, 256–57. Winkler was 81 per cent Mennonite; Gretna was a customs station with an English-Canadian population of about 15 per cent, where the younger generation "speak English almost exclusively among themselves."

58 "Committee to Investigate Youth Problems in Toronto," *The Labour Gazette* (February 1935): 98.

59 L. Marsh, *Canadians In and Out of Work: A Survey of Economic Classes and Their Relation to the Labour Market* (Toronto: Oxford University Press, 1940), 165.

60 H. Barone, "We Knew How to Have Fun," in *Freedom to Play: We Made Our Own Fun,* ed. N. Lewis (Waterloo, ON: Wilfrid Laurier University Press, 2001), 109–10. The son of Italian immigrants, Barone grew up in Toronto during the interwar years.

61 Editorial, *The Canadian Guider* (January 1932): 7. See also Public Archives of Nova Scotia, MG 898, Girl Guides of Canada, Nova Scotia Council, Canadian Council of the Girl Guides Association, *Annual Report for the Year Ending April 1939*, 34.

62 F.T. Sharpe, "Stopping before Starting," *Child Welfare News* (January 1934): 43–44. The classic contemporary survey is K.H. Rogers, *Street Gangs in Toronto: A Study of the Forgotten Boy* (Toronto: Ryerson Press, 1945). On the importance of recreation for unemployed youth, see also Public Archives of Nova Scotia, MG 20, Box 413, file 4, Halifax Welfare Council, *Report of The Recreation Committee*, November 1935, 3–4; also Recreation Committee, Minutes, Meeting of December 7, 1935: 2–3.

63 M. McLeachy, "The Effect Upon Young People of the Economic Depression and Unemployment," *Child and Family Welfare* (November 1935): 15; E. Muncaster, "Strengthening Family Ties through Recreation," *Child and Family Welfare* (November 1933): 47; see also Library and Archives Canada, Canadian Welfare Council papers, Canadian Council on Child and Family Welfare, Division on Leisure Time and Educative Activities, "Relief Is Not Enough: The Idle Time of Compulsorily Idle Canadians," *Bulletin* 1 (25 September 1933): 1–4; "Will Canada Have a Youth Movement?" *The Canadian Doctor* (January 1939): 17–18.

64 S. Brent, "Reinforcing Family Strengths by the Provision of Leisure Time Activities," *Child and Family Welfare* (September 1931): 53; W.R. Cook, "Getting Down to Brass Tacks in Community Planning for Leisure Time," *Child and Family Welfare* (March 1938): 10–11; "Relief Is Not Enough," 1–4.

65 W. Bowie, "The Character of a Nation," *Social Welfare* (July 1931): 199.

66 "The New Canada Movement," editorial, *Waterford Star*, February 8, 1934, 3.

67 Library and Archives Canada, Canadian Welfare Council papers, "Survey of Social Agencies: Ottawa, 1929," 1–5.

68 A.P. Woollacott, "Junior G-Men of Canada," *Maclean's* (January 1939): 14–27. Within the first year of its operation, the club had a membership of 2,300 in Vancouver, with branches "in every section of the city and half a dozen in other parts of the province." Branches were also started in Edmonton, Alberta, and Brantford, Ontario.

69 Public Archives of Nova Scotia, MG 898, Girl Guides of Canada, Nova Scotia Council, Canadian Council of the Girl Guides Association, *Annual Report Ending April 1937*, 1–3. Guiding began in Canada in 1911; Canada had the third largest membership of Girl Guides in the world by the 1930s. On the CYC, see P. Axelrod, "The Student Movement of the 1930s," in *Youth, University and Canadian Society: Essays in the Social History of Higher Education*, ed. P. Axelrod and J.G. Reid (Montreal: McGill-Queen's University Press, 1989), 219–20. In the late 1930s, the CYC had a total constituent membership of over 400,000, mostly in the 18–24 age range.

70 "Declaration of Rights Passed by Congress," *Ottawa Journal*, May 26, 1936, 1; the newspaper is reporting on the congress held in Toronto on 24–25 May 1935. Representing 201 youth organizations from Toronto and district, the group gathered in the Toronto Technical School to discuss "pressing problems affecting youth in this time." Of 389 delegates, 45 were church and bible-class representatives, 25

represented the YM/YWCA, 20 represented trade unions, and 23 were from student and school-affiliated study groups; the rest included representatives from a number of athletic, political, pacifist, settlement, and unemployment organizations.

71 "Canadian Youth Act Will Be Submitted to Parliament," *Toronto Star*, May 26, 1936, 6.

72 University of British Columbia Archives, Special Collections, Canadian Youth Congress, *Democracy, Civil Liberties, Economic Conditions*, Montreal, July 1940, 1–8.

73 "Fifty-Fourth Annual Convention of the Trades and Labour Congress of Canada," *The Labour Gazette* (October 1939): 1013–15. See also "Congress Pledged Support for CYC," *The Labour Gazette*, (October 1938): 1101–106. See also McMaster University Archives, Canadian Youth Congress fonds, Kenneth Woodsworth, "Brief on a National Youth Administration," 2–5; Woodsworth was co-secretary of the Canadian Youth Congress. The final conference was held in 1940; see Axelrod, "The Student Movement," 216–46. For a fascinating discussion of the CYC and other youth groups deemed subversive by the RCMP, see P. Axelrod, "Spying on the Young in Depression and War: Students, Youth Groups and the RCMP, 1935–42," *Labour/Le travail* 35 (Spring 1995): 43–63.

74 National Council of Young Men's Christian Associations of Canada, Young Men's Committee, Submission to the Royal Commission on Dominion-Provincial Relations, Toronto, April 1938, 3.

75 Each was published by the late 1940s; their findings are summarized in B. Davies, *Youth Speaks Its Mind* (Toronto: Ryerson, 1948); also Canadian Youth Commission, *Youth in Your Town* (Ottawa: Queen's Printer, 1950); J. Keshen, *Saints, Sinners, and Soldiers: Canada's Second World War* (Vancouver: University of British Columbia Press, 2004), 161, 214–16. The only detailed historical examination of the commission is L. Ambrose, "The Canadian Youth Commission: Planning for Youth and Social Welfare in the Post-war Era," PhD dissertation, University of Waterloo, 1992.

76 Public Archives of Nova Scotia, MG 898, Girl Guides of Canada, Nova Scotia Council, Canadian Council of the Girl Guides Association, *Annual Report Ending April 1940*, 10.

77 Letter from Mary Kett, age fourteen, from Marshall, Saskatchewan, published in "Pathfinders," a regular column for young people in the *Free Press Prairie Farmer*, June 3, 1943, in *"I Want to Join Your Club": Letters from Rural Children, 1900–1920*, ed. N. Lewis (Waterloo, ON: Wilfrid Laurier University Press, 1996), 98–99.

78 "Boy Scout Week," Pathfinders page, *Free Press Prairie Farmer*, February 16, 1944, in *"I Want to Join Your Club,"* 100–101.

79 Hubbert, *Since the Day I Was Born*, 227.

80 J. Carroll, "Montreal Police Juvenile Clubs," *National Home Monthly* (April 1950): 24. See also "Montreal's Girl Delinquents," *National Home Monthly* (April 1950): 13.

81 L. Dempsey, "Teen-Age Special: What Are the Causes of Juvenile Delinquency," *Chatelaine* (June 1946): 10, 55, 63. On wartime scares about juvenile delinquency, see Keshen, *Saints, Sinners and Soldier*, especially chapter 8, 194–227.

82 Dempsey, "What Are the Causes," 10.

83 "Organizes Teen-Age Club," *Toronto Star*, January 30, 1945, 6.

84 Coca-Cola advertisement, *Toronto Star*, January 31, 1945, 5; "Three City Teen-Age Clubs Report a Good Time Was Had by All," *Toronto Star*, April 16, 1946, 5.

85 "Community Centre Scheme Cuts Juvenile Delinquency," *Toronto Star*, April 26, 1946, 4. Judge Hawley S. Mott of the Toronto family court had just issued an annual report "in which he records that cases of juvenile delinquency before his court in 1945 were the fewest documented in any year in the past quarter century"; he attributed this to the spread of community facilities for teenage clubs. On the community centre movement, see S. Tillotson, *The Public at Play: Gender and the Politics of Recreation in Post-war Ontario* (Toronto: University of Toronto Press, 2000).

86 "No Discrimination in 'Teen-Age Clubs: Social and Racial Differences Absent in Youth Recreation Centres," *Simcoe Reformer*, June 28, 1945, 2. Simcoe is a rural town in southwestern Ontario.

87 W. Hicks, "Oakville Teen-Town Builds Citizenship for Tomorrow," *Toronto Star*, March 30, 1946, 8. Two years earlier, 200 Oakville high school students had petitioned the Rotary Club for support; the club had about 250 "citizens" who paid fifty cents per month membership fees and elected a mayor and a council of 10 each year. See also "Teen-Agers 'Running' Town of Bracebridge," *Toronto Star*, April 16, 1946, 8.

88 R. Mah, "Rob Mah's Teen Town Memories, 1947–50," Victoria, BC, January 20, 2001; http://www.teentown.ca. Mah grew up in Port Alberni, became a public school teacher, and taught in the area for thirty years. The Alberni Valley Teen Town flourished from the mid-1940s to the late 1960s.

89 Ibid.

90 Ibid.

91 G. McKnight, "Teen Town Memories," ibid. McKnight believes that the Teen Town movement was brought down by the costs of bands, hall rentals, and so on; by "organized community recreation commissions with paid staff and a structured system which was not teen-member driven and operated"; and by the rise of other commercial venues, such as discotheques.

92 "Jive, Boogie Rhythms Rule 10,300 at Teen Town Time," *Toronto Star*, May 7, 1946, 8. The proceeds of $2,575 were presented to club representatives to continue their programs.

93 "Leaside Teen Club Rowdyism! Where? When?" *Toronto Star*, December 6, 1946, 10; see also *Toronto Star*, December 17, 1946, 8.

94 Wetherell and Kmet, *Useful Pleasures*, xxi; Williams, *Culture and Society*, 320; Peiss, *Cheap Amusements*, 4–8.

Conclusion

1 See the discussion of youth as a social formation in J. Austin and M.N. Willard, "Introduction: Angels of History, Demons of Culture" in *Generations of Youth: Youth Culture and History in Twentieth Century America*, ed. J. Austin and M.N. Willard (New York: New York University Press, 1998), 7. Mannheim makes this point in "The Problem of Generations" (1927), in K. Mannheim, *Essays on the Sociology of Knowledge* (London: Routledge and Kegan Paul, 1972; originally published 1928), 320; M. Danesi discusses juvenilization in *Forever Young: The "Teen-Aging" of Modern Culture* (Toronto: University of Toronto Press, 2003), especially 11–20.

2 Mannheim, "The Problem of Generations," 283. See also P. Kecskemeti, "Introduction," in Mannheim, *Essays on the Sociology of Knowledge*, 21–22; Mannheim, "The Problem of Generations," 302, 309–10. Turner, "Strategic Generations: Historical Change, Literary Expression, and Generational Politics," in *Generational Consciousness, Narratives, and Politics*, ed. J. Edmunds and B.S. Turner (Lanham, MD: Rowman and Littlefield, 2002), contends that "war and its social consequences have been a particularly important lever for the formation of generational consciousness and leadership."

3 J. Springhall, *Youth, Popular Culture and Moral Panics: Penny Gaffs to Gangsta-Rap, 1830–1996* (New York: St. Martin's Press, 1998), especially 1–10.

4 J. Wyn and R. White, "Negotiating Social Change: The Paradox of Youth," *Youth and Society* 32 (2000): 169.

5 M. Danesi, *Cool: The Signs and Meanings of Adolescence* (Toronto: University of Toronto Press, 1994), 34–5.

6 G. Neufeld and G. Maté, *Hold On to Your Kids: Why Parents Matter* (Toronto: A. Knopf, 2004), 3. See also P. Ariès, "Les ages de la vie," *Contrepoint* 1 (May 1970): 23–30; Ariès envisioned adolescence as the "breaking point" of a late twentieth-century variant of the ongoing crisis in the family. See also R.T. Vann, "The Youth of *Centuries of Childhood*," *History and Theory* 21 (1982): 89–97; P.H. Hutton, "Late-Life Historical Reflections of Philippe Ariès on the Family in Contemporary Culture," *Journal of Family History* 26 (2001): especially 398–99.

7 A.R.M. Lower, "Our Present Discontents," *The Dalhousie Review* 13 (1933): 97.

Bibliography

Archival Collections

National and Provincial

LIBRARY AND ARCHIVES CANADA
Canadian Council on Social Development
Canadian Youth Commission
Council on Child and Family Welfare

ARCHIVES OF BRITISH COLUMBIA
Department of Education
Department of Labour
Department of Health

ARCHIVES OF NEW BRUNSWICK
Inter-provincial Home for Young Women
Department of Education
Department of Health

ARCHIVES OF NOVA SCOTIA
Halifax Welfare Council
Nova Scotia Girls' Work Boards
Boys' Club, Meetings of the Directors
Girl Guides of Canada, Nova Scotia Council
Alexander Mowat collection
Department of Education
Department of Health

ARCHIVES OF ONTARIO
YM/YWCA Toronto
Department of Agriculture, Agricultural Representatives Office, Junior Farmers
Department of Agriculture, Extension Branch
Department of Health
Public Health Nursing Division
Department of Education
Royal Commission: Ottawa Collegiate Institute Inquiry, 6 January 1927
Department of Labour
Ontario Board of Censors
Historical Pamphlets Collection

University and Library Collections

Dalhousie University Archives
McMaster University Archives
McGill University Archives
Queen's University Archives
University of Alberta Archives
University of British Columbia Archives
University of Guelph Archives
University of Manitoba Archives
University of New Brunswick Archives
University of Toronto Archives
University of Waterloo Archives
University of Western Ontario Archives

Other Depositories

City of Vancouver Archives
City of Toronto Archives
Grey County Museum and Archives [Ontario]
Guelph Public Library Archives
Huron County Museum and Archives [Ontario]
Kitchener Public Library Archives
Wellington County Museum and Archives [Ontario]

Newspapers, Periodicals, and Annuals

Berlin Daily Telegraph
Berlin News Record
Calgary Eye-Opener
Canada Yearbook, 1920–1950
Canadian Boy
Canadian Doctor
Canadian Guider
Canadian Medical Association Journal
Canadian Medical Monthly
Canadian Mentor
Canadian Nurse
Canadian Practitioner
Canadian Public Health Journal
Canadian Unionist
Canadian Welfare Summary
Chatelaine
Child and Family Welfare
Child Welfare News
Dalhousie Review
Dawn of Tomorrow
Edmonton Journal

Globe and Mail
Grain Growers' Guide
Guelph Daily Mercury
Halifax Evening Mail
Halifax Herald
Health
House of Commons Debates, 1919–1950
Industrial Canada
Labour Gazette
Maclean's
Montreal Gazette
National Home Monthly
Ottawa Journal
Queen's Quarterly
Saturday Night
Scout Leader
Simcoe Reformer
Social Welfare
Statutes of Canada
Toronto Star
Toronto World
Vancouver Sun
Waterford Star

High School Publications

Acta Nostra, Guelph Collegiate and Vocational Institute, Guelph, ON
Adventure, Magee High School, Vancouver, BC
Challenger, St. John Vocational School, St. John, NB
Collegiate Oracle, Fort William Collegiate and Technical Institute, Fort William (Thunder Bay), ON; *FWCI Oracle* after 1930
En Avant, Alexandra High School, Medicine Hat, AB
The Grumbler, Kitchener Collegiate Institute, Kitchener, ON
Oak Bay Annual, Oak Bay High School, Victoria, BC
The Souvenir, John Oliver High School, Vancouver, BC
Vox Scholae, Fergus High School, Fergus, ON
Wings, Sangudo High School, Sangudo, AB

Books and Anthologies

Published Historical Material, Memoir, and Oral History

Abella, Irving, ed. *The Canadian Worker in the Twentieth Century*. Toronto: Oxford University Press, 1978.
Adams, R.A. *The Social Dance*. Kansas City, Kansas: R.A. Adams, 1921.
Addams, Jane. *The Spirit of Youth and the City Streets*. New York: Macmillan, 1909.
Anderson, Allan. *Remembering the Farm: Memories of Farming, Ranching, and Rural Life in Canada, Past and Present*. Toronto: Macmillan, 1979.

Anderson, J.T.M. *The Education of the New Canadian.* Toronto: J.M. Dent and Sons, 1918.

Baden-Powell, R. *Scouting for Boys.* London: Horace Cox, 1908.

Baden-Powell, A. *The Handbook for Girl Guides or How Girls Can Help Build the Empire.* London: Thomas Nelson and Sons, 1912.

Banks, L. A. *A Manly Boy: A Series of Talks and Tales for Boys.* Toronto: William Briggs: 1900.

Blanchard, Phyllis, and Carolyn Manassas. *New Girls For Old.* New York: Macaulay, 1930.

Bliss, Michael, and L. Grayson, eds. *The Wretched of Canada.* Toronto: University of Toronto Press, 1971.

Boyle, Harry J. *With a Pinch of Sin.* New York: Doubleday, 1966.

Broadfoot, Barry, ed. *Ten Lost Years, 1929–1939: Memories of Canadians Who Survived the Depression.* Don Mills, ON: General, 1973.

Calverton, V.F., and Samuel D. Schmalhausen, eds. *The New Generation: The Intimate Problems of Modern Parents and Children.* New York: Macaulay, 1930.

Canada, Honorary Advisory Council for Scientific and Industrial Research. *Survey of General Conditions of Industrial Hygiene in Toronto.* Ottawa: Privy Council of Canada, 1921.

Canada, Department of Labour. *The Employment of Children and Young Persons in Canada.* Ottawa: King's Printer, 1930.

Canadian Youth Commission. *Youth and Jobs in Canada.* Toronto: Ryerson Press, 1945.

Canadian Youth Commission. *Youth, Marriage and the Family.* Toronto: Ryerson Press, 1947.

Canadian Youth Commission. *Youth Speaks Out on Citizenship.* Toronto: Ryerson Press, 1948.

Canadian Youth Commission. *Youth in Your Town.* Ottawa: Queen's Printer, 1950.

Collins, Robert. *You Had to Be There: An Intimate Portrait of the Generation That Survived the Depression, Won the War, and Re-Invented Canada.* Toronto: McClelland and Stewart, 1997.

Daniel, W.A. *The Adolescent Patient.* St. Louis, MO: C.V. Mosby, 1970.

Davis, Katherine Bement. *Factors in the Sex Life of 2200 Women.* New York: Harper and Row, 1929.

Davies, Blodwen. *Youth Speaks Its Mind.* Toronto: Ryerson, 1948.

Dawson, Carl. *Group Settlement: Ethnic Communities in Western Canada.* Toronto: Macmillan, 1936.

Duvall, Evelyn Mills. *Facts of Life and Love for Teenagers.* Toronto: Popular Library, 1950.

Dyde, W.F. *Public Secondary Education in Canada.* New York: Columbia University, 1929.

Elias, Norbert. *The Civilizing Process.* New York: Urizen, 1978.

Erikson, E. H. *Identity and the Life Cycle.* New York: W.W. Norton, 1959.

Erikson, E.H. *Identity, Youth and Crisis.* New York: W.W. Norton, 1968.

Exner, M.J. *The Question of Petting.* New York: American Social Hygiene Association, 1926

Gallagher, J.R. *Your Son's Adolescence.* Boston: Little, Brown, 1951.

Gallagher, J.R. *Medical Care of the Adolescent.* 2nd ed. New York: Appleton-Century-Crofts, 1966.

Garner, Hugh. *Cabbagetown.* Toronto: Holt Rinehart, 1977.

Hall, Granville Stanley. *Adolescence: Its Psychology and Its Relation to Physiology, Anthropology, Sociology, Sex, Crime, Religion and Education.* New York: D.E. Appleton, 1904.

Hall, Granville Stanley. *Youth: Its Education, Regimen and Hygiene.* New York: D.E. Appleton, 1907.

Hoar, Victor, ed. *The Great Depression.* Toronto: Copp Clark, 1969.

Hubbert, Mildred Young. *Since the Day I Was Born.* Thornbury, ON: Conestoga, 1991.

Jaques, Edna. *Uphill All the Way: An Autobiography.* Saskatoon, SK: Western Producer Prairie Books, 1977.

Johnston, Basil. *Indian School Days.* Toronto: Key Porter Books, 1988.

Kealey, Greg, ed. *Canada Investigates Industrialism: The Royal Commission on the Relations of Labor and Capital, 1889.* Toronto: University of Toronto Press, 1973.

Kirkendall, Lester, and A. Ruth Farnham Osborne. *Dating Days*. Chicago: Science Research Associates, 1949.

Kugelmass, I.N. *Adolescent Medicine: Principles and Practice*. Springfield, IL: Charles C. Thomas, 1975.

Lewis, Norah. ed. *"I Want to Join Your Club": Letters from Rural Children, 1900–1920*. Waterloo, ON: Wilfrid Laurier University Press, 1996.

Lewis, Norah. ed. *Freedom to Play: We Made Our Own Fun*. Waterloo, ON: Wilfrid Laurier University Press, 2002.

Livesay, Dorothy. *Right Hand, Left Hand*. Erin, On.: Press Porcepic, 1977.

Livesay, Dorothy. *Journey with My Selves: A Memoir, 1909–1963*. Vancouver, BC: Douglas and McIntyre, 1991.

MacGill, Helen Gregory. *The Work of the Juvenile Court*. Vancouver, BC: Moore, 1943.

Mannheim, Karl. *Essays on the Sociology of Knowledge*. London: Routledge and Kegan Paul, 1972; originally published 1952.

Marsh, Leonard. *Employment Research*. Toronto: Oxford University Press,1935.

Marsh, Leonard. *Canadians in and out of Work: A Survey of Economic Classes and Their Relation to the Labour Market*. Toronto: Oxford University Press, 1940.

McCutcheon, J.M. *Public Education in Ontario*. Toronto: Best, 1941.

McNeil, Bill. *Voices of a War Remembered: An Oral History of Canadians in World War II*. Toronto: Doubleday Canada, 1991.

Melendy, M.R. *Vivilore: The Pathway to Mental and Physical Perfection*. Toronto: J.L. Nichols, 1904.

Miner, Horace. *St. Denis, a French-Canadian Parish*. Chicago: University of Chicago Press, 1939.

Peate, Mary. *Girl in a Sloppy Joe Sweater: Life on the Canadian Home Front during World War II*. Montreal: Optimum, 1988.

Phillips, C.E. *The Development of Education in Canada*. Toronto: W.J. Gage, 1957.

Porter, John. *The Vertical Mosaic: An Analysis of Social Class and Power in Canada*. Toronto: University of Toronto Press, 1965.

Ramsay, Terry. *A Million and One Nights: A History of the Modern Motion Picture*. New York: Simon and Schuster, 1926.

Read, D., and R. Hann, eds. *The Great War and Canadian Society: An Oral History* Toronto: New Hogtown Press, 1979.

Richler, Mordecai. *The Street*. Toronto: McClelland and Stewart, 1969.

Richter, L. ed. *Canada's Unemployment Problem*. Toronto: Macmillan, 1939.

Riesman, David. *The Lonely Crowd*. New Haven: Yale University Press, 1950.

Robbins, J. E. *Dependency of Youth*. Census Monograph no. 9, Dominion Bureau of Statistics, Ottawa: King's Printer, 1937.

Rogers, K. R. *Street Gangs in Toronto: A Study of the Forgotten Boy*. Toronto: Ryerson, 1945.

Ross, A.H.D. *A Short History of the Arnprior High School*. Ottawa: Popham, 1922.

Sharp, Rosalie, Irving Abella, and Edwin Goodman, eds. *Growing Up Jewish: Canadians Tell Their Own Stories*. Toronto: McClelland and Stewart, 1997.

Strange, K.R. *With the West in Her Eyes*. Toronto: George J. McLeod, 1937.

Taylor, Claire Drainie. *The Surprise of My Life: An Autobiography*. Waterloo, ON: Wilfrid Laurier University Press, 1998.

Thom, D.A. *Normal Youth and Its Everyday Problems*. New York: D. E. Appleton, 1932.

Thomas, W.I. *The Unadjusted Girl, with Cases and Standpoint for Behavior Analysis*. Boston, MA: Little, Brown, 1923.

Wargon, Sylvia T. *Children in Canadian Families*. Ottawa: Statistics Canada, 1979.

Webster, E.C. *Guidance for the High School Student*. Montreal: McGill University Social Research Series, no. 8, 1939.

Wile, Ira S., ed. *The Sex Life of the Unmarried Adult: An Inquiry into and an Interpretation of Current Sex Practices*. New York: Garden City, 1940.

Williams, F. E. *Adolescence, Studies in Mental Hygiene*. New York: Appleton-Century, 1932.
Young, Charles H. *The Ukrainian Canadians: A Study in Assimilation*. Toronto: Thomas Nelson and Sons, 1931.
Young, Charles H., and Helen Y. Reid. *The Japanese Canadians*. Toronto: University of Toronto Press, 1938.

Secondary Sources

Adams, Mary Louise. *The Trouble with Normal: Postwar Youth and the Making of Heterosexuality*. Toronto: University of Toronto Press, 1997.
Aitken, Stuart. *Geographies of Young People: The Morally Contested Spaces of Identity*. London: Routledge, 1999.
Allahar, A.L., and J.E. Cote. *Generation on Hold: Coming of Age in the Late Twentieth Century*. Toronto: Stoddart, 1994.
Ariès, Philippe. *Centuries of Childhood: A Social History of Family Life*. New York: Knopf, 1962.
Arnup, Katharine. *Education for Motherhood: Advice for Mothers in Twentieth-Century Canada*. Toronto: University of Toronto Press, 1994.
Austin, Joe, and Michael Nevin Willard, eds. *Generations of Youth: Youth Culture and History in Twentieth Century America*. New York: New York University Press, 1998.
Axelrod, Paul. *Making a Middle-Class: Student Life in English Canada during the Thirties*. Montreal: McGill-Queen's University Press, 1991.
Axelrod, P., and J.G. Reid, eds. *Youth University and Canadian Society: Essays in the Social History of Higher Education*. Montreal: McGill-Queen's University Press, 1989.
Axelrod P. *The Promise of Schooling: Education in Canada*. Toronto: University of Toronto Press, 1997.
Ayto, John. *Twentieth Century Words*. London: Oxford University Press, 1999.
Bailey, Beth. *From Front Porch to Back Seat: Courtship in Twentieth-Century America*. Baltimore, MD: Johns Hopkins University Press, 1988.
Bailey, Peter. *Leisure and Class in Victorian England: Rational Recreation and the Contest for Control, 1830–1885*. Toronto: University of Toronto Press, 1978.
Benstock, Shari, ed. *The Private Self: Theory and Practice of Women's Autobiographical Writing*. Chapel Hill, NC: University of North Carolina Press, 1988.
Berger, Carl. *The Sense of Power: Studies in the Ideas of Canadian Imperialism, 1867–1914*. Toronto: University of Toronto Press, 1970.
Berman, Marshall. *All That Is Solid Melts into Air*. New York: Simon and Schuster, 1982.
Bernier, Serge, ed. *L' Impact de la Deuxième Guerre mondiale sur les sociétés canadienne et québécoise*. Montreal/Ottawa: Université du Québec à Montréal et la Direction Histoire et patrimoine de la Défense nationale, Ottawa, 1998.
Betcherman, Lita-Rose. *The Swastika and the Maple Leaf: Fascist Movements in Canada*. Toronto: Fitzhenry and Whiteside, 1975.
Bibby, Reginald. *Canada's Teens: Today, Yesterday and Tomorrow*. Toronto: Stoddart, 2001.
Blake, R.B., and J. Keshen, eds. *Social Welfare Policy in Canada*. Toronto: Copp Clark, 1995.
Bourdieu, Pierre. *Outline of a Theory of Practice*. Cambridge, UK: Cambridge University Press, 1977.
Bourdieu, Pierre. *Reproduction in Education, Society and Culture*, 2nd ed. London: Sage, 1990.
Bourdieu, Pierre. *Sociology in Question*. London: Sage, 1993.
Bradbury, Bettina. *Working Families: Age, Gender and Daily Survival in Industrializing Montreal*. Toronto: McClelland and Stewart, 1993.
Brake, Michael. *Comparative Youth Culture*. London: Routledge and Kegan Paul, 1985.
Buss, Helen. *Mapping Our Selves: Canadian Women's Autobiography*. Montreal: McGill-Queen's University Press, 1993.

Cassel, Jay. *The Secret Plague: Venereal Disease in Canada, 1838–1939*. Toronto: University of Toronto Press, 1987.

Carrigan, Owen. *Crime and Punishment in Canada*. Toronto: McClelland and Stewart, 1991.

Carrigan, Owen. *Juvenile Delinquency in Canada: A History*. Concord, ON: Irwin, 1995.

Chambers, Lori, and E.-A. Montigny, eds. *Family Matters: Papers in Post-Confederation Canadian Family History*. Toronto: Canadian Scholars' Press, 1998.

Childs, Michael. *Labour's Apprentices*. Montreal: McGill-Queen's University Press, 1993.

Christie, Nancy, and M. Gauvreau. *A Full-Orbed Christianity: The Protestant Churches and Social Welfare in Canada, 1900–1940*. Montreal: McGill-Queen's University Press, 1996.

Chudacoff, H.P. *How Old Are You? Age Consciousness in American Culture*. Princeton, NJ: Princeton University Press, 1989.

Chunn, Dorothy. *From Punishment to Doing Good: Family Courts and Socialized Justice in Ontario, 1880–1940*. Toronto: University of Toronto Press, 1993.

Cohen, Stanley. *Folk Devils and Moral Panics*. Oxford: Basil Blackwell, 1990.

Comacchio, Cynthia R. *"Nations Are Built of Babies": Saving Ontario's Mothers and Children, 1900–40*. Montreal: McGill-Queen's University Press, 1993.

Comacchio, Cynthia R. *The Infinite Bonds of Family: Domesticity in Canada, 1850–1940*. Toronto: University of Toronto Press, 1999.

Cook, Ramsay, and R. Brown. *Canada, 1896–1921: A Nation Transformed*. Toronto: McClelland and Stewart, 1974.

Cross, Gary. *Time and Money: The Making of Consumer Culture*. New York: Routledge, 1993.

Danesi, Marcel. *Cool: The Signs and Meanings of Adolescence*. Toronto: University of Toronto Press, 1994.

Danesi, Marcel. *Forever Young: The "Teen-Aging" of Modern Culture*. Toronto: University of Toronto Press, 2003.

Doherty, Thomas. *Teenagers and Teenpics: The Juvenilization of American Movies in the 1950s*. Winchester MA: Unwin Hyman, 1988.

Dubinsky, Karen. *Improper Advances: Rape and Heterosexual Conflict in Ontario, 1880–1929*. Chicago: University of Chicago Press, 1993.

Elder, Glen. *Children of the Great Depression: Social Change in Life Experience*. Chicago: University of Chicago Press, 1974.

Elder, Glen, and S.E. Dragastin, eds. *Adolescence in the Life Cycle: Psychological Change and Social Context*. New York: Halsted Press, 1975.

Edmunds, June, and Bryan S. Turner, eds. *Generational Consciousness, Narrative, and Politics*. Lanham, MD; Rowman and Littlefield, 2002.

Eksteins, Modris. *Rites of Spring: The Great War and the Birth of the Modern Age*. Toronto: Lester and Orpen Dennys, 1989.

Enstad, Nan. *Ladies of Labor, Girls of Adventure: Working Women, Popular Culture and Labor Politics at the Turn of the Twentieth Century*. New York: Columbia University Press, 1999.

Everdell, William R. *The First Moderns*. Chicago: University of Chicago Press, 1997.

Fass, Paula. *The Damned and the Beautiful: American Youth in the 1920s*. New York: Oxford University Press, 1977.

Fass, Paula. *Outside In: Minorities and the Transformation of American Education*. New York: Oxford University Press, 1989.

Fass, Paula, and M.A. Mason, eds. *Childhood in America*. New York: New York University Press, 2000.

Foot, David K. *Boom, Bust and Echo: How to Profit from the Coming Demographic Shift*. Toronto: Macfarlane Walter and Ross, 1996.

Fowler, David. *The First Teenagers: The Lifestyle of Young Wage-Earners in Interwar Britain*. London: Woburn Press, 1995.

Fox, R.W., and T. Jackson Lears, eds. *The Power of Culture: Critical Essays in American History*. Chicago: University of Chicago Press, 1993.

Freeman, Mark. *Rewriting the Self: History, Memory, Narrative*. London: Routledge, 1993.

Fussell, Paul. *The Great War and Modern Memory*. New York: Oxford University Press, 1975.

Gidney, R.D., and W. Millar. *Inventing Secondary Education: The Rise of the High School in Nineteenth-Century Ontario*. Montreal: McGill-Queen's University Press, 1990.

Gillis, John. *Youth and History*. New York: Academic Press, 1974.

Goldstein Ruth M., and Edith Zornow. *The Screen Image of Youth: Movies about Children and Adolescents*. New York: Scarecrow Press,1980.

Goodson, Ivor F., and Christopher J. Anstead, eds. *Through the Schoolhouse Door: Working Papers*. Toronto: Garamond, 1993.

Graff, Harvey. *Conflicting Paths: Growing Up in America*. Cambridge, MA: Harvard University Press, 1995.

Gurney, Helen. *Girls' Sports: A Century of Progress in Ontario High Schools*. Don Mills, ON: OFSAA, 1979.

Hampton, Benjamin B. *History of the American Film Industry from Its Beginnings to 1931*. New York: Dover, 1970.

Heap, Ruby, and A. Prentice, eds. *Gender and Education in Ontario: An Historical Reader*. Toronto: Canadian Scholars' Press, 1991.

Hendrick, H. *Images of Youth: Age, Class and the Male Youth Problem, 1880–1920*. London: Oxford University Press, 1990.

Hollander, Stanley C., and Richard Germain. *Was There a Pepsi Generation Before Pepsi Discovered It? Youth-Based Segmentation in Marketing*. Lincolnwood, IL: NTC Business Books, 1992.

Horn, Michiel, and R. Sabourin, eds. *Studies in Canadian Social History*. Toronto: McClelland and Stewart, 1974.

Iacovetta, Franca, and M. Valverde, eds. *Gender Conflicts: New Essays in Women's History*. Toronto: University of Toronto Press, 1992.

Ishwaran, K., ed. *Childhood and Adolescence in Canada*. Toronto: McGraw-Hill Ryerson, 1979.

Jacobs, Lewis. *The Rise of the American Film: A Critical History, 1921–47*. New York: Teachers College Press of Columbia University, 1939; 1948; 1967.

James, A., and A. Prout, *Constructing and Reconstructing Childhood: Contemporary Issues in the Sociological Study of Childhood*. London: Falmer, 1990.

Johnson, F. *A Brief History of Canadian Education*. Toronto: McGraw-Hill, 1968.

Johnston, Russell. *Selling Themselves: The Emergence of Canadian Advertising*. Toronto: University of Toronto Press, 2001.

Jones, D.C., N.M. Sheehan, and R.M. Stamp, eds. *Shaping the Schools of the Canadian West*. Calgary: Detselig, 1979.

Jowett, Garth S., Ian C. Jarvie, and Kathryn H. Fuller. *Children and the Movies: Media Influence and the Payne Fund Controversy*. Cambridge, UK: Cambridge University Press, 1996.

Kalaidjian, Walter. *American Culture between the Wars: Revisionary Modernism and Post-Modern Critique*. New York: Columbia University Press, 1993.

Kamman, Michael. *The Mystic Chords of Memory: The Transformation of Tradition in American Culture*. New York: Vintage, 1991.

Keshen, Jeffrey. *Saints, Sinners and Soldiers: Canada's Second World War*. Vancouver, BC: University of British Columbia Press, 2004,

Kett, Joseph. *Rites of Passage: The Invention of Adolescence, 1900 to the Present*. New York: Basic Books, 1977.

Kidd, Bruce. *The Struggle for Canadian Sport*. Toronto: University of Toronto Press, 1996.

Kinsman, Gary. *The Regulation of Desire: Sexuality in Canada*. Montreal: Black Rose, 1987; 2nd edition, 1996.

Knockwood, Isabelle. *Out of the Depths: The Experiences of Mi'kmaw Children at the Indian Residential School at Shubenacadie, Nova Scotia*. Lockeport, NS: Roseway, 1992.

Leach, William. *Land of Desire: Merchants, Power and the Rise of a New American Culture*. New York: Vintage Books, 1993.

Lears, T. Jackson. *No Place of Grace: Antimodernism and the Transformation of American Culture, 1880–1920*. Chicago: University of Chicago Press,1981.

Lears, T. Jackson. *Fables of Abundance: A Cultural History of Advertising in America*. New York: Basic Books, 1994.

Levesque, Andrée. *Le Norme et les déviantes: Des femmes au Québéc pendant l'entre-deux-guerres*. Montreal: Editions du Rémue-Ménage, 1989; trans. Y. Klein. *Making and Breaking the Rules: Women in Quebec, 1919–1939*. Toronto: McClelland and Stewart, 1994.

Levine, Allan. *The Devil in Babylon: The Fear of Progress and the Birth of Modern Life*. Toronto: McClelland and Stewart, 2005.

Levitt, C., and W. Shaffir. *The Riot at Christie Pits*. Toronto: Lester and Orpen Dennys, 1987.

Linton, D. *Who Has the Youth Has the Future*. Cambridge, MA: Harvard University Press, 1990.

McLaughlin, E., J. Muncie, and G. Hughes, eds. *Youth Justice: Critical Readings*. London: Sage, 2002.

Macleod, D. *Building Character in the American Boy: The Boy Scouts, YMCA and Their Forerunners, 1870–1920*. Madison, WI: University of Wisconsin Press, 1983.

Magder, Ted. *Canada's Hollywood: The State and the Feature Film Industry in Canada*. Toronto: University of Toronto Press, 1993.

Marshall, David. *Secularizing the Faith: Canadian Protestant Clergy and the Crisis of Belief, 1850–1940*. Toronto: University of Toronto Press, 1992.

Marshall, Dominique. *The Social Origins of the Welfare State: Quebec Families, Compulsory Education and Family Allowances*. trans. Nicola Danby. Waterloo, ON: Wilfrid Laurier University Press, forthcoming.

Mazon, Mauricio. *The Zoot-Suit Riots: The Psychology of Symbolic Annihilation*. Austin, TX: University of Texas Press, 1984.

McCarty, John. *Hollywood Gangland: The Movies' Love Affair with the Mob*. New York: St. Martin's Press, 1993.

McIntosh, Robert. *Boys in the Pits: Child Labour in Coal Mines*. Montreal: McGill-Queen's University Press, 2000.

McKay, Ian. *The Quest of the Folk: Antimodernism and Cultural Selection in Twentieth-Century Nova Scotia*. Montreal: McGill-Queen's University Press, 1994.

Mennell, Stephen. *Norbert Elias: An Introduction*. Oxford, UK: Blackwell, 1982.

Miller, Mark. *Such Melodious Racket: The Lost History of Jazz in Canada, 1914 to 1949*. Toronto: Mercury Press, 1997.

Mitchinson, Wendy. *The Nature of Their Bodies: Women and Their Doctors in Victorian Canada*. Toronto: University of Toronto Press, 1991.

Montigny, E.A., and L. Chambers, eds. *Family Matters: Papers in Post-Confederation Canadian Family History*. Toronto: Canadian Scholars' Press, 1998.

Modell, John. *Into One's Own: From Youth to Adulthood in the United States*. Berkeley, CA: University of California Press, 1988.

Morton, Suzanne. *Ideal Surroundings: Domestic Life in a Working-Class Suburb in the 1920s*. Toronto: University of Toronto Press, 1995.

Moss, Mark. *Manliness and Militarism: Educating Young Boys in Ontario for War*. Toronto: Oxford University Press, 2001.

Mott, M., ed. *Sports in Canada: Historical Readings*. Toronto: Copp Clark Pitman, 1989.

Mungham, G., and G. Pearson, eds. *Working Class Youth Culture*. London: Routledge and Kegan Paul, 1976.

Muus, Rolf E. *Theories of Adolescence*, 5th ed. New York: Random House, 1988.

Pagan, Eduardo Obregon. *Murder at Sleepy Lagoon: Zoot Suits, Race and Riot in Wartime L.A.* Charlotte, NC: University of North Carolina Press, 2003.

Nasaw, David. *Going Out: The Rise and Fall of Public Amusement*. Cambridge, MA: Harvard University Press, 1993.

Neubauer, J. *The Fin-de-Siecle Culture of Adolescence*. New Haven, CT: Yale University Press, 1992.

Neufeld, Gordon, and Gabor Maté. *Hold On to Your Kids: Why Parents Matter*. Toronto: Alfred Knopf Canada, 2004.

Nicholls, Peter. *Modernisms: A Literary Guide*. Berkeley, CA: University of California Press, 1995.

Owram, Doug. *Born at the Right Time: A History of the Baby Boom Generation*. Toronto: University of Toronto Press, 1996.

Palladino, Grace. *Teenagers: An American History*. New York: Basic Books, 1996.

Parr, Joy, ed. *Childhood and Family in Canadian History*. Toronto: McClelland and Stewart, 1982.

Parr, Joy. *Labouring Children: British Immigrant Apprentices to Canada, 1869–1924*, 2nd ed. Toronto: University of Toronto Press, 1994.

Peiss, Kathy. *Cheap Amusements: Working Women and Leisure in New York City, 1880–1920*. Philadelphia: Temple University Press, 1986.

Petrik, P., and E. West, eds. *Small Worlds: Children and Adolescents in America, 1850–1950*. Lawrence, KS: University Press of Kansas, 1993.

Piva, Michael, ed. *History of Ontario: Selected Readings*. Toronto: McClelland and Stewart, 1985.

Prescott, Heather Munro. *A Doctor of Their Own: The History of Adolescent Medicine*. Boston, MA: Harvard University Press, 1998.

Rains, P., and E. Teram. *Normal Bad Boys: Public Policies, Institutions, and the Politics of Client Recruitment*. Montreal: McGill-Queen's University Press, 1992.

Randall, D. *Kipling's Imperial Boy: Adolescence and Cultural Hybridity*. New York: Palgrave, 2000.

Riess, Steven A. *City Games: The Evolution of American Urban Society and the Rise of Sports*. Chicago, IL: University of Illinois Press, 1991.

Rosenthal, M. *The Character Factory: Baden-Powell and the Origins of the Boy Scout Movement*. London: Collins Press, 1986.

Ross, Dorothy. *G. Stanley Hall: The Psychologist as Prophet*. Chicago: University of Chicago Press, 1983.

Ross, Dorothy, ed. *Modernist Impulses in the Human Sciences*. Baltimore, MD: Johns Hopkins University Press, 1994.

Rothman, Ellen K. *Hands and Hearts: A History of Courtship in America*. New York: Basic Books, 1984.

Rubin, David C., ed. *Autobiographical Memory*. Cambridge, UK: Cambridge University Press, 1986.

Sangster, Joan. *Regulating Girls and Women: Sexuality, Family, and the Law in Ontario, 1920–1960*. Don Mills, ON: Oxford University Press, 2001.

Sangster, Joan. *Girl Trouble: Female Delinquency in English Canada*. Toronto: Between the Lines, 2002.

Shore, Marlene. *The Science of Social Redemption: McGill, the Chicago School, and the Origins of Social Research in Canada*. Toronto: University of Toronto Press, 1987.

Shutt, Greta. *The High Schools of Guelph*. Toronto: University of Toronto Press, 1961.

Sklar, Robert. *Movie-Made America: A Cultural History of American Movies*. New York: Vintage Books, 1994.

Springhall, John. *Youth, Empire and Society: British Youth Movements, 1883–1940*. London: Croom Helm, 1977.

Springhall, John. *Coming of Age: Adolescence in Britain, 1860–1960*. London: Oxford University Press, 1986.

Springhall, John. *Youth, Popular Culture and Moral Panics: Penny Gaffs to Gangsta-Rap, 1830–1996*. New York: St. Martin's Press, 1998.

Strange, Carolyn. *Toronto's Girl Problem: The Perils and Pleasures of the City, 1880–1930*. Toronto: University of Toronto Press, 1995.

Strauss, William, and Neil Howe, eds. *Generations: The History of America's Future*. New York: William Morrow, 1991.

Strong-Boag, Veronica. *The New Day Recalled: Lives of Girls and Women in English Canada, 1919–1939*. Markham, ON: Penguin, 1988.

Strong-Boag, Veronica, Mona Gleason, and Adele Perry, eds. *Rethinking Canada: The Promise of Women's History*. Toronto: Oxford University Press, 2002.

Struthers, James. *No Fault of Their Own: Unemployment and the Canadian Welfare State, 1914–1941*. Toronto: University of Toronto Press, 1983.

Studlar, Gaylyn. *This Mad Masquerade: Stardom and Masculinity in the Jazz Age*. New York: Columbia University Press, 1996.

Sutherland, Fraser. *The Monthly Epic: A History of Canadian Magazines, 1789–1989*. Toronto: Fitzhenry and Whiteside, 1989.

Sutherland, Neil. *Growing Up: Childhood in English Canada from the Great War to the Age of Television*. Toronto: University of Toronto Press, 1997.

Sutherland, Neil. *Children in English Canadian Society, 1880–1920: Framing the Twentieth-Century Consensus*. Toronto: University of Toronto Press, 1976; Waterloo, ON: Wilfrid Laurier University Press, 2000.

Swyripa, Frances. *Wedded to the Cause: Ukrainian-Canadian Women and Ethnic Identity, 1891–1991*. Toronto: University of Toronto Press, 1993.

Taylor, Jeffery. *Fashioning Farmers: Ideology, Agricultural Knowledge and the Manitoba Farm Movement, 1890–1925*. Regina: Canadian Plains Research Centre, 1994.

Tillotson, Shirley. *The Public at Play: Gender and the Politics of Recreation in Post-War Ontario*. Toronto: University of Toronto Press, 2000.

Thompson, John Herd, and Allan Seager. *Canada, 1922–1939: Decades of Discord*. Toronto: McClelland and Stewart, 1985.

Trattner, Walter I., ed. *Biographical Dictionary of Social Welfare in America*. New York: Greenwood Press, 1986.

Turner, Bryan S., ed. *Theories of Modernity and Post-modernity*. London: Sage, 1990.

Turner, Bryan S., ed. *Citizenship and Social Theory*. London, UK: Sage, 1993.

Ueda, R. *Avenues to Adulthood: The Origins of the High School and Social Mobility in an American Suburb*. Cambridge, UK: Cambridge University Press, 1987.

Vance, Jonathan. *Death So Noble: Memory, Meaning and the First World War*. Vancouver, BC: University of British Columbia Press, 1997.

Van Krieken, Robert. *Norbert Elias*. London, UK: Routledge, 1998.

Vipond, Mary. *The Mass Media in Canada*. Toronto: James Lorimer, 2000.

Vipond, Mary. *Listening In: The First Decade of Canadian Broadcasting, 1922–1932*. Montreal: McGill-Queen's University Press, 1992.

Waiser, W.A. *"All Hell Can't Stop Us": The On-to-Ottawa Trek and Regina Riot*. Calgary, AB: Fifth House, 2003.

Walden, Keith. *Becoming Modern: The Industrial Exhibition and the Shaping of a Late Victorian Culture*. Toronto: University of Toronto Press, 1997.

Watson, Peter. *A Terrible Beauty: The People and Ideas That Shaped the Modern Mind*. London: Phoenix Press, 2000.

Wegs, R. *Growing Up Working Class: Youth in Vienna, 1870–1920*. Philadelphia, PA: University of Pennsylvania Press, 1989.

Weintraub, William. *City Unique: Montreal Days and Nights in the 1940s and '50s*. Toronto: McClelland and Stewart, 1996.

Wetherell, D.G., and I. Kmet. *Useful Pleasures: The Shaping of Leisure in Alberta, 1896–1945*. Regina, SK: Canadian Plains Research, 1990.

Williams, Raymond. *Culture and Society, 1780–1950*. London: Chatto and Windus, 1967.

Zeller, Suzanne. *Inventing Canada: Early Victorian Science and the Idea of a Transcontinental Nation*. Toronto: University of Toronto Press, 1987.

Internet Sites

American Silent Films, www.silentsaregolden.com
Canadian Encyclopedia of Music, www.canadianencyclopedia.ca
Canadian Popular Music since 1900, http://collections.ic.gc.ca/heirloom_series/
Department of National Defence, www.dnd.ca
Living History Oral History Project, Riverview Health Centre, Winnipeg, MB, 1999,
     http://www.riverviewhealthcentre.com/
Library and Archives Canada, www.archives.ca
National Adult Literacy Database, Learning for Life Project, http://www.nald.ca/
Prince George, BC, Oral History Page, http://www2.pgohg.org
Teen Towns in Canada, www.teentown.ca

Index

Books in the Studies in Childhood and Family in Canada Series
Published by Wilfrid Laurier University Press

Making Do: Women, Family, and Home in Montreal during the Great Depression
by Denyse Baillargeon, translated by Yvonne Klein • 1999 / xii + 232 /
ISBN: 0-88920-326-1 / ISBN-13: 978-0-88920-326-6

Children in English-Canadian Society: Framing the Twentieth-Century Consensus
by Neil Sutherland with a new foreword by Cynthia Comacchio • 2000 /
xxiv + 336 pp. / illus. / ISBN: 0-88920-351-2 / ISBN-13: 978-0-88920-351-8

Love Strong as Death: Lucy Peel's Canadian Journal, 1833-1836 edited by
J. I. Little • 2001 / x + 229 pp. / illus. / ISBN: 0-88920-389-X /
ISBN-13: 978-0-88920-389-1

The Challenge of Children's Rights for Canada by Katherine Covell and R. Brian
Howe • 2001 / x + 244 pp. / ISBN: 0-88920-380-6 / ISBN-13: 978-0-88920-380-8

NFB Kids: Portrayals of Children by the National Film Board of Canada, 1939-1989
by Brian J. Low • 2002 / 288 pp. / illus. / ISBN: 0-88920-386-5 /
ISBN-13: 978-0-88920-386-0

*Something to Cry About: An Argument against Corporal Punishment of Children in
Canada* by Susan M. Turner • 2002 / xix + 317 pp. / ISBN: 0-88920-382-2 /
ISBN-13: 978-0-88920-382-2

Freedom to Play: We Made Our Own Fun edited by Norah L. Lewis • 2002 /
xiv + 210 pp. / ISBN: 0-88920-406-3 / ISBN-13: 978-0-88920-406-5

The Dominion of Youth: Adolescence and the Making of Modern Canada, 1920–1950
by Cynthia Comacchio • 2006 / x + 302 / illus. / ISBN: 0-88920-488-8 /
ISBN-13: 978-0-88920-488-1